LAW AND THE REGULATION OF MEDICINES

The principal purpose of this book is to tell the story of a medicine's journey through the regulatory system in the UK, from defining what counts as a medicine, through clinical trials, licensing, pharmacovigilance, marketing and funding. While the UK's regulatory regime is the principal focus, the question of global access to medicines is addressed not only because of its political importance, but also because it is an issue which places the question of whether medicines are a private or a public good in particularly stark focus. Two further specific challenges to the future of medicines regulation are examined separately: first, pharmacogenetics, or the genetic targeting of medicines to subgroups of patients, and second, the possibility of using medicines to enhance wellbeing or performance, rather than treat disease. Throughout, the emphasis is upon the role of regulation in shaping and influencing the operation of the medicines industry, an issue which is of central importance to the promotion of public health and the fair and equitable distribution of healthcare resources.

Law and the Regulation of Medicines

Emily Jackson

·HART·
PUBLISHING

OXFORD AND PORTLAND, OREGON
2012

Published in the United Kingdom by Hart Publishing Ltd
16C Worcester Place, Oxford, OX1 2JW
Telephone: +44 (0)1865 517530
Fax: +44 (0)1865 510710
E-mail: mail@hartpub.co.uk
Website: http://www.hartpub.co.uk

Published in North America (US and Canada) by
Hart Publishing
c/o International Specialized Book Services
920 NE 58th Avenue, Suite 300
Portland, OR 97213-3786
USA
Tel: +1 503 287 3093 or toll-free: (1) 800 944 6190
Fax: +1 503 280 8832
E-mail: orders@isbs.com
Website: http://www.isbs.com

© Emily Jackson 2012

Emily Jackson has asserted her right under the Copyright, Designs and Patents Act 1988,
to be identified as the author of this work.

British Library Cataloguing in Publication Data
Data Available

ISBN: 978-1-84946-179-5

Typeset by Hope Services, Abingdon
Printed and bound in Great Britain by
TJ International Ltd, Padstow, Cornwall

In memory of my brother, Rupert Jackson
1968–2002

ACKNOWLEDGEMENTS

Sabbatical leave enabled me to write this book, and I am grateful to the London School of Economics and especially to my colleagues in the Law Department for giving me the time to devote to this project. I (nearly) finished the manuscript during a three-week stay at the Fondation Brocher, outside Geneva, and I am very grateful to the Brocher Foundation and to its staff for the opportunity. I would also like to thank my fellow researchers, in particular Jessica Mozersky, Linsey McGoey, Reed Pyeritz and Bob Cook-Deegan, for helping to make it such a productive stay. Linsey McGoey also deserves thanks for stimulating my interest in what has been a new area of research for me, and for sustaining it with many illuminating conversations and helpful suggestions.

Thanks too, as ever, to Robert Phillips, Alison Cox (who also gave me some helpful advice on chapter seven, for which I am very grateful), Ciarán O'Meara, Duncan Paterson and Matthew Weait, and to Douglas, Sue, Emma and Sophie Jackson.

TABLE OF CONTENTS

PREFACE

In some quarters, there continues to be scepticism over medical law's claim to be a distinctive area of legal scholarship, as opposed to a melting pot of tort, criminal, family and public law with some applied ethics thrown in for good measure. What is uncontroversial, on the other hand, is that some medico-legal questions have received much more academic commentary and analysis than others. Lawyers are often drawn to the complex issues that arise in malpractice litigation and in applications for judicial review, and it is easy to see why academics, as well as the general public, are fascinated by the complex and thorny ethical issues that arise at the beginning and end of life. Clashes between and autonomy and other values, such as beneficence or the public good, are played out in debates over the best way to solve the organ shortage. Medicines regulation, in contrast, has attracted comparatively little attention.

I do not mean to suggest that the regulation of medicines has been ignored altogether, although it is noteworthy that, within the UK, sociology journals are more likely than law journals to contain articles devoted to defects or gaps in the regulation of medicines. There are a number of scholarly works which explain the increasingly complex web of European Directives; indeed, given the impact of the EU on medicines regulation, it has clearly represented an important case study in the field of European law. There is also a burgeoning literature, much of it coming from the US, describing alarming, not to say shoddy or even downright illegal practices in the pharmaceutical industry.

At the risk of drastic over-simplification, analysis of medicines regulation tends to fall into one of two camps. Either it explains, describes and evaluates existing regulation, or it draws attention to the negative consequences of drug companies' relentless pursuit of profit. My purpose in this book is to try to steer a course between these two poles by concentrating on the way in which regulation shapes behaviour. It should not surprise anyone that a for-profit company, which is under a duty to maximise shareholder value, will strive to increase its profits within the rules that constrain its activities. Those rules are therefore critical, since both their content and their implementation will largely determine the limits of what the pharmaceutical industry can do, and therefore does, in its pursuit of the bottom line.

To take a concrete example: many commentators are critical of the fact that drug companies often seem to be more interested in developing 'me-too' drugs – that is, new versions of existing profitable medicines – than they are in discovering novel treatments for neglected diseases. In practice, however, castigating drug companies for acting in the best interests of their shareholders diverts attention away from the role that the law plays in *facilitating* and *encouraging*, albeit not intentionally, the development of drugs that do not offer much, if any, improvement over existing and well-tolerated medicines. Rather than worrying about why drug companies do not behave more like charities, we should instead focus upon the regulatory framework which specifies the essential prerequisites for receiving a licence to market a new medicine. If it is only necessary to prove that a drug is safe and marginally more effective than nothing, then this is what clinical trials will set out to prove. There is no point in lamenting the fact that many new drugs offer no improvement over established medicines if such a requirement is absent from the criteria which must be satisfied before a marketing authorisation can be granted.

The pharmaceutical industry is a global one: a series of mergers towards the end of the twentieth century means that a handful of supranational companies are now responsible for developing and supplying almost all branded medicines worldwide. These companies are extraordinarily powerful, and countries which institute hostile regulatory regimes may find that important sources of employment and tax revenues simply move abroad. It would probably be impossible to institute a uniform global regulatory system, although attempts at harmonisation of certain aspects of the licensing process do exist. Nevertheless, while this book concentrates on the UK, and inevitably also the European legal framework, the way in which the development and supply of medicines is regulated in other parts of the world is also important. Clinical trials, for example, commonly cross national borders, taking place in many countries simultaneously. If a UK-based company is carrying out research in India, the Ukraine and Japan, for a medicine which it intends to market worldwide, whose rules should govern the conduct of those trials?

Although it is important not to ignore the global reach of the pharmaceutical industry, the UK offers an especially interesting site for investigation of what might be described as a clash of cultures between for-profit drug companies and state-run healthcare provision. At the time of writing, there is much greater private involvement in the supply of healthcare in other high-income countries than there is in the UK. In Australia and in most European countries, state funding for healthcare exists in tandem with private insurance, and reimbursement schemes are more common than Aneurin Bevan's vision of the NHS as a comprehensive healthcare system, free at the point of use. Of course, in the US, the healthcare system is thoroughly saturated with for-profit companies that provide health services, manage care and offer insurance schemes.

It seems likely that recent reforms to the NHS will give a greater role to private providers, but nevertheless the UK has a long and proud history of publicly funded and state-run healthcare provision. Obviously, the treatment we receive within the NHS is not limited to medicines, but equally they are an important aspect of the care which the NHS provides, and critically, they are developed and supplied by the private sector. Imagine that an orthopaedic surgeon working in the NHS develops a promising new way to treat torn knee cartilage. The surgeon's first step will not be to obtain a patent for his new technique and prevent anyone else from carrying out surgery in the same way for 20 years. Rather, the surgeon is likely to seek to publish his results in a medical journal and discuss them with colleagues. In contrast to this public-service ethos, the development of a new medicine is treated as a private good, to be patented and profited from, even though, like the innovative surgeon's salary, it will be paid for by public funds.

The lack of fit between the private and public good models of healthcare provision is an important theme that emerges in several different contexts in this book. One particular point of pressure is the moment at which a medicine's chemical formulation moves from being a trade secret, protected by patent law, to being part of the publicly available 'knowledge commons'. Deciding to grant manufacturers 20 years of patent protection enables them to recoup their costs and make a profit, but it inevitably does so at the expense of making medicines available cheaply more quickly. Of course, in theory the patent system also protects public health by creating an incentive towards innovation. In practice, however, because it is possible to patent medicines which do not represent a 'step-change' for patients, patents incentivise the development of profitable medicines, and these are not always necessarily especially innovative.

The chief purpose of this book is to tell the 'story' of a medicine's journey through the regulatory system in the UK. First, it is necessary to define what a medicine is, and what it is not, and this means contemplating where alternative and complementary medicines might fit within the regulatory scheme. Next, the medicine must successfully complete the various phases of clinical trials in order to gather evidence sufficient for it to be granted a marketing authorisation. Once a medicine is licensed for use, it continues to be monitored, and if safety problems emerge, litigation is possible. After licensing, the medicine's manufacturer will market its new product, to both prescribers and consumers, and decisions must be taken within the NHS about its affordability.

While the UK's regulatory regime is this book's principal focus, it quickly became apparent that a book on medicines regulation which ignored global access to medicines would fail to address an issue of growing political importance, and one where the question of whether medicines should be treated as a private or a public good comes into particularly stark focus. As a result, the chapter on the funding of medicines within the UK is followed by one which addresses global access to medicines and vaccines.

Two further specific challenges exist to the future of medicines regulation, and these are dealt with separately in the final two chapters. First, it is possible that pharmacogenetics might end the blockbuster model of drug development, whereby medicines are developed for the population as a whole. Genetic testing could enable medicines to be targeted much more specifically to subgroups of the population in whom they are likely to be safe and effective, and while this could have obvious health benefits for patients who receive effective treatment more quickly, by shrinking the potential market for new medicines, it also raises a number of distinctive issues. What will happen to people with rare genotypes for whom it will not be profitable to develop medicines? Unlike genetic testing that can identify future susceptibility to disease, pharmacogenetic testing might reveal that someone will be largely untreatable in the future. Routine pre-prescription genetic testing might also raise new confidentiality issues, and although patients would have the right to refuse testing, this might decrease their access to medicines.

Second, we normally think of medicines as something we take when we are ill, to restore us to health or to alleviate our symptoms. Of course there have always been exceptions to this: the contraceptive pill is a good example of a medicine which is intended to improve quality of life by enabling women to control their fertility. The development of more medicines which are intended to enhance well-being or performance, rather than treat disease, has led to interest in whether we might be entering a new era of cosmetic pharmacology, in which taking medicines may be a lifestyle choice, rather than a public health good. Does enhancement medication raise any special ethical issues – is it cheating, for example, and should it be routinely available within the NHS?

Throughout, I hope to demonstrate that law and regulation are important 'actors' in the development and supply of medicines. This is not to anthropomorphise law, rather it is to argue that those responsible for the content of the regulatory regime, and the way in which it is administered, play a crucial role in shaping the development, supply and marketing of medicines. If we believe that drug companies devote too much energy to developing new treatments for obesity and male-pattern baldness, and not enough to finding cures for sleeping sickness and dengue fever, we should acknowledge that the regulatory framework may help to create or sustain incentives towards the former, and disincentives towards the latter. If we are concerned about the indirect marketing of medicines to consumers, through disease awareness campaigns for example, then attention should be paid to the existence of easily exploitable loopholes in regulations which are supposed to restrict the advertising of medicines.

In sum, we all benefit from the wide availability of safe and effective medicines, which may be facilitated by creating the background conditions in which the pharmaceutical industry can flourish and be productive. At the same time, the pursuit of profit will sometimes be in tension with the promotion of public health. We need to be alive not only to the intended but also to the unintended consequences of regulation, and to the understandable tendency of large multi-national companies to seek out and exploit any potentially profitable loopholes and cracks in the regulatory regime. We should not be surprised that for-profit companies are motivated by the pursuit of profit, rather our focus should be on the role of regulation in shaping and influencing the way the medicines industry works. This is not to say that regulation is the only relevant factor, nor that changing the status quo will always be easy, or even possible. Rather, what I hope this book will demonstrate is that regulating the development and supply of medicines is not only a complex and challenging task, but also one that should be of central importance to anyone interested in the promotion of public health and the fair and equitable distribution of healthcare resources.

1

What are Medicines and why are they Special?

OBVIOUSLY, THERE ARE points of similarity between the design and manufacture of pharmaceutical drugs and other products. Computer manufacturers are also under considerable commercial pressure to come up with new and improved computers, and novel technological gadgets. Like drug companies, they must continually innovate in order to remain profitable. The food industry makes products for human ingestion, and, in common with the pharmaceutical industry, its reputation will be badly affected if an unsafe product causes its consumers to become ill.[1] Despite the existence of similarities with other industries, one of the key assumptions underlying this book is that there is something distinctive about medicines which necessitates a special regulatory regime.

This chapter begins by examining, in very general terms, what it is that makes medicines special. Next, it considers how medicines are defined by law, and the difficulties that can sometimes arise in telling the difference between medicines and other products, like vitamin supplements and homeopathic remedies. The line the law attempts to draw between medical and non-medical products depends both upon the claims made for a product's efficacy, and upon the nature of the substance itself. Complementary and alternative medicines are subject to a special regulatory regime, where the burden of proof of efficacy is different from that which applies to conventional medicines. This chapter will conclude by arguing that the reasons which justify treating medicines differently from other products apply whenever someone claims to be able to cure disease or relieve symptoms, and that, as a result, purveyors of alternative medicines should either have to prove effectiveness in the same way as manufacturers of conventional medicines or stop making medical claims for their products.

I Why Medicines are Special

The claim that medicines are unlike other products has two components. First, there are the *intrinsic* properties of medicines, which must be powerful enough to

---

[1] I Sample, 'E Coli Outbreak: German Organic Farm Officially Identified' *The Guardian* 19 June 2011.

alleviate symptoms or alter disease progression. Any compound which is potent enough to have these positive effects may also be potent enough to cause adverse side effects in some users. Even common and generally safe drugs like aspirin are not safe for everybody: in children, aspirin can cause Reye's disease. And treatments for life-threatening diseases, like cancer, are so toxic that they cause extremely unpleasant side effects in almost everyone. The sort of risk-benefit calculation that makes it acceptable to market a drug which has very serious side effects, even when taken exactly according to instructions, would not make sense in relation to other products for human ingestion. A substance which is inert enough never to cause adverse side effects is also likely to be too inert to cure disease. If every licensed medicine had to be wholly safe for the entire population, there would be few treatment options available. The question then becomes whether a medicine is *safe enough* to license for use in humans, rather than whether it is 100 per cent safe for everyone.

The second and related aspect of the claim that medicines are special relates to how they are purchased and used. Here there are important differences between medicines depending upon how consumers obtain them. Some medicines require a prescription written by a doctor or a nurse prescriber; others can be purchased, but only in a pharmacy staffed by a qualified pharmacist; others are available for general sale, in pharmacies but also in supermarkets and convenience stores. Chapter three considers this subdivision in more detail. For now, the important point is that general sale medicines, like paracetamol and ibuprofen, are not that different from other consumer products. People can purchase and take them without the intervention of a professional intermediary. Limits on packet size and on how many packets may be purchased simultaneously are intended to discourage overdose, but it is clear that these are ineffective obstacles to someone who is determined to obtain large quantities of, say, paracetamol. The local chemist may only be prepared to sell me two packets of sixteen tablets, but I could very easily visit a number of other shops in order to amass sufficient pills to cause serious harm to myself.

Pharmacy medicines are subject to slightly more control. For example, the sale of a commonly used pharmacy-available sleep-aid will be accompanied by a reminder that it is for occasional use only. Where there is a contraindication to the use of a pharmacy-available medicine, the pharmacist will be able to ask the customer whether they have diabetes, say, or high blood pressure. Of course, the pharmacist is not able to insist upon proof that the person buying the medicine is telling the truth, so this level of control, while more intensive than that which exists in relation to general sale medicines, is still imperfect. This means that where medicines are available for sale in pharmacies, they should not be so unsafe that there are likely to be very serious consequences if they are used either by people with contraindications, or more frequently than is advisable.

It is the category of prescription-only drugs which are sold, purchased and consumed in a wholly different way from any other consumer product. When a medicine is prescribed by a doctor, the person who makes the purchasing decision is not its ultimate consumer. A person may visit their doctor and ask to be prescribed antibiotics or sleeping pills, but they have no right to a prescription. If the doctor believes that antibiotics would be useless, or that sleeping pills might be used in order to take an overdose, the patient is likely to leave the surgery empty-handed.

In addition, in relation to prescription medicines, the medicine is paid for neither by the person who makes the purchasing decision, nor by its ultimate consumer. The vast majority of patients in the United Kingdom pay nothing for their medicines. Prescription charges have been abolished in Wales, Northern Ireland and Scotland, and in England, because children, the elderly and the unemployed are exempt, only a minority of patients actually pay the prescription charge. Even for those English patients who do have to pay £7.40 per prescription, this will commonly be a fraction of the real cost of the drugs, which are funded instead through the NHS budget, and ultimately through general taxation.

Doctors decide which drugs to prescribe, but they do not pay for them. Patients do not decide which drugs they are prescribed, and again, they will rarely pay the full cost. Of course there are other situations when people buy things for others' consumption, but it must be admitted that in the context of prescription drugs, normal market relationships between manufacturers of products and their ultimate consumers are distorted, to say the least. In chapter five, this issue will be revisited in relation to the implications it has for advertising and marketing.

Doctors act as the gatekeepers to prescription medicines, and this is important in relation to the risk-benefit calculation that must be carried out when deciding whether a medicine is safe enough to be licensed for use in patients. If a medicine is effective in curing a very serious condition, but known to cause terrible side effects in some users, doctors should, in theory, be able to ensure that it is prescribed only to people in whom it can be used safely. An extreme example might be the drug thalidomide, which was withdrawn from use after evidence emerged that it caused extremely serious birth defects. In recent years, there have been indications that thalidomide can be effective in the treatment of leprosy and certain cancers. Its side effects mean that it is unthinkable that thalidomide would ever be available 'over-the-counter', but the doctor as intermediary is able to ensure that its use is limited to people who are gravely ill and who are informed in clear and direct terms that they must not expose themselves to even the smallest risk of pregnancy while taking the drug.

Of course, while the prescription system should enable a high level of third-party control over the consumption of medicines, the rise of online pharmacies poses a new challenge to what has been called the 'learned intermediary' rule.[2] If you type 'buy Valium' or 'buy Ritalin' into Google, there is no shortage of sites, frequently based offshore or with no information about their location,[3] offering prescription-only medicines for sale and shipping without a prescription. Indeed, 'buy Viagra without prescription' comes up with 20.9 million hits on Google.

[2] *Sterling Drug v Cornish* (370 F.2d 82, 85) 1966.
[3] TL Bessell et al, 'Quality of Global E-pharmacies: Can we Safeguard Consumers?' (2002) 58 *European Journal of Clinical Pharmacology* 567–72.

Although there are certainly examples of good practice in online pharmacies,[4] and they may be especially attractive to patients who find their symptoms embarrassing,[5] one of the principal reasons for a drug being 'prescription-only' is precisely that self-medication is inappropriate, usually on safety grounds. There is evidence that some online pharmacies are willing to supply medicines to patients in whom they are clearly contraindicated. Eysenbach, for example, found it remarkably easy to obtain Viagra online, despite pretending to be an obese 69-year-old woman suffering from coronary artery disease and hypertension.[6] Online pharmacies are also helping to blur the line between illegal drugs and prescription medicines. As discussed further in chapter nine, prescription painkillers are increasingly used for recreational purposes, rather than to treat symptoms.[7] This trend is undoubtedly facilitated by the existence of websites where it is possible to buy these drugs anonymously, without a prescription.

II The Development of a Special Regulatory Regime for Medicines

The use of plant and animal preparations to treat disease and relieve symptoms has a very long history, dating back (at least) to the fourth century BC, when the Sumerians used plants like liquorice, mustard, myrrh and opium in the treatment of disease. Aspirin, a very commonly used analgesic, is also a very old drug. Two thousand years ago the bark and leaves of the willow tree (which contain salicylic acid, the active ingredient in aspirin) were widely used in Greece in order to alleviate pain and fever.[8]

The regulation of medicines in the UK probably began in the fifteenth century, and was limited to inspecting the premises of apothecaries and their wares in order to ensure that they were not defective or contaminated.[9] Another early regulatory technique was the publication of a pharmacopoeia, a book which contains a list of pharmaceutical products and sets out their prescribed formulae and methods of preparation. The *Pharmacopoeia Londinensis* was published in 1618, and the British Pharmacopoeia, now produced by the British Pharmacopoeia Commission

---

[4] MJ Jones, 'Internet-Based Prescription of Sildenafil: A 2104-Patient Series' (2001) 3 *Journal of Medical Internet Research* E2; B Arruñada, Quality Safeguards and Regulation of Online Pharmacies' (2004) 13 *Health Economics* 329–44.

[5] N Glover-Thomas and J Fanning, 'Medicalisation: The Role of E-pharmacies in Iatrogenic Harm' (2010) 18 *Medical Law Review* 28–55.

[6] G Eysenbach, 'Online Prescribing of Sildanefil (Viagra) on the World Wide Web' (1999) 1 *Journal of Medical Internet Research* E10.

[7] R Sandhill, 'Prescription Drugs: Legal and Lethal' *The Sunday Times* 24 February 2008, available at www.timesonline.co.uk/tol/life_and_style/health/article3403941.ece.

[8] MR Tramèr, 'Aspirin, Like All other Drugs, is a Poison: We Do Not Know Who Should be Given what Dose and For How Long' (2000) 321 *British Medical Journal* 1170.

[9] Pharmacy Wares, Drugs and Stuffs Act of 1540. See also JP Griffin, 'Venetian Treacle and the Foundation of Medicines Regulation' (2004) 58 *British Journal of Clinical Pharmacology* 317–25.

Secretariat of the Medicines and Healthcare products Regulatory Agency (MHRA), is still the official collection of standards for UK medicinal products and pharmaceutical substances.[10]

More recent regulation of the supply of medicines has taken a number of forms including restrictions on who may supply medicines: the Pharmacy Act 1868 contained a list of drugs, including opium, which could only be sold by pharmaceutical chemists and the Dangerous Drugs Act 1920 further restricted supply, by specifying that some drugs could only be supplied on prescription.

In the 1950s, thalidomide's UK manufacturers, Distillers, claimed that it could 'be given with complete safety to pregnant women and nursing mothers without adverse effect on mother or child'.[11] Unfortunately, this claim was wrong, and between 1956 and 1961 12,000 children were born in over 30 countries with very severe limb and other birth defects. One-third of these 'thalidomide' babies died within a month. Although interest in regulating the safety of medicines existed before the thalidomide tragedy, there is no doubt that in the UK it played an important part in the drive towards the regulation of the safety and efficacy of medicines, in addition to their quality. The Medicines Act 1968 was the result, and, as amended, it continues to apply today. Its role in the licensing of medicines is considered in detail in chapter three.

Before the Medicines Act came into force in 1971, regulation of the supply of medicines was limited to control over their quality, and did not address questions of safety or efficacy.[12] It might be thought that 'quality' and 'safety' are essentially similar requirements – and hence that the pre-1968 system of regulation went some way to protect patient safety. There can, however, be an important difference between quality and safety, as illustrated by the US experience with Elixir Sulfanilamide. Sulfanilamide had been used successfully to treat streptococcal infections. Responding to demand for the drug in liquid form, in the 1930s its manufacturer's chief chemist discovered that sulfanilamide would dissolve in diethylene glycol. Raspberry flavouring was added, and the new medicine – Elixir Sulfanilamide – was widely marketed. Unfortunately, while there was no doubt as to the *quality* of the ingredients, diethylene glycol is poisonous, and Elixir Sulfanilamide killed more than one hundred people, many of them children in whom it had been used to relieve sore throats. This incident prompted the instigation of *safety*-based medicine requirements in the United States in 1938, and this – along with the stoic refusal of one Food and Drug Administration employee, Frances Kelsey, to approve thalidomide[13] – helped the US to avoid the thalidomide tragedy which occurred, mainly in Europe, three decades later.

---

[10] *The British Pharmacopoeia 2011* available at www.pharmacopoeia.co.uk/.

[11] P Ferguson, *Drug Injuries and the Pursuit of Compensation* (London, Sweet & Maxwell, 1996) 5.

[12] Sale of Food and Drugs Act 1875.

[13] In 2010, at the age of 95, Frances Kelsey was presented with an award from the Food and Drug Administration (FDA). Andrew Jack, 'Perils for Pill Pushers' *Financial Times* London, September 22, 2010.

III What is a Medicine?

The Medicines Act 1968, and the series of EU Directives which have been incorporated into UK law since it came into force, apply only to medicinal products, and it is therefore critically important to be able to tell when a substance is and is not a medicine. While there is a clear and obvious difference between a blister pack of antibiotics and a lettuce, sometimes the line between foodstuffs and medicines is much less clear. Dietary supplements often look like medicines – they often come in the form of pills and capsules – and people generally take them because they believe they will have a positive impact upon their health. So how do manufacturers tell whether or not the product they wish to market is a medicine, and hence requires a marketing authorisation based on proof of quality, safety and efficacy, or whether it is a foodstuff, and hence subject to food safety regulations which are concerned only with safety and hygiene?[14]

'Medicinal products' are defined in the Codified Pharmaceutical Directive, as amended,[15] as follows:

(a) Any substance or combination of substances presented as having properties for treating or preventing disease in human beings; or

(b) Any substance or combination of substances which may be used in or administered to human beings either with a view to restoring, correcting or modifying physiological functions by exerting a pharmacological, immunological or metabolic action, or to making a medical diagnosis.

What is important about this definition is that it gives two separate routes for classifying a product as a medicine: *presentation* and *function*. If a product is marketed for the treatment or prevention of disease, or if it is used for diagnostic purposes, or to alter physiological function, it is a medicinal product. It does not matter if the claims made for the product are, in fact, groundless and it will have no impact at all on physiological function, it is still to be treated as a medicinal product, and be judged against the standards required of medicines. The point of the regulatory system is not just to protect the public against actively dangerous products, but also from useless ones.

The body charged with deciding whether a product is a medicine is the Medicines and Healthcare products Regulatory Agency (MHRA), previously the Medicines Control Agency (MCA). When determining whether a product is *presented* for the treatment of disease, the MHRA will consider medical claims – both explicit and implicit — which have been made for it, and will additionally look at the presentation of the product, including its labelling, packaging and advertising.[16] Also relevant will be whether the product *looks like* a medicine, perhaps because it is

---

[14] Food Safety Act 1990, as amended; The General Food Regulations 2004, as amended.

[15] Codified Pharmaceutical Directive 2001/83/EEC, OJ L – 311, 28/11/2004 67–128.

[16] Medicines and Healthcare products Regulatory Agency, *A Guide to What is a Medicinal Product* (MHRA Guidance Note 8, revised 2007).

supplied in tablet or capsule form. When deciding whether a product should be classified as a medicine, the European Court of Justice has taken into account the *impression* that 'average well informed consumers' are likely to form as a result of the product's presentation.[17]

Claims that a product relieves symptoms, such as stress or anxiety, will be regarded as medicinal claims.[18] The reference to 'prevention' means that products which claim to 'protect against' disease will similarly be treated as medicinal products.[19] In contrast, the statement that a product 'helps to maintain a healthy lifestyle' has not been regarded by the MHRA as a medicinal claim.[20]

The second route to classification as a medicine refers to the *action* of the product. Here it is enough that the product contains active ingredients which are known to have a physiological effect. It is not necessary for the product to also be presented as a medicine, nor does it matter if no claims are made for the product's beneficial effects. Hence, a herbal remedy which has a pharmacologically active ingredient in a therapeutic dose, will fall within the definition even if it does not claim to be a medicine. In relation to vitamins, it will commonly be the size of the dose which will distinguish between medicinal products, which need a marketing authorisation, and dietary supplements that do not. Generally, vitamins are sold in relatively small quantities.[21] However, where vitamin or multi-vitamin preparations are taken in sufficiently large doses that they may modify physiological function – an example might be the use of vitamin D in the treatment of rickets – a vitamin supplement may be classified as a medicinal product. From the point of view of manufacturers of vitamin supplements, the rather unsatisfactory conclusion is that it is only possible to decide whether a product will be regarded as a medicinal product by function on a case-by-case basis, having regard to the pharmacological properties of each vitamin preparation.[22]

It is clear that the MHRA has a broad discretion when deciding whether or not a product is a medicine. In *R v Medicines Control Agency, ex parte Pharma Nord*,[23] the Court declined to interfere with the Agency's decision that melatonin was a medicinal product and should be available only on prescription. Pharma Nord applied for judicial review arguing that the MCA's reasons for classifying melatonin as a medicinal product were inadequate, and not in accordance with the relevant EC Directive.[24] Recognising that they were unlikely to succeed in proving *Wednesbury*[25] unreasonableness – that is, that the decision was so unreasonable that no reasonable regulator could have taken it – Pharma Nord applied for a full trial on the merits of whether melatonin should be considered a medicinal

---

[17] *Van Bennekom* [1983] ECR 3883.
[18] MHRA n 16 above.
[19] ibid.
[20] ibid.
[21] *Van Bennekom* n 17 above.
[22] *Hecht-Pharma GmbH v Staatliches Gewerbeaufsichtsamt Lüneburg* [2009] 2 CMLR 23 [73].
[23] *R v Medicines Control Agency, ex p Pharma Nord* (1998) 44 BMLR 41.
[24] Directive 65/65 EEC, the first European pharmaceutical directive, OJ L No 22 of 9. 2. 1965, 369.
[25] *Associated Provincial Picture Houses v Wednesbury Corporation* [1948] 1 KB 223.

product. Collins J refused to exercise his discretion to transfer the case to the civil courts, and the Court of Appeal dismissed the applicant's appeal. Lord Woolf MR found that only if the 'MCA could not reasonably have come to the decision which it did' would it be legitimate for the Court to interfere with its expert decision-making.

The Agency's discretion is not absolute, however. In *Re Garlic Preparations in Capsule Form: Commission of the European Communities v Germany*[26] the European Court of Justice held that the German Regulatory Agency's classification of garlic supplements as a medicine was contrary to the Directive. Their decision had been challenged by the European Commission on the grounds that it restricted free trade within the EU. The supplements were marketed as foodstuffs in other Member States and contained nothing but garlic, which, in its natural state, is self-evidently a food and not a medicine. While the garlic supplement was supplied in capsule form, this was not, on its own, sufficient to bring it within the first limb of the definition of a medicinal product. The supplements could only be categorised as medicines under the second limb if they had identifiable pharmacological properties, which garlic did not.

IV Complementary and Alternative Medicines

The simple binary system for classification of a product as a medicine, which needs a marketing authorisation from the MHRA, and a non-medicine, or foodstuff, which does not, is complicated significantly by special schemes covering herbal and homeopathic medicines. While these can, and in some cases are, treated as ordinary medicinal products, which can be granted a marketing authorisation from the MHRA in the same way as other drugs, they can also be licensed for sale via an exceptional regime. This section first sets out how these exceptional licensing processes work in practice, before turning to the more fundamental question of whether it is acceptable to treat unconventional medicines differently from conventional medical products. It is clear that complementary and alternative medicine which could not obtain an ordinary marketing authorisation because there is insufficient proof of efficacy nevertheless sometimes 'work' in the sense that they may make consumers feel better. The evidence that this is due to anything other than the placebo effect is, however, extremely weak. This leads on to the important question of whether it is acceptable to prescribe what are effectively placebo treatments to patients, either privately or within the NHS.

---

[26] *Re Garlic Preparations in Capsule Form: Commission of the European Communities v Germany* [2008] 1 CMLR 36.

A Licensing Herbal Medicines

There are three ways in which herbal medicines can be marketed in the UK. The first is that they can be treated as ordinary medicines and their manufacturers can obtain a marketing authorisation from the MHRA, for which they will have to establish proof of safety, quality and efficacy. Approximately 500 herbal medicines currently hold ordinary marketing authorisations.[27] The second route is more controversial and involves the Traditional Herbal Medicines Registration Scheme (THMRS), which has been in operation since October 2005. Products are required to meet specific standards of safety and quality *but not efficacy*, and are accompanied by agreed indications, based on traditional usage.[28]

The exemption from the need to prove efficacy is in some ways simply a practical recognition that the sort of evidence of effectiveness which would normally be needed to satisfy the MHRA is seldom available for herbal medicines because large-scale randomised controlled trials, which are the norm in relation to conventional medicines, are uncommon. Even when trials *have* been carried out, they will seldom be sufficiently rigorous to offer the sort of robust evidence the MHRA requires before it licenses a new product. For example, St John's Wort has been tested in over 30 controlled trials involving approximately 3000 patients with depression. However, these studies have involved different extracts of the herb, with different concentrations of the active ingredient, and the research subjects have been suffering from different types of depression. The data generated by these trials do not then provide evidence for the efficacy of one defined extract, or for one specific indication.[29]

In order to apply for the registration of a traditional medicinal product under the THMRS, applicants must submit a review of safety data and an expert report on quality, in addition to evidence of at least 30 years of traditional use, 15 of which should have been within the EU. In exceptional circumstances, registration will be possible even if the product has not been in use in the EU for 15 years, but it will still be necessary to prove that it has been used elsewhere for at least 30 years. The assumption behind the 'traditional use' requirement is that there must be some degree of efficacy if the remedy has been used for this length of time. The product label must inform the consumer that the basis for registration is traditional use, rather than clinical trial data, with the following warning: 'The safety and efficacy of the product rely exclusively on information obtained from its long-term use and experience'.

The assumption that proof of longevity of use offers some evidence of effectiveness is problematic, to say the least. People have been reading horoscopes and

---

[27] MHRA, *Placing a Herbal Medicine on the UK Market* (MHRA, 2011), available at www.mhra.gov.uk.

[28] The Traditional Herbal Medicinal Products Directive (EC) 2004/24 [2004] OJL136/85. Details of the Scheme are available at www.mhra.gov.uk.

[29] J Barnes, 'Quality, Efficacy and Safety of Complementary Medicines: Fashions, Facts and the Future. Part II: Efficacy and Safety' (2003) 55 *British Journal of Clinical Pharmacology* 331–40.

having their palms 'read' for many years, but this does not amount to evidence that astrologers and palm readers are capable of predicting the future. Rather, and this may be true in relation to traditional medicines too, it may instead offer compelling evidence of the remarkable durability of gullibility.

In order to avoid the submission of duplicate evidence, the Committee for Herbal Medicinal Products (CHMP), which is part of the European Medicines Agency (EMA), has developed a 'positive list' of ingredients. Establishing that a product contains an ingredient which is on the indicative list does not necessarily mean that an application for registration will be successful, but it will mean that applicants do not need to submit detailed evidence of safety or traditional use. Evidence of the quality of the particular product will still be necessary.

Finally, the third way in which herbal medicines can be marketed is the special exemption for non-manufactured herbal medicines, which are supplied to an individual consumer. Under section 12(1) of the Medicines Act 1968, herbal remedies which contain only plant materials are exempt from the requirement to obtain a marketing authorisation if the herbal remedy was made up on the premises from which it was supplied, and if it was prescribed after a one-to-one consultation. This provision is problematic insofar as it does not set any requirements at all for safety or quality, nor are there any restrictions on who can prescribe and sell non-manufactured herbal products. As the MHRA itself explains, 'anyone – irrespective of qualifications or experience – can practise herbal medicine and, after making a diagnosis and forming a judgement about the treatment required, can make up and supply an unlicensed herbal medicine'.[30] There are no grounds for thinking that a non-manufactured product is necessarily safer than a manufactured one. On the contrary, given that herbal medicines – including those that have been individually prepared – can be toxic and unsafe, as well as harmless and/ or useless, this exemption seems unwarranted.

Section 12(2) of the Medicines Act 1968 used to also contain an exemption for pre-prepared over-the-counter remedies, provided they were not sold under any brand name and did not make any written therapeutic claims, but this 'unlicensed' route has been phased out, and since April 2011, any manufactured herbal remedies must either be registered under the THMRS or have an ordinary marketing authorisation.

B Homeopathic Medicines

Homeopathy involves taking highly diluted substances, usually in tablet form. Proponents believe that it works in two ways. The first, known as 'like-cures-like', involves using a diluted form of a substance which causes a symptom in order to treat the same symptom. Secondly, 'ultra-dilution' is based upon the claim that the more dilute a substance the more potent it is, in part as a result of the way in which

[30] MHRA, *Unlicensed Herbal Remedies Made up to Meet the Need of Individual Patients: Section 12(1) of the Medicines Act 1968* (MHRA, 2011).

solutions are shaken, also known as 'succussion'. The general claim is that home-opathy stimulates the body's capacity to heal itself. It is, however, scientifically improbable. In his evidence to the House of Commons Science and Technology Committee, Professor David Colquhoun stated bluntly: 'If homeopathy worked the whole of chemistry and physics would have to be overturned'.[31]

When the Medicines Act 1968 came into force, Product Licences of Right (PLRs) were issued to all medicines which were then on the market. Some homeo-pathic medicines would have been covered by this provision, and may still be marketed with indications for use. The MHRA has attempted to phase out PLRs by encouraging manufacturers to apply for their medicines to be covered by the more appropriate Simplified Registration Scheme, and now the National Rules, but they have not gone so far as to withdraw all PLRs.

New homeopathic medicines could, in theory, be eligible for marketing author-isations in the same way as ordinary medicines, but they are unlikely to meet the efficacy requirements. There have been studies which appear to show some advantage to homeopathic medicines when compared with a placebo treatment, but these have been methodologically flawed.[32] When only the most rigorous methodological studies are taken into account, they consistently demonstrate no benefit over placebo.[33]

There are currently then two ways in which new homeopathic products can be registered. First, the Simplified Registration Scheme for homeopathic medicines was introduced in 1992 by an EU Directive.[34] Under this Scheme, manufacturers must establish the safety and quality of products, and must make no therapeutic claims. The Scheme only applies to medicines for oral or external use, and prod-ucts must be sufficiently dilute to guarantee safety.

Second, the National Rules Scheme was introduced in 2006.[35] It enables homeo-pathic medicinal products to be marketed for the relief or treatment of minor symptoms and conditions, defined as those that can be relieved or treated without the supervision or intervention of a doctor. Homeopathic products must not be

---

[31] Science and Technology Committee – Fourth Report of session 2009–10, *Evidence Check 2: Homeopathy* para 59.

[32] K Linde and D Melchart, 'Randomised Controlled Trials of Individualised Homeopathy: A State-of-the-Art Review' (1998) 4 *Journal of Alternative and Complementary Medicine* 371–88.

[33] ibid; K Linde *et al*, 'Impact of Study Quality on Outcome in Placebo-Controlled Trials of Homeopathy' (1999) 52 *Journal of Clinical Epidemiology* 631–36; J Kleijnen, P Knipschild and G ter Riet, 'Clinical Trials of Homoeopathy' (1991) 302 *British Medical Journal* 316–23; JP Boissel et al, *Critical Literature Review on the Effectiveness of Homoeopathy: Overview of Data from Homoeopathic Medicine Trials: Homoeopathic Medicine Research Group Report to the European Commission* (Brussels, 1996) 195–210; M Cucherat et al, 'Evidence of Clinical Efficacy of Homeopathy: A Meta-Analysis of Clinical Trials' (2000) 56 *European Journal of Clinical Pharmacology* 27–33; A Shang et al, 'Are the Clinical Effects of Homoeopathy Placebo Effects? Comparative Study of Placebo-Controlled Trials of Homoeopathy and Allopathy' (2005) 366 *The Lancet* 726–73.

[34] 92/73/EC Council Directive 92/73/EEC of 22 September 1992 widening the scope of Directives 65/65/EEC and 75/319/EEC on the approximation of provisions laid down by Law, Regulation or Administrative Action relating to medicinal products and laying down additional provisions on home-opathic medicinal products, OJ L 297, 13.10.1992, 8–11.

[35] The Medicines for Human Use (National Rules for Homoeopathic Products) Regulations 2006 SI 1952.

marketed for serious conditions. Applications under the National Rules Scheme must establish quality, safety *and efficacy*. This does not, however, mean that companies must submit trial data in the same way as for a conventional medicine. Rather, the applicant must provide study reports in relation to the product *or* published scientific literature *or* what are referred to as 'homoeopathic provings'. The MHRA has suggested that, 'whatever data is provided, it should be sufficient to demonstrate that UK homeopathic practitioners would accept the efficacy of the product for the indications sought'.[36] It is not clear that this latter requirement is sufficient to establish efficacy. Instead, it looks like the claim that a homeopathic medicine works if other people, who believe in homeopathy, believe that it works. To return to the analogy of horoscopes, presumably there are astrologers who believe that knowledge of a person's date and time of birth can help them predict how the following year is likely to turn out for them. Even if it could be established that a very large number of astrologers honestly believe that horoscopes can predict the future, this does not make it true.

C Licensing Complementary and Alternative Medicine

There are clearly good reasons for bringing complementary and alternative medicine (CAM), like herbal medicines and homeopathy, within the regulatory regime which applies to other products which make medicinal claims. The MHRA can enforce safety and quality requirements, and can require proof of efficacy. A system where there was no control over CAM would be self-evidently undesirable, leading to unqualified individuals prescribing potentially dangerous and/or useless medicines to people who might die or be seriously injured as a result, either because of the toxicity of the medicine itself, or because taking it means they do not receive effective conventional treatment for their condition.[37]

On the other hand, there may be dangers in treating CAM as an exceptional case within the regulatory regime for medicines. Weakening the requirements to prove efficacy, while at the same time licensing or registering these products, gives them an unwarranted stamp of official legitimacy. Of course, there is no reason why only chemically synthesised compounds should be treated as medicines, and the manufacturers of herbal and homeopathic medicines can apply for marketing authorisations in the same way as other makers of medicines. Some herbal medicines undoubtedly work – senna is an effective treatment for constipation, for example – and these products can and should be treated in the same way as other effective medicinal products. What is objectionable is that the manufacturers of herbal and homeopathic medicines have alternative *and less demanding* routes for the formal recognition of their products when there is no robust evidence that they work, other than as a result of the placebo effect.

---

[36] MHRA, *The Homeopathic National Rules Scheme: Brief Guidance for Manufacturers and Suppliers* (MHRA, 2006).

[37] House of Lords Select Committee on Science and Technology, *Complementary and Alternative Medicine* Session 1999–2000, 6th Report (Parliament, 2000) para 4.21.

In addition to the questionable assumption that proof of traditional use offers some proof of efficacy, two further assumptions underpin the problematic but common view that CAM – while not necessarily very effective – is essentially harmless. First, it is often assumed that anything that is herbal or natural is necessarily safe, when compared with artificial chemical compounds. This is simply wrong. Many plants are potent and/or toxic. Digoxin, for example, is extracted from foxgloves and is used in a number of conventional medicines for the treatment of heart disease; in large quantities, however, it can be fatal. The common but mistaken assumption that 'natural' remedies cannot cause harm is also partly responsible for the significant under-reporting of adverse side effects caused by CAM: unlike side effects experienced after taking conventional medicines, consumers of herbal remedies are less likely to connect their unpleasant symptoms with the herbal medicine they have been taking, and they are less likely to report adverse side effects.

Second, it is also often assumed that CAM is used principally by the worried well, who may be wasting their money on ineffective 'natural' remedies, but who are not likely to suffer any serious ill effects as a result. Again, this assumption is mistaken and it is common for people with extremely serious illnesses, like cancer, to consult alternative medical practitioners. Lippert et al questioned 190 patients with prostate cancer and found that 43 per cent had used complementary and alternative medicines.[38] Ernst and Cassileth conducted a meta-analysis of published studies on the use of alternative medicine by cancer patients and found that the proportion of patients who said that they had used CAM in the treatment of their cancer varied from 7–64 per cent, with an average prevalence of 31.4 per cent.[39] In their study of patients undergoing cardiac surgery Liu et al found that the overall rate of CAM use was 75 per cent, or 44 per cent if prayer and vitamins were excluded.[40] If someone facing a very serious diagnosis chooses to rely on alternative medicine, access to effective, evidence-based treatment may be delayed or foregone altogether, with serious consequences for the person's health. There is, for example, evidence that homeopaths who recommend ineffective homoeopathic prophylaxis for malaria also sometimes undermine and criticise the use of conventional malaria prophylaxis, and do not necessarily give simple advice on bite prevention.[41]

Alternative medicines are also often taken by people who are taking other sorts of conventional medication, and given that the overwhelming majority of patients (87 per cent in Liu et al's study) do not tell their doctors about their use of alternative

---

[38] MC Lippert et al, 'Alternative Medicine Use in Patients with Localised Prostate Cancer Treated with Curative Intent' (1999) 86 *Cancer* 2642–48.

[39] E Ernst and BR Cassileth, 'The Prevalence of Complementary/Alternative Medicine in Cancer: A Systemic Review' (1998) 83 *Cancer* 777–82.

[40] EH Liu et al, 'Use of Alternative Medicine by Patients Undergoing Cardiac Surgery' (2000) 120 *Journal of Thoracic and Cardiovascular Surgery* 335–41.

[41] B Goldacre, 'Benefits and Risks of Homoeopathy' (2007) 370 *The Lancet* 1672–73.

medicines,[42] perhaps fearing censure or disapproval, the risk of drug/herb adverse reactions may be significant. St John's Wort, for example, interacts with a number of conventional medicines, in some cases reducing the conventional medicine's effectiveness.

Edzard Ernst has argued that the conditions that are most likely to drive patients to some sort of alternative medicine are first, 'chronic benign complaints', like back pain or arthritis, and, second, 'incurable life-threatening diseases such as cancer or AIDS'. Their use by these groups is prompted in part by dissatisfaction with what conventional medicine can offer them, as well as by the promises made by CAM practitioners.[43]

D Satisfaction with CAM and the Placebo Effect

Use of CAM is common, and users often report being satisfied with its results. There are a number of reasons for its popularity, which can be broadly divided into 'push' factors, mainly involving dissatisfaction with conventional medicine,[44] and 'pull' factors, in which consumers feel positive about the supposedly natural or holistic approach to treatment.

There are a number of reasons why patients may feel dissatisfied with conventional medicine. The fear of being sued may make doctors more cautious and less relaxed with their patients, and it is rare for patients to have a long-term relationship with a family doctor. Increased bureaucracy and paperwork can make patients feel as though they are being 'processed' within the system.[45] Conventional medicine is also not well suited to dealing with patients who have what is sometimes referred to as 'illness without pathology'; that is, people who feel unwell despite the fact that tests suggest that there is nothing wrong with them.

It is clear that patients do feel better after using CAM.[46] A survey of 6,500 patients over a six-year period conducted by the Bristol Homeopathic Hospital found that 70 per cent of patients reported improved health, with 50 per cent reporting a major improvement. A survey of 500 patients treated at the Royal London Homeopathic Hospital found that 81 per cent said their main problem had improved very much, moderately or slightly. Of the patients who had been taking prescription medicines when they first attended, 29 per cent had stopped, and 32 per cent had reduced their intake.[47] Of course, these surveys do not neces-

---

[42] ibid. A Ranzini, A Allen and YL Lai, 'Use of Complementary Medicines and Therapies Among Obstetric Patients' (2001) 97 *Obstetrics & Gynecology* S46.

[43] E Ernst, 'We Must Give Patients the Evidence on Complementary Therapies' (2006) 333 *British Medical Journal* 308.

[44] FMC Sharples, R van Haselen and P Fisher 'NHS Patients' Perspective on Complementary Medicine: A Survey' (2003) 11 *Complementary Therapies in Medicine* 243–48.

[45] See also C Vincent and A Furnham, *Complementary Medicine: A Research Perspective* (Chichester, Wiley & Sons, 1997).

[46] House of Lords Select Committee on Science and Technology n 37 above, 1.

[47] Sharples et al n 44 above.

sarily provide evidence that homeopathy is effective in treating disease and relieving symptoms, rather they could instead demonstrate the extraordinary power of the placebo effect.

It is important to remember that the placebo effect which is at work here is not limited to the positive impact of believing that you have received effective medicine. A number of other features of alternative medicine may result in an enhanced placebo response. First, CAM is commonly used to treat symptoms that often clear up on their own, like pain. If I have an acute headache, and take an ultra-diluted preparation of belladonna (deadly nightshade), I may be convinced that any improvement I experience is the result of the homeopathic remedy, rather than something that would have happened anyway. In addition, some of the conditions which homeopaths claim to be able to treat, such as anxiety and irritable bowel syndrome, may be especially susceptible to placebo responses.

Second, the decision to consult a CAM practitioner is a conscious and deliberate one, and patients clearly hope that it will provide relief from their symptoms which they may not have received so far from conventional medicine. Since admitting that the alternative treatment made no difference would cast doubt on the wisdom of that choice, purchasers of CAM therapies may be more invested in experiencing a positive improvement than users of conventional medicine. Indeed, much CAM claims to work by harnessing the body's own healing capacities. Admitting it has not worked might even appear to be an admission of failure.

Indeed, some critics have accused CAM of bolstering essentially conservative ideologies of personal responsibility and blame for the state of one's health. In their study of CAM's approach to breast cancer, which commonly involves locating the cause of the cancer within the woman's life experiences and choices, Sered and Agigian comment acerbically that:

> While coding the interviews, we couldn't help noting that if a breast cancer patient had to resolve her issues with self-esteem, anger, nurturing, work-family balance, and her relationship with her mother, not to mention transforming her negative or toxic thoughts into positive energy, meditating, doing special exercises, overhauling her diet and rearranging her furniture while navigating a positive female gender role in a society in which gender roles are rapidly changing, she easily could die of old age before becoming well.[48]

While CAM is sometimes available within the NHS, most is provided within the private sector. This will mean that the premises are often more comfortable and welcoming, which in itself can make patients feel better about their decision to consult a CAM therapist. It has also been suggested that 'paying for healthcare increases patients' involvement in their own recovery and provides additional motivation, which leads in turn to greater treatment compliance and a greater degree of satisfaction'.[49]

---

[48] S Sered and A Agigian, 'Holistic Sickening: Breast Cancer and the Discursive Worlds of Complementary and Alternative Practitioners' (2008) 31 *Sociology of Health and Illness* 616–31.

[49] House of Lords Select Committee n 37 above, para 3.6.

Finally, and perhaps most importantly, CAM medicine often *does* provide something which busy conventional doctors are unable to offer, namely time, sympathy, warmth and hope.[50] Waiting for 30 minutes in a cramped and noisy waiting room, in order to spend seven minutes with an overworked and rushed GP, who sends you away with the inconclusive and frustrating advice to come back if you feel no better in a month's time, is unlikely to induce a placebo response in anyone.

It should not be at all surprising that someone feels better after talking to a CAM therapist, who will be interested in how she feels, and who will discuss and take seriously all of her complaints and symptoms, however trivial. In their study of three 'placebo' treatments for irritable bowel syndrome: observation while being placed on a waiting list; having fake acupuncture with an uncommunicative doctor and having fake acupuncture with a warm and empathetic practitioner, Kaptchuk et al found that it was the quality of the practitioner's interaction with the patient which made the most difference to the apparent relief of symptoms following placebo treatment.[51] In another study, the high placebo response in all treatments for irritable bowel syndrome (42 per cent) was greater still (as much as 72 per cent) where the treatment involved more office visits.[52]

Baarts and Pedersen found that patients 'became convinced of the positive benefits of CAM, even in cases where CAM did not relieve them of their symptoms'.[53] This at first sight rather surprising finding is explained by the fact that using CAM encouraged people to 'regard the body as a natural phenomenon involving bodily energies, which they regard as potential self-healing resources'.[54] The satisfaction patients report following CAM is not necessarily because it has altered the progression of their disease, rather it may simply have enhanced their much more subjective sense of 'wellbeing'.[55]

Here perhaps is the central dilemma in relation to CAM. On the one hand, it is self-evident that people's health and wellbeing can be enhanced by things other than conventional medicines. The beneficial effects of exercise, for example, are well known. Most people have personal experience of the therapeutic effects of a relaxing holiday. If CAM does make people feel better, it is possible that conventional medicine may have something to learn about what Laurence has called the 'power of care'.[56] Spending time talking to patients, and treating them with respect

---

[50] K Resch, S Hill, and E Ernst, 'Use of Complementary Therapies by Individuals with Arthritis' (1997) 16 *Clinical Rheumatology* 391–95; Jonathan Waxman, 'Shark Cartilage in the Water' (2006) 333 *British Medical Journal* 1129.

[51] TJ Kaptchuk et al, 'Components of Placebo Effect: Randomised Controlled Trial in Patients with Irritable Bowel Syndrome' (2008) 336 *British Medical Journal* 999–1003.

[52] SD Dorn et al, 'A Meta-Analysis of the Placebo Response in Complementary and Alternative Medicine Trials of Irritable Bowel Syndrome' (2007) 19 *Neurogastroenterology and Motility* 630–37.

[53] C Baarts and IK Pedersen, 'Derivative Benefits: Exploring the Body through Complementary and Alternative Medicine' (2009) 31 *Sociology of Health and Illness* 31 719–33.

[54] ibid.

[55] E Soint, 'The Search for Wellbeing in Alternative and Complementary Health Practices' (2006) 28 *Sociology of Health and Illness* 330–49.

[56] J Laurance, 'Magic is Acceptable' (2010) 375 *The Lancet* 885.

and concern can undoubtedly help them to feel better.[57] On the other hand, much CAM claims to be having a physiological effect upon disease progression, where the evidence base is dubious, if not non-existent. The claim that extremely diluted substances can alter the progress of disease is not substantiated, and diverts attention away from the much more important insight that the quality of the practitioner/patient interaction has a significant impact upon health outcomes.

E CAM on the NHS

It has been estimated that around half of all general practitioners provide some access to complementary medicine within the NHS.[58] Homeopathy has been provided in the NHS since its inception, and there are currently four homeopathic hospitals in the UK, in London, Bristol, Liverpool and Glasgow. In his evidence to the Science and Technology Committee in 2010, Health Minister Mike O'Brien estimated that the total spent on homeopathy by the NHS was 'probably less than £12 million . . . but not too much less'.[59]

It would be a mistake to rule out any NHS funding of CAM, since there are a few techniques which are demonstrably more effective than placebo. Ernst et al compiled what they described as a 'meagre list' of 20 interventions which 'are backed by positive and sound evidence', including melatonin for insomnia and Co-enzyme Q10 for hypertension.[60] Excluded from this list were the majority of CAM treatments that are safe but do not work (such as Bach flower remedies and homeopathy), and the few which do work but are unsafe (such as kava-kava).

The principal issue raised by spending NHS funds on CAM is whether it is acceptable to pay for treatments which may work, but only because of the placebo effect. On the one hand, it could be argued that harnessing the placebo response to restore health and wellbeing is an appropriate use of NHS resources: patients feel better and these satisfied patients may impose fewer costs on other parts of the NHS.[61] Studies have suggested that the use of placebos – most commonly vitamins and over-the-counter analgesics – in ordinary medical practice is not uncommon.[62] In the US, one study suggested that 80 per cent of US hospital clinicians occasionally used placebo medicines, and the reasons they gave included satisfying

[57] W Grant Thompson, *The Placebo Effect and Health: Combining Science and Compassionate Care* (Amherst, NY, Prometheus Books, 2005).

[58] KJ Thomas, P Coleman and JP Nicholl, 'Trends in Access to Complementary or Alternative Medicines via Primary Care in England: 1995–2001 Results from a Follow-Up National Survey' (2003) 20 *Family Practice* 575–77.

[59] House of Commons Science and Technology Committee *Evidence Check 2: Homeopathy* Fourth Report of Session 2009–10, para 14.

[60] E Ernst, 'Complementary and Alternative Medicine: What the NHS Should be Funding?' (2008) 58 *British Journal of General Practice* 208–09.

[61] WA Brown, 'The Placebo Effect' (1998) 278 *Scientific American* 90–95.

[62] JC Tilburt et al, 'Prescribing "Placebo Treatments": Results of National Survey of US Internists and Rheumatologists' (2008) 337 *British Medical Journal* a1938.

the demanding patient and proving to themselves that the patient's symptoms were, in fact, psychogenic and had no organic origin.[63]

On the other hand, others might argue that the deliberate prescription of placebo medicines is unethical, because it will generally work only if patients are led to believe that they are receiving a physiologically effective drug, rather than an inert substance.[64] This necessity to deceive the patient about what has been prescribed could be said to be inconsistent with the partnership model of medical decision-making, with its increasing emphasis upon ensuring that patients give their informed consent to treatment. Even if the doctor states, honestly, to a patient that 'some people feel better after undergoing this treatment', she is still relying upon the patient's assumption that her doctor *must* be giving her some sort of 'real' treatment.

So far, the National Institute for health and Clinical Excellence, whose role we consider in more detail in chapter six, has not systematically evaluated CAM. Many commentators have argued that such a review is necessary in order to establish definitively which treatments represent good value for money, and hence might properly be provided within the NHS, and which do not.[65] This raises the further question of what is properly provided by a national *health* service, given that medical treatment is not the only factor which contributes to a person's state of health or wellness. We cannot expect the NHS to provide everything that might be able to make us feel better. Exercise undoubtedly has a positive impact upon health, but I cannot expect the NHS to pay for the expensive running shoes which I have to replace each year.

CAM may contribute to its users' sense of wellbeing. If they are paying for it themselves, the information provided to the patient will be critical. Advertising should not be misleading, for example, and consumers must be properly informed of the evidence base, or lack of it, in order to make an informed choice about whether to spend their money on non-evidence-based treatment. If treatment is provided within the NHS, as *medical* treatment, it should meet the same standards as other treatment. Proof of safety and efficacy should be a prerequisite, and NICE should robustly rule out NHS provision of any CAM therapies which do not meet the standards it sets for the more conventional treatments it assesses.

---

[63] G Gray and P Flynn 'A Survey of Placebo Use in a General Hospital' (1981) *General Hospital Psychiatry* 199–203.

[64] House of Commons Science and Technology Committee *Evidence Check 2: Homeopathy* n 59 above, para 94; A Hróbjartsson, 'Clinical Placebo Interventions are Unethical, Unnecessary and Unprofessional' (2008) 19 *Journal of Clinical Ethics* J 66–69.

[65] L Franck, C Chantler and M Dixon, 'Should NICE Evaluate Complementary and Alternative Medicine?' (2007) 334 *British Medical Journal* 506–07.

V Conclusion

The next chapter turns to the regulation of the sort of clinical trials that must be carried out before a medicine can receive a marketing authorisation from the MHRA. Although the requirement to prove efficacy for a specified indication is much more rigorously enforced than is the case in the weaker 'registration' scheme for CAM, it is not without difficulties. Chapter three will address the licensing regime for conventional medicines, and it is evident that proof of efficacy greater than placebo – while clearly much more robust than a 'traditional use' requirement – can facilitate the marketing of medicines that are of marginal effectiveness, and no better than existing medicines. If these rules were to be further strengthened, so that manufacturers had to establish that any new medicine offered a real and substantial improvement to patients, and if this were additionally to apply whenever anyone makes a medical claim about their product, much CAM would disappear. While such a move might be grounded in a desire to protect consumers from wasting their money on useless or unsafe interventions, it is clear that it would not be popular with CAM enthusiasts who believe that they do benefit – in real and concrete ways – from their interactions with CAM practitioners.

The central paradox is that modern, conventional medicine is not the only way to make people feel better. Harnessing the beneficial effects of warmth, care and hope may be good for patients, but it is not medicine. The irony is that part of the reason people's wellbeing improves after consulting a CAM practitioner is precisely because they mistakenly believe that it works, in a physiological rather than a psychological way. The positive effects of the placebo response would be threatened if CAM practitioners had to admit that all they have to offer is time and kindness. And yet – with very few exceptions, when CAM could in any event reach the standards we require of conventional medicines – it is fundamentally misleading to pretend otherwise.

2

Clinical Trials

IN THE PREVIOUS chapter, the deficiencies of the system for registering alternative medicines were discussed. This chapter is concerned instead with conventional medical products, and the regulation of the trials which must be carried out before a new medicine can be licensed for use in humans. The licensing process itself is the subject of the next chapter.

Of course, clinical trials in human subjects are by no means the first stage in the long process of drug discovery. Years before a medicine reaches the clinical trial stage, the drug company will usually have acquired a patent, that is an exclusive monopoly right to make, sell and market the chemical compound for a minimum of 20 years.[1] Once its commercial interests in its product have been protected, trials must take place in order to establish safety and efficacy. It is possible to test medicines on animals, and more recently there has been progress in using human stem cell lines for *in vitro* toxicology testing,[2] but it is impossible to know whether a medicine is safe and effective for use in humans unless trials have taken place involving human beings. If no one was ever subjected to the risks of being among the first people to take a new drug, it would be impossible to develop innovative ways to treat disease. Medical progress therefore depends upon some people being exposed to the risks of research, and one of the most basic questions for regulation is how to strike the right balance between the need to generate useful data and the need to protect research participants' welfare.

The abuse of research subjects has a long and undistinguished history. The most infamous abuses took place in Nazi Germany, where concentration camp inmates were used in dangerous and sometimes fatal 'experiments', often designed to serve the war effort.[3] After the end of the Second World War, some of the Nazi doctors and scientists who had participated in these experiments were prosecuted at

---

[1] World Trade Organisation, *Agreement on Trade-Related Aspects of Intellectual Property Rights* (WHO, 1994). Patents can be granted in the UK under s 1 of the Patents Act 1977 for inventions that are (a) new, (b) involve an inventive step (this means a step that is not obvious to someone with knowledge and experience in the area), and (c) are capable of industrial application. Under s 14(3), an application for a patent must be accompanied by a specification which discloses the invention 'in a manner which is clear enough and complete enough for the invention to be performed by a person skilled in the art'. See further *Pharmacia v Merck* [2001] EWCA Civ 1610.

[2] S Bremer and T Hartung, 'The Use of Embryonic Stem Cells for Regulatory Developmental Toxicity Testing In Vitro – The Current Status of Test Development' (2004) 10 *Current Pharmaceutical Design* 2733–47.

[3] T Taylor, *The Anatomy of the Nuremberg Trials: A Personal Memoir* (New York, Little Brown, 1993).

Nuremberg, and in its judgment, the Nuremberg Court set out a Code for the future conduct of medical research, with its first principle being that 'the voluntary consent of the human subject is absolutely essential'.[4]

The Nazis' experiments were breathtaking in their lack of concern for human life, but abuse of research subjects certainly did not begin in the 1930s and end in 1945. In the eighteenth and nineteenth centuries, research was carried out on orphans, prostitutes, and other 'expendable' social groups, and it is clear that the Nuremberg Code did not eliminate unethical research practices.[5] One of the most infamous examples was the Tuskegee study, which took place between 1932 and 1972, in which effective treatment for syphilis was deliberately withheld from 400 poor and uneducated black men so that the disease's natural progression could be observed. They were not told that they had syphilis, nor that they were taking part in an experiment. On the contrary, the men believed that they were receiving free health care from the US government. One of the doctors involved in this study also carried out syphilis research in Guatemala, which involved sending prostitutes known to be infected with syphilis into prisons in order to have sex with prisoners, who could then be given prophylactic treatment to test whether it was capable of preventing infection.[6]

Although the symbolic importance of the Nuremberg Code cannot be overstated, it did not have much impact upon medical practice, perhaps because most clinicians assumed it applied *in extremis,* to doctors who would deliberately kill and injure their patients in the interests of science. More user-friendly, and much more detailed, has been the World Medical Association's Helsinki Declaration, a statement of ethical principles for medical research involving human subjects. It has been updated eight times since it was first adopted in 1964, and its principles have been embedded in UK law, via the EU Clinical Trials Directive.[7]

This chapter begins with a description of different stages or 'phases' of clinical trials, through which toxicity is initially investigated using a small number of subjects, before efficacy and the acceptability of side effects are established in larger groups of patients. Next, it considers what justifies enrolling someone in a trial. For competent adults, this is commonly said to be their fully informed consent to participation. For children and for adults who lack capacity, it is harder to justify subjecting them to risks when the intention is not to benefit them but to generate new and generalisable knowledge. On the other hand, if it was only possible to

---

[4] *United States v Karl Brandt.* Trials of War Criminals before the Nuremberg Military Tribunals under Control Council Law No 10, vol 2 181–2. US Government Printing Office (Washington, DC 1949).

[5] See further HK Beecher, 'Ethics and Clinical Research' (1966) 274 *New England Journal of Medicine* 1354–60 and MH Pappworth, *Human Guinea Pigs: Experimentation on Man* (Beacon Press, Boston, 1967).

[6] SM Reverby, '"Normal Exposure" and Inoculation Syphilis: A PHS "Tuskegee" Doctor in Guatemala 1946–48' (2011) 23 *Journal of Policy History* 6–28.

[7] (2001) Directive 2001/20/ EC of the European parliament and of the council of 4 April 2002 on the approximation of the laws, regulations and administrative provisions of the Member States relating to the implementation of good clinical practice in the conduct of clinical trials on medicinal products for human use. OJ L121, 34–44.

carry out research on those who are able to give consent, illnesses which only affect individuals who lack capacity would be effectively untreatable.

The development costs of a new drug are enormous – a common, although not undisputed figure is $800 million,[8] or around £550 million.[9] Most investigational compounds fail at some point during the testing process, and the costs of these failures must be recouped from medicines which do eventually reach the marketplace. There is obviously considerable economic pressure on the pharmaceutical industry to obtain data from clinical trials that justify their investment by demonstrating safety and efficacy. It is, however, vitally important that the results of trials which show that a new compound does not work, or that it is unsafe are made public. Trials which do not show efficacy are plainly not as interesting as those which report a dramatic medical breakthrough, and they are less commercially advantageous for the drug's manufacturer. They also appear to receive much less publicity and are reported less frequently in specialist medical journals than positive results, despite being an essential component of the total evidence base which should inform decisions about the licensing, funding and prescription of medicines.

Finally, there have been a number of recent changes to the organisation of clinical trials. Instead of scientists and clinicians recruiting research participants, for-profit contract research organisations commonly fulfil this role and do much of the planning and running of clinical trials. It is also now common for medical writing agencies, again operating commercially, to prepare both applications to licensing authorities and manuscripts for publication. Clinical research is increasingly 'outsourced' to low and middle-income countries, raising important questions about whether this is done for clinical reasons – as in the case of treatments for conditions, like malaria, which are prevalent only in poorer tropical regions of the world – or whether it is simply easier and cheaper to conduct research in places where regulations may be weaker and less strictly enforced.

I What are Clinical Trials?

Clinical trials in humans are subdivided into phases I–IV. Phase I trials involve a small number of healthy volunteers (commonly between 20–80), who are given the drug so that researchers can study its toxicity, and the way in which it is absorbed and metabolised. Next, in a phase II trial, the drug is given to a larger group of people suffering from the condition which it is intended to treat in order to evaluate its effectiveness, as compared with a 'control' group, who receive either a placebo or the standard treatment for the condition. The tolerability of the proposed dosage and presence of any side effects will also be monitored. Phase II trials

---

[8] DM Cutler, 'The Demise of the Blockbuster?' (2007) 356 *New England Journal of Medicine* 1292–93; M Goozner, *The $800 Million Pill: The Truth Behind the Cost of New Drugs* (Berkeley, University of California Press, 2004).

[9] Association of the British Pharmaceutical Industry, *Annual Report 2009–10* (ABPI, 2010).

are usually randomised, controlled and double-blinded (see below), and involve a few hundred individuals. Phase III trials, also usually randomised, controlled and double-blinded, will involve monitoring a larger group of patients, from several hundred to several thousand, who take the medicine for a longer period of time, and again outcomes will be judged against those of the patients who were allocated to the control group. It has been estimated that for every 100 drugs which enter phase I, 70 will make it to phase II, 33 to phase III, 25 to regulatory submission and 20 to final approval.[10] Phase IV trials take place after a medicine has been licensed for use in humans, in order to study longer-term efficacy and safety or to investigate new indications for a licensed medicine.

A Phase I Trials

The twin assumptions behind the use of phase I trials to test for toxicity are first, that safety should be assessed at the outset, *before* drugs are tested for efficacy, and, second, that safety can be properly determined using healthy volunteers, rather than patients suffering from the condition the drug is intended to treat. These assumptions are seldom questioned,[11] even though it could be argued that a phase I trial which shows that drug X can be safely taken by healthy people has not generated *clinically* useful information. It has not shown that drug X works, and it has not shown that it can safely be taken by *patients*. Proving that a new medicine is safe when taken by a group of fit and strong men in their twenties does not establish that it will also be safe for the elderly women with hypertension who may be its intended users. Nevertheless, it seems to be generally accepted that detecting toxicity in humans is best done with a small group of healthy volunteers, *before* enrolling patients.

Dramatic evidence of the risks of non-therapeutic phase I trials emerged in the UK in 2006, when eight healthy male volunteers were enrolled in a phase I trial (of monoclonal antibody TGN1412 – thought to have potential uses in the treatment of arthritis, leukaemia and multiple sclerosis) at Northwick Park Hospital in north London. Primate toxicology studies had not shown any adverse effects, and it was wrongly assumed that TGN1412 would be well-tolerated in humans. The six men who had been given an active dose immediately suffered life-threatening multiple organ failure. The other two men had been given a placebo. None of the affected men died, but one of them was subsequently diagnosed with the early stages of an aggressive lymphoma, and all of them face an elevated risk of suffering from incurable auto-immune diseases in the future.[12]

---

[10] ABPI Report of Seminar, *Medicines; Tried and Tested – or an Unknown Risk?* 2 Nov 2000,available at www.abpi.org.uk/amric/tried_&_tested.pdf.

[11] A notable exception is R Wachbroit, 'Assessing Phase I Clinical Trials' (2010) 9 *Law, Probability and Risk* 179–86.

[12] D Leppard, 'Elephant Man Drug Victims told to Expect Early Death' *The Sunday Times* 30 July 2006.

A report into the incident by an expert scientific group made a number of rec-ommendations about how to protect participants' safety in 'first in man' studies.[13] When deciding on the dose, the Expert Group suggested that investigators should always err on the side of caution, and should give careful consideration to both the route and rate of administration. Slow infusion, which can be stopped immedi-ately at the first sign of any adverse effects, should generally be preferred. The TGN1412 trial was further criticised for giving all six men the active dose within minutes of each other: 'New agents in first-in-man trials should be administered sequentially to subjects with an appropriate period of observation between dosing of individual subjects'.[14]

Ironically, this incident prompted an *increase* in the numbers of people making inquiries about taking part in clinical trials.[15] Media coverage had reported that the men had received £2000 each for taking part, and this stimulated interest in other phase I trials, which might be equally lucrative but, since this case was clearly an aberration, might be assumed to be safer.

B Phase II and III Trials

Sometimes it will not be acceptable to enrol healthy volunteers in phase I trials. When a new treatment is known to be toxic – chemotherapeutic agents for use in the treatment of cancer, for example – there could be no justification for exposing healthy volunteers to the risks and side effects of treatment. Trials of highly toxic drugs must therefore involve patients from the outset. Normally, however, once phase I trials establish that a drug is reasonably safe, the next stage is to involve patients in a phase II trial.

As phase II trials become better designed and larger, the justification for carry-ing out phase III trials may be lost.[16] If a phase II trial can pick up common side effects and offer proof of efficacy, it may not be ethical to continue to enrol patients in further research. Certainly it is true that evidence of effectiveness in a phase II trial will sometimes be so overwhelming that it would be inappropriate to waste time conducting a phase III trial before making the demonstrably beneficial med-icine available to patients. This happened in the US with the first HIV/AIDS drug zidovudine (brand name AZT). In the phase II trial, one patient who had been given zidovudine died, compared with 19 deaths among the patients who had been given a placebo. The results were so dramatic, and the public health need so press-ing, that the US Regulatory Agency, the Food and Drug Administration (FDA), approved zidovudine immediately, without requiring further data.[17]

---

[13] Department of Health, *The Expert Group on Phase One Clinical Trials: Final Report* (DH, 2006), available at www.dh.gov.uk.

[14] ibid.

[15] S Knight, 'Surge in Drug Volunteers despite Trial Tragedy' *The Times* 16 March 2006.

[16] TC Jones, 'Call for a New Approach to the Process of Clinical Trials and Drug Registration' (2001) 322 *British Medical Journal* 92.

[17] C-J Lee, LH Lee and C-H Lu, *Development and Evaluation of Drugs: From Laboratory through Licensure to Market* (CRC Press, 2003).

This raises the additional question of when trials should be stopped. Clearly if there is evidence of serious harm to participants, the trial must be ended immediately. But positive evidence of efficacy may also require the trial to cease before it has run its course. If there is statistically significant proof that the new intervention works, the justification for the trial may be lost, and, once that happens, it must be brought to an end. Stopping early may have risks, however. Longer-term safety problems may not have been detected, and the study is unlikely to pick up anything other than extremely common side effects. In addition, it is possible that any ostensible benefit the new medicine appeared to offer might also turn out to be short-lived.

C Phase IV Trials

After licensing, the drug will continue to be monitored before it can be categorised as an 'established' medicine, and this post-licensing surveillance is sometimes referred to as a phase IV trial. Phase IV trials involve looking at how drugs work 'in the real world', and will therefore include patients who are routinely excluded from clinical trials, such as pregnant women and people with comorbidities like diabetes or heart disease. The limitations of the data generated in clinical trials – where the drug is tested on a carefully selected group of patients over a relatively short period of time – mean that post-licensing trials are vital in order to find out whether the drug really is safe and effective when used in real patient populations. In practice, however, there is no legal requirement to carry out phase IV trials. Indeed, as is explained further in chapter four, trials carried out after licensing will commonly be done not in order to generate important long-term safety data, but rather to expand the drug's market by testing for new indications.[18]

D Randomised Controlled Trials

In order to demonstrate efficacy, in phase II and III trials, double-blind randomised controlled trials (RCTs) are generally considered to be the 'gold standard'.[19] In an RCT, the research participants, who will usually be patients suffering from the condition the new drug is intended to treat, are randomly allocated by computer to the control or the active arm of the study. Neither the patient, nor their doctor, nor the trial investigator knows who is in the active arm, and has been given the new medicine, and who is in the control group.

Patients in the control group are given either an inert placebo or the best standard treatment for their condition. Some patients may have got better anyway, regardless of whether they received effective medication. Others will be likely to

---

[18] HE Glass and DW Dalton, 'Profiles of Phase IV Investigators and Subsequent Prescribing of the Study Drug' (2006) 17 *Journal of Pharmaceutical Marketing and Management* 3–17.

[19] For criticism of the concept of the 'gold standard', see N Cartwright, 'Are RCTs the Gold Standard?' (2007) 2 *BioSocieties* 11–20.

report an improvement which has been triggered by the placebo effect, that is, a beneficial effect that arises from the patient's expectations of the treatment rather than from the treatment itself. In a placebo-controlled trial, if the patients in the active arm demonstrate a significantly greater improvement than those in the control arm, this suggests that the new medicine actually works. Interestingly, there is evidence that patients in placebo-controlled phase II and III trials are remarkably tolerant of side effects, since they interpret these as evidence that they have received an active dose.[20] Patients who suffer side effects, perhaps ironically, may be *more* likely to continue in the trial and not withdraw prematurely than patients who suffer no side effects, and who therefore reason that they must have been 'fobbed off' with a sugar pill.[21]

In an active-controlled trial, where the control group are given the best standard treatment, the aim may be to show superiority – that is, that the new treatment is *better* than the standard treatment, or, more controversially, that it is not inferior, or *no worse* than the standard treatment. The acceptability of non-inferiority trials is considered in more detail below.

Results can be obtained more quickly, using fewer participants if a placebo control is used. Proof that a new agent works more effectively, or no less effectively, than an existing treatment will take longer, because it might be expected that the difference between the two groups will be less striking than if the control group is given a sugar pill. On the other hand, withholding effective treatment from a sick patient in order to obtain results more quickly would appear to breach one of the first principles of the Helsinki Declaration and the Clinical Trials Regulations, namely that 'the rights, safety and well-being of the trial subjects shall prevail over the interests of science and society'.[22] As a result, if a doctor believes that a new drug would be the best treatment for his patient's condition, carrying out a placebo-controlled RCT, in which the patient may receive no treatment at all, or even an active-controlled trial where the patient might receive an old drug, which the doctor believes to be less good than the new one, may be problematic. Using a computer to randomly allocate a sick patient to either the active or control arm of a study might also appear to be incompatible with the doctor's normal duty to tailor treatment to the needs of the individual patient. It is therefore often said that an RCT will be ethical only if there is what is known as 'equipoise', that is, there must be genuine uncertainty about which treatment is best.[23]

Strictly speaking, the equipoise requirement would mean it is only acceptable to use an inert placebo if there is *no* treatment for the patient's condition, in which case there is equipoise between doing nothing and giving the patient the untested drug. It has, however, been suggested that this is unduly restrictive where the

---

[20] JA Fisher, *Medical Research for Hire: The Political Economy of Pharmaceutical Clinical Trials* (Rutgers University Press, 2009) 192.

[21] ibid.

[22] Medicines for Human Use (Clinical Trials) Regulations 2004 Sch 1 pt 2 para 1. Helsinki Declaration (2008) para 6.

[23] AJ London, 'Equipoise and International Human Subjects Research' (2001) 15 *Bioethics* 312–32.

patient's condition is not serious and where the patient consents to being denied effective treatment for a relatively short period of time. Giving a sugar pill to a patient with hayfever would cause only temporary discomfort and so, provided the patient consents to take part in a randomised, placebo-controlled trial of a new treatment for hayfever, the use of a placebo would be acceptable.[24]

Using the concept of equipoise in order to justify random allocation in a placebo-controlled trial is not as straightforward as is sometimes assumed. First, if there really was genuine uncertainty over whether a new medicine offered any chance of improving the patient's condition, it could be argued that the justification for carrying out a trial *at all* is not made out. A trial involving human subjects is only justifiable if animal and other preliminary studies suggest that the new medicine is *expected to work*. Of course, the researchers do not yet know for sure that the treatment will be effective in humans, but they must have evidence that it is likely to be, otherwise they should not be exposing the participants to the risks of taking part in research. In short, in order to conduct a trial involving humans, the state of scientific knowledge cannot be in complete equipoise between the new treatment and doing nothing.

Second, even if the clinician conducting the research is, remarkably, in a state of absolute equipoise perhaps between the new treatment and an existing one, or even in rare cases between the new treatment and a placebo, this is very unlikely to be the case once the results start to come in.[25] At some point before statistically significant results have been obtained, she is likely to have formed a view as to whether the new drug is an improvement or not, and *her* equipoise may therefore have been lost. One way around this problem might be to say that while an individual clinician may have lost her prior belief that there is nothing to choose between the new treatment and whatever the control group are taking, she should not yet act on this change of view because as yet she lacks definitive evidence, provided by a well conducted RCT, of efficacy. *She* may no longer be indifferent, but her newly acquired preference for the treatment under investigation has not yet been backed up by robust evidence from a randomised controlled trial in human subjects.

Perhaps one solution to the difficulties raised by the equipoise requirement would be a reformulation, intended to capture the 'mischief' which it is supposed to address, without insisting on the researcher being blind both to pre-trial data and to the trial's initial results. The purpose of the equipoise requirement is to ensure that people are not enrolled in a trial when it is positively against their interests to be allocated randomly to the control or the active arm of a study. Participation in the trial – where there is a chance of being allocated to the study's control arm – should not leave the patient *worse* off than she would have been if

[24] World Medical Association, *Declaration of Helsinki: Ethical Principles for Medical Research Involving Human Subjects* (6th version adopted at the 59th WMA General Assembly, Seoul, South Korea Oct 2008), available at www.wma.net, para 32.

[25] R Ashcroft, 'Equipoise, Knowledge and Ethics in Clinical Research and Practice' (1999) 13 *Bioethics* 314–26.

she had chosen not to participate. To enrol a person who has just been diagnosed as HIV positive in a study of a new anti-retroviral drug would be unethical if it would leave her worse off than if she was given standard combination therapy. It would therefore be unethical to use a placebo control. Trials may have shown that the new drug is extremely promising, and the researcher may not be indifferent to its potential benefits. But by enrolling a patient in a trial, in which she may receive standard combination therapy or she may receive the new medicine, the patient who ends up in the control arm of the trial is not left worse off than she would have been if she had refused to take part, when she would simply have been given the standard treatment.

In addition to potentially conflicting with a clinician's duty of care towards her patients, randomised controlled trials could also be said to pose a challenge to our normal understanding of what is demanded by the principle of patient autonomy.[26] The whole point of an RCT is the patient does not know what treatment she will be taking, and, as a result, she can play no part in the decision about what treatment she will receive. In an ordinary medical encounter, the doctor should give the patient information about her alternatives, including not having any treatment at all, so that the patient can make her own choice about which option best suits her needs and preferences. Of course, in an RCT the patient consents to randomisation and to not being able to participate in decisions, although, as explained in more detail below, randomisation may be hard for patients to understand. Importantly, too, it could be argued that the interference with autonomy which is an essential prerequisite of an RCT is justifiable only if that RCT is capable of contributing towards scientific and medical knowledge. Where the results of a trial are not publicly disseminated (discussed in more detail later in this chapter), it may be harder to justify overriding the patient's normal right to be actively involved in decisions about her care.

E Non-inferiority Trials

The purpose of a non-inferiority trial is to establish that a new drug is no less effective than an existing drug, within a predetermined non-inferiority margin. The setting of a non-inferiority margin means that the new drug may, in fact, be less effective than an existing drug, but just not so much that the difference falls outside whatever margin has been specified in advance. This means that a non-inferiority trial might be described more accurately as a 'not *too* inferior' trial, or even as a 'just a little bit worse' trial. For obvious reasons, the non-inferiority margin *must* be set in advance. If researchers could choose a margin of, say, 20 per cent, after results are in which establish that the new drug is 18 per cent less effective, then clearly they have not *proved* anything at all, rather they have selected a

---

[26] MS Stein and J Savulescu, 'Welfare versus Autonomy in Human Subjects Research (2011) 38 *Florida State University Law Review* 303.

definition of non-inferiority which, with the benefit of hindsight, is guaranteed to establish non-inferiority in their product.

In an active-controlled trial, it is also generally important to decide in advance whether one is trying to establish superiority or non-inferiority. Switching outcomes from proof of non-inferiority to proof of superiority could be sensible, if the results unexpectedly establish that the new drug is more effective than the control drug. It is more problematic to switch from a protocol which is intended to prove superiority, but which fails to do so, and then decide, after the event, that the trial has, in fact, established non-inferiority. Because of the unacceptable risk of bias if the margin of non-inferiority is chosen when the results are known, the European Medicines Agency (EMA)'s guidance is that, if there is any prospect of proof of non-inferiority being an outcome of potential value in a trial, then a non-inferiority margin should be defined in advance, even if the original goal is to prove superiority.[27]

There are a number of reasons for carrying out non-inferiority trials. For drugs like antibiotics where resistance to medication is a problem, having a range of equally effective medicines from which to choose may be important:[28] it is not then necessary to prove that a new antibiotic is better than existing ones, only that it is not demonstrably inferior. Non-inferiority trials might also be carried out when it would be unethical to use a placebo control – perhaps in a trial of a new chemotherapeutic agent for the treatment of cancer. If the new drug is believed to be less toxic than existing treatments, it might be important to carry out a non-inferiority trial in order to establish that it is, in addition, no less effective.

Non-inferiority trials can be problematic for a number of reasons, the most important of which is that it could be argued that they are incapable of proving efficacy, because the efficacy of the control drug is taken for granted. Efficacy is said to be proved *indirectly* because the new drug is no worse than a control drug, in which efficacy has already been established satisfactorily. But if the new drug is simply proved to be no worse than the control drug, that does not amount to proof that both work. Unless the trial contains a placebo control arm, in addition to the active control arm, proof that the new drug is not inferior to the existing drug could mean that neither drug works. While a three arm trial may be able to establish efficacy, by comparing both of the active arms with a placebo control, this would mean recruiting more participants and would inevitably add to the trial's cost.

The problem of taking the efficacy of the control drug for granted may be magnified over time if the drug that was licensed on the grounds of proof that it was no worse than an existing drug is itself then used as the control for the trial of a new drug. This new drug will then be proved to be no worse than a drug whose own proof of efficacy was just that it was no worse than another drug, and so on.

---

[27] Committee for Medicinal Products for Human Use, *Points to Consider on Switching between Superiority and Non-Inferiority* (European Medicines Agency (EMA), 2000).

[28] C Chuang-Stein, M Beltangady, M Dunne and B Morrison 'The Ethics of Non-Inferiority Trials' (2008) 371 *The Lancet* 895–96.

When coupled with the existence of the margin of inferiority, which means that a non-inferiority trial may establish that the new drug is slightly less effective than the existing drug, the successive use of non-inferiority trials may lead to the licensing of steadily decreasingly effective medicines, a process that has been described as 'biocreep'.[29]

It has also been argued that non-inferiority trials are unethical because they involve enrolling patients in a trial – with all the risks that that entails – when the goal may not be to improve treatment options for patients, but just to bring another drug, of a similar type to ones which are already available, to the market.[30] Given that the new drug inevitably has a less well-established safety record, then unless it is capable of offering some demonstrable advantage to patients – fewer side effects, for example – it could be argued that there is no clinical justification for the trial.

The choice of the non-inferiority margin is clearly critical, since if a margin of 10–15 per cent is regarded as tolerable, the new drug may be demonstrably less effective than existing treatments, but because the decreased efficacy falls within the non-inferiority margin, then the sponsor of the trial can claim that non-inferiority has been proved.[31] Within the EU, the Committee for Medicinal Products for Human Use has issued a guideline on the choice of the inferiority margin.[32] A wider non-inferiority margin for efficacy may be justifiable, according to the guideline, 'if the product has an advantage in some other aspect of its profile', but at the same time the 'margin should not, however, be so wide that superiority to placebo is left in doubt'. The guideline also specifies that a three-armed trial with an active arm, a control arm *and a placebo arm* 'is the recommended design and should be used wherever possible'. Non-inferiority trials are not always acceptable, according to the guideline, and the 'decision to perform a non-inferiority trial should be justified considering both the therapeutic area and the profile of the [new] product'.

F Vaccine Trials

An exception to the normal model of enrolling patients in phase II and III trials is vaccine research. Vaccines are given to healthy people in order to protect them against future exposure to disease, so all phases of vaccine trials will generally involve healthy volunteers. Phase I vaccine trials will investigate short-term safety and toxicity, in the same way as trials of new drugs. Phase II vaccine trials will be

---

[29] RB D'Agostino, JM Massaro and LM Sullivan, 'Non-Inferiority Trials: Design Concepts and Issues – the Encounters of Academic Consultants in Statistics' (2003) 22 *Statistics in Medicine* 169–86.

[30] S Garattini and V Bertele', 'Non-Inferiority Trials are Unethical because they Disregard Patients' Interests (2007) *The Lancet* 370, 1875–77.

[31] JH Powers, CK Cooper, D Lin and DB Ross, 'Sample Size and the Ethics of Non-Inferiority Trials' (2005) *The Lancet* 366, 24–25.

[32] Committee for Medicinal Products for Human Use, *Points to Consider on Switching between Superiority and Noninferiority* (EMA, 2000).

used to determine dosage and the administration route in larger groups of healthy individuals, but this time including the population expected to use the vaccine, which commonly includes children. Finally, phase III vaccine RCTs will have to take place over many years in order to demonstrate that the vaccine works, as against placebo or the best currently available vaccine, in preventing the spread of disease.

The number of people needed to prove the efficacy of a vaccine is much larger than when testing a new medicine. Many of the people in the study will never be exposed to the infectious agent or other disease vector. In order to be confident that sufficient people in the trial *have* been exposed to the disease, more people must take part for much longer than is the case when the task is to work out whether a medicine has a positive physiological impact on the condition of a group of patients all known to have a particular disorder. It would therefore not be uncommon to enrol 40–50,000 individuals, often children, in a vaccine trial.[33]

It will be acceptable to use a placebo in the control group of a vaccine trial only if no effective vaccine currently exists for the condition. In relation to HIV/AIDS, for example, vaccine trials could currently use a placebo control, however the obligation to place the interests of research subjects above the interests of science and society means that the researchers should be under an obligation to offer advice on how to prevent HIV transmission and free condoms to all participants, even though it must be admitted that if the research participants are universally successful in preventing HIV infection as a result of practising safer sex and refraining from other unsafe practices like sharing needles, the trial will generate no useful information.

As explained in more detail below, research participants find the concept of randomisation especially difficult to understand when giving consent to take part in research. Clearly if the vaccine is to be tested against a placebo control, explaining that some participants will have no chance at all of being protected against the disease which is targeted by the new vaccine is especially important. Even if they happen to be in the active arm, the vaccine being tested has not yet been proved to offer effective protection against infection. For a condition like HIV/AIDS, ensuring participants understand the concept of randomisation is vital since if participants wrongly assume that they have received an active and effective vaccine, they might engage in riskier behaviour than they would otherwise, which could leave them worse off than they would have been if they had not taken part in the trial.

II Regulating Trials

Before a drug's manufacturer can carry out a clinical trial in human beings, they must have a clinical trial authorisation from the Medicines and Healthcare

---

[33] C Grady, 'Ethics of Vaccine Research' in AS Iltis (ed) *Research Ethics* (Routledge, 2006) 22–31.

products Regulatory Agency (MHRA), one condition of which is that they must have received a favourable opinion from a properly constituted Research Ethics Committee (REC),[34] discussed in more detail below. The MHRA will grant a clinical trial authorisation only if the proposed research complies with the requirements of the Medicines for Human Use (Clinical Trials) Regulations 2004, which transposed an EU Directive into English law.

The Regulations specify that trials 'shall be conducted in accordance with the ethical principles that have their origin in the Declaration of Helsinki, and that are consistent with good clinical practice and the requirements of these Regulations'.[35] What this means in practice is fleshed out in Schedule 1, parts 1–5. As we have seen already, the first and overarching principle is that 'the rights, safety and well-being of the trial subjects shall prevail over the interests of science and society'. Although taking part in research cannot be guaranteed to be risk-free, the Regulations also provide that:

> Before the trial is initiated, foreseeable risks and inconveniences have been weighed against the anticipated benefit for the individual trial subject and other present and future patients. A trial should be initiated and continued only if the anticipated benefits justify the risks.[36]

Of course, since the outcome of research is, by definition, unknown, this sort of risk-benefit calculation inevitably involves a degree of guesswork.

The MHRA has the power to suspend a clinical trial if it has grounds for believing that the conditions set out in the original request for authorisation are no longer satisfied, or if it receives information raising doubts about the conduct, safety or scientific validity of the trial. Regulations 32–35 provide for notification, within strict time limits, of actual and suspected serious adverse events. Sponsors are required to provide an annual list of all serious adverse events, and a report on the safety of the trial's subjects. Regulations 49 and 50 create a number of criminal offences, punishable by up to two years imprisonment: it is, for example, an offence to start a clinical trial in the absence of a favourable ethics committee opinion.

The Regulations also contain detailed provisions on the processes which must be in place in order to ensure that competent participants give informed consent, and the circumstances in which it may be acceptable to carry out research on participants who cannot give consent.

A Informed Consent

The Medicines for Human Use (Clinical Trials) Regulations 2004 set out a number of conditions which apply when the research participant is a competent adult, the

---

[34] Medicines for Human Use (Clinical Trials) Regulations 2004 reg 12.
[35] ibid Sch 1 pt 2 para 1.
[36] ibid Sch 1 pt 2 para 2.

first and most important of which is that the subject must have given his informed consent to taking part in the trial.[37] The Regulations specify that this must involve having had an interview in which he is 'given the opportunity to understand the objectives, risks and inconveniences of the trial and the conditions under which it is to be conducted'.[38] He must be provided with a contact point from whom he may obtain further information.[39] Subjects must also be told of their right to withdraw from the trial at any time,[40] and must be able to do so without suffering any detriment.[41]

Of course, the need to obtain 'informed consent' begs the question of exactly how much information is needed before consent can be considered 'informed'. Clearly the participant needs to understand that he is taking part in research, rather than receiving medical treatment. He must be told about the risks of taking part, and, if the trial is an RCT, the process of random allocation must be explained. In the case of other sorts of information – such as whether the person who recruited them was paid to do so – it is less clear that disclosure is the norm. If the trial is not the first one involving this drug, should participants be told exactly what happened in any previous trials? Insofar as this may provide material information about risks and benefits, it would seem only fair to tell potential participants about previous studies and their outcomes. It is by no means clear that this always happens in practice,[42] however, and it is easy to see why recruiters might be reluctant to disclose this sort of information. If data from the first trial were not promising, subjects might be unwilling to take part in a second trial. Alternatively, if the results from the first trial were good, subjects might be unwilling to subject themselves to randomisation in which they are not guaranteed access to the new drug.

The fact that disclosing information about the results from trials that have already been carried out is not a standard feature of the consent process is grounded in the tendency to treat each trial as a one-off event. In practice, there will often be many different trials of the same drug taking place, often in many different countries, at the same time or sequentially. What is known so far about the drug is clearly information relevant to the risks associated with taking part in subsequent trials, but it does not appear to be standard practice to disclose this information to subjects. An especially worrying example of this is the Paxil Japanese Post Marketing Paediatric Study in Depression, registered on Clinicaltrials.gov, which took place between 2009 and 2011.[43] The primary purpose of this trial was 'to compare the efficacy of oral paroxetine 10 to 40 mg/day (initial dose: 10 mg/day) versus placebo administered once daily (after evening meal) for 8 weeks in

---

[37]   ibid Sch 1 pt 3 para 3.
[38]   ibid Sch 1 pt 3 para 1.
[39]   ibid Sch 1 pt 3 para 5.
[40]   ibid Sch 1 pt 3 para 2.
[41]   ibid Sch 1 pt 3 para 4.
[42]   J Savulescu, I Chalmers and J Blunt, 'Are Research Ethics Committees Behaving Unethically? Some Suggestions for Improving Performance and Accountability' (1996) 313 *British Medical Journal* 1390.
[43]   Paxil Japanese Post Marketing Paediatric Study in Depression http://clinicaltrials.gov/ct2/show/study/NCT00812812.

children and adolescents with major depressive disorder'. 56 children between the ages of 7 and 17 took part before the trial was prematurely terminated due to an inability to achieve sufficient enrolment

The clinical trials registry does not give any details about the information which was provided to children and their parents prior to enrolment. It seems unlikely, however, that they were informed that existing trial data (discussed later in this chapter and in chapter three) have indicated that paroxetine not only does not work in under-18s, but that it also presents a risk of suicidal ideation sufficiently serious that paroxetine is now contraindicated for use in children in the UK. It is hard to imagine that 56 Japanese children and their parents would have been willing to take part in this trial if there had been full disclosure about the results of these previous trials.

The standard informed consent process is also grounded in the misassumption that a person will decide whether or not to take part in a trial *after* he has been provided with information and has had the opportunity to ask questions. Evidence suggests, however, that most people have made up their mind to take part *before* they attend the consultation at which they are given information. As a result, even if participants welcome the chance to find out more about the trial, they do not generally use this information in order to weigh the pros and cons of participation.[44] For both would-be participants and trial investigators, there is a danger that the informed consent process is perceived to be a time-consuming, bureaucratic hurdle – which must be overcome before participation can begin – rather than as an essential precursor to the making of an informed decision about whether or not to take part in the trial.

In addition, consent to take part in a trial should not be limited to the moment when the participant signs a consent form, after receiving an information sheet but before the trial begins. Rather the better understanding of consent is that it is an ongoing agreement to participate, and the person's interest in information relevant to their decision to *carry on participating* continues after the trial has started. In trials involving patients, this raises difficulties, however, since the participant has a clear interest in being told as soon as there is *any* evidence that the new medicine is effective, or more effective than the standard treatment. For the individual patient, this is undoubtedly material information which would be likely to affect their willingness to continue to be enrolled in the trial. However, if participants are informed of any preliminary evidence of effectiveness or ineffectiveness, the results may not yet be statistically significant and the trial might come to an end – as a result of patients withdrawing from it in large numbers – before robust proof of efficacy has been obtained. Again, there is a tension between the good of society, which requires a sound evidence base for new drugs, and the good of the individual research participant, who does not want to be in a randomised, controlled trial when there is evidence that one treatment is superior.

---

[44] Fisher n 20 above, 163.

In a phase I trial involving healthy volunteers, ensuring they understand that they are taking part in research will generally be straightforward. They will have been recruited specifically to take part in a clinical trial, often by a contract research organisation, and they will commonly be receiving some form of compensation or payment in return. This is so unlike ordinary medical treatment that it would be very difficult to confuse the two.

The situation is different for patients who are recruited to phase II and III trials. Here the suggestion that they take part in a trial may come from a healthcare professional, and by this stage the researchers hope that the drug being tested will prove to be an effective treatment for the condition from which they suffer. This leads to what is sometimes referred to as the 'therapeutic misconception': patients who are asked to take part in a trial commonly assume that participation is straightforwardly in their best interests.[45]

Even when they have apparently given 'informed consent' to participation, some people do not realise that they have taken part in a trial. Random allocation is so contrary to what we normally expect from healthcare professionals that participants often struggle to understand that a clinician is proposing to let a computer arbitrarily determine what treatment they should receive.[46] This is especially true when the potential research participants are extremely ill, and even more so if their reason for taking part in the trial is that they have exhausted conventional medical treatments for their condition. In their research into the understanding of stroke patients who had been asked to take part in a trial of thrombolytic treatment, Mangset et al found that many of them 'interpreted the invitation as a special recommendation for them and believed that they were offered the very best treatment available'.[47] Seriously and terminally ill patients do not want to consider the possibility that taking part in the trial is unlikely to help them. As Frances Miller puts it, 'these desperate souls want to believe in the omnipotence of medicine'.[48]

In Jill Fisher's interviews with research coordinators, discussed in more detail below, some of them explained how hard they sometimes found it to communicate the difference between research and care:

> Even though he'd read the informed consent and we'd explained it to him, he didn't understand it well: 'How would they pick me to not get the drug when I'm so bad?' . . .

---

[45] PS Appelbaum, LH Roth and C Lidz, 'The Therapeutic Misconception: Informed Consent in Psychiatric Research'(1982) 5 *International Journal of Law and Psychiatry* 319–29; A Charuvastra and SR Marder, 'Unconscious Emotional Reasoning and the Therapeutic Misconception' (2008) 34 *Journal of Medical Ethics* 193–97.

[46] K Featherstone and JL Donovan 'Random Allocation or Allocation at Random? Patients' Perspectives of Participation in a Randomised Controlled Trial' (1998) 317 *British Medical Journal* 1177–78; C Snowdon, J Garcia and D Elbourne, 'Making Sense of Randomisation; Responses of Parents of Critically Ill Babies to Random Allocation of Treatment in a Clinical Trial' (1997) 45 *Social Science and Medicine* 1337–55.

[47] M Mangset et al, '"I don't Like that, it's Tricking People too Much . . .": Acute Informed Consent to Participation in a Trial of Thrombolysis for Stroke' (2008) 34 *Journal of Medical Ethics* 751–56.

[48] FH Miller, 'Trusting Doctors: Tricky Business When it Comes to Clinical Trials' (2001) 81 *Boston University Law Review* 423.

He still seemed a little dumbfounded by it because you're in a medical setting, *sort of* ... We're doing medical tests and they're still expecting medical treatment *appropriate* for their [conditions], even though you've told them otherwise (Coordinator B).[49]

Some participants assume that the time spent talking to them before the trial is intended to ensure that they receive a personalised treatment plan, rather than to obtain their informed consent to taking part in an experiment.[50] There is also evidence that people tend to forget what they have been told about risks more quickly than they forget about any potential benefits of participation.[51]

Even if potential subjects do understand that they are being asked to take part in a trial, from which they may derive no benefit, some patients may feel grateful to the people treating them and find it difficult to say 'no' to a request to take part in research.[52] For patients with some chronic conditions, this problem may be especially acute. As Fitten explains: 'Chronic care institutions tend to breed a loss of self-esteem, learned helplessness and dependence in residents that may lead to fears, real or imagined, about the consequences of not pleasing their caregivers'.[53]

Although it will be easy to ensure that healthy volunteers understand that they are taking part in a trial, there are those who argue that offering a substantial sum of money in return for participation might compromise the voluntariness of their agreement in a different way. In other legal contexts, consent may be vitiated if it was obtained as a result of coercion or undue influence.[54] Does offering a few hundred or a few thousand pounds to take part in a trial amount to coercion or undue influence? It would be difficult to argue that an attractive financial offer amounts to a 'coercion of the will such as the apparent consent is not a true consent'.[55] In order to establish this, the person volunteering for the trial must have had no alternative but to give consent. Since there is no *right* to take part in a trial, and a would-be participant may find herself excluded, it would be hard to prove that the offer of money meant that a person had no alternative but to take part in the trial. Of course, trial participants are undoubtedly influenced by the offer of money, but it is not clear that this is necessarily illegitimate. Deep sea fishermen, soldiers, miners and cycle couriers, among many others, accept a level of risk at work in return for their wages, and we do not generally believe that this threatens their ability to freely choose this line of employment.

---

[49] Fisher n 20 above.

[50] K Featherstone and JL Donovan, 'Why Don't they Just Tell me Straight, Why Allocate it?' The Struggle to Make Sense of Participating in a Randomised Controlled Trial' (2002) 55 *Social Science and Medicine* 709–19.

[51] E Wager et al, 'How To Do It: Get Patients' Consent to Enter Clinical Trials' (1995) 311 *British Medical Journal* 734.

[52] FJ Ingelfinger, 'Informed (But Uneducated) Consent' (1972) 287 *New England Journal of Medicine* 466.

[53] LJ Fitten, 'The Ethics of Conducting Research with Older Psychiatric Patients' (1993) 8 *International Journal of Geriatric Psychiatry* 33–39.

[54] See, for example, the Matrimonial Causes Act 1973 s 12: A marriage ... shall be voidable on the following grounds ... (c) that either party to the marriage did not validly consent to it, whether in consequence of duress, mistake, unsoundness of mind or otherwise.

[55] *Pao On v Lau Yiu Long* [1980] AC 614.

Trial participation is not generally regarded as a job, however, and the regulation of trials is grounded in the construction of the decision to take part in research as a single or occasional act of altruism. Participants give their informed consent to participation; they do not sign an employment contract. There is nevertheless evidence that some people are effectively professional 'guinea pigs', with the payments from trial participation forming their main source of income. In Roberto Abadie's ethnographic study of self-identified professional guinea pigs, some volunteers had taken part in more than 80 phase I trials.[56] The existence of a pool of experienced trial subjects is undoubtedly useful for drug companies: these participants understand what is expected from them, which may reduce the time needed to explain what is involved in a trial and help to maximise compliance. Of course, repeated participation in phase I trials may also pose a risk to subjects' health. If it was admitted that trial participation is sometimes a form of employment, subjects, or rather employees, would benefit from employment protection legislation, which might be a better way to protect their interests than the fiction that this is an occasional altruistic act, justified by the subject's informed consent.[57]

In addition to persuading people to volunteer for phase I trials, payments offer an incentive to would-be recruits to be less than completely frank about characteristics that might disqualify them from participation, such as alcohol or drug use, or the fact that they are taking other medication. This may increase the health risks of participation, and it could also distort the trial's results.[58]

Payments inevitably also skew the representativeness of trial populations, by ensuring that poorer sections of society, such as students and the unemployed, are overrepresented. In an empirical study of phase I participants, Pamela Ferguson found that they conformed to 'the stereotype of the typical phase I volunteer'. Nearly three quarters were male and aged between 18 and 45. A minority (23 per cent) was in full-time employment.[59] Of course, establishing that a medicine can safely be taken by healthy, young men does not necessarily offer evidence that it will also be safe in the drug's target population, who are, for obvious reasons, more likely to be older, and to suffer from more comorbidities.

In addition, it is not just payments which might influence someone to agree to take part in research. Medical students or junior employees may feel pressure to agree to participate in their teachers' or employers' research projects. As a result, the Helsinki Declaration requires researchers to be particularly cautious if the subject is in a dependent relationship, and to ensure that consent is taken by an independent physician.[60]

---

[56] R Abadie, *The Professional Guinea Pig: Big Pharma and the Risky World of Human Subjects* (Duke University Press, 2010).

[57] T Lemmens and C Elliott, 'Justice for the Professional Guinea Pig' (2001) 1 *American Journal of Bioethics* 51–53.

[58] JP Bentley and PG Thacker, 'The Influence of Risk and Monetary Payment on the Research Participation Decision Making Process' (2004) 30 *Journal of Medical Ethics* 293–98.

[59] PR Ferguson, 'Clinical Trials and Healthy Volunteers' (2008) 16 *Medical Law Review* 23–51.

[60] Helsinki Declaration para 26.

B Participants who Lack Capacity

In relation to both adults and children who lack capacity, the decision about what medical treatment they should be given is governed by the 'best interests' test.[61] Parents normally consent on behalf of their child, but their consent or refusal can be overridden by the courts, acting in the child's best interests.[62] When deciding what medical treatment should be given to adults who lack capacity, in the absence of a 'valid and applicable' advance refusal of medical treatment,[63] doctors should treat the patient in their best interests.[64]

These rules would not appear to facilitate the participation of children and incapacitated adults in medical research. In some cases, where there is a chance of receiving therapy for an otherwise untreatable condition, trial participation could plausibly be said to be in the best interests of someone who lacks capacity. More commonly, however, and invariably in the case of phase I trials, there are risks associated with trial participation which mean that it is not necessarily in the subject's best interests.

A blanket ban on research involving patients who lack capacity would avoid this problem, but would create another one: if no trials can ever take place involving children and mentally incapacitated adults, members of these groups will have access only to inadequately tested treatments. Historically this has undoubtedly been the case. It has been estimated that two-thirds of all children in hospital,[65] and 90 per cent of sick newborn babies,[66] have been given medicines which are not licensed for use in children. Off-label prescription inevitably means an increased likelihood of adverse side effects,[67] but in relation to children it has tended to be the norm, rather than something to be tried only in exceptional circumstances. More recently, the EU has issued a new set of rules, known as the 'Paediatric Regulation',[68] which provides incentives for carrying out high-quality paediatric trials, in order to facilitate both the development and the availability of medicines for children. The European Medicines Agency (EMA) offers free scientific advice and protocol assistance to companies on the design and conduct of trials necessary to demonstrate the quality, safety and efficacy of a medicinal product in children. A new committee at EMA, the Paediatric Committee, is responsible for reviewing and agreeing applications for paediatric investigation plans (PIPs), and provided

---

[61] Children Act 1989 s 1; Mental Capacity Act 2005 s 1.

[62] See, for example, *Re C (A Child) (HIV Testing)* [2000] Fam. 48.

[63] Mental Capacity Act 2005, ss 25 and 26.

[64] Mental Capacity Act 2005 ss 1 and 4.

[65] S Conroy et al, 'Survey of Unlicensed and Off-Label Drug Use in Paediatric Wards in European Countries' (2000) 320 *British Medical Journal* 79–82.

[66] S Conroy, J McIntyre and I Choonara 'Unlicensed and Off-Label Drug Use in Neonates' (1999) 80 *Archives of Disease in Childhood Fetal and Neonatal Edition* F142–F145.

[67] S Turner, AJ Nunn, K Fielding and I Choonara, 'Adverse Drug Reactions to Unlicensed and Off-Label Drugs on Paediatric Wards: A Prospective Study' (1999) 88 *Acta Paediatrica* 965–68.

[68] Regulation (EC) No 1901/2006, on medicinal products for paediatric use, OJ L 378, 27.12.2006, 1

there is compliance with the PIP, companies may be entitled to an additional six months of patent protection.

It would not be acceptable to enrol mentally incapacitated adults in phase I trials that could easily be done on volunteers who are able to give informed consent, or in phase II or III trials for conditions which also affect patients with capacity, such as arthritis or cancer. If, however, a new drug is intended to treat a condition which impedes its sufferers' mental capacity, it would be impossible to carry out phase II and phase III trials *without* the participation of patients who lack capacity.

The Clinical Trial Regulations contain slightly different rules depending on whether the potential subject is a child or an adult who lacks capacity, but in both cases the first stage is to obtain the consent of the subject's legal representative.

i Obtaining the Consent of a Legal Representative

Under Schedule 1, parts 4 and 5 of Medicines for Human Use (Clinical Trials) Regulations 2004, where a person cannot give consent to participation, consent must be obtained from their 'legal representative'. Normally, the person who should act as a potential research subject's legal representative should be someone close to them. For a child, the personal legal representative should be a person with parental responsibility. The personal legal representative of an incapacitated adult should be someone with whom they have a close personal relationship, who themselves has capacity. Where it is impossible to find a suitable personal legal representative, the patient's doctor can act as a 'professional legal representative', unless she is 'connected with the conduct of the trial', in which case another healthcare professional must be nominated.

The personal or professional legal representative is responsible for giving consent to the potential subject's participation in the clinical trial. Their decision should be based upon what the child or adult who lacks capacity would have wanted: what the Regulations call their 'presumed will'.[69] If the representative is not a personal one, and does not know anything about the subject's values or beliefs, they can, subject to the duty to respect the patient's confidentiality, consult people who do. The representative must have an opportunity to be properly informed about the trial; be given a contact point from whom he can obtain further information about the trial, and be informed that he has the right to withdraw the subject from the trial at any time.[70] Once the personal or professional legal representative's consent to participation in research has been obtained, slightly different rules apply depending upon whether the research participant is a child or an adult.

---

[69] Medicines for Human Use (Clinical Trials) Regulations 2004 Sch 1 pt 4 para 13, and pt 5 para 12.
[70] ibid Sch 1 pt 4 paras 1–3 and pt 5 paras 1–3.

ii Children

Before a child participates in research, she must be given information about the trial, appropriate to her level of understanding;[71] her explicit wish not to participate, or to be withdrawn from the trial must be 'considered';[72] and no financial incentives should be given, either to her or to anyone with parental responsibility for her.[73] The trial must either relate to a condition from which the minor suffers or must be one which can only be carried out on minors, and the Clinical Trial Regulations further specify that 'some direct benefit for the group of patients involved in the clinical trial is to be obtained from that trial'.[74]

Two criticisms might be made of these criteria. First, it seems extraordinary that the minor's explicit wish not to participate must simply be 'considered' by the investigator.[75] Because minors are defined in the Regulations as anyone under the age of 16, this means that a mature 15-year-old, who would be judged capable of consenting to medical treatment, could, in theory at least, be forced to participate in a clinical trial against her will. In practice, this is unlikely to happen. The GMC's guidance to doctors states that: 'Children and young people should not usually be involved in research if they object or appear to object in either words or actions, even if their parents consent'.[76] And more recently, the European Commission's Ad Hoc Working Group on the implementation of the Clinical Trials Directive issued further recommendations for research on children.[77] While reiterating the need for the informed consent of the minor's legal representative, the document recommends that in addition, the child's 'assent' should be sought. If the child wishes to withdraw from the trial, the recommendation is that their 'will should be respected'.[78]

Second, the requirement that some direct benefit 'is to be obtained' by participants makes it very difficult to justify any research on children, since clinical trials, by definition, involve some *uncertainty* about whether the participants will benefit. If the investigator has sufficient evidence to *know* that the child participants will benefit from taking the new drug, there could be no justification for carrying out a clinical trial. In practice, the Regulations are not interpreted literally, and there must generally simply be a realistic possibility that participants may benefit from participation.

---

[71] ibid Sch 1 pt 4 para 6.

[72] ibid para 7.

[73] ibid para 8.

[74] ibid para 9.

[75] E Cave, 'Seen but not Heard? Children in Clinical Trials' (2010) 18 *Medical Law Review* 1–27.

[76] General Medical Council, *Consent to Research* (2010) available at www.gmc-uk.org, para 38.

[77] *Ethical Considerations for Clinical Trials on Medicinal Products Conducted with the Paediatric Population* (2008), available at http://ec.europa.eu/enterprise/pharmaceuticals/eudralex/vol-10/ethical_considerations.pdf.

[78] ibid.

iii Adults who Lack Capacity

In relation to adults who lack capacity, participants must once again be given information about the trial, appropriate to their level of understanding;[79] the explicit wish of the subject not to participate must be 'considered';[80] and no financial incentives should be provided.[81] In addition, the Regulations provide that the trial must relate 'directly to a life-threatening or debilitating clinical condition from which the subject suffers', and that research can take place only if 'there are grounds for expecting that administering the medicinal product to be tested in the trial will produce a benefit to the subject outweighing the risks or produce no risk at all'.[82]

Again, these provisions could be criticised. First, it could be argued that the requirement only to 'consider' the explicit wish of the subject not to participate fails to give their wishes sufficient weight. Indeed, the GMC guidance goes further and suggests that their wishes should be decisive:

> You must make sure that a participant's right to withdraw from research is respected. You should consider any sign of objection, distress or indication of refusal, whether or not it is spoken, as implied refusal.[83]

In relation to intrusive research not covered by the Regulations – that is, not clinical trials – the Mental Capacity Act 2005 applies and interestingly this Act also gives more weight to the wishes of the person who lacks capacity: 'if he indicates (in any way) that he wishes to be withdrawn from the project he must be withdrawn without delay'.[84] The Mental Capacity Act further provides that:

> Nothing may be done to, or in relation to, him in the course of the research to which he appears to object (whether by showing signs of resistance or otherwise) except where what is being done is intended to protect him from harm or to reduce or prevent pain or discomfort.[85]

It is perhaps odd to have this double standard in the regulation of research, in which adults who lack capacity have fewer rights in relation to clinical trials than they do if they take part in other sorts of 'intrusive research'. Of course, doctors who are involved in clinical trials should comply with GMC guidance, and so it could be argued that the relative weakness of the protection for adults who lack capacity in the Clinical Trials Regulations has limited practical significance for participants. Nevertheless, this is a clear instance of good practice guidance, backed up by the threat of a challenge to a doctor's fitness to practise, imposing more rigorous obligations than the law.[86]

---

[79] Medicines for Human Use (Clinical Trials) Regulations 2004 Sch 1 pt 5 para 6.
[80] ibid para 7.
[81] ibid para 8.
[82] ibid para 9.
[83] GMC, *Consent to Research* (2010) (n 75) para 30.
[84] Mental Capacity Act 2005 s 33(4).
[85] Section 33(2).
[86] See further, E Jackson, 'Informed Consent and the Impotence of Tort' in S McLean (ed), *First Do No Harm* (Aldershot, Ashgate, 2006) 273–86.

Second, the requirement that the medicinal product will produce a benefit or no risk at all for the participant who lacks capacity may be at odds with the principle of equipoise, according to which research is ethical only if there is *genuine uncertainty* as to whether the treatment to be tested is better than the alternative. The requirement that research which is not likely to benefit the incapacitated adult should 'produce no risk at all' means that it would be very difficult to justify carrying out *any* non-therapeutic procedures on incapacitated adults. Additional blood tests or X-rays would satisfy a 'minimal risk' condition, but this is not what the Regulations say. Extra blood tests and X-rays are not completely risk-free and so if a strict, literal interpretation of the Regulations were to be adopted, they might appear to be prohibited.

III Ethical Review

The Medicines for Human Use (Clinical Trials) Regulations 2004 specify that the favourable opinion of a research ethics committee (REC) is a precondition of a clinical trial authorisation.[87] The process of ethical review is coordinated by the National Research Ethics Service (NRES), and governed by the *Governance Arrangements for Research Ethics Committees* (GAfREC), published by the UK Health Departments.[88]

According to GAfREC, RECs should have no more than 18 members, and at least a third of each REC's members should be 'lay', that is, with no professional involvement in the provision of care services. RECs consider research proposals at meetings which the applicants may attend in order to answer questions from committee members. A minority of applications results in straightforward and unconditional approval; it is more common for the REC to decide that it requires further information, or assurances from the applicant, before approving the project.[89]

In recent years, there has been a move towards what is known as proportionate review, whereby research proposals that do not raise serious ethical issues can be subject to 'light-touch' review within NRES, with full REC review being reserved for proposals that *do* raise significant ethical issues. Of course, this move rests upon the assumption that 'serious ethical issues' are always easy to spot on the face of a proposal, rather than sometimes emerging only after a rigorous ethical review process.[90]

---

[87] Medicines for Human Use (Clinical Trials) Regulations 2004 reg 12.

[88] UK Health Departments, *Governance Arrangements for Research Ethics Committees* (GAfREC) (DH, 2011).

[89] UK NHS, *Management Information* (UK NHS, London, 2007), available at www.nres.npsa.nhs.uk/news-and-publications/publications/corporate-publications/management-information/; M Dixon-Woods, E Angell, RE Ashcroft, A Bryman, 'Written Work: The Social Functions of Research Ethics Committee Letters' (2007) 65 *Social Science and Medicine* 792–802.

[90] D Hunter, 'Proportional Ethical Review and the Identification of Ethical Issues' (2007) 33 *Journal of Medical Ethics* 241–45.

RECs are charged with judging whether research is ethical and with ensuring that the interests of research participants are protected. According to GAfREC:

> Researchers must satisfy a research ethics committee that the research they propose will be ethical and worthwhile. The committee has to be assured that any anticipated risks, burdens or intrusions will be minimised for the people taking part in the research and are justified by the expected benefits for the participants or for science and society.[91]

It is often said that RECs review the ethics of research, not the quality of the science,[92] but it is not always easy to draw a clear distinction between these two considerations. If research is scientifically invalid and, as a result, will not generate any useful data, then this is also an *ethical* issue, because the 'anticipated benefits' to society do not justify the risks to the research subjects. Certainly there is evidence that a considerable proportion of REC letters to applicants, which raise issues that must be addressed before approval is given, are concerned with scientific matters: in one study of REC decisions in relation to proposed trials in the field of oncology, 71 per cent raised scientific design issues.[93]

So how effective are RECs? There is certainly evidence of inconsistent decision-making,[94] which may suggest that there is a degree of subjectivity in their judgements about what counts as a reason to reject a proposal. This is probably inevitable given that, although instances of plainly unethical research do exist, the question 'what is ethical?' is not necessarily one to which there is only one right answer. RECs do not operate with any system of binding precedent, rather each REC makes its own decision on an application and it is not bound to follow, or even take into account, what other RECs have decided in relation to similar issues in the past.[95] Inconsistency in REC decisions is undoubtedly frustrating for applicants, especially since they have little option but to accept the REC's recommendations. It is possible to appeal against REC decisions, but the process is so cumbersome that it will generally be easier and simpler to just do what the REC has requested in order to obtain a favourable opinion.[96]

It would obviously make sense to try to minimise easily avoidable inconsistencies in REC decision-making, such as those which result from committees having members with different expertise. A committee which has a statistician as a member may identify issues which another committee which does not have anyone with expertise in statistics may miss. There is no requirement that RECs should contain a lawyer. GAfREC is clear that the obligation to ensure that research is conducted in accordance with the law lies with researchers and sponsors, not with

---

[91] UK Health Departments, GAfREC (2011) (n 88) para 1.2.2.

[92] ibid para 5.4.3(a).

[93] M -Woods et al, 'What do Research Ethics Committees Say about Application to do Cancer Trials?' (2008) 9 *Lancet Oncology* 700–01.

[94] E Angell, A Sutton, K Windridge and M Dixon-Woods, 'Consistency in Decision-Making by Research Ethics Committees: A Controlled Comparison' (2006) 32 *Journal of Medical Ethics* 662–64.

[95] CH Coleman, 'Rationalizing Risk Assessment in Human Subject Research' (2004) 46 *Arizona Law Review* 1–51.

[96] Dixon Woods et al (2007) n 89 above.

the REC and that '[i]t is not the role of the REC to offer a legal opinion on research proposals'.[97] Nevertheless RECs may 'advise the researcher, sponsor or host organisation whenever it considers that legal advice might be helpful to them'.[98] A committee which happens to have a lawyer as a member may be more likely to spot issues of legal significance, and therefore more likely to recommend that the researchers seek legal advice.

Because of their access to the original protocol, RECs might be thought to be well placed to monitor researchers' adherence to the ethical standards upon which the REC's approval was based. GAfREC specifies that RECs should reconsider their favourable opinion if they subsequently receive information that would have altered their initial view of the project.[99] But while they are expected to receive and consider annual progress reports, RECs do not proactively monitor the researchers' compliance with their original protocol, or even satisfy themselves that the research has taken place and been properly reported. This is problematic insofar as the REC is specifically charged with satisfying itself that the research is 'worthwhile'. Research which is not published or otherwise made publicly accessible,[100] is unethical, cannot be worthwhile and may amount to scientific misconduct.[101] When Pich et al went back to look at what happened to the trials approved by their Spanish ethics committee, they found that only 64 per cent of trials 'were finally implemented and finished in accordance with the original protocol', leading them to conclude that the other 36 per cent 'cannot have a special social value'.[102]

Unsurprisingly, given the emphasis placed on informed consent and minimising risks to participants in the Regulations, these tend to be the 'ethical issues' raised most frequently by RECs. The issue of publication bias, considered in more detail in the following section, does not figure highly in REC decision-making, even though if research is not published, it is impossible for society to benefit from the research subjects' participation, and hence any risks to which they were subjected could not be justified by the trial's benefits to society. On the contrary, participation in research which is not publicly disseminated was, with the benefit of hindsight, based upon a misunderstanding of the trial's aims. It could even be argued that a failure to publicly disseminate the findings of research is a breach of the researchers' 'implied contract' with the participants.[103] RECs are used to concerning themselves with physical risks of harm to research participants, but they seldom consider the less tangible harm which may result from a breach of the trust

---

[97] UK Health Departments, GAfREC (2011) (n 88) para 3.2.11.

[98] ibid.

[99] ibid para 3.2.17.

[100] H Mann, 'Research Ethics Committees and Public Dissemination of Clinical Trial Results' (2002) 360 *The Lancet* 406–08.

[101] I Chalmers, 'Underreporting Research is Scientific Misconduct' (1990) 263 *Journal of the American Medical Association* 1405–08.

[102] X Pich et al, 'Role of a Research Ethics Committee in Follow-Up and Publication of Results' (2003) 361 *The Lancet* 1015–16.

[103] G Antes and I Chalmers, 'Under-Reporting of Clinical Trials is Unethical' (2003) 261 *The Lancet* 978–79.

participants placed in the researchers that the trial was likely to lead to valuable information, capable of improving treatment options for patients.[104]

RECs, which are supposed to ensure that research is 'ethical and worthwhile', tend to rely only upon what researchers tell them they are planning to do *before the research begins*. This suggests that the whole focus of REC review is skewed towards ethical issues that arise in the planning of a trial and away from ethical issues that arise later on, even though the question of whether a trial is ethical is not limited to whether the informed consent processes and arrangements for data storage and so on, are satisfactory. A failure to publish the complete evidence base puts future patients at risk of harm, and increases the chance that unsafe research will be duplicated in the future. For the ethical review process to effectively turn a blind eye to such a basic prerequisite of ethical research suggests that current REC practice, with its emphasis upon trial planning rather than trial completion, may be flawed.

All the evidence suggests that when RECs *do* investigate whether approved trials, in fact, led to publication, they find that a minority of trials is actually published. Suñe-Martin and Montoro-Ronsano followed up the publication status of all trials considered by an ethics committee (again in Spain) over a two year period, and found that, after a median follow-up period of 976 days, only 20 per cent of the approved trials had resulted in a publication.[105] This finding is backed up by Pich et al's study, mentioned above, which found that the results of only 21 per cent of the completed clinical trials had been published in peer reviewed journals.[106] There is no reason to believe that this is a distinctively Spanish phenomenon: on the contrary, widespread non-publication of clinical trials appears to be a worldwide problem.[107]

It is worth remembering that REC members must, according to the Governance Framework, be unpaid volunteers, and that RECs already have a very large workload. Without changing the way in which RECs are staffed and run, it would be difficult to insist that they play a robust role in the ongoing scrutiny of trials and that they effectively monitor and police instances of publication bias. The fact that RECs are often overstretched and under-resourced is not a good reason for preserving the status quo, however. It would be easy and straightforward to require a commitment, in writing, to publish the results of a trial as a condition of REC approval. Monitoring compliance could be achieved through a random audit process. After approval the REC does not have the same bargaining power or 'teeth' that it had before approval is granted, when refusal to give a favourable opinion is an option, but it would be possible to ensure that researchers who fail

---

[104] RS Saver, 'Medical Research and Intangible Harm' (2006) 74 *University of Cincinnati Law Review* 941.

[105] P Suñe-Martin and JB Montoro-Ronsano 'Role of a Research Ethics Committee in Follow-Up and Publication of Results' (2003) 361 *The Lancet* 2245–46.

[106] ibid.

[107] Mann, 'Research Ethics Committees and Public Dissemination of Clinical Trial Results' (2002) (n 100).

to publicly disseminate their data are unable to have future research protocols approved.[108]

In any event, if a lack of capacity is the principal reason for RECs' failure to ensure that the research they approve meets one of the most basic and fundamental criteria of ethical research – namely that it is capable of serving some useful purpose – this suggests that we may need to rethink the idea that the rigorous scrutiny of research can properly be achieved by well-meaning volunteers, in their spare time. Instead, perhaps the task of ethical review should be treated as a full-time job for a specially selected group of people with a range of specific expertise,[109] as well as sufficient time and administrative support to vigorously police protocol compliance and selective publication. The professionalisation of ethics committees would also make it easier to insist that each REC contains members with certain professional or academic qualifications, thus minimising inconsistencies in decision-making which simply result from the fact that one REC has a lawyer or a statistician as a member, while another does not.

IV Trials and Industry

A Conflicts of Interest

Conventionally, discussion of research ethics has tended to concentrate on the need to ensure that participants are not subjected to unacceptable risks, and that they have given fully informed consent to participation. Equally important, but often comparatively neglected, is the question of how to manage the conflicts of interest that arise throughout the whole process of designing and carrying out clinical trials, and publishing their results. A conflict of interest arises whenever someone has interests which threaten their ability to carry out their duties in a fair and impartial way. An obvious example might be if a judge is asked to adjudicate on a dispute between two companies when he is a major shareholder in one of them. The only appropriate response here is to say that his financial interest disqualifies the judge from being involved in the case.

At its most basic, there is obviously a potential conflict of interest whenever a body that will profit from the sales of a new medicine sponsors research into that medicine's safety and efficacy. Positive results could lead to enormous profits, while negative results may mean that the investment to date in the drug's development has been a waste of money. Similarly, if a researcher is paid to recruit research participants, he has a financial interest in ensuring that a prospective recruit decides to take part in the trial. If he puts too many potential recruits off, perhaps

---

[108] Savulescu et al n 42 above.

[109] J Savulescu, 'Two Deaths and Two Lessons: Is it Time to Review the Structure and Function of Research Ethics Committees?' (2002) 28 *Journal of Medical Ethics* 1–2.

by being completely frank about the risks and disadvantages of taking part, he will make less money.

Of course, it would be a mistake to imply that these sorts of conflicts of interest inevitably lead to unethical research practices. Clearly, a pharmaceutical company which falsified results in order to bring unsafe and ineffective medicines to the market is not, in fact, furthering its own financial interests. The way to maximise profits is to market safe and effective medicines, and it is obviously in a company's interests to discover if a new drug is unsafe and/or ineffective as early in the research process as possible. Marketing an unsafe medicine is likely to lead to its early withdrawal from the marketplace and perhaps also to costly legal claims from injured patients.[110] A researcher who fails to disclose the risks of taking part in a trial, in order to maximise his income from recruitment fees, might also be sued by participants and find it hard to recruit anyone in the future. Again, following good practice in the recruitment of research subjects is in the recruiter's longer-term best interests. Nonetheless, it is insufficient to rely on perceived self-interest in order to manage the risks posed by conflicts of interest. It would not be in a judge's interests to gain a reputation for corruption, but it would be absurd to suggest that self-interest offers a sufficient constraint against judicial bias. If self-interest is not enough, it is therefore important to consider what steps should be taken to ensure that endemic conflicts of interest do not compromise the ethical integrity and the scientific objectivity of research.

In relation to clinical trials, without dramatic changes to the funding of research, it would be impractical to disallow any company with an interest in the profitability of medicines to sponsor clinical trials. Currently the pharmaceutical industry carries out more healthcare-related research in the UK than every other source combined: it carries out six times as much as the Department of Health; five times as much as medical charities and eight times as much as the Medical Research Council (MRC).[111] The fact that the largest investors in trials are drug companies inevitably skews research towards pharmaceutical solutions to health problems. A drug company has an interest in funding research into anti-arthritic medicines, but no incentive to investigate other things – better walking sticks perhaps – which might improve the quality of life of people with arthritis.[112]

Because 90 per cent of clinical trials are industry-funded,[113] it would be impossible to remove this source of funding overnight. Instead, one of the principal ways in which potential conflicts of interest are currently managed in relation to clinical trials is through their disclosure. If the author of a journal article reporting the results of a clinical trial of a new medicine has received funding from its manufac-

---

[110] Although note that chapter four will consider the difficulty of mounting a successful action against a drug's manufacturer in the UK.

[111] House of Commons Health Select Committee *The Influence of the Pharmaceutical Industry* Fourth Report of Session 2004–05, para 160.

[112] J Collier and I Iheanacho, 'The Pharmaceutical Industry as an Informant' (2002) 360 *The Lancet* 1405–09.

[113] House of Commons Select Committee n 111 above, para 21.

turer, this must be disclosed.[114] The assumption is that readers will then scrutinise the article's methodology and conclusions more closely.

It is not clear that a requirement that authors disclose their conflicts of interest helps to eliminate bias, however. There is evidence that interests are not always disclosed,[115] but even when they are, it is not clear that declarations of conflicts of interest make much difference in practice to the weight readers place on the content of journal articles. If most journal articles are accompanied by funding declarations, the force that such a declaration might have if it was unusual is diluted. Silverman et al carried out a study in which physicians were presented with both conflicted and non-conflicted research papers. They found that whether a study's authors had received money from the company that stood to benefit from the trial made no difference to doctors' judgements, and their interviewees certainly did not discount information from conflicted sources.[116] Their conclusion was that disclosure is 'only an illusory solution to the bias associated with industry-sponsored and presented research'.[117]

If the researcher and/or his employer own substantial stocks in the company which is sponsoring the trial, in addition to a disclosure declaration on any subsequent publications, should this also be disclosed to individual research subjects? This issue arose in the case of Jesse Gelsinger, an 18-year-old with a rare liver disorder, who died as a result of taking part in a gene therapy study at the University of Pennsylvania's Institute for Human Gene Therapy. In its investigation into Jesse's death, the US drugs regulator, the Food and Drug Administration (FDA), found that his liver function was so poor that he should not have been enrolled in the study. The FDA also criticised the trial on the grounds that the director of the Institute owned stock in the company, Genovo, which had funded the research, and that, along with the former dean of the medical school, he also owned patents on parts of the procedure. Whether or not disclosure of this fact would have made a difference to Jesse's decision to participate is, however, open to question. Weinfurt et al found that, out of 470 cardiac patients, only five per cent of those who were informed about a hypothetical investigator's equity interest in a clinical trial claimed that disclosure of this fact would lead them to refuse to participate in the trial.[118]

It could also be argued that it is insufficient to effectively delegate responsibility for how to manage this sort of conflict of interest to research participants like Jesse

---

[114] International Committee of Medical Journal Editors, *Uniform Requirements for Manuscripts Submitted to Biomedical Journals: Writing and Editing for Biomedical Publication* (October 2008), available at www.icmje.org/urm_main.htm.

[115] S Krimsky et al, 'Financial Interest of Authors in Scientific Journals: A Pilot Study of 14 Publications' (1996) 2 *Science and Engineering Ethics* 395–410; S Krimsky and L Rothenberg, 'Financial Interest and its Disclosure in Scientific Publications' (1998) 280 *Journal of the Americal Medical Association* 25–26.

[116] GK Silverman et al, 'Failure to Discount for Conflict of Interest when Evaluating Medical Literature: A Randomised Trial of Physicians' (2010) 36 *Journal of Medical Ethics* 265–70.

[117] ibid.

[118] KP Weinfurt et al, 'Disclosure of Financial Relationships to Participants in Clinical Research' (2009) 361 *New England Journal of Medicine* 916.

Gelsinger. Simply informing participants that staff involved in the trial have a financial interest in the outcomes of that trial, and leaving it up to them what they do with that information, is an extremely weak way to protect the interests of research participants. As discussed earlier, patients often unwittingly put a positive spin on the information they are given during the informed consent process. In the context of disclosures of financial interests, for example, there seems to be some evidence that participants might actually be *encouraged* by the disclosure that the investigator has a financial stake in the product to be tested, assuming that this demonstrates that he has a great deal of confidence in its therapeutic advantages.[119]

Given the weight of evidence that interpreting what they are told before they consent to take part in research is already difficult for participants in general, and patient participants in particular, it is unacceptable to devolve to them the task of controlling conflicts of interest through their decisions to consent or refuse to take part in a trial in which a financial conflict of interest has been declared. Again, to return to the courtroom analogy, it is inconceivable that anyone would consider that the dangers posed by a financial conflict of interest would have been acceptably managed so long as the judge disclosed his financial interest to the other party, who then gave his 'informed consent' to proceed to trial, despite the judge's interest in his opponent's finances. In other areas of public life simply disclosing a financial interest is not judged sufficient to eliminate the conflict that arises as a result. Carl Elliott argues that disclosure is also insufficient in the context of research funding:

> Disclosure is an empty ritual designed to ease the consciences of academics unable to wean themselves from the industry payroll. Its only purpose is to serve as a warning signal, like a fire alarm in a burning building. Disclosure does nothing to fix the underlying problem of pharma funding, which is not secrecy but power.[120]

B Results and Publication Bias?

A further neglected issue in relation to research relates to how scientific data are interpreted and disseminated. Positive results are often widely circulated, and equivocal results may receive a positive 'spin'. Negative results sometimes disappear without trace.[121] Taken together, this has led Richard Horton, former editor of *The Lancet,* to make the alarming claim that 'journals have devolved into information laundering operations for the pharmaceutical industry'.[122]

---

[119] KP Weinfurt et al, 'Views of Potential Research Participants on Financial Conflicts of Interest: Barriers and Opportunities for Effective Disclosure' (2006) 21 *Journal of General Internal Medicine* 901–06.

[120] C Elliott, 'Pharma Goes to the Laundry: Public Relations and the Business of Medical Education' (2004) 34 *Hastings Center Report* 18–23.

[121] D Blumenthal et al, 'Withholding Research Results in Academic Life Science: Evidence from a National Survey of Faculty' (1997) 277 *Journal of the American Medical Association* 1224–28.

[122] R Horton, 'The Dawn of McScience' (2004) 51 *New York Review of Books* 7–9.

Medical journals are often heavily dependent upon advertising income. There is evidence that adverts for medicines (which, as we see in chapter five, can be directed only at healthcare professionals) sometimes make dubious and unsupported claims.[123] While doctors may be more influenced by adverts in medical journals than they would care to admit, we are all accustomed to the one-sided marketing message delivered by what are clearly advertisements. A more important consequence of the ubiquity of advertisements for prescription medicines is that they enable journals like the *British Medical Journal* to be sent free of charge to all doctors, thus ensuring a much wider readership than would be the case if doctors had to purchase the journal for themselves.

This wide readership is important because of the more insidious way in which the pharmaceutical industry influences the content of medical publications. The evidence is now overwhelming that a significant proportion of articles which are published in leading medical journals, and which receive the journal's stamp of approval and authenticity via the peer review process,[124] are themselves biased.

A preliminary problem is that the trial's results may be interpreted by the researchers themselves, who understandably and often laudably 'believe fervently in the importance of their subject matter'.[125] This leads to what John Dewey has called the 'fallacy of selective emphasis',[126] or a tendency to unintentionally exaggerate. Investigators only initiate trials because they believe that they will lead to interesting results, and this prior belief may unwittingly colour their interpretation of the data. The popular media almost certainly contributes to skewed interest in positive trial results. A dramatic breakthrough in the search for a treatment for secondary liver cancer will be newsworthy in a way that a study that shows that a new compound is ineffective is not. The entertainment function of the news media clearly does not promote the unbiased and comprehensive presentation of clinical research, some of which may result in the unexciting but nonetheless important information that a new treatment does not work.

More sinister than the researchers' and the media's understandable enthusiasm for exciting results is that there appears to be systematic and irrefutable evidence that industry-sponsored research is more likely – generally between three and five times more likely – to lead to the publication of positive findings than research which is not sponsored by industry.[127]

---

[123] P Villanueva et al, 'Accuracy of Pharmaceutical Advertisements in Medical Journals' (2003) 361 *The Lancet* 27–32.

[124] R Smith, 'Medical Journals Are an Extension of the Marketing Arm of Pharmaceutical Companies' (2005) 2 *PLoS Medicine* e138.

[125] G Trotter, 'Interpreting Scientific Data Ethically: A Frontier for Research Ethics' in Ana Smith Iltis (ed), *Research Ethics* (Routledge, 2006) 165–77, 169.

[126] J Dewey, 'The Later Works 1925–1953: Volume 1 1925' in JA Boydston (ed), *Experience and Nature* (Southern Illinois UP, 1988).

[127] P M Ridker and J Torres, 'Reported Outcomes in Major Cardiovascular Clinical Trials Funded by For-Profit and Not-for-Profit Organisations 2000–2005' (2006) 295 *Journal of the American Medical Association* 2270–76; B Als-Nielsen et al, 'Association of Funding and Conclusions in Randomised Drug Trials' (2003) 290 *Journal of the American Medical Association* 921–28; B Djulbegovic et al, 'The Uncertainty Principle and Industry-Sponsored Research' (2000) 356, *The Lancet* 635–38; L Bero et al, 'Factors Associated with Findings of Published Trials of Drug-Drug Comparisons: Why Some Statins

There are a number of possible explanations for this. First, the trials themselves may be designed in order to increase the chance of obtaining positive results.[128] It is easier to prove efficacy when comparing a new drug to nothing, rather than comparing it to a proven therapeutic agent, which may be why industry-sponsored trials are more likely to use placebo controls.[129] It is also possible to increase the chance of a successful outcome by using an inappropriate comparison drug, such as an old drug which is known to be ineffective.[130] Alternatively, an inappropriate dosage of the comparator drug might be used: too low a dose might exaggerate the efficacy of the new drug, or too high a dose might mean that the control group appears to suffer from more or worse side effects.[131] As one recruiter has explained:

> In my recruitment strategy, I can use subject inclusion criteria that are so selective that I can 'engineer out' the possibility of adverse events being seen. Or I can demonstrate that my new drug is better by 'engineering up' a side effect in another drug (by doubling its dose for example).[132]

Using a higher dose of the drug to be tested may make it easier to demonstrate efficacy, and while using excessive doses is also likely to increase the risk of side effects, these may not be captured in a relatively short trial.[133] Indeed, running any trial for a relatively short period of time means it is unlikely that any but the most glaringly obvious side effects will be picked up.[134] Alternatively, the recording of adverse events can be split into smaller subgroups so that none looks statistically significant.[135]

Rigorous selection and exclusion policies are used to ensure that only patients who are most likely to benefit from the drug are enrolled in the trial.[136] There is, for example, a preference for recruiting what are sometimes referred to as

Appear More Efficacious Than Others' (2007) 4 *Public Library of Science* 1–10; JE Bekelman et al, 'Scope and Impact of Financial Conflicts of Interest in Biomedical Research' (2003) 289 *Journal of the American Medical Association* 454–56; S Sismondo, 'How Pharmaceutical Industry Funding Affects Trial Outcomes: Causal Structures and Responses' (2008) 66 *Social Science and Medicine* 1909–14.

[128] S Sismondo n 127 above.

[129] Djulbegovic et al n 127 above.

[130] HK Johansen and PC Gotzsche, 'Problems in the Design and Reporting of Trials of Antifungal Agents Encountered During Meta-analysis' (1999) 282 *Journal of the American Medical Association* 1752–59.

[131] J Safer, 'Design and Reporting Modifications in Industry-Sponsored Comparative Psychopharmacology Trials' (2002) 190 *Journal of Nervous and Mental Disease* 583–92;

[132] A Petryna, *When Experiments Travel Clinical Trials and the Global Search for Human Subjects* (Princeton University Press, 2009) 25.

[133] J Busfield, 'Pills, Power, People: Sociological Understandings of the Pharmaceutical Industry' (2006) 40 *Sociology* 297–314.

[134] BM Psaty and D Rennie, 'Clinical Trial Investigators and Their Prescribing Patterns' (2006) 295 *Journal of the American Medical Association* 2787–90; B Hrachovec and M Mora, 'Reporting of 6-month vs 12-month Data in a Clinical Trial of Celecoxib' (2001) 286 *Journal of the American Medical Association* 2398–99.

[135] DW Light, 'Bearing the Risks of Prescription Drugs' in Donald W Light (ed), *The Risks of Prescription Drugs* (Columbia UP, 2010) 1–39, 16.

[136] P Farahani et al, 'Clinical Data Gap between Phase III Clinical Trials (Pre-Marketing) and Phase IV (Post-Marketing) Studies: Evaluation of Etanercept in Rheumatoid Arthritis' (2005) 12 *Canadian Journal of Clinical Pharmacology* e254–e263.

'treatment naïve' subjects, that is, patients who have not been using medication to manage their condition. The effect of a new drug on a treatment naïve population is likely to be more dramatic than it would be if it is taken by people who have already been taking medication to control their illness.[137] Trial sponsors also try to ensure that only patients who are likely to comply to the letter with the treatment regime are included: there is evidence that sponsors of trials for new treatments for HIV/AIDS have preferred to recruit university-educated white, homosexual males, whom they perceive to be more likely to follow instructions (and demonstrate the drug's success), than people from low-income or minority groups, who may nevertheless be among the medicine's ultimate users.[138]

A trial can also use a 'surrogate' end-point, which can sometimes distort results. For example, if bone-density is used as a surrogate end-point for a trial of a treatment for osteoporosis, fluoride would appear to be effective. However, as well as increasing bone-density, fluoride also makes bones brittle and more likely to fracture, which in fact rules it out as appropriate treatment for osteoporosis.

Skewed trial design is only part of the explanation, however.[139] Even more significantly, selective publication may mean that only positive results are widely disseminated.[140] Evidence of the underreporting of negative trial results is now overwhelming. Friedberg et al found that industry-funded studies are eight times less likely to report unfavourable conclusions than non-industry-funded research.[141] Indeed, White's cross-industry analysis found that the pharmaceutical industry suppressed data more frequently than the tobacco industry.[142]

Turner et al compared trials that were in the public domain with the data, which included both published and unpublished trials, on anti-depressant efficacy which had been submitted to the FDA. Their findings were stark: 'According to the published literature, it appeared that 94 per cent of the trials conducted were positive. By contrast, the FDA analysis showed that only 51 per cent were positive'.[143]

---

[137] Fisher n 20 above.

[138] VJ Burroughs, 'Racial and Ethnic Inclusiveness in Clinical Trials in Ethics and the Pharmaceutical Industry' in MA Santoro and TM Gorrie (eds), *Ethics and the Pharmaceutical Industry* (Cambridge University Press, 2005).

[139] J Lexchin et al, 'Pharmaceutical Industry Sponsorship and Research Outcome and Quality: Systematic Review' (2003) 326 *British Medical Journal* 1167–70; L Kjaergard and B Als-Nielsen, 'Association between Competing Interests and Authors' Conclusions: Epidemiological Study of Randomised Clinical Trials Published in the BMJ' (2002) 325 *British Medical Journal* 249.

[140] M Wynia and D Boren, 'Better Regulation of Industry-Sponsored Clinical Trials is Long Overdue' (2009) 37 *Journal of Law, Medicine and Ethics* 410; K Dickersin et al, 'Factors Influencing Publication of Research Results' (1992) 267 *Journal of the American Medical Association* 374–78; A-W Chan et al, 'Empirical Evidence for Selective Reporting of Outcomes in Randomised Trials: Comparison of Protocols to Published Articles' (2004) 291 *Journal of the American Medical Association* 2457–65.

[141] M Friedberg et al, 'Evaluation of Conflict of Interest in Economic Analyses of New Drugs Used in Oncology' (1999) 282 *Journal of the American Medical Association* 1453–57.

[142] J White, 'Corporate Manipulation of Research: Strategies are Similar Across Five Industries' (2010) 67 *Stanford Law and Policy Review* 105.

[143] EH Turner et al, 'Selective Publication of Antidepressant Trials and its Influence on Apparent Efficacy' (2008) 358 *New England Journal of Medicine* 253. See also K Rising, P Bacchetti and L Bero, 'Reporting Bias in Drug Trials Submitted to the Food and Drug Administration: Review of Publication and Presentation' (2008) 5 *PLoS Medicine* e217.

Similarly, Bourgeois et al found that industry-funded trials reported positive outcomes in 85.4 per cent of publications, compared with 50 per cent for government-funded trials. In a study of all psychiatric drugs trials published in four leading journals over a two year period, out of 162 randomised, double-blind, placebo-controlled studies, those which disclosed a conflict of interest with the pharmaceutical company that manufactured the drug were also nearly five times more likely to report positive results.[144] When coupled with the finding that a minority of industry-funded trials are actually published within two years of study completion, it is hard to avoid the conclusion that there is systematic and selective non-publication of certain trial results.[145] Indeed the leaked GlaxoSmithKline memo, referred to in chapter four, concerning how to 'manage' the data from paediatric trials of paroxetine (Seroxat) 'in order to minimise any potential negative commercial impact', stated that 'there are no plans to publish data from Study 377'.[146]

In addition to the widespread under-reporting of negative results, positive results may be published multiple times.[147] This is extraordinarily significant because the presence of double counting of positive results, and the absence of negative data, will mean that the published data is not representative of the *total* body of evidence. Meta-analyses, which tend to use only publicly available data, will then magnify and exaggerate this publication bias.[148] In their study of ondansetron (brand name Zofran), a drug used to prevent post-operative vomiting, Tramèr et al found that there had been multiple publication of the same positive trial data. They calculated that the inclusion of these duplicate publications in meta-analyses had led to a 23 per cent over-estimation of ondansetron s efficacy.

If both prescribing and funding decisions are made on the basis of distorted meta-analyses, the consequences of over-publication of positive results and under-publication of negative data will be both inferior treatment of patients and the wasteful use of healthcare resources. Inappropriate prescribing poses a risk to patient health, and means that scarce NHS resources are spent on drugs which may not be as effective, and hence as cost-effective, as they appear from the distorted evidence base.[149]

It is difficult for the editors of medical journals to know whether articles submitted to them duplicate data that is already in the public domain. As Richard Smith, former editor of the *British Medical Journal,* explains:

[144] RH Perlis et al, 'Industry Sponsorship and Financial Conflict of Interest in the Reporting of Clinical Trials in Psychiatry' (2005) 162 *American Journal of Psychiatry* 1957–60.

[145] FT Bourgeois, S Murthy, and KD Mandl, 'Outcome Reporting Among Drug Trials Registered in ClinicalTrials.gov' (2010) 153 *Annals of Internal Medicine* 158–66.

[146] GlaxoSmithKline, *Seroxat/Paxil Adolescent Depression: Position Piece on the Phase III Clinical Studies,* available at at www.ahrp.org/risks/SSRI0204/GSKpaxil/index.php.

[147] MR Tramèr et al, 'Impact of Covert Duplicate Publication on Meta-Analysis: A Case Study' (1997) 315 *British Medical Journal* 635.

[148] H Melander et al, 'Evidence B(i)ased Medicine – Selective Reporting from Studies Sponsored by Pharmaceutical Industry: Review of Studies in New Drug Applications' (2003) 326 *British Medical Journal* 1171–73.

[149] S Lock and F Wells, 'Preface to the Second Edition' in S Lock and F Wells (eds), *Fraud and Misconduct in Medical Research* (London, BMJ Publishing Group, 1996) xi–xii; G Antes and I Chalmers, n 102 above.

editors have no other mechanism to know what other unpublished studies exist. It's hard even to know about related studies that are published, and it may be impossible to tell that studies are describing results from some of the same patients. Editors may thus be peer reviewing one piece of a gigantic and clever marketing jigsaw – and the piece they have is likely to be of high technical quality.[150]

The quality of articles published in leading medical journals is supposed to be ensured by the peer review process. If 'peer review' meant that an eminent scientist replicated the trial, in order to test the accuracy of the results presented in the paper, then it might be able to act as a robust filter on the publication of poor research. More frequently 'peer review' simply means that the article is sent to two experts who advise acceptance, rejection or resubmission. A peer reviewer who recommends publication will essentially be saying: 'it looks OK to me', meaning that the research described simply appears to be plausible. Richard Smith describes a study carried out by the *British Medical Journal* in which major errors were inserted into articles sent out for peer review. No reviewers spotted all of the errors, and most reviewers identified only about a quarter of them.[151] According to Smith, the peer review process is ineffective:

> In addition to being poor at detecting gross defects and almost useless for detecting fraud, [peer review] is slow, expensive, profligate of academic time, highly subjective, something of a lottery, prone to bias and easily abused.[152]

Smith also points out that editors may themselves have a conflict of interest when it comes to decisions about publication: 'Publishers know that pharmaceutical companies will often purchase thousands of dollars' worth of reprints, and the profit margin on reprints is likely to be 70 per cent'.[153] Reprints can be distributed to doctors as part of the drug's marketing strategy, but with the 'badge' of respectability and objectivity that comes from being published by a journal, rather than being distributed straightforwardly as marketing material. The *New England Journal of Medicine* sold 929,400 reprints of the article which described the now discredited VIGOR study which Merck used to promote Vioxx, a drug which was subsequently withdrawn because it increased the risk of heart attacks and strokes.[154]

Journal supplements, often paid for by pharmaceutical companies, tend to be subject only to light-touch or minimal peer review.[155] They often contain papers that were delivered at an industry-sponsored symposium, where the speakers are paid and are chosen either because their positive views about a particular drug are well known, or because 'they have a reputation for being adaptable in attitude

---

[150] R Smith n 124 above.

[151] R Smith, *The Trouble with Medical Journals* (Royal Society of Medicine, 2006) 89.

[152] ibid.

[153] ibid. See also The *PLoS Medicine* Editors, 'Increased Responsibility and Transparency in an Era of Increased Visibility' (2010) 7 *PLoS Medicine* e1000364.

[154] C Elliott, *White Coat Black Hat: Adventures on the Dark Side of Medicine* (Boston, Beacon Press, 2010) 41.

[155] PA Rochon et al, 'Evaluating the Quality of Articles Published in Journal Supplements Compared with the Quality of those Published in the Parent Journal' (1994) 272 *Journal of the American Medical Association* 108–13.

toward the needs of the company paying their fee'.[156] The resulting collection of papers is then offered to a reputable medical journal to be published as a supplement, in return for a significant sum of money, which may 'run into hundreds of thousands of dollars'.[157] The former editor of *The Lancet*, Richard Horton explains:

> Publication of the supplement appears to benefit all parties. The sponsor obtains a publication whose content it has largely if not wholly influenced, but which now appears under the imprint of a journal that confers on the work a valuable credibility that the company has bought, not earned. The publisher receives a tidy high-margin revenue from the deal.[158]

If disclosure policies and the peer review process cannot stop the publication of biased research results, what other steps might be able to achieve this result? Smith himself proposes the radical step of journals refusing to publish trial results, which could instead be disseminated directly by the companies themselves via the internet.[159] Journals, he suggests, would then devote themselves to the critical evaluation of evidence, rather than the presentation of it.[160]

The root of the problem may be industry funding of trials, leading Matthew Wynia and David Boren to argue that:

> the number and variety of ways in which industry funding can affect research are so great and so difficult to detect that it will not be possible to manage these conflicts effectively without building a professional firewall between industry funding and the design, conduct, and reporting of clinical trials.[161]

If trials were instead carried out by an independent body, and the raw data were made freely available, manufacturers would have far less scope to influence the presentation of trial results. This would, however, require a complete overhaul of the system of carrying out and funding clinical trials and, since the clinical trials industry is a global one, international cooperation would be necessary. I shall return to this point below.

C Clinical Trials Registration

A simpler solution to the problem of selective reporting of research results might be to require every clinical trial to be registered *in advance* so that it is not possible for results that are 'commercially unacceptable' to disappear without trace.[162] Pre-trial registration is also intended to protect the interests of research participants, many of whom would not participate if they thought the research was intended

---

[156] Horton n 122 above. See also MK Cho and LA Bero, 'The Quality of Drug Studies Published in Symposium Proceedings' (1996) 124 *Annals of Internal Medicine* 485–89.
[157] Horton n 122 above.
[158] ibid.
[159] Smith n 124 above.
[160] ibid.
[161] Wynia and Boren n 140 above.
[162] J Simes, 'Publication Bias: The Case for an International Registry of Clinical Trials' (1986) 4 *Journal of Clinical Oncology* 1529–41.

only to generate data that would be treated as 'trade secrets'.[163] Initially, the pharmaceutical industry was hostile to the idea of compulsory registration, regarding the existence of trials and their results as commercially sensitive information, in which the trial sponsor alone had a proprietary right. There was also concern that registration would add yet another layer of time-consuming bureaucracy to the process of carrying out research.

In recent years, however, the industry has been forced to embrace pre-trial registration, and there has been substantial progress in instituting a system of compulsory registration. The Declaration of Helsinki now states that 'Every clinical trial must be registered in a publicly accessible database before recruitment of the first subject'.[164] In 2004, the International Committee of Medical Journal Editors (ICMJE) published a statement, which unequivocally required pre-trial registration as a condition of publication:

> The ICMJE member journals will require, as a condition of consideration for publication, registration in a public trials registry. Trials must register at or before the onset of patient enrollment.[165]

Of course, pre-trial registration is not the same as the compulsory publication of all data, but it should make it more difficult to conceal the existence of trials with inconvenient results.

So how successful has pre-trial registration been? Two years after the ICMJE's statement, the Committee published a reevaluation of its policy. It found that there had been rapid take-up of registration, with approximately 200 new trial registrations each week, and that registration – having previously been the exception – was now the rule.[166] In the EU, the Clinical Trials Register is a searchable, publicly available registry of all clinical trials taking place in the EU.[167] At the time of writing, it contains detailed information about 11,619 trials.

Simply registering the initiation of a trial may not be sufficient, however. If other important information – such as the trial's proposed duration and its outcomes – are not registered, simply knowing that a trial has begun does not necessarily allow disinterested observers to find out what the trial has contributed to scientific knowledge. Ross et al analysed a random sample of trials that had been registered with ClinicalTrials.gov, and found that only 40 per cent of the industry-sponsored registered trials had published their results, and of those, only a third had the citation recorded on ClinicalTrials.gov. So – despite registration – the results of the majority of trials are still not published.[168] Even when they are, in

---

[163] D Rennie, 'Trial Registration A Great Idea Switches From Ignored to Irresistible' (2004) 292 *Journal of the American Medical Association* 1359–62.

[164] Helsinki Declaration 2008 para 19.

[165] C De Angelis et al, 'Clinical Trial Registration: A Statement from the International Committee of Medical Journal Editors' (2004) 351 *New England Journal of Medicine* 1250–51.

[166] C Laine et al, 'Clinical Trial Registration: Looking Back and Moving Ahead' (2007) 147 *Annals of Internal Medicine* 275–77.

[167] www.clinicaltrialsregister.eu/.

[168] JS Ross et al, 'Trial Publication after Registration in ClinicalTrials.Gov: A Cross-Sectional Analysis' (2009) 6 *PLoS Medicine* e1000144.

most cases it would be impossible to know this by consulting the trial register. It is also uncommon for published papers to include the trial registration numbers, again making it hard for an observer to draw a connection between the published data and registered trials.

Obviously the peer review process may mean that not every trial will be the subject of an article which is accepted for publication, but that is an argument in favour of publicly available registries of results, with compulsory submission being a standard REC requirement. Mandatory reporting of results in trial registries, as opposed to just requiring the initial registration of a trial, might then appear to be a vital next step, and in the US, the FDA Amendments Act 2007 provides that, in addition to compulsory pre-trial registration, 'basic results' of phase II and III trials must be submitted to ClinicalTrials.gov no later than one year after the primary completion date, defined as when 'the last subject was examined or received intervention for purposes of final collection of data for the primary outcome'.[169] Efforts are underway within the EU to include a similar requirement to publish results.[170]

There continues to be evidence of discrepancies between the primary outcomes which are registered before the trial begins, and the primary outcomes that are subsequently reported. Mathieu et al found that, not only were a minority (45.5 per cent) of trials adequately registered, with the primary outcome clearly specified in advance, even among those trials where pre-trial registration was adequate, in a third of cases the outcomes published were different from the outcomes that had been registered. Al-Marzouki et al analysed articles which had been accepted for publication in *The Lancet* and found similar rates of inconsistency between protocols and published reports. In 30 per cent of the trials they analysed, they found 'major differences between the protocols and the reports for primary outcomes'.[171] Even when results are reported, the problem of selective disclosure of outcomes remains.[172]

People who agree to participate in trials, and funding agencies that provide support for research, do so because they believe that the research is capable of enhancing and extending understanding. Data that are not disseminated cannot make a contribution to scientific knowledge.[173] As argued above, because this is a critical *ethical* issue, there might be a role for research ethics committees in ensuring and

[169] See further http://clinicaltrials.gov/ct2/info/results.

[170] European Commission, Health and Consumers Directorate-General Implementing Technical Guidance – List of Fields for Results-Related Information to be Submitted to the 'EudraCT' Clinical Trials Database, and to be Made Public, in Accordance with Article 57(2) of Regulation (EC) No 726/2004 and Article 41 of Regulation (EC) No. 1901/2006 and their Implementing Guidelines 2008/ C168/02 and 2009/C28/01. 1 June 2010 (http://ec.europa.eu/health/files/clinicaltrials/technical_ guidance_en.pdf.)

[171] S Al-Marzouki et al, 'Selective Reporting in Clinical Trials: Analysis of Trial Protocols Accepted by *The Lancet*' (2008) 372 *The Lancet* 201.

[172] S Mathieu et al, 'Comparison of Registered and Published Primary Outcomes in Randomised Controlled Trials' (2009) 302 *Journal of the American Medical Association* 977–84.

[173] S Hopewell et al, 'Publication Bias in Clinical Trials due to Statistical Significance or Direction of Trial Results' (2009) 1 *The Cochrane Library* 1–26.

monitoring the extent to which trial sponsors comply with the requirement both to register the trial, and to make its results publicly accessible.

D Outsourcing Research and Publications

In the relatively recent past, pharmaceutical companies were dependent upon academic institutions in order to carry out and disseminate research. Physicians working in large teaching hospitals were needed to design trials, recruit patients and publish the results in medical journals. A drug's manufacturer might have funded the trial, but it would exercise little control over the research process. While companies might hope that 'their product would look good . . . they had no way of knowing for sure'.[174]

Now much more control is exercised by the pharmaceutical industry at every stage of the process. Even when research is carried out in academic centres, contracts frequently contain 'gag' clauses, which give the trial sponsor exclusive control over the results, meaning that researchers may be unable to use their own unpublished data.[175] This occurred in the case of Nancy Olivieri, a Canadian paediatric haemotologist, who had discovered that deferiprone (Ferriprox), a drug she was testing in patients with thalassaemia, caused serious side effects. She informed the research ethics board, and indicated her intention to inform patients and the Canadian regulator. Apotex, the trial sponsor, threatened legal action against her if she made her concerns public, citing a confidentiality clause in her research contract.[176] At the time of this dispute, Apotex and Olivieri's employer, the University of Toronto, were in negotiations over a $30 million donation to the University for the construction of a new biomedical research centre.[177] For the University, defending the academic freedom of one of its employees could prove extremely costly.[178] Although she was ultimately exonerated, the University's initial, and heavily criticised, response was to conduct an internal inquiry, later found to have been flawed, which found fault with Olivieri's conduct and led to her dismissal.

Contracts may also give the sponsor the right to stop the trial at any time, for any reason, perhaps because initial results look unpromising.[179] In their comparison of Danish trial protocols and the subsequent publication of these trials' results,

---

[174] G Edmond, 'Judging the Scientific and Medical Literature: Some Legal Implications of Changes to Biomedical Research and Publication' (2008) 28 *Oxford Journal of Legal Studies* 523–561.

[175] R Steinbrook, 'Gag Clauses in Clinical-trial Agreements' (2005) 352 *New England Journal of Medicine* 2160–62.

[176] A Schafer, 'Biomedical Conflicts of Interest: A Defence of the Sequestration Thesis – Learning from the Cases of Nancy Olivieri and David Healy' (2004) 30 *Journal of Medical Ethics* 8–24.

[177] F Baylis, 'The Olivieri Debacle: Where were the Heroes of Bioethics?' (2004) 30 *Journal of Medical Ethics* 44–49.

[178] DG Nathan and DJ Weatherall, 'Academic Freedom in Clinical Research' (2002) 347 *New England Journal of Medicine* 1368–71.

[179] P Gøtzsche et al, 'Constraints on Publication Rights in Industry-initiated Clinical Trials' (2006) 295 *Journal of the American Medical Association* 1645–46, 1646.

Gøtzsche et al found constraints on publication rights in 91 per cent of the protocols; 50 per cent of protocols noted that the sponsor owned the data and/or needed to approve any manuscript describing its results. None of the resulting publications disclosed these constraints.[180]

In relation to trial design, patient recruitment and the publication of results, there has also been a shift towards employing a new layer of 'middle men'. There are now companies which run clinical trials, known as contract research organisations (CROs), and medical writing agencies are employed to write up the results, which in addition to being submitted to regulators as part of the licensing process, are also submitted to medical journals, commonly in the name of established doctors.

i Contract Research Organisations

There are sound commercial reasons for pharmaceutical companies to employ CROs to conduct clinical trials, rather than relying upon doctors working in busy teaching hospitals. The process of running a trial and obtaining approval for a new medicine is cumbersome and time-consuming, and delays are extremely costly for drug companies. In the US it has been estimated that for each day's delay in obtaining FDA approval, the manufacturer of a medicine will lose, on average, $1.3 million.[181] It therefore makes economic sense to employ a contract research organisation which can design and complete trials more speedily than over-stretched academic doctors.[182]

Outsourcing to CROs is now the norm, rather than the exception in relation to clinical trials. 70 per cent of clinical trials are now managed by these private companies.[183] Quintiles, one of the largest CROs, has 23,000 employees in 60 countries, and claims to have helped develop or commercialise *all* of the world's 30 best-selling drugs.[184] Covance, with 10,000 employees, again in 60 countries, claims to have developed one-third of all prescription medicines currently on the market.[185]

CROs tend to rely upon research coordinators, rather than doctors, in order to manage the consent process. 90 per cent of research coordinators are female, and they often have a background in nursing.[186] They are responsible for recruiting and enrolling patients, and for 'maintenance', that is ensuring continued participation and compliance with the research protocol. In order to maximise the economic efficiency of trials, it is vital that the time and money spent on recruitment and obtaining informed consent is not wasted by a high drop-out rate, or high rates of

---

[180] ibid.

[181] T Bodenheimer, 'Uneasy Alliance – Clinical Investigators and the Pharmaceutical Industry' (2000) 342 *New England Journal of Medicine* 1539–44.

[182] JA Fisher, 'Co-Ordinating "Ethical" Clinical Trials: The Role of Research Coordinators in the Contract Research Industry' (2006) 27 *Sociology of Health and Illness* 678–94.

[183] C Elliott 'The Mild Torture Economy' (2010) 32 *London Review of Books* 26–27.

[184] www.quintiles.com/.

[185] www.covance.com/.

[186] Fisher n 182 above.

non-compliance. At the outset, then, it is important that recruits know what is expected of them, and Jill Fisher's interviews with coordinators found that they used the informed consent session primarily to emphasise the *obligations* of participation, in order to ensure that potentially non-compliant participants are weeded out before the trial begins.[187]

Outsourcing has not completely bypassed the need for doctors' involvement in recruiting patient subjects for phase II and III trials. Doctors undoubtedly still have a role to play in identifying potential research subjects, and for this they can be paid what are known in the US as 'finders' fees'. It is difficult to know how common this practice is in the UK,[188] but it undoubtedly goes on: GP practices are commonly paid several thousand pounds for every research subject they successfully recruit.[189] These payments will seldom be described as recruitment fees, but instead as reimbursement for the administrative costs associated with recruiting patients.[190] Since 'administration costs' do not look like an incentive to recruit, the conflict of interest that may exist if doctors are paid to recruit research subjects may be disguised, and need not be disclosed. Yet if, as is now common, a GP practice can receive more money from recruiting its patients to a research trial than it can from simply treating them, there is a clear incentive to recruit as many patients as possible.[191]

While outsourcing to CROs, which may pay doctors to help find willing patients for phase II and III trials, is undoubtedly economically efficient, these organisations are employed by drugs' manufacturers to speed up their approval times; they are not employed to investigate, in a completely disinterested way, how best to treat a particular condition. Again, CROs have a classic financial conflict of interest: their profitability will depend upon the extent to which they can satisfy the needs of their commercial clients. Adriana Petryna interviewed one contract researcher who documented her concerns about the safety of a drug being tested, but was ignored by the trial's sponsor. She told Petryna: 'We never got a contract from that manufacturer again.' The drug in question was successfully submitted for approval, but was subsequently withdrawn on safety grounds.

---

[187] Fisher n 20 above, 173.

[188] J Raftery et al, 'Payment to Healthcare Professionals for Patient Recruitment to Trials: Systematic Review and Qualitative Study' (2008) 12 *Health Technology Assessment* 1–128; J Bryant, and J Powell, 'Payment to Healthcare Professionals for Patient Recruitment to Trials: A Systematic Review' (2005) 331 *British Medical Journal* 1377.

[189] JN Rao and LJ Sant Cassia, 'Ethics of Undisclosed Payments to Doctors Recruiting Patients in Clinical Trials' (2002) 325 *British Medical Journal* 36.

[190] PB Miller and T Lemmens, 'The Human Subjects Trade: Ethical and Legal Issues Surrounding Recruitment Incentives' (2003) 31 *Journal of Law, Medicine and Ethics* 398–418.

[191] KM Boozang et al, *Conflicts of Interest in Clinical Trial Recruitment & Enrollment: A Call for Increased Oversight* (White Paper for the Center for Health & Pharmaceutical Law & Policy, Seton Hall Law School, 30 November 2009).

ii Medical Writing Agencies

A second type of outsourcing relates to the writing of journal articles. There are now a number of firms which write medical manuscripts, liaise with the formally identified 'authors' and submit these articles to prestigious medical journals. Because the whole process is shrouded in secrecy, much of the evidence of this ghost authoring of research papers comes from legal proceedings, in which companies are obliged to hand over documents which, for obvious reasons, they would prefer not to put into the public domain. In 2009 the *New York Times* published 'A Case Study in Medical Writing', using documents released in a personal injury action against Wyeth.[192] These documents revealed that Wyeth had paid DesignWrite, a medical writing company, $25,000 to draft an outline for an article about the treatment of vasomotor symptoms (hot flushes and sweating) in menopausal and premenopausal women. The author was to be determined later. This outline was subsequently sent to an eminent gynaecology professor. She vetted the outline and agreed to be its author, suggesting a change of title and a possible journal for submission. A first draft was then sent to the now identified author, with her name attached. She made one correction, but otherwise declared it to be 'excellent . . . an A plus article!'. The article was then published in *The Journal of Reproductive Medicine*, without any declaration of any conflict of interest.

Also as a result of involvement in litigation, psychiatrist David Healy obtained access to a document which listed 85 manuscripts which had been managed by a medical writing agency about sertraline (brand name Zoloft), an anti-depressant.[193] Not only did these manuscripts represent a significant proportion of the published literature about sertraline, it is noteworthy that the papers which had been produced by the writing agency had been *more* prominently published and *more* frequently cited than articles which were not written and 'managed' by agencies employed by the drug's manufacturer.[194]

Sismondo and Doucet are sharply critical of the 'ghost management' of medical publications, arguing that it 'makes apparently scientific research a marketing tool'.[195] Indeed, it could be argued that the most sophisticated way to promote drugs to doctors is to disguise advertising so that it looks like part of the peer reviewed evidence base. It is impossible to tell how many journal articles have been ghostwritten – estimates have included 10 per cent,[196] 50 per cent[197] and

---

[192] http://documents.nytimes.com/design-write-medical-writing#document/p15.

[193] D Healy and D Cattell, 'Interface between Authorship, Industry and Science in the Domain of Therapeutics' (2003) 183 *British Journal of Psychiatry* 22.

[194] ibid.

[195] S Sismondo and M Doucet, 'Publication Ethics and the Ghost Management of Medical Publication' (2010) 24 *Bioethics* 273–83. See also S Sismondo, 'How Pharmaceutical Industry Funding Affects Trial Outcomes: Causal Structures and Responses' (2008) 66 *Social Science and Medicine* 1909–14.

[196] A Flanagin et al, 'Prevalence of Articles with Honorary Authors and Ghost Authors in Peer-Reviewed Medical Journals' (1998) 280 *Journal of the American Medical Association* 222–24.

[197] House of Commons Health Select Committee, *The Influence of the Pharmaceutical Industry* (Fourth Report of Session 2004–05) para 196.

75 per cent.[198] Regardless of whether ghostwriting is unusual or the norm, the significance of this for research ethics cannot be overstated. Rather than containing disinterested, objective reports of well executed research, the goal of which is the 'open-minded pursuit of truth',[199] a significant proportion of the peer reviewed evidence base contained in leading medical journals is, in fact, just a particularly sophisticated form of marketing.

Medical writing agencies do not just write up original clinical research results on behalf of drugs companies, but they may also be employed to write 'letters to the editors' and review articles, which promote a different but equally important marketing message. Carl Elliott gives the example of an article produced by a medical writing agency on the interaction between dietary supplements and warfarin (a cheap generic anticoagulant).[200] This at first sight does not look like marketing, but in fact AstraZeneca was developing its own anticoagulant and part of its promotional strategy was to highlight defects with warfarin, so that when its new drug reached the market, physicians would recall reading that warfarin might not be safe for all users and therefore might be more likely to try their patients on this newly available, and much more expensive, branded drug.

Ghost authorship of articles also raises the question of the ethical responsibility of the honorary 'authors' who allow their names to be attached to articles which they may have reviewed, but which they did not write themselves.[201] Students who put their name to papers they have not written are guilty of plagiarism, for which the penalties can be extremely serious. Likewise, Carl Elliott has argued that ghost-written articles should be treated as straightforward instances of scientific fraud.[202]

This problem is exacerbated by the trend towards increasingly long lists of authors on scientific papers. Sole-authored research papers in medical journals are now unusual, and it is much more common for an article to be 'authored' by a long list of individuals, some of whose contributions may have been minimal, to say the least. This trend towards multiple authorship is, according to Shapiro et al, 'associated with a dilution of the meaning of authorship'.[203] It remains to be seen whether the recent initiative by many medical journals to require every published article to be accompanied not only by a disclosure of financial interests, but also by a signed declaration of each author's specific contribution to the final article will change this. Where, as often happens, the authors simply declare that they all 'contributed equally to the work', honorary authorship and ghostwriting may remain undetected.[204] Of course, if an author is subsequently revealed to have

---

[198] D Healy, 'Shaping the Intimate: Influences on the Experience of Everyday Nerves' (2004) 34 *Social Studies of Science* 219–45.

[199] TO McGarity and WE Wagner, *Bending Science: How Special Interests Corrupt Public Health Research* (Harvard UP, 2008) 8.

[200] Elliott n 154 above, 37.

[201] ibid.

[202] n 120 above.

[203] D Shapiro, N Wenger and M Shapiro, 'The Contributions of Authors of Multiauthored Biomedical Research Papers' (1994) 271 *Journal of the American Medical Association* 438–42.

[204] D Rennie, V Yank and L Emanuel, 'When Authorship Fails: A Proposal to make Contributors Accountable' (1997) 278 *Journal of the American Medical Association* 579–85.

made a false claim of authorship, the consequences for her future career might be extremely serious. But this is the case anyway, irrespective of the existence of a signed declaration of authorship, and it seems clear that relying upon authors' perceived self-interest is a weak and ineffective way to prevent the practice of ghostwriting.

V The Global Trials Industry

The clinical trials industry increasingly operates globally. The proportion of trials carried out outside the US and Western Europe increased dramatically at the start of the twenty-first century: from 10 per cent in 1991 to 40 per cent in 2005. The larger CROs have facilities in many different countries, enabling them to carry out transnational studies with ease. Generally this is done on the grounds of cost: the cost of recruitment is much less in Eastern Europe, India, Russia, Brazil and China than it is in the UK or the US. Jean-Paul Garnier, a former CEO of GlaxoSmithKline, has reported that a trial conducted in Romania costs as little as $3000 per participant compared with $30,000 each in the United States.[205] There may also be scientific advantages: 'treatment naïve' populations are less likely to suffer drug-drug interactions, and it may be easier to obtain positive results more quickly. It is, however, hard to find patients who are middle-aged or older in high-income countries who are *not* taking several different types of medication simultaneously, as one of Adriana Petryna's interviewees put it: 'people live on pills in the west'.[206]

India has become an especially attractive site for trials because it has a large treatment naïve population, who are increasingly likely to suffer from non-communicable diseases, like diabetes and cancer. An Indian CRO advertises what it calls the 'Indian Advantage', claiming that India represents a 'largely untapped resource for clinical trials'. It lists India's diseased patient populations as '40 million asthmatic; 34 million diabetic; 8–10 million people HIV positive; 3 million cancer patients; 2 million cardiac related deaths; 1.5 million patients with Alzheimer's disease and 1 per cent of population suffers from schizophrenia'.[207] Most Indian doctors speak English, and many have been trained in the UK or the US. What India lacks, however, is a robust and comprehensive ethical review system.[208] Only about half of its large hospitals have ethical review committees, and many of these lack expertise.[209]

---

[205] A Lustgarten, 'Drug Testing Goes Offshore' Fortune 2005 (August 8 2005), available at http://money.cnn.com/magazines/fortune/fortune_archive/2005/08/08/8267653/index.htm.

[206] Petryna n 132 above, 21.

[207] J Cekola, 'Outsourcing Drug Investigations to India: A Comment on US, India and International Regulation of Clinical Trials in Cross-Border Pharmaceutical Research' (2007) 28 *North Western Journal of International Law and Business* 125.

[208] SB Bhat and TT Hegde, 'Ethical international research on human subjects research in the absence of local institutional review boards' (2006) 32 *Journal of Medical Ethics* 535–53.

[209] S Nundy, M Chi and CM Gulhati, 'A New Colonialism? – Conducting Clinical Trials in India' (2005) 352 *New England Journal of Medicine* 1633–36.

Of course, there can be advantages to the host countries of clinical trials, as well as to the pharmaceutical industry and CROs. If clinical trials enable otherwise underserved patients to receive treatments at no cost, taking part in research may mean some people receive medical care which would not normally be available to them.[210] Trials in which doctors are paid to recruit patients can also be lucrative for poorly paid healthcare professionals. A contract research executive told Adriana Petryna that 'In Russia, a doctor makes $200 a month ... [in this trial] he is going to make $5000 per Alzheimer's patient.'[211] The existence of a powerful financial incentive to recruit as many patients as possible is self-evident.

Enrolling participants from low and middle-income countries is often said to take unfair advantage of their vulnerability, perhaps by exploiting their lack of understanding of what research entails. An example might be Pfizer's decision to fly researchers to Kano in Nigeria during a meningitis epidemic in order to test its investigational antibiotic trovafloxacin (brand name Trovan) against ceftriaxone, a proven treatment for meningitis. Shortage of medical supplies meant that Médecins Sans Frontières agreed to use Trovan in a group of children with meningitis, and to use ceftriaxone in others. The parents were not told that this was an experiment, and allegations surfaced later that the health of the children in the control group was put at risk because they were given an inadequate dose of ceftriaxone, in order to ensure that Trovan appeared more effective.[212]

In arguing that carrying out research in poorer countries may be exploitative, Alisa Carse and Margaret Oliver Little argue that an important feature of exploitative transactions is that they are *morally asymmetrical.*[213] By this they mean that there may be something wrong with exploiting another's vulnerability, even if his decision to participate is, in fact, both rationally and morally defensible. There are three ways in which exploitation is said to occur in the outsourcing of clinical trials to low and middle-income countries: through the standard of care offered to the control group; through challenges in obtaining informed consent; and through a failure to ensure that the community in which the trial takes place has any chance of benefiting from the research.

A The Standard of Care Debate

As described earlier, if there is no treatment for a person's condition, it is acceptable to carry out a placebo-controlled trial. This then begs the question of whether it is acceptable to carry out a placebo-controlled trial where treatment *exists*, but is unavailable. A good example of this problem came from the decision to carry out placebo-controlled clinical trials in nine low-income countries in order to test

---

[210] Petryna n 132 above, 10.

[211] ibid.

[212] C Elliott n 154 above.

[213] A Carse and MO Little, 'Exploitation and the Enterprise of Medical Research' in Jennifer S Hawkins and Ezekiel J Emanuel, *Exploitation and Developing Countries: The Ethics of Clinical Research* (Princeton UP, 2008) 206–45, 214.

a low-cost intervention to reduce perinatal (mother to baby) HIV transmission.[214] In 1994, when these trials took place, there was an effective way to prevent HIV transmission during pregnancy which was already standard treatment in most high-income countries. This treatment, known as the 076 protocol, involved oral and intravenous doses of an antiretroviral drug (zidovudine) to pregnant women throughout pregnancy and during childbirth; abstaining from breastfeeding; and the provision of zidovudine to babies for six weeks after birth. The 076 protocol could reduce transmission rates from 25 per cent to eight per cent, and when accompanied by other measures such as caesarean delivery, only about one per cent of babies born to HIV positive mothers will be infected with the virus.

For a number of reasons, the 076 protocol was not standard treatment in low-income countries. First and most obviously, it was too expensive: in 1994 the 076 protocol cost about $1000 per woman; in Uganda the total health expenditure per person was less than $3 per annum. Second, the 076 protocol requires health interventions – like early pregnancy testing and the possibility of providing drugs intravenously during childbirth – which may not be available in low-income countries. Third, without a reliable supply of clean water, using formula milk may pose a more immediate threat to a baby's life than HIV transmission.

Since the 076 protocol was unavailable to women in low-income countries, researchers were interested in whether a cheaper and simpler course of treatment might also be able to reduce transmission rates. In order to test this hypothesis, 15 randomised controlled trials were set up in which one group of HIV positive pregnant women was to receive a short course of zidovudine during the last four weeks of pregnancy, while a control group was given a placebo. Preliminary results from a trial in Thailand demonstrated that this short course of zidovudine halved transmission rates, and so the trial was stopped in order to make this treatment more widely available.

This looks, at first sight, like a wholly positive outcome: the trial established that a low-cost and simple intervention could save babies' lives. Nevertheless some commentators, most notably Peter Lurie and Sidney Wolfe in a seminal article in the *New England Journal of Medicine*, argued that the trial should never have taken place. Their complaint was that it introduced an unacceptable double standard in research,[215] because if this trial had been carried out in a high-income country, the researchers would have had to give the women in the control group the best standard treatment (namely the 076 protocol), rather than a placebo. Lurie and Wolfe maintained that permitting this sort of double standard inevitably provided pharmaceutical companies with a powerful incentive to carry out trials in low-income countries, where they would be able to offer trial subjects a lower, and hence cheaper standard of care.[216]

---

[214] P Lurie and SM Wolfe, 'Unethical Trials of Interventions to Reduce Perinatal Transmission of the Human Immunodeficiency Virus in Developing Countries' (1997) 337 *New England Journal of Medicine* 853–56.

[215] ibid.

[216] ibid.

In contrast, defenders of the trials maintained that it was important to find locally affordable solutions to HIV transmission in pregnancy. No one who took part in the trial was actually worse off than they would have been if they had not taken part, and using a placebo control meant that statistically significant results could, and indeed were, obtained quickly. The researchers were trying to find out if a short course of zidovudine was better than nothing, which was what women in these countries were receiving before the trial took place. An active-controlled trial would be likely to have told them only that a short course of zidovudine was not as effective as the 076 protocol. Evidence that a short course of zidovudine is inferior to the 076 protocol would clearly not be useful information when deciding what treatment to offer HIV positive pregnant women in low-income countries.

Lie et al have suggested that there is, in fact, a 'consensus view' that it is sometimes 'ethically justifiable to conduct a trial in a developing country in which the participants are provided medical interventions that are less than the worldwide best standard of care', provided three conditions are met.[217] First, there must be a valid scientific reason for using a lower standard of care than that which is available in richer countries: this condition might be satisfied if giving the control group the established effective intervention would not yield scientifically reliable results *relevant to the health needs of the study population*. Second, the proposed research must have the potential to provide a clear health benefit for the host community: its intention must be the delivery of an effective *and locally deliverable* treatment. Third, there must be an acceptable balance of risks and potential benefits for the individual participants in the trial. This, they argue, would be satisfied if the participants will be no worse off than they would have been if they had not enrolled in the trial. All three conditions would appear to have been met in the trials which sparked this controversy.

In the debates over the ethical legitimacy of these trials, the prohibitive cost of the optimum treatment was often taken for granted. It is, however, important to remember that, while it may have cost a lot to develop, zidovudine is not, in fact, expensive to manufacture, and could have been made cheaply by local generic drug manufacturers. Of course, there were other obstacles to the local provision of the 076 protocol, such as the absence of basic health services, but the move to allow generics manufacturers in poorer countries to market generic versions of patented drugs, an issue discussed in more detail in chapter seven, is an important adjunct to the standard of care debate.

B Informed Consent

It has been argued that informed consent presents particular challenges in low and middle-income countries for three reasons. First, it may be more difficult to ensure

---

[217] RK Lie et al, 'The Standard of Care Debate: The Declaration of Helsinki Versus the International Consensus Opinion' (2004) *Journal of Medical Ethics* 190–19.

that the participants have understood the information presented to them.[218] Illiteracy may pose challenges to obtaining adequately informed consent. If the information has to be translated into the subjects' own language, there may not be words for some scientific concepts. Moreover, if it is challenging to explain the concept of randomisation and the use of placebos to generally well-informed, western research subjects, this may be almost impossibly difficult in low and middle-income countries.[219] In their interviews with the subjects in a South African vaccine trial, for example, Moodley et al found that fewer than a fifth of the participants understood that being given a placebo meant receiving no active medicine.[220]

Patients in high-income countries find it hard to believe that doctors would suggest participation if it was not in their best interests, and this 'therapeutic misconception' is even more acute in low and middle-income countries, where there may be especially high levels of trust in healthcare professionals.[221] In their study of attitudes towards research participation in northern India, DeCosta et al found that one of the most important reasons for people's willingness to take part in research 'was an implicit faith in doctors and the medical system'.[222] This confidence in the medical profession led a significant minority (17.5 per cent) of their interviewees to report that they would not want *any* information before deciding whether to participate. One subject explained that 'we'll only take the new agent because doctors are telling us to. If they tell us to take a particular medicine, we will surely do so even if it is poisonous'. Another said he believed that 'doctors are in a way godly. Who would know better than them?'[223]

In addition, in populations in which the concept of patient autonomy is not as dominant as it is in the West, people may not understand that they have a right *not* to take part in research, and that such a refusal will not jeopardise the care they will receive. In their study of Bangladeshi women taking part in a trial of iron supplementation, Lynoe et al found that a majority of participants believed that the trial was part of their routine medical care, and most women did not understand that they were free to withdraw their consent to participation at any time.[224]

Second, incentives may work differently in poorer countries. If participants lack basic healthcare, the prospect of receiving *any* attention from medically qualified investigators offers a powerful incentive to take part. Of course the fact that a

---

[218] DW Fitzgerald et al, 'Comprehension during Informed Consent in a Less-Developed Country' (2002) 360 *The Lancet* 1301–02.

[219] C Pace et al, 'Quality of Parental Consent in a Ugandan Malaria Study' (2005) 95 *American Journal of Public Health* 1184–89.

[220] K Moodley, M Pather and L Myer, 'Informed Consent and Participant Perceptions of Influenza Vaccine Trials in South Africa' (2005) 31 *Journal of Medical Ethics* 727–32.

[221] Z Hill et al, 'Informed Consent in Ghana: What do Participants Really Understand?' (2008) 34 *Journal of Medical Ethics* 48–53.

[222] A DeCosta et al, 'Community Based Trials and Informed Consent in Rural North India' (2004) 30 *Journal of Medical Ethics* 318–23.

[223] ibid.

[224] N Lynöe et al, 'Obtaining Informed Consent in Bangladesh' (2001) 344 *New England Journal of Medicine* 460–61.

person has few options does not render them incompetent to consent to any of them. But participants' lack of alternative ways to access healthcare may make it easy for recruiters to persuade them to take part, perhaps against their better judgement.

Third, in some low and middle-income countries, it may be usual practice for important decisions to be taken by the leader of the community, or a senior (and probably male) family member, rather than by the individuals who will ultimately take part in the research. It has been suggested that in order to show respect for a community's culture, it might sometimes be appropriate to seek consent from a third party, but this should not replace the need to also obtain the participant's informed consent.[225] Indeed the Nuffield Council on Bioethics' report on research in developing countries suggests if an individual does not wish to take part, then even if the community leader has agreed, researchers should have a duty to facilitate the reluctant individual's non-participation.[226]

C Community Benefit

It is often said that locating trials in poorer countries is acceptable only if there is a reasonable prospect of the intervention benefiting the community in which the research takes place. This requirement has two limbs. First, the drug being tested must be one which could reasonably be expected to be *useful* to the community in which the trial takes place. Conducting a phase I trial for a new anti-obesity drug in sub-Saharan Africa would, on this view, be unacceptable since the trial does not attempt to address a health need in that region. This restriction is plainly paternalistic, since it rules out the research participant him or herself as the best judge of whether to take part in a trial. If a subject in Malawi, say, is to be paid $100 to take part in a phase I trial of an anti-obesity drug, and chooses to do so, their choice may be informed and rational, and a refusal to allow them to make this choice suggests that we think there is something wrong with the offer the company running the trial has made to them, perhaps because it takes unfair advantage of the subject's poverty.

Second, if people in the trial have benefited from taking the new medicine during the trial, it would be unacceptable to deprive them of this effective treatment once the trial is over. This may prove extremely expensive for pharmaceutical companies if the successful drug is one which has to be taken long-term, as is the case with antiretroviral drugs used in the treatment of HIV/AIDS. A distinction might be drawn here between continuing to provide the beneficial drug for the trial subjects – when withdrawing effective medication would be unacceptable, regardless of the costs to the drug company – and an obligation to provide the

---

[225] Council for International Organisations of Medical Sciences (CIOMS), *International Ethical Guidelines for Biomedical Research Involving Human Subjects*, available at www.cioms.ch/.
[226] Nuffield Council on Bioethics, *The Ethics of Research Related to Healthcare in Developing Countries* (NCOB, 2002) para 6.22.

beneficial medication to the whole community, which drug companies might more reasonably claim is unaffordable.

Some might argue that this restriction also embodies a rather narrow notion of the benefits and burdens of trial participation. There may be benefits to a community from taking part in research other than any health benefits provided by the drug itself, such as the training of local health care personnel and the construction of an infrastructure for delivery (what is collectively referred to as 'capacity building'). Emanuel et al therefore argue that a 'fair benefits' framework would be more effective than a 'reasonable availability' requirement in ensuring populations are not exploited.[227]

VI Conclusion

The central problem which underlies many of the issues discussed in this chapter would seem to be that the regulatory system depends on companies testing their own products in order to establish their safety and efficacy, which – if proven – will lead to potentially huge profits. Drug companies have a clear financial interest in the outcomes of the trials that they carry out and it should not surprise us that trials are designed in order to increase the chances of a positive outcome. Nor is it surprising that drug companies are more keen to publicise trials which have a positive outcome than they are when the results are, from the company's point of view, disappointing.

If the regulator did not just have to rely on data submitted by the company which wishes to market a drug, but instead had the resources to carry out its own independent trials, it would be possible to be much more confident that it had access to an objective and complete evidence base when licensing a new product. As Jan Vandenbroucke has explained:

> in usual clinical or epidemiologic research, studies are repeated by others, in different settings and by different means, looking for biases, flaws, and ways of remedying them ... That is the essence of open scientific debate and criticism, which is the only guarantee for progress. That is no longer possible with pharmaceutical products because the monopoly of the pharmaceutical industry of studies of its own products leads to persistently one-sided studies that can no longer be questioned by studies from other sides. Moreover, the one-sidedness cannot be seen from the public record, that is the published papers. Without the possibility of open debate, science simply ceases to exist.[228]

[227] EJ Emanuel, 'Addressing Exploitation: Reasonable Availability versus Fair Benefits' in Jennifer S Hawkins and Ezekiel J Emanuel, *Exploitation and Developing Countries: The Ethics of Clinical Research* (Princeton UP, 2008) 286–313.

[228] JP Vandenbroucke, 'Without New Rules for Industry-Sponsored Research, Science Will Cease to Exist'. (Rapid response on bmj.com, posted 14 December 2005) [http://bmj.bmjjournals.com/cgi/eletters/331/7529/1350.

The problem is not only that conflicts of interest threaten the objectivity of science, but also because funding decisions and prescribing decisions are made on the basis of the publicly available evidence base, publication bias leads to worse patient care and the wasteful use of NHS resources.

The time has then come to treat 'under-reporting of research as just as serious a form of scientific misconduct as fabrication of data'.[229] To this end, the process of ethical review needs to be overhauled so that it is not directed solely towards the ethical status of the original protocol, with its informed consent procedures and patient information sheets, but instead is capable of identifying research which, with the benefit of hindsight, is proven to be unethical, *because it is unpublished*. The legacy of the research abuses of the twentieth century was a regulatory system which emphasises the need to ensure that participants give their informed consent to take part in research. It is to be hoped that the legacy of the more recent recognition of the research abuses of selective publication and endemic conflicts of interest, will be to reduce the commercial secrecy that surrounds clinical trials. Regulation should ensure that trials take place within a transparent system which is capable of minimising both selective publication and the publication of articles which turn out to be advertising in disguise, each of which is the antithesis of good science.

The clinical trials industry is just that, an industry, whereas it is regulated 'as if it were a charitable practice with a pure humanitarian mission'.[230] Financial conflicts of interest exist at every stage of a drug's development, and are often missed by a regulatory system that assumes that a subject's informed consent to participation is sufficient to make research ethical. Instead, whenever someone who is involved in designing a trial, recruiting subjects, carrying out research and writing up the results has a financial stake in the outcome of the trial, there is a danger that the integrity of the research enterprise is threatened.

---

[229] I Chalmers, 'From Optimism to Disillusion about Commitment to Transparency in the Medico-Industrial Complex' (2006) 99 *Journal of the Royal Society of Medicine* 337.

[230] T Lemmens, 'Leopards in the Temple: Restoring Scientific Integrity to the Commercialised Research Scene' (2004) 32 *Journal of Law, Medicine and Ethics* 641–57.

3

Licensing

I The Significance of a Marketing Authorisation

BEFORE ANY MEDICINAL product (including generic equivalents of established drugs) can be made available for public use, it must have a marketing authorisation.[1] In a drug's journey from experimental compound to marketable product, the moment at which it receives a marketing authorisation from the regulator is a critical one. It is at this point that its manufacturer can stop engaging in research and start engaging in marketing. The people taking the medicine move from carefully selected research participants, to any patient who happens to be prescribed the medicine, or depending upon its classification, who happens to purchase it herself from a pharmacist or a general sale outlet. The fact of approval gives the new medicine an official badge of reliability, which prescribing doctors rely upon when deciding whether to prescribe it to their patients. The moment of approval should ideally be viewed as one very important 'snapshot' in a medicine's life span, with research into safety and efficacy continuing for some time after the medicine reaches the marketplace. But in practice, the binary system of drugs regulation, in which medicines are either safe or not safe, effective or ineffective, means that the point at which a medicine receives a marketing authorisation is the moment when it is formally designated as a safe and effective drug.

II Applying for a Marketing Authorisation

Within the EU, there are a number of different routes for acquiring a marketing authorisation. First, there is the centralised procedure, in which a single application is made directly to the European Medicines Agency (EMA). Once granted, a centralised (or 'Community') marketing authorisation is valid throughout the European Union and in European Economic Area/European Free Trade Area states (namely Iceland, Liechtenstein and Norway).

---

[1] Medicines Act 1968 s 7(2).

The centralised procedure is compulsory for products derived from biotechnology and other high technology processes, and for all medicines intended for the treatment of HIV/AIDS, cancer, diabetes, neurodegenerative diseases, autoimmune and other immune dysfunctions, viral diseases and 'orphan medicines' for the treatment of rare diseases. Manufacturers can choose to use the centralised procedure for a medicine that falls outside this list, provided it constitutes a significant therapeutic, scientific or technical innovation, or if its authorisation would be in the interest of public health.

Once a centralised application has been made, it will be evaluated by the relevant scientific committee at EMA, most commonly the Committee for Medicinal Products for Human Use (CHMP). The CHMP will determine whether or not the medicine meets the necessary quality, safety and efficacy requirements.[2] This process can take up to 210 days, after which the committee will adopt an 'opinion' on whether the medicine should be marketed or not. This opinion is then transmitted to the European Commission, which has the ultimate authority for granting marketing authorisations in the EU. For every medicine it assesses, the CHMP publishes a European public assessment report (EPAR), setting out in considerable detail the grounds for its opinion, either favourable or unfavourable. EPARs are freely available on EMA's website.

Second, for medicines which are not compulsorily subject to the centralised procedure, applications can be made to one or more members states' national licensing authorities. Under the decentralised procedure, companies apply for simultaneous authorisation in more than one EU state. More commonly, under the mutual recognition procedure, a medicine is first authorised in one EU member state, after which other EU countries grant marketing authorisations which recognise the validity of the original authorisation.

The mutual recognition procedure places European licensing authorities in competition with each other for regulatory business. Where use of the mutual recognition procedure is an option, it will make commercial sense for manufacturers to choose to first license their product in the country which has the shortest time-lag between application and authorisation. Because licensing authorities are either in part or wholly funded by the fees paid by applicants, there is an economic incentive for regulators to speed up their processes.

There is evidence that approval times have been dropping throughout Europe,[3] which is undoubtedly good news for the pharmaceutical industry. Faster approval times can also be in the interests of patients by making new drugs available more quickly than they would if the approval process was more cumbersome and time-

---

[2] In accordance with EU legislation, particularly Directive 2001/83/EC of the European Parliament and of the Council of 6 November 2001 on the Community Code Relating to Medicinal Products for Human Use, OJ L – 311, 28/11/2004, 67–128.

[3] J Abraham and G Lewis, *Regulating Medicines in Europe* (London, Routledge, 2000); P Edmonds, D Dermot and C Oglialoro, 'Access to Important New Medicines' (2000) 13 *European Business Journal* 146–58.

consuming.[4] In the early days of the AIDS pandemic, for example, activists argued bluntly that, by delaying access to potentially life-saving medications, protracted regulatory approval processes were costing lives:

> there is no question on the part of anyone fighting AIDS that the FDA [the US drugs regulator] consists of the single most incomprehensible bottleneck in American bureaucratic history - one that is actually prolonging the roll call of death.[5]

But while speedier access to medicines may improve health outcomes, especially where the new medicine is for a previously untreatable condition, reduced drug approval times can also pose a risk to patients. If the analysis of the trial data is less thorough, a faster licensing process may result in the licensing of medicines which a more rigorous review would have identified as unsafe.[6] Olsen reports that even a one month reduction in the time taken to approve a new drug results in a significantly elevated risk of adverse drug reactions (ADRs), some of which may be extremely serious.[7] According to Olsen, 'a 12 month reduction in a drug's review time is associated with an increase of 10.92 ADR hospitalisations and 7.68 ADR deaths per drug'.[8]

Mutual recognition agreements also exist between the EU and Switzerland, Canada, Australia, and New Zealand, and the International Conference on Harmonisation (ICH) has even broader scope. Initially intended to harmonise technical requirements for the licensing of medicines in Europe, Japan and the US,[9] other countries with limited or no drug regulatory capacity have chosen to adopt agreed ICH standards.[10] ICH has developed over 50 specific guidelines which are intended to eliminate duplication in drug development and registration by ensuring that a single data set and common technical documentation can be used to demonstrate the quality, safety and efficacy of a new medicinal product when applying to different regulatory agencies. Again some commentators have suggested that international harmonisation may have been successful at speeding up the licensing of new medicines, but that this has sometimes been at the expense of safety standards.[11]

---

[4] DP Carpenter, 'The Political Economy of FDA Drug Review' (2004) 23 *Health Affairs* 52–63.

[5] L Kramer, 'The FDA's Callous Response to AIDS' *The New York Times* 23 March 1987 A19.

[6] J Abraham and G Lewis, 'Harmonising and Competing for Medicines Regulation: How Healthy are the EU's Systems of Drug Approval?' (1999) 48 *Social Science and Medicine* 1655–67.

[7] MK Olson, 'The Risk we Bear: The Effects of Review Speed and Industry User Fees on Drug Safety' (2008) 27 *Journal of Health Economics* 175–200.

[8] MK Olson, 'Pharmaceutical Policy Change and the Safety of New Drugs' (2002) 45 *The Journal of Law and Economics* 615–42.

[9] www.ich.org.

[10] World Health Organisation *Effective Medicines Regulation: Ensuring Safety, Efficacy and Quality, WHO Policy Perspectives on Medicines* WHO/EDM/2003.2 (WHO, Geneva, 2003).

[11] J Abraham and T Reed, 'Reshaping the Carcinogenic Risk Assessment of Medicines: International Harmonisation for Drug Safety, Industry/Regulator Efficiency or Both?' (2003) 57 *Social Science & Medicine* 195–204.

III Grounds for Licensing Decisions

A Proof of Efficacy, Safety and Quality

When applying for a marketing authorisation, the pharmaceutical company must submit data from all of the trials it has carried out. The manufacturer must also provide information about the manufacturing process and quality control mechanisms, and must explain how it is proposing to market the product, and submit the patient information leaflet which will be supplied with it. Whether the application is made to EMA or the Medicines and Healthcare products Regulatory Agency (MHRA), the decision to grant a marketing authorisation will be based upon company data, presented as a series of detailed assessment reports, often put together by the professional medical writing agencies and contract research organisations (CROs) described in the previous chapter. The licensing authority will seldom analyse the raw data itself. Companies have argued that this is commercially sensitive, and hence confidential information. Under section 118(1) of the Medicines Act 1968, it is an offence for anyone to disclose to any other person any information obtained through the regulatory process. Licensing decisions are publicly available, but the data upon which they are based are not. I shall return to this point below.

So what factors are relevant to the decision to grant a new medicine a marketing authorisation? The Medicines Act 1968 specifies that the licensing authority shall in particular take into consideration a medicinal product's safety, efficacy and quality.[12] Safety and efficacy will be established using clinical trial data, while proof of quality means establishing that there is an effective pharmaceutical quality assurance system in place, which is compliant with Good Manufacturing Practice (GMP) standards.[13] Price is not relevant; the fact that a medicine is prohibitively expensive is not a good reason to deny it a marketing authorisation. Of course, it might subsequently be decided that a medicine is too expensive to be prescribed within the NHS, but if it is safe, effective and there are processes in place to ensure that it will be of sufficient quality, it should receive a marketing authorisation.

Efficacy, according to the licensing regime, is an 'all or nothing' concept: a drug either works or it does not work. In practice, however, efficacy clearly exists on a spectrum, from extremely effective to slightly better than nothing. Proof of efficacy can, as explained in the previous chapter, often amount to no more than proof that the new medicine is marginally more effective than a placebo in a specially selected group of trial participants. Given the freedom a drug's manufacturer has in designing a trial so that its product is likely to look good, the requirement

---

[12] Medicines Act 1968 s 19(1).

[13] Directive 91/412/EEC laying down the principles and guidelines of good manufacturing practice for veterinary medicinal products OJ L 228, 17.8.1991, 70–73 and Directive 2003/94/EC laying down the principles and guidelines of good manufacturing practice in respect of medicinal products for human use and investigational medicinal products for human use, OJ L 262, 14.10.2003, 22–26.

that a drug is 'more effective than nothing' in a trial which has been designed in order to prove efficacy is not especially demanding.[14] Efficacy also varies between different patients – a drug might work very well in a few patients, quite well in a handful of others, and not at all in most people. The licensing regime does not make this sort of distinction. If doctors and patients rely upon a marketing authorisation's badge of approval, all approved drugs are essentially equal in terms of proof of efficacy, even though the reality will be very different.[15]

When judging safety, it is important not only to consider the safety of a medicine when taken exactly according to the manufacturer's instructions, but also the drug's safety when, as is in practice common,[16] consumers fail to follow those instructions to the letter. To take an extreme example, if a medicine is safe in its normal dose, say when the patient takes one pill every four hours, but extremely dangerous if the patient takes it slightly more frequently, perhaps by taking one pill every two hours, then it would not be sufficiently safe for human use, since it can be predicted that some people will make this mistake. It would not be reasonable for manufacturers to have to establish that a drug is safe even when taken in wholly unreasonable quantities, however. Paracetamol, for example, is safe at normal and also slightly higher than normal doses. It is not safe if someone takes the contents of four packets in one go. On the other hand, although it is not necessary to prove that a drug is safe when a patient takes an overdose, if a drug is not toxic when a patient overdoses, this may be information which is relevant to its overall safety profile, especially if there are other drugs in the same class in which overdose is extremely dangerous.[17]

A new drug's first marketing authorisation lasts for five years, after which it has to be renewed once, and then continues indefinitely. The five year review should be an opportunity to evaluate the safety and efficacy of the drug when used 'in the real world', but this does not necessarily happen in practice, and, provided there are no obvious safety issues with a medicine, renewal is essentially automatic.[18]

B 'Me-too' Drugs

Section 19(2) of the Medicines Act 1968 specifies that the licensing authority 'shall leave out of account any question whether medicinal products of another description would or might be equally or more efficacious for that purpose'. A drug company therefore only has to prove that the new medicine works better than placebo, it does not have to establish that it represents an improvement on existing treat-

[14] T Lemmens, 'Leopards in the Temple: Restoring Scientific Integrity to the Commercialised Research Scene' (2004) 32 *Journal of Law, Medicine and Ethics* 641–57.
[15] B Falit, 'The Path to Cheaper and Safer Drugs: Revamping the Pharmaceutical Industry in the Light of GlaxoSmithKline's Settlement' (2005) 33 *Journal of Law, Medicine and Ethics* Spring 174.
[16] R Sykes, *New Medicines, The Practice of Medicine, and Public Policy* (Nuffield Trust, London, 2000).
[17] *Organon v Department of Health and Social Security, The Times* 6 Feb 1990.
[18] House of Commons Health Select Committee, *The Influence of the Pharmaceutical Industry* Fourth Report of Session 2004–05, para 301, available at www.publications.parliament.uk.

ments, nor does it have to demonstrate that the medicine meets a demonstrable health need. This facilitates the licensing of what are known as 'me-too' drugs, that is, medicines which are essentially new versions of existing ones, such as new angiotensin-converting-enzyme (ACE) inhibitors; calcium-channel blockers and selective serotonin reuptake inhibitor antidepressants.

There are no UK statistics for the number of newly approved drugs which are essentially 'me-too' drugs, as opposed to those which offer a significant therapeutic advance, but in the US, the Food and Drug Administration (FDA) separates new medical entities into those that deserve priority review (because they offer a potentially significant therapeutic advance over existing medicines), and those which receive a standard review (because they do not). The proportion of new medical entities requiring priority review each year is falling, and has been as low as 23 per cent, meaning that 77 per cent of the drugs licensed by the FDA that year may have been 'me-too' drugs, many of which will have been virtually identical, in terms of chemical composition, to the originals. The Canadian Patented Medicine Prices Review Board, which assesses the therapeutic novelty of every patented medicine, appraised 1147 newly patented drugs between 1990 and 2003, and found that only 68 (5.9 per cent) qualified as breakthrough drugs, defined as 'the first drug to treat effectively a particular illness or which provides a substantial improvement over existing drug products'.[19]

Because the pharmaceutical industry is global, there is no reason to believe that the picture is any different in Europe. On the contrary, there is considerable evidence that throughout the world, the number of entirely new medicinal products being brought to the market is falling,[20] and it has been estimated that 68 per cent of all new chemical entities marketed worldwide in the last 25 years have been 'me-too' products.[21]

'Me-too' drugs are not the same thing as generic versions of patented drugs, which are chemically identical to the drug whose patent has expired, and which can be sold only because the original is now out of its period of patent protection. 'Me-too' drugs have to be different in some way from the original medicine in order to qualify for their own period of patent protection. Unlike generic medicines, which are a fraction of the price of the patented original – Prozac cost $2.50 per capsule, generic fluoxetine costs $0.25[22] – 'me-too' drugs are themselves expensive patented medicines.[23]

Of course, there may be good reasons for refining existing therapeutic advances

[19] SG Morgan et al, '"Breakthrough" Drugs and Growth in Expenditure on Prescription Drugs in Canada' (2005) 331 *British Medical Journal* 815

[20] D Taylor, 'Fewer New Drugs from the Pharmaceutical Industry' (2003) 326 *British Medical Journal* 326, 408–40; R Joppi, V Bertele and S Garattini, 'Disappointing Biotech' (2005) 331 *British Medical Journal* 895.

[21] P Trouiller et al, 'Drug Development for Neglected Diseases: A Deficient Market and a Public-Health Policy Failure' (2002) 359 *The Lancet* 2188–94.

[22] JA Dimasi and C Paquette, 'The Economics of Follow-On Drug Research and Development: Trends in Entry Rates and the Timing of Development' (2004) 22 *Pharmacoeconomics* Supplement 2 1–14.

[23] SG Morgan et al n 19 above.

by producing new versions of existing drugs. Sometimes the first drug in a thera-peutic class may be defective in some way, and a subsequent version may be more effective or have fewer or milder side effects. Small therapeutic advantages are not necessarily worthless, especially for patients who may not be able to tolerate the first medicine of its type, and who are much better served by the second or third one. There are many examples of classes of drugs where later versions have dem-onstrable advantages over the first one. Tagamet, for example, was one of the first H_2 antagonists used for the treatment of heartburn, Zantac is a 'me-too' H_2 antag-onist, but it has fewer interactions with other medicines, which means it can be safely taken by more patients. For some classes of drugs, like antibiotics, to which it can be expected that some disease strains may become resistant, it could even be said that there is a pressing health *need* to continually develop new and therefore effective versions of existing medicines.

Because of the time it takes from the first isolation of a new compound to licens-ing, it is likely that different companies will be working on the same lines of research simultaneously, so it is unsurprising that similar products will reach the licensing stage within a short time of each other. The second and third drugs of their type to reach the market are not necessarily copies of the first one, cynically produced by manufacturers seeking to cash in on the first drug's commercial suc-cess. Rather the 'me-too' drug's subsequent entry to the marketplace may simply indicate that its manufacturer lost the race to be first. Di Masi and Paquette, for example, found that by the time a 'first-in-class' product is licensed, most 'follow on' products are already in the later stages of clinical development.[24]

It might also be assumed that the competitiveness of the market for 'me-too' drugs would drive prices down and quality up, with each new entrant to the mar-ket having to be cheaper and/or better than existing products in order to win a share of the already crowded market.[25] In fact, it appears that sometimes compa-nies are able to gain from the common assumption that 'what is newer is better', and therefore worth more, even when, in practice, it offers no therapeutic advan-tage over established treatments.[26] In Sweden, for example, Ekelund and Perssson found that 'me-too' versions of existing drugs tended to be introduced at about twice the price of the original drugs.[27]

There may additionally be health risks from 'me-too' drugs. If there are already effective and well-tolerated medicines to treat a condition, and the 'me-too' drug does not offer any therapeutic advantages over these tried and tested medicines, developing and marketing a new drug with potentially unknown side effects may be dangerous for both research subjects – who will be subjected to the risks of taking part in a clinical trial when there is no obvious scientific or clinical

---

[24] Dimasi and Paquette n 22 above.

[25] TH Lee, '"Me-Too" Products – Friend or Foe?' (2004) 350 *New England Journal of Medicine* 211–21.

[26] DA Kessler et al, 'Therapeutic-Class Wars – Drug Promotion in a Competitive Marketplace' (1994) 331 *New England Journal of Medicine* 1350–53.

[27] M Ekelund and B Persson, 'Pharmaceutical Pricing in a Regulated Market' (2003) 85 *Review of Economics and Statistics* 298–306.

justification for it – and for patients. Rare side effects may not come to light until some time after the drug is first approved, and hence a new drug may pose as yet unknown risks to patients, which will be worth taking if it is a new treatment for an otherwise untreatable condition, but not if it has no advantages over safe and well-established treatments. It has been estimated that while only one in seven new drugs offers patients a therapeutic advantage over existing drugs, two in seven result in serious adverse events.[28] If they offer no improvement over existing treatments, but bring with them the possibility of unknown side effects, Jerry Avorn has argued that 'me-too' drugs should be labelled with the following 'revenue-crippling' warning:

> This new medication has not been shown to be any better than currently available products, and has a much more limited safety record. There is no evidence that its higher price is accompanied by any demonstrated therapeutic advantage.[29]

A good example of a 'me-too' drug which posed serious safety risks to patients is Vioxx. Its withdrawal from the market on safety grounds is described in more detail in the following chapter, but it is worth noting here that, when it was licensed, Vioxx was simply another anti-inflammatory painkiller, which did not, in fact, offer a significant therapeutic advantage to patients over existing treatments, but which was estimated to have caused between 88,000 and 130,000 heart attacks or strokes before it was withdrawn.[30]

It is unsurprising that companies, which are under a duty to their shareholders to maximise profits, favour the development and production of 'me-too' drugs. It is clearly riskier to develop an entirely novel treatment, which is much more likely to fail, or to be found to have unacceptable side effects than a compound which is similar to a treatment which is already known to be safe and effective. Each new medicine, even if it does not represent an improvement on existing treatments, receives 20 years of patent protection. When the medicine in question is genuinely innovative, at least half of this time is likely to expire while the drug is being developed and tested. If a company is simply developing a new version of an existing chemical compound, it will need to do less testing, at lower risk, since a different version of the compound has already satisfied the criteria for obtaining a marketing authorisation. The new drug is therefore likely to be able to benefit from a longer period of 'on the market' patent protection. Developing more 'me-too' drugs is therefore undoubtedly an efficient way to spend a company's research and development (R&D) budget.

Not only are there economic incentives towards pursuing 'me-too' drug research, it could further be argued that allowing many competitors to enter the market soon after a new therapeutic advance actually disincentivises genuinely

---

[28] DW Light, 'Bearing the Risks of Prescription Drugs' in D W Light (ed) *The Risks of Prescription Drugs* (Columbia UP, 2010) 1–39, 11.

[29] J Avorn, *Powerful Medicines: The Benefits, Risks, and Costs of Prescription Drugs* (New York, Knopf, 2004) 365.

[30] DW Light n 28 above, 12.

innovative research. 'Me-too' drugs will take some of the market share away from the original innovator.[31] Why bother to spend a great deal of money making a genuinely new discovery if there is no obstacle to your competitors introducing very similar products during your innovative drug's period of patent protection? The manufacturer of the first statin, for example, received much less reward for its innovation than would have been the case if the statin market was not immediately flooded with imitators. By *splitting* the market, 'me-too' drugs effectively reduce the commercial benefits of innovation. It has been estimated that 'me-too' drugs reduce the period of market exclusivity each new medicine enjoys – from 10.2 years on average in the 1970s, to 1.2 years in the 1990s.[32]

C 'Evergreening'

In order to delay or block competition from generic versions when a medicine is coming to the end of its period of patent protection, the manufacturer of the original medicine may engage in a process known as 'evergreening'. This involves the submission of a new application for an ostensibly novel product, which is in fact only very slightly different from the one which is about to lose its patent protection. The 'new' product can then receive a further 20 years of patent protection. The difference between the old drug and the new one can simply be a change of dosage (from four times a day to once a day, for example), or a change in presentation (from bulky capsule to slimline tablet).[33] Evergreening can also involve no more than a new indication for an old medicine. For example, when Prozac (fluoxetine) was about to lose its patent protection, it was rebranded as Sarafem, a new, patented treatment for premenstrual dysphoric disorder.

If the new product, which will often have a slightly more convenient method of delivery, is introduced before the patent on the original version expires, attempts might be made to persuade doctors to switch their patients to the newer product, with the longer running patent.[34] The best way to ensure that patients are switched onto the new medicine is to remove the original product from the market before generic competitors can enter it. If the patient is already taking the new branded medicine once generic versions of the old one become available, they are more likely to carry on taking it than if the rebranding takes place *after* cheaper, generic versions have become available.

The principal purpose of evergreening is to increase the profitability of medicines: it 'is an exercise in marketing, not science'.[35] Of course, to obtain a fresh

[31] F Lichtenberg and T Philipson, 'The Dual Effects of Intellectual Property Regulations: Within- and between-Patent Competition in the US Pharmaceuticals Industry' (2002) 45 *Journal of Law and Economics* 643–72.

[32] DiMasi and Paquette n 22 above.

[33] House of Commons Health Select Committee (2004–05) n 18 above.

[34] RG Frank, 'The Ongoing Regulation of Generic Drugs' (2007) 357 *New England Journal of Medicine* 1993–96.

[35] D Henry and J Lexchin, 'Patent Law' (2003) 361 *The Lancet* 1059.

patent, there must be genuine novelty, and there have been cases where courts have declared patents invalid on the grounds that there is really no difference between the new product and one already in circulation.[36] Drug companies may argue that altering the route of delivery, or the dosage, may improve patient compliance, and hence lead to better health outcomes, but the evidence for this claim is in fact weak.[37] There is, however, substantial evidence that evergreening imposes significant costs on the NHS. It has, for example, been estimated that the evergreening of six medicines (omeprazole, amlodipine, doxazosin, loratadine, mirtazapine, and ramipril) resulted in little or no therapeutic benefit for patients, but cost the NHS up to £369 million.[38]

D Data Exclusivity

It might be thought that the patent system is the only way in which drug manufacturers can effectively block competition from generics manufacturers, but there is, in practice, a further route through which competition can be delayed, namely by restricting generics companies' ability to rely upon the original trial data. Although in theory generics companies are free to conduct their own clinical trials, the prices they will be able to charge for their products will not be sufficient to recoup the costs of doing so. It might also be said to be unethical for a generics company to conduct fresh trials in animals and in human subjects of a substance that has already been adequately tested. As a result, when applying for a marketing authorisation a generics company must rely indirectly on the original manufacturer's trial data by demonstrating that its product is the same as the original.[39]

The data are not actually disclosed to the generics manufacturer, rather the regulator will compare the generic application with the original trial data. If the generic product contains the same active substance and is judged to be bioequivalent, that is, its effects, both in terms of efficacy and safety, are expected to be essentially the same, then the regulator can grant a marketing authorisation to the generics manufacturers based upon the data submitted to support the original drug's application for a marketing authorisation. Unless the regulator can rely upon the trial data that were submitted by the original manufacturer, it cannot grant the generics company a marketing authorisation for its product, and so generic competition will be delayed. If the original manufacturer is able to restrict access to its trial data after the patent expires, it may be able to extend de facto the period of patent protection.[40]

---

[36] *Les Laboratoires Servier v Apotex Inc* [2008] EWCA Civ 445.

[37] DA Hughes, 'Less is More: Medicines that Require Less Frequent Dosing Improve Adherence, but are they Better?' (2006) 24 *Pharmacoeconomics* 211–23.

[38] House of Commons Health Select Committee (2004–05) n 18 above, 92.

[39] Article 10 of Directive 2001/83/EC as amended by Directive 2004/27/EC.

[40] JH Reichman, 'Rethinking the Role of Clinical Trial Data in International Intellectual Property Law: The Case for a Public Goods Approach' (2009) 13 *Marquette Intellectual Property Law Review* 1.

The period of what is known as 'data exclusivity' within the EU is rather complicated. The start of the data (and market) exclusivity periods is the date when the first marketing authorisation was granted within the EU. Since 2004, the EU Pharmaceutical Legislation has created a harmonised EU eight-year data exclusivity provision with an additional two-year period of market exclusivity. Market exclusivity is the period of data exclusivity, plus the time it takes to register and market the generic medicine, which is a further one to three years. Effectively then there is a 10-year period of market exclusivity. Matters are made even more complicated because this 10-year period can be further extended by an additional year if, during the first eight years, the marketing authorisation holder obtains an authorisation for a new therapeutic indication which delivers a significant clinical benefit in comparison with existing treatments. In practical terms, this means that a generic application for a marketing authorisation can be submitted after year eight, but the product cannot be marketed until after year 10, or 11 if there has been a new therapeutic indication.

In *R (on the application of Merck Sharp & Dohme) v Licensing Authority*,[41] the drug company sought to argue that when it changed the dosage of one of its products, the new dosage should benefit from a new period of data exclusivity, even though the active substance was identical to that of the original product, for which the period of data exclusivity had expired. Merck Sharp and Dohme (MSD) held marketing authorisations for Fosamax 5mg, 10mg (product A) and Fosamax Once Weekly, 70mg (product B), both of which were used to treat osteoporosis. A generics company wished to rely on their data in order to obtain a marketing authorisation for a drug (product C) which was identical to product B. Product B (which was essentially seven times the dose of the daily version, to be taken weekly) had not been in circulation for 10 years. MSD therefore argued that the generics company could not rely upon the trial data which established the safety and efficacy of product A, which had been in circulation for more than 10 years, because product C was the same as product B, rather than product A. Moses J rejected this claim, since its effect might be that the generics company would have to carry out wholly unnecessary tests on an active ingredient which had already been fully tested, and which was known to be safe in the dosage it was proposing to manufacture.

Market exclusivity is independent of the patent system, so it can be used to protect clinical trial data for products which are not sufficiently innovative to benefit from patent protection. Data exclusivity is granted simply because the company expended effort and resources in carrying out trials: there is no requirement to establish that those trials resulted in any technological or scientific achievement. In relation to medicines, however, it is common for market exclusivity and patent protection to exist in tandem, and much will therefore depend upon the relative timing of the award of the patent and the granting of a marketing authorisation.

---

[41] *R (on the application of Merck Sharp & Dohme) v Licensing Authority* [2005] EWHC 710 (Admin).

It is, of course, possible that the period of market exclusivity will have expired during the product's period of patent protection, in which case, its existence will make no difference to generics' manufacturers' ability to enter the marketplace immediately after the patent expires. If, for example, the original product receives its marketing authorisation six years after the patent was first granted, market exclusivity will have expired four years before patent expiry. But as discussed earlier, it is quite common for a significant proportion of the 20 years of patent protection to have been used up while the new compound is being developed. If the original product receives its first marketing authorisation 12 years after it received its patent, the data/market exclusivity rules will, in practice, block generic competition for a further two years after patent expiry.

In some ways, this outcome is precisely what is intended by granting a period of data exclusivity, the purpose of which is to offer an incentive to carry out expensive trials when delays in obtaining a marketing authorisation may restrict a company's ability to profit from those trials. In practice, however, by further delaying generic competition and offering an additional period of de facto patent protection, data exclusivity offers an additional benefit to drug companies, at the expense of the NHS. It could also be argued that it contributes to the prevalent assumption that clinical trial data are a private, as opposed to a public good. Treating trial data as commercially sensitive and privately acquired information means that secrecy and confidentiality are the norm. Instead, it could be argued that clinical trial data are also a public good,[42] and that restricting access to them for any longer than the period which is already guaranteed by the patent system prioritises private interests in income generation over public interests in drug safety.

E Confidentiality of Data

In addition to the narrow issue of data exclusivity rights as a way of extending the de facto period of patent protection, much of the information produced by drug companies during the many stages of drug development is treated as commercially sensitive and hence confidential. An application for a marketing authorisation will be accompanied by a great deal of data: one of the largest dossiers submitted to the UK regulator contained 100,000 pages of information.[43] Very little of this information is made publicly available, meaning that it is difficult for external observers to scrutinise the basis of licensing decisions. Of course, the results of trials may be written up and published in medical journals, but as was evident in the previous chapter, the published data will seldom offer a complete picture of all of the information gathered during clinical trials.

In 2011, Peter C Gøtzsche and Anders W Jørgensen published a case study of their attempt, between 2007 and 2010, to obtain the data from five placebo-

---

[42] Reichmann n 40 above.
[43] J Collier, and I Iheanacho, 'The Pharmaceutical Industry as an Informant' (2002) 360 *The Lancet* 1405–09.

controlled trials of two anti-obesity drugs, rimonabant (Acomplia) and orlistat (Xenical), from the European Medicines Agency. They explained to the Agency that they wanted to 'explore the robustness of the results by adjusting for the many missing data on weight loss and to study selective publication by comparing protocols and unpublished results with those in published reports'.[44] This is a particularly important issue in relation to anti-obesity drugs because their risk-benefit profile is controversial: the beneficial effects on weight can be fairly marginal and the harms, which have included cardiac and pulmonary complications, can be substantial. EMA turned down this request, citing the commercial sensitivity of the data, but Gøtzsche and Jørgensen persisted. They complained to the European Ombudsman, who repeatedly asked EMA for a satisfactory explanation of their refusal. EMA continued to refuse access, additionally citing the workload that would be involved in redacting the documents, that is, removing personal, confidential information from them. Eventually the Ombudsman inspected the documents himself and declared that they were not commercially sensitive: he held that the risk of an economic interest being undermined must be reasonably foreseeable and not purely hypothetical. The Ombudsman therefore made a finding of maladministration against EMA, after which the documents were released.[45]

EMA had cited three different categories of commercially confidential information: intellectual property; trade secrets; and commercial confidences. Because the trial data were submitted as part of an application for a marketing authorisation, for drugs that were already covered by patent protection, the Ombudsman found that they did not contain information which needed to be kept confidential in order to protect intellectual property rights. The requested documents did not contain any information about the formulae of the drugs, or their manufacturing process, so they did not represent 'trade secrets'. Nor did they contain 'commercial confidences', such as information about the companies' proposed marketing strategy. EMA had additionally argued that disclosure would give competitors valuable information about the long-term clinical development strategy of the drugs' manufacturers. Again, this was rejected by the Ombudsman: given that the outcome of the application for a marketing authorisation would be in the public domain, the fact that these companies had been developing anti-obesity drugs could hardly be said to reveal confidential information about their long-term drug development strategy.

In response to this case, the European Medicines Agency revised its policy on access to documents, which in the initial stages involves responding to requests for disclosure, but is ultimately intended to ensure that EMA proactively places as much of its documentation as possible on its website.[46] While the policy spells out

[44] PC Gøtzsche and AW Jørgensen, 'Opening up Data at the European Medicines Agency' (2011) 342 *British Medical Journal* d2686.

[45] European Ombudsman. *Draft Recommendation of the European Ombudsman in his Inquiry into Complaint 2560/2007/BEH against the European Medicines Agency* (7 June 2010), available at www.ombudsman.europa.eu/cases/draftrecommendation.faces/en/4883/html.bookmark.

[46] European Medicines Agency, *European Medicines Agency Policy on Access to Documents (Related to Medicinal Products for Human and Veterinary Use)* (EMA, 2010).

EMA's commitment to openness and transparency, it also specifies that, in relation to documents containing 'information of commercial interest', in responding to requests for disclosure, 'the Agency has to strike the balance between the right of the applicant to gain access to documents and the interest of industry to have commercial confidential information duly protected'. For the purposes of its policy, the Agency defines commercial confidential information as 'any information which is not in the public domain or publicly available and where disclosure may undermine the economic interest or competitive position of the owner of the information'.

Of course, much depends upon how this is interpreted. As the Ombudsman's inspection of the documents in the above case demonstrated, trial data are very unlikely to contain descriptions of the chemical properties of the drug and explanations of its synthesis. On the contrary, the medicine will be referred to by a combination of letters and numbers which will tell competitors nothing about how it was produced and how it works. Moreover, because the data which the company submits to the regulator should contain both published and unpublished results, they are likely to be less positive about the medicine than information which is in the public domain, and so might be thought to be less likely to prompt competitors to instigate the development of similar drugs. Ironically, information that *is* of commercial value – such as the results of *in vitro*, animal, and early human studies – are frequently made publicly available in order to attract investors.

Although Gøtzsche and Jørgensen had grounded their application for access to data from these trials in their legitimate interest in evaluating the evidence base for anti-obesity drugs, given that these drugs appear to have a rather marginal risk-benefit profile, it could be argued that the Ombudsman's finding that these trial data were not commercially sensitive applies to any medicine, when the submission to the regulator is very unlikely to contain information about drug composition or long-term development strategy. If this judgment were to lead to a presumption that the submitted data should be made publicly available in all cases, this could potentially help address the problem, discussed in the previous chapter, that the published evidence base is not complete and, as a result of selective publication, is skewed towards the over-representation of positive results.

F Generic Drugs

Once a medicine loses its patent protection, anyone can apply for a marketing authorisation to manufacture and sell a generic alternative. Generic drugs manufacturers are not trying to recoup the original R&D investment, and nor do they spend much money on marketing. Because generic drugs are made by a number of different manufacturers simultaneously, none has an incentive to spend money on marketing which would, in practice, also benefit their competitors. As a result, generic drugs are much cheaper than the original branded version. Unsurprisingly, therefore, there has been considerable pressure within the NHS to switch, where possible, from branded to generic prescription drugs. Compared with other countries, levels of generic prescriptions in the UK are high – 83 per cent of prescribed drugs are generics. It has, however, been estimated that five per cent of all prescriptions are for branded medicines when a generic version is also available, and that this unnecessary prescription of branded drugs represents a significant proportion of the £9 billion a year the NHS currently spends on branded medicines.[47]

One way to promote generic prescription would be to provide doctors with incentives towards writing prescriptions for generic substitutes. Such a scheme was introduced in the UK in order to address the very high levels of prescriptions of atorvastatin (brand name Lipitor) by GPs, despite the availability of the first generic statin (simvastatin). Ironically, this scheme was challenged by the Association of the British Pharmaceutical Industry (ABPI) on the grounds that it was contrary to regulations which are intended to ensure that *drug companies* do not offer financial incentives to doctors to prescribe their medicines. The relevant provision provided that:

> Where medicinal products are being promoted to persons qualified to prescribe or supply them, no gifts, pecuniary advantages or benefits in kind may be supplied, offered or promised to such persons unless they are inexpensive and relevant to the practice of medicine or pharmacy.[48]

The High Court referred the interpretation of this provision to the European Court of Justice (ECJ), which held that prescription incentive schemes, organised by national public health authorities, are motivated by legitimate budgetary concerns, rather than by profit-maximisation, and hence are not contrary to these regulations. It is, of course, true that the Department of Health is not motivated by profit when it devises a prescription incentive scheme, but it is less clear that this is the case for the partners within GP practices, who do benefit financially from these sorts of incentives.[49]

In 2010, the Department of Health consulted on whether to go beyond persuasion and incentives in primary care, and instead move towards automatic generic substitution by pharmacists. 80 per cent of doctors and 64 per cent of NHS organisations supported the Department of Health's preferred option for the automatic generic substitution of drugs on a defined list. Automatic generic substitution was, unsurprisingly, supported by only 10 per cent of trade bodies. It was also unpopular among a well-organised patient lobby of epilepsy sufferers who responded to the consultation in large numbers, using template responses. Small variations in the absorption of epilepsy medication can result in significant differences in their

---

[47] Department of Health, *The Proposals to Implement 'Generic Substitution' in Primary Care, Further to the Pharmaceutical Price Regulation Scheme (PPRS) 2009* (DH, 2010).

[48] Article 94(1) of Directive 2001/83/EC of the European Parliament and of the Council on the Community Code Relating to Medicinal Products for Human Use was introduced into domestic law by Article 21(1) of the Medicines (Advertising) Regulations 1994/1932.

[49] J Fanning and N Glover-Thomas, 'Take this Medicine: The Legality of Prescription Incentive Schemes' (2010) 18 *Medical Law Review* 417.

therapeutic effect, but this might have been an argument for saying that epilepsy is a special case where generic substitution may not be appropriate, and hence that epilepsy medication should not be on the defined list, rather than an argument against automatic generic substitution per se.

Following this consultation, the government rejected automatic generic substitution on 'patient safety' grounds.[50] A significant number of respondents to the Department of Health's consultation, among them many trade bodies, had argued that generic substitution could lead to confusion and anxiety, especially among vulnerable patients, and that this might lead to non-compliance, and in turn to poorer health outcomes.[51] This confusion would be likely to be exacerbated by frequent changes in the appearance of the same medicine: pharmacies try to buy the cheapest generic versions, which can mean that they frequently change suppliers. Patients collecting the same drug from the same pharmacist might then find that its packaging and presentation varies.[52]

It was also argued that patients might suffer a kind of reverse placebo effect when their medication changes in appearance, even if it is chemically identical to the branded medicine. Patients might perceive the medicine to be less good than the branded medicine, and as a result, they might report more side effects and decreased efficacy. As the National Pharmacy Association put it: 'Even if these are only perceived effects they are very real to the patient and may lead to reduced compliance.'[53] It was also argued, principally by pharmaceutical companies, that automatic generic substitution 'would have a negative impact on the viability of the UK pharmaceutical industry and on innovation in new or improved medicines'.[54]

The obvious response to the patient safety fears identified by respondents to the consultation would be to make sure that generic versions of branded medicines not only contain the same active ingredient as the original, but that they also try, as far as possible, to mimic the way the medicine looks, is packaged and is taken. While the active ingredient in a generic medicine will be the same as in the original, the stabilising, bulking, flavouring, colouring, and sweetening agents may be different, and these can sometimes cause allergies or intolerance.[55] Again, ensuring the generic version also contains the same non-active ingredients could ensure more perfect substitutability. This approach, while sensible, may be problematic in practice if the manufacturer of the original medicine has taken out a series of 'evergreening' patents on the way a medicine is packaged, 'bulked out' and marketed.[56]

---

[50] Department of Health n 47 above.
[51] Department of Health, 'Consultation on the Proposals to Implement "Generic Substitution" in Primary Care: Analysis of Responses For Department of Health By Greenstreet Berman' (DH, 2010).
[52] RE Ferner, 'Controversy Over Generic Substitution' (2010) 340 *British Medical Journal* c2548.
[53] Department of Health n 51 above.
[54] ibid.
[55] Ferner n 52 above.
[56] M Angell and AS Relman, 'Patents, Profits and American Medicine: Conflicts of Interest in the Testing & Marketing of New Drugs' (2002) *Daedalus* 102–11.

Generic versions of existing drugs, if sold in sufficient numbers, can be highly profitable. But for the manufacturer of the original version, competition from generic versions of a profitable patented medicine is generally unwelcome. As a result, a number of strategies have been used in order to attempt to delay the introduction of generic competition, such as launching multiple patent applications or infringement actions, both of which create uncertainty for generics manufacturers.[57] Because patents not only cover a medicine's active ingredient, but can also be taken out on other features, such as the colour of the pill, each drug can be the subject of several patents which, if taken out at different times during the drug's original period of patent protection, make it difficult for generics manufacturers to know exactly when they are free to market a new version of the drug. The European Generics Medicines Association suggests that brand-name manufacturers commonly 'stockpile' patent protection by obtaining separate 20-year patents on multiple attributes of a single product, including aspects of the manufacturing process, tablet colour, dosing route, mechanism of action, etc.[58]

If a generics manufacturer decides to produce a new generic version when there is some doubt over whether any of these 'evergreening' patents are still extant, they could be sued by the original manufacturer, and even if the generics manufacturer ultimately wins, this sort of litigation takes time and delays the entry of generic competition. The profits that can be made by the original manufacturer as a result of delayed generic entry will often more than pay for any damages that may be awarded against them.

Before they come to court, it is not uncommon for these cases to be settled, with the companies making agreements which, in some cases, come very close to bribes paid to the generics manufacturer to delay the release of their generic version of the branded medicine. In the US, the manufacturer of the heart drug Cardizem CD (diltiazem) was reported to have paid a generics company almost $100 million to keep its version off the market, and the manufacturer of the antihypertensive and prostate drug Hytrin (terazosin) had apparently offered to pay $54 million to delay the release of a generic version.[59]

This sort of behaviour is plainly anti-competitive and may fall foul of competition law. Within the EU, the European Commission fined Astra Zeneca €60 million for anti-competitive behaviour in trying to delay the market entry of generic versions of Losec, its best-selling proton pump inhibitor. Astra Zeneca had provided misleading information to European patent offices in order to obtain an additional period of patent protection, which it then used in order to launch patent infringement actions against generics manufacturers. It had also deregistered Losec capsules, and launched Losec tablets, in countries where generics manufacturers would

---

[57] AB Engelberg, AS Kesselheim, and J Avorn, 'Balancing Innovation, Access, and Profits – Market Exclusivity for Biologics' (2009) 361 *New England Journal of Medicine* 1917–19.

[58] European Generics Association (EGA), *Evergreening* (EGA, 2004), available at www.egagenerics. com/gen-evergrn.htm.

[59] M Shuchman, 'Delaying Generic Competition – Corporate Payoffs and the Future of Plavix' (2006) 355 *New England Journal of Medicine* 1297–300.

have to rely on the original marketing authorisation for Losec capsules in order to obtain a marketing authorisation for their generic alternative.[60] Astra Zeneca appealed against this decision, and, although it did annul one aspect of the EC's decision, the ECJ upheld the Commission's central finding that Astra Zeneca had abused its dominant position.[61]

The European Commission investigated anti-competitive practices in the pharmaceutical industry in 2008–09. It found that there was, on average, a delay of seven months between a medicine's loss of patent exclusivity and the entrance of a generic alternative, and that the savings from generic entry would be 20 per cent higher if this delay could be eliminated. The Commission found that much of this delay was due to the practices of pharmaceutical companies, including 'patent settlements' in which generic manufacturers had agreed to restrictions on their freedom to market their products in return for total payments of around €200 million. Many of these agreements were made in the year before patent exclusivity was lost, and they placed restrictions on the marketing of generics for, on average, more than two years after patent expiry.[62] Agreements like this are clearly anti-competitive. Their purpose will often be to share profits between the original manufacturer and the generic manufacturer, at the expense of the purchasers of medicines. The compensation payable may fully reimburse the generic manufacturer for its losses as a result of its product's delayed entry to the market, but it does not reimburse consumers and public health systems like the NHS, whose interests are not represented in these settlement negotiations.

Since 2009, the European Commission has carried out annual monitoring of the number of problematic patent settlements within the EEA. Its original inquiry had found that 22 per cent of all patent settlements in the pharmaceutical sector were problematic, but in its first monitoring exercise, this had decreased significantly, to 10 per cent.[63] It is unclear whether greater scrutiny of anti-competitive practices is the cause of this decrease, and it remains to be seen whether this downward trend will continue.

IV Relationship between Regulators and Industry

The MHRA necessarily has a close relationship with the pharmaceutical industry, but some critics have argued that it is too close and too cosy.[64] It is inevitable that

---

[60] N Fagerlund and SB Rasmussen, 'AstraZeneca: The First Abuse Case in the Pharmaceutical Sector' (2005) 3 *EC Competition Policy Newsletter* 54–56.

[61] *AstraZeneca AB v European Commission* (T-321/05) [2010] 5 CMLR 28.

[62] ibid.

[63] EU Press Release, *Antitrust: Commission Launches Second Monitoring Exercise of Patent Settlements in Pharma Sector* (Europa, 17 January 2011).

[64] I Iheanacho, 'Drug Regulation: A Sometimes Unhealthy Coalition' (2010) 340 *British Medical Journal* c2613; R Evans and S Boseley 'The Drugs Industry and its Watchdog: A Relationship too Close for Comfort' *The Guardian* 4 October 2004.

people who work for the MHRA will have had links with the industry. The previous chapter explained that managing conflicts of interest raises important and often neglected ethical issues in the context of clinical trials. The same is true in relation to drugs regulation. New members and chairs of committees of the MHRA are bound by a Code of Practice which gives them three months to dispose of their financial interests in the industry, after which they can participate fully in the work of committees. This assumes that disposing of the interest removes the conflict.[65] In practice, loyalties towards and relationships with previous employers may persist after financial ties are broken. These other personal interests should be declared at meetings, and it is up to the relevant committee chair to decide how to manage them.

A more complicated conflict of interest, and one that is harder to manage, arises not when an individual who is involved in a licensing decision has a personal or financial link with the product's manufacturer, but rather when those involved in regulation have, as a result of long-term exposure, a general 'affinity with the industry'.[66] Currently, however, conflicts of interest are assumed to arise only when decisions are taken about specific products to which MHRA members and experts have an identifiable connection.

It has been argued that the relationship between the pharmaceutical industry and its regulator amounts to what is known as 'regulatory capture'.[67] This can result from lobbying and through the co-opting of experts from industry, but is perhaps best illustrated by what has been described as the 'revolving door':

> regulatory officials begin their careers in industry, then work for some years in the regulatory agency until they are promoted back into the higher echelons of industry.[68]

Officials who assume that their next job may involve working in the industry that they are currently regulating may, understandably, be especially keen to maintain cordial relationships with future colleagues or employers. Because 'capture' implies that regulation was initiated without this industry influence, and has only subsequently been 'captured', John Abraham prefers to describe the relationship between industry and the regulator as one of 'corporate bias', by which he means that the industry has had, *from the outset*, 'privileged strategic access' to the regulator and to policy makers, over and above that of any other interest group.[69]

A contrary argument, put forward by Richard Epstein, suggests that regulators may in fact be too *tough* on drug companies, because they are more anxious to avoid a false positive (where a dangerous drug is wrongly categorised as safe, or an ineffective drug is wrongly judged to be effective) than a false negative (where a

---

[65] J Lexchin and O O'Donovan, 'Prohibiting or 'Managing' Conflict of Interest? A Review of Policies and Procedures in Three European Drug Regulation Agencies' (2010) 70 *Social Science and Medicine* 643–47.

[66] ibid.

[67] J Braithwaite, *Corporate Crime in the Pharmaceutical Industry* (London, Routledge, 1984).

[68] J Abraham, 'Sociology of Pharmaceuticals Development and Regulation: A Realist Empirical Research Programme' (2008) 30 *Sociology of Health and Illness* 869–85.

[69] ibid.

safe drug is wrongly categorised as dangerous, or an effective drug is wrongly judged to be ineffective).[70] Epstein maintains that the public consequences of the first type of error are more severe for regulators than the second type. No one wants to be responsible for licensing another thalidomide, whereas if a useful medicine is wrongly kept out of the market, while real people may suffer or even die as a result, they are unidentifiable and hence the negative consequences of this sort of error are less visible than when people are injured by a defective medicine. The focus on avoiding licensing bad medicines, at all costs, in Epstein's view, prolongs trials and erodes a drug's patent life. Epstein goes further and argues that drugs which are unsafe or ineffective will not be used by patients, whereas if safe and effective drugs are not approved for use, this 'mistake' cannot be rectified by the consumers themselves.[71]

Epstein is surely right that there is a balance to be struck between the mirror-image risks, first of approving drugs too quickly, with the risk that dangerous drugs will be allowed into the marketplace, and second, approving drugs too slowly, with the risk that access to effective medicines will be delayed.[72] It would, however, be a mistake to assume that these risks carry the same weight for every new medicine. Where a new medicine is genuinely a significant therapeutic advance, and might offer treatment for a currently untreatable disease, the consequences of undue delay in approval processes could be extremely serious. There might then be good reasons for attempting to speed up approval times where the condition the medicine is intended to treat is life-threatening or extremely serious, and where no other effective medicine is currently available. In contrast, where the new medicine is essentially a 'me-too' drug, or might represent a marginal improvement on existing treatment, the risk of approving it too hastily may outweigh the risk of delaying access.

V Classification of Medicines

In addition to deciding whether to grant a marketing authorisation, the MHRA also classifies medicines into one of three categories: prescription-only medicines (POM); medicines which can be bought from a pharmacist without prescription (P) and general sale list medicines, which can be sold in ordinary retail outlets and do not need to be dispensed by a pharmacist (GSL).

The factors which should be taken into account when deciding whether a medicine should be prescription-only are whether the medicine:

---

[70] RA Epstein, *Overdose: How Excessive Government Regulation Stifles Pharmaceutical Innovation* (New Haven, Yale University Press, 2006). See also H Teff, 'Regulation under the Medicines Act 1968: A Continuing Prescription for Health' (1984) 47 *Modern Law Review* 303–23.

[71] Epstein n 70 above.

[72] A Daemmrich and G Krücken, 'Risk versus Risk: Decision-making Dilemmas of Drug Regulation in the United States and Germany' (2000) 9 *Science as Culture* 505–34.

- is likely to present a direct or indirect danger to human health, even when used correctly, if used without the supervision of a doctor or dentist; or
- is frequently and to a very wide extent used incorrectly, and as a result is likely to present a direct or indirect danger to human health; or
- contains substances or preparations of substances of which the activity requires, or the side effects require, further investigation;
- is normally prescribed by a doctor or dentist for parenteral administration [that is, intravenously or by injection];[73]
- is likely, if incorrectly used, to present a substantial risk of medicinal abuse, lead to addiction or be used for illegal purposes.[74]

It is possible for medicines to be reclassified, in order to restrict or broaden access. If new risks are identified which require a doctor to be involved in order to ensure safe usage, the MHRA might reclassify a medicine previously sold in pharmacies as prescription-only, or if information emerges which suggests that the medicine should not be supplied without a pharmacist first checking that it is safe for the patient, again it would be possible for a medicine on the general sale list to be reclassified as pharmacy-only.

It is, however, much more common for reclassification to broaden access to medicines – by moving them from prescription-only to pharmacy (POM to P) status, or from pharmacy to general sale (P to GSL) – as a result of evidence that the medicine does not pose the risk to health which justified its original classification. It will generally be more convenient for consumers to be able to buy medicines over-the-counter,[75] and self-medication will save the NHS money and use up fewer GP appointments.

The drive to reclassify medicines so that more can be sold over-the-counter has a number of consequences. First, the leaflets supplied with medicines become more important, since they may represent the only information the patient receives about how to take the medicine safely. When a medicine has to be prescribed by a doctor, she is responsible for ensuring that the medicine is appropriate for the individual patient. Pharmacists are supposed to ask about contraindications for certain medicines, and give some information about safe usage, but this is a far less rigorous system of control. Second, where the pharmacist must ask personal information prior to selling a P medicine – the morning-after pill is a good example – there may be implications for a person's privacy, since few chemist shops have private facilities in which to hold consultations.

Third, pharmacy and general sale medicines can, unlike prescription-only medicines, be marketed directly to consumers. When a prescription-only medicine's patent expires, and it faces competition from generic manufacturers, if its status can be downgraded to pharmacy-available, advertising it under its brand name is one way to attempt to maintain sales.[76]

---

[73] Medicines Act 1968 s 58A(2).

[74] ibid s 58A(3).

[75] D Prayle and M Brazier, 'Supply of Medicines: Paternalism, Autonomy and Reality' (1998) 24 *Journal of Medical Ethics* 93–98.

[76] ibid.

VI Buying Prescription Drugs Online

The system for the classification of medicines rests on the assumption that it is possible to exercise considerable control over access to prescription-only medicines. If a doctor must write a prescription, it is – in theory at least – possible to ensure that the medicine is only taken by someone for whom it is clinically indicated and in whom it is likely to be safe. Although labels on prescription drugs specify that the medicine should be taken only by the person for whom it was prescribed, in practice it is impossible to exercise much control over the bottle or packet of pills once the person for whom it was prescribed has taken it home. It is difficult to know how common it is for people to share or steal their friends' or relatives' prescription medicines, but there are obvious health risks if drugs which have been classified as prescription-only on the grounds that self-medication poses a risk to health are taken by people to whom they were not prescribed.

The rise of online pharmacies dramatically increases the risk of inappropriate use of prescription medicines. Some online pharmacies which operate in the UK are registered by the Royal Pharmaceutical Society of Great Britain (RPGB), and supply prescription-only medicines where the purchaser has a valid prescription from a registered medical practitioner. Other sites offer private virtual consultations, which sometimes amount to no more than filling in a questionnaire. Doctors employed by the owners of these websites then prescribe and dispense medicines without a face-to-face encounter with the patient. It is hard to see how this is compatible with a doctor's duty of care. According to General Medical Council (GMC) guidance, good clinical care must include 'adequately assessing the patient's conditions, taking account of the history (including the symptoms, and psychological and social factors), the patient's views, and where necessary examining the patient'.[77] Without seeing the patient, there must be doubts about whether their condition can be adequately assessed online, especially given how easy it is to disguise one's identity on the internet. Someone who presents himself online as a 50-year-old man with erectile dysfunction could, in fact, be a 16-year-old boy. More specifically still, GMC good practice guidance instructs doctors that:

> In providing care you must . . . prescribe drugs or treatment, including repeat prescriptions, only when you have adequate knowledge of the patient's health, and are satisfied that the drugs or treatment serve the patient's needs.[78]

It is difficult to see how a doctor can be 'satisfied' that drugs serve a patient's needs when the person buying the prescription medicine has simply filled out a form online, and there is no guarantee that they have done so accurately. In addition to serious doubts about whether an online consultation can effectively rule out inappropriate prescribing, there are also websites which proudly advertise the fact that

---

[77] General Medical Council, *Good Medical Practice* (GMC, 2006) paras 2 and 3.
[78] ibid.

there is 'no need for a prescription', and in these cases control over access to prescription-only medicines, or counterfeit products which are sold as such, is non-existent.

Buying medicines online is an attractive option for some patients. The medicines which are most commonly purchased online are for conditions or symptoms which may be embarrassing or attract some sort of stigma. People might also seek access to medicines online if they are worried that their doctor will be unsympathetic to their request for medication. If the medicines which are supplied are generally safe, allowing people to buy them online may have the same advantages to patients as reclassification from prescription-only status to pharmacy availability, but crucially this takes place without the prior judgement of the MHRA that self-medication is safe enough to justify declassification.

Unregistered online pharmacies do not necessarily require a healthcare professional to determine whether the medicine is appropriate for its would-be purchaser. In the absence of a professional gatekeeper, the risk that medicines will be taken by people for whom they are inappropriate is high. There is no way to ensure that the purchaser's self-diagnosis is accurate, nor that they are an appropriate candidate for the treatment they have decided to buy. They may be taking other medication which may interact with the self-purchased drug, and because they may be reluctant to tell their doctors about their internet drug purchases, legitimately prescribed medicines may also prove unsafe if they interact with the drug which was purchased online. Buying antibiotics without a prescription from a healthcare professional poses health risks not just for the individual patient, but for the population as a whole by increasing antibiotic resistance in the community.

If drugs are purchased from an unregistered online pharmacy, there is also a significant risk that they will be fake: as many as 62 per cent of drugs purchased online are counterfeit medicines,[79] and this may pose a serious risk to consumers' health, both because the substance itself may be dangerous, or in a dangerous dosage, and because access to effective treatment may be delayed. It is impossible to know how many adverse reactions result from drugs purchased online. Consumers may be too embarrassed to tell their doctors that they have taken drugs which they bought online, perhaps because they fear censure, but also because privacy is one of the most important reasons for seeking out drugs on the internet.

Despite these risks, it appears that it is increasingly common for people to buy prescription drugs online. One survey found that 15 per cent of British adults had bought a prescription-only medicine online without a prescription. It can be predicted that the numbers of people buying medicines online is likely to increase significantly in the future. Currently, the group of people most likely to be taking many different medicines, namely the very elderly, is also the section of society which is least likely to be familiar with the internet, and more specifically with using the internet to self-diagnose and manage health problems. As people who

[79] S Mayor, 'More than Half of Drugs Sold Online are Fake or Substandard' (2008) 337 *British Medical Journal* a618.

are familiar with the internet grow older, and therefore more likely to suffer from a number of different health problems, use of online pharmacies will almost certainly become much more common.

Such sanctions as exist in relation to online drug supply are focused on the supplier and not the purchaser. Unless the medicine is a controlled substance – when importing into the UK is subject to particular restrictions – it is not an offence to buy prescription drugs online from an overseas website. It is a criminal offence for someone who is not properly qualified and registered to prescribe and supply a prescription-only medicine. The MHRA monitors online pharmacies, and if sites are based in the UK, and not registered, their owners may be prosecuted, and the MHRA publishes details of all prosecutions for the illegal supply of medicines on its website. If the MHRA is concerned about a site that is registered abroad, it will inform the relevant regulatory authority in that country, but it is clearly impossible for the MHRA to control the activities of internet pharmacies that are based overseas.

Both the MHRA and the RPGB attempt to influence consumers' behaviour by the provision of information and warnings, strongly advising people to seek advice from their doctor rather than buying drugs online. For example, 'You've got life-threatening email' was a campaign which was intended to inform the public about the dangers of responding to spam emails which purport to offer prescription drugs for sale. Evidence was gathered by collecting spam emails received by a random section of the population and, whenever they offered prescription medication, drugs were purchased. The medicines obtained as a result were extremely dangerous. Some contained ingredients that had been withdrawn on safety grounds. None came with a patient information leaflet and many were inadequately packaged in tin foil or folded paper.[80]

VII Conclusion

The Medicines Act provides that a medicine can receive a marketing authorisation if it is marginally more effective than a placebo, and no more effective than existing and well-established medicines. In order to persuade companies to invest in research into drugs which are significantly safer or more effective than established medicines, it could be argued that companies should have to establish that a new medicine offers some non-negligible therapeutic advantage before it can receive a marketing authorisation.

Drug companies might argue that this would be unfair, since a new medicine's advantages may not come to light until some years after it has been licensed for use, when it becomes clear that its long-term safety profile is better than the alter-

---

[80] www.mhra.gov.uk/Safetyinformation/Generalsafetyinformationandadvice/Adviceandinformation forconsumers/BuyingmedicinesovertheInternet/CON019610.

natives. But of course, the reverse may also be true, and the new medicine may prove to be much less safe than alternatives, with the result that many patients will have been harmed unnecessarily while long-term safety data is gathered. Clearly there are limits to how definitive the judgement of a 'non-negligible therapeutic advantage' could be at the point of licensing, but this is an argument for robust post-licensing trials and data gathering, rather than a justification for permitting onto the market lots of drugs which are no better than established medicines but which have much more limited safety profiles.

The task faced by licensing authorities, including national authorities like the MHRA and cross-national ones like EMA, is undoubtedly a difficult one, not least because pharmaceutical regulation within the EU is intended to serve two goals which will sometimes come into direct conflict with each other. Drug regulation is supposed to protect patient safety, by ensuring that only drugs which have passed the intense scrutiny of the licensing regime make it to the marketplace, but at the same time, it has a parallel aim of promoting a flourishing European pharmaceutical industry. Within the EU, there has been considerable concern that Europe might be lagging behind the US as a site for pharmaceutical innovation. A High Level Group on Innovation and the Provision of Medicines, then called G-10 Medicines, was set up in 2001, and it made a number of recommendations, many of which were adopted by the European Commission in 2003. The 2003 Communication – revealingly entitled *A Stronger European-Based Pharmaceutical Industry for the Benefit of the Patient* – was clear that: 'The Commission's objective is to retain and develop a dynamic and thriving EU-based pharmaceutical industry to help meet our challenging economic, social and public health goals', and one of its key proposals was that 'Member States at their national level must ensure that new medicines are made available to their patients as quickly as possible'.[81] Speedy approval times will sometimes coincide with patients' interests in access to new and innovative medicines, but at other times it is clear that the continual drive to reduce approval times is not necessarily the best way to promote the safety of medicines.

---

[81] European Commission, *A Stronger European-Based Pharmaceutical Industry for the Benefit of the Patient – A Call for Action* (EC, 1 July 2003).

4

Pharmacovigilance and Liability for Dangerous Drugs

T HIS CHAPTER IS concerned with what happens after a drug has reached the marketplace. Because of the inevitable limitations of clinical trial data, it is vitally important that interest in a drug's safety profile does not disappear once its manufacturer has obtained a marketing authorisation. Yet while systems are in place to monitor safety after a medicine has been licensed for use, in practice these are much less robust and effective than the requirement to prove safety and efficacy prior to licensing. This chapter also looks at the issue of unsafe medicines from the perspective of the individual patient, and considers the patient's chances of bringing a successful legal claim against a drug's manufacturer.

I Post-marketing Surveillance

A Adverse Drug Reactions

An adverse drug reaction (ADR) is defined by the Medicines and Healthcare products Regulatory Agency (MHRA) as:

> an unwanted or harmful reaction experienced following the administration of a drug or combination of drugs, [which] is suspected to be related to the drug. The reaction may be a known side effect of the drug or it may be new and previously unrecognised.[1]

Of course, the fact that the consumer of a medicine experiences unpleasant symptoms does not mean that these were caused by the drug that she has taken. Establishing that an adverse reaction was triggered by a particular drug can be extremely difficult, not least because the person taking the medicine is often already feeling unwell, and their reaction could be a symptom of their underlying condition, rather than an ADR. Sick people also often take a number of different medicines at the same time, so it may be hard to pinpoint which one, or which combination of medicines, led to the ADR.

---

[1] Medicines and Healthcare products Regulatory Agency *Healthcare Professional Reporting: Adverse Drug Reactions* (MHRA, 2010), available at www.mhra.gov.uk.

Clinical trials are carried out on a relatively small number of people, which means that they will usually only be able to detect common and spontaneous adverse reactions. If 2000 people are involved in the trial of a new medicine, a sudden adverse reaction which occurs in one in every 10 users will probably be picked up, but one which only happens to one patient in every two thousand is unlikely to be identified. Longer-term consequences, such as increasing the risk of cancer, will not be detected during trials of relatively short duration. In addition, clinical trials are often carried out on 'treatment naïve' subjects, that is people who are not simultaneously taking other medicines. Trials will therefore seldom pick up ADRs which are caused by interactions between different drugs, which may be identified only once the drug is being taken by patients in the real world.

The limitations of clinical trial data mean that evaluations of drug safety cannot stop once a medicine has been granted a marketing authorisation. On the contrary, post-marketing pharmacovigilance is essential in order to ensure that drugs which have met the requisite safety threshold in a relatively small and specially selected group of research participants are in fact safe when taken by the entire patient population. Drugs should then be rigorously monitored after they have been marketed, in order to identify adverse reactions which could not have been identified during the trial, such as long-term safety hazards and ADRs which occur when the drug is taken by people who will have been excluded from clinical trials, such as pregnant women and people with multiple comorbidities.

B Voluntary Reporting of ADRs

So how is the safety of a medicine monitored after a medicine has received a marketing authorisation? One imperfect but important technique is the spontaneous reporting of ADRs. As we see below, manufacturers are under a duty to keep a record of all reported ADRs and to report these to the MHRA. The General Medical Council places doctors under a duty to report adverse drug reactions and cooperate with requests for information from public health organisations.[2] Under the 'yellow card scheme' GPs, nurses, midwives, health visitors and patients can report ADRs electronically.[3] For established drugs, only serious suspected ADRs must be reported. In contrast, all new drugs (denoted by an inverted black triangle) are more intensely monitored for a minimum of two years, during which time *all* suspected ADRs should be reported. The black triangle is not necessarily removed after two years: it will be retained if the need for monitoring remains. Black triangle status can also be re-assigned to an existing drug if it is marketed for a new indication or given a new route of administration. All ADRs which occur in children and pregnant women, in whom drugs historically have been inadequately tested, should continue to be reported after the drug loses its black triangle status.

---

[2] General Medical Council, *Good Medical Practice*, 4th edn (GMC, 2006) para 14.
[3] www.yellowcard.gov.uk.

In 1996 the yellow card scheme was extended to include unlicensed herbal products. Monitoring ADRs from herbal remedies has proved particularly difficult, however, since patients are often reluctant to consult their GP if they suspect an adverse reaction and are also less likely to report ADRs themselves. In 2009, only 58 ADRs associated with the use of herbal medicines were reported, 20 of which were received from patients.

In 2010, a total of 24,029 ADRS were reported in the UK: 47 per cent of reports were received via industry, 45 per cent from healthcare professionals, and 8 per cent from patients.[4] 85 per cent of these ADRs were classified as 'serious'.[5] This figure, while clearly not insignificant, is also a massive underestimate.[6] It has been estimated that only 10 per cent of serious reactions and between two and four per cent of non-serious reactions are reported via the yellow card scheme.[7] Taken together, these statistics would suggest that over 200,000 serious adverse drug reactions happen each year in the UK, a 'man-made epidemic' of staggering proportions.[8]

Why are so few of these adverse reactions reported? Some of this non-reporting may be due to patients not suspecting an adverse reaction and so failing to tell their doctor about their symptoms, or report an ADR themselves.[9] This is not a complete explanation, however, and it is clear that the most significant obstacle to comprehensive reporting is the failure of doctors to report ADRs. The problem is certainly not uniquely British, and under-reporting occurs wherever notification schemes exist.[10]

A number of studies have been carried out to try to work out why doctors consistently under-report ADRs. One obvious reason might be if the doctor has no reason to believe that the patient's symptoms are the result of a reaction to the medicine she is taking. This is especially likely if the adverse event is one which is already relatively common among patients with the condition the medicine is intended to treat. Phen-fen, for example, was a combination of weight loss drugs phentermine and fenfluramine. It was eventually withdrawn from the market because it caused primary pulmonary hypertension. If an obese patient taking phen-fen suffered a heart attack, it is easy to see why their doctor would assume their obesity was the primary cause, and hence would not report a suspected ADR.

[4] MHRA, *Medicines Act Advisory Bodies Annual Report 2010* (MHRA, 2011) para 144, available at www.MHRA.gov.uk.

[5] ibid para 143.

[6] RM Martin et al, 'Underreporting of Suspected Adverse Drug Reactions to Newly Marketed ("Black Triangle") Drugs in General Practice: Observational Study' (1998) 317 *British Medical Journal* 119–12.

[7] M Rawlins, 'Pharmacovigilance: Paradise Lost, Regained or Postponed?' (1994) 29 *Journal of the Royal College of Physicians of London* 1.

[8] DW Light, 'Toward Safer Prescribing and Better Drugs' in DW Light (ed), *The Risks of Prescription Drugs* (Columbia UP, 2010) 140–64, 160.

[9] N Jarernsiripornkul et al, 'Patient Reporting of Adverse Drug Reactions: Useful Information for Pain Management?N (2003) 7 *European Journal of Pain* 219–24.

[10] M Backstrom, T Mjorndal and R Dahlquist, 'Under-Reporting of Serious ADRs in Sweden' (2004) 13 *Pharmacoepidemiology and Drug Safety* 483–87.

Where a drug has side effects, like dizziness or drowsiness, which may result in a person falling or crashing her car, it is very unlikely that the drug will be picked up as the cause of the person's injuries, which will instead be attributed to the fall or car accident.

Other reasons for under-reporting include a series of common but mistaken assumptions about the duty to report ADRs. Apparently it is not uncommon for GPs to wrongly believe that they should only report ADRs if they are certain about causation. Some GPs only ever report ADRs that they judge to be serious, even though for new drugs, *all* suspected ADRs should be reported.[11] GPs frequently but incorrectly believe that there is no need to report an ADR if the reaction is already well known.[12] It also appears to be common for GPs to worry that admitting that a patient has suffered an adverse event could result in them being sued in negligence. Even when GPs understand that they ought to report an ADR, pressures on their time or simple inertia may prevent them from doing so.[13]

The yellow card scheme cannot then provide accurate statistics on the total number of ADRs each year, rather its purpose is to generate data which the MHRA can use, along with other data gathering mechanisms, to identify 'signals' of emerging drug safety problems. The ability to detect these signals is enhanced by cross-European collection of information on drug safety. EudraVigilance is an electronic database, maintained by the European Medicines Agency (EMA), which contains adverse reaction reports from all EU regulatory agencies and from pharmaceutical companies. It facilitates the electronic exchange of information about suspected adverse reaction reports, and is continuously monitored and evaluated by EMA to ensure the early detection of safety signals.

Even with cross-national reporting mechanisms, partial reporting means the data are inevitably incomplete. As a result, a variety of other sources of information are analysed by the regulatory authorities, including post-marketing clinical trials which drugs companies carry out principally for marketing purposes; case reports in medical journals and epidemiological research using large-scale databases of patient information.[14] Perhaps the most useful such database in the United Kingdom is the General Practice Research Database (GPRD), which is the world's largest database of anonymised longitudinal medical records from primary care GP practices. Currently there are 500 participating practices, and they supply the GPRD with a wide range of information about their five million patients. In addition to recording the use of medication, the GPRD data includes information

---

[11] E Heeley et al, 'Prescription-Event Monitoring and Reporting of Adverse Drug Reactions' (2001) 358 *The Lancet* 1872–73.

[12] J Hasford et al, 'Physicians' Knowledge and Attitudes Regarding the Spontaneous Reporting System for Adverse Drug Reactions' (2002) 55 *Journal of Clinical Epidemiology* 945–50.

[13] K Belton et al, 'Attitudinal Survey of Adverse Drug Reaction Reporting by Medical Practitioners in the United Kingdom' (1995) 39 *British Journal of Clinical Pharmacology* 223–26; I Elland et al, 'Attitudinal Survey of Voluntary Reporting of Adverse Drug Reactions' (1999) 48 *British Journal of Clinical Pharmacology* 623–27.

[14] Academy of Medical Sciences, *Safer Medicines* (The Academy of Medical Sciences, 2005).

about co-prescription, comorbidity, dosage details, off-label prescription, and patient demographics (age, sex etc), which permits a wide range of drug safety studies to be carried out.

Also important is the Drug Safety Research Unit (DSRU) in Southampton, which monitors the safety of new drugs used in general practice by collecting data on all prescriptions for the first 20,000 to 50,000 patients given a new drug. The DSRU sends a form to every prescribing doctor on which they are asked to report all 'events' recorded in the patient's notes during a specific time period since the patient started treatment with the new medicine. Prescription event monitoring removes the need for the prescribing doctor to give an opinion about whether an event might have been caused by the medicine, and therefore enables the identification of unsuspected, as well as suspected adverse events. Not all doctors comply with requests from the DSRU, however. In fact fewer than 50 per cent of GPs do so, but despite this, the data generated nevertheless provide invaluable information on the outcomes for at least 10,000 patients who have been prescribed a new drug. Both the GPRD and the DSRU databases, while useful, only cover prescription drugs in primary care, and provide no information on medicines used in hospitals, where patients are often more seriously ill and the risks of ADRs may be greater. Preliminary data from the Royal Liverpool University Hospital has suggested that the rate of ADRs among hospital inpatients is approximately 16 per cent.

Other ways to calculate the total number of ADRs involve analysis of hospital admissions. One such study found that each year, as many as 250,000 patients – amounting to four per cent of total hospital bed capacity and costing the NHS approximately £500 million each year[15] – are admitted to hospital as a result of suffering serious adverse reactions to medicines, most commonly to aspirin, diuretics, warfarin, and non-steroidal anti-inflammatory drugs. More than two per cent of patients admitted to hospital with an ADR died as a result.[16]

Of course, ADRs are not the only safety issue which may arise post-marketing. It is also possible that a medicine, or a particular batch, may be defective in some way, perhaps because it was contaminated during the manufacturing process. The MHRA's Defective Medicines Report Centre (DMRC) provides an emergency assessment and communications system to deal with the risk defective medicines may pose to public health. Where a risk is identified, the DMRC will grade it according to seriousness and the drug's manufacturer is responsible for recalling the affected medicines or, in extreme cases, removing all batches of the product from the market. Manufacturers are under a duty to inform the MHRA of any suspected quality defect in a medicinal product that might pose a risk to health.

---

[15] House of Commons Health Select Committee, *The Influence of the Pharmaceutical Industry* Fourth Report of Session 2004–05 para 5.
[16] M Pirmohamed et al, (2004) 'Adverse Drug Reactions as Cause of Admission to Hospital: Prospective Analysis of 18,820 Patients' (2004) 329 *British Medical Journal* 15–19.

C A Life-cycle Approach to Medicine's Risk-Benefit Profile

It is, of course, important to acknowledge that there is no such thing as a 'safe drug': all drugs may be unsafe in some doses, or for some patients. A new medicine which causes terrible side effects might be 'safe enough' if it offered a cure for secondary liver cancer, for example, or HIV/AIDS. Exactly the same side effects would render a new statin or oral contraceptive pill insufficiently safe for use in humans. Pharmacovigilance is vitally important, but it will only ever be able to *refine* the risk-benefit profile of a medicine, rather than establish proof of absolute safety.[17]

Proper evaluation of medicines requires what might be called a 'life-cycle' approach to each medicine's risk-benefit evaluation.[18] Currently, the decision to approve a medicine effectively signals an end to the gathering of meaningful and reliable information as to safety. This is problematic, however, because the limits of clinical trial data mean that attention to both efficacy and safety *after* approval is the only way to adequately protect public health. The moment of approval does not signal a 'singular moment of clarity about the risks and benefits associated with a drug'.[19] Rather it represents one admittedly important *stage* in a drug's life cycle, when a decision is made that, on the basis of the evidence gathered *so far,* it is safe enough to market to a wider group of patients. But this judgement is not the final word on the medicine's safety when it is taken for longer periods of time, by people who may be older or younger than the trial participants, or who have other comorbidities, or are taking other medicines at the same time.

D The 'Weak Link' in Regulation?

The central problem, then, is that the only way to be confident that safety signals have been properly quantified and evaluated would be to conduct very large-scale randomised controlled trials, over very long periods of time. If such trials had to be done before licensing, the costs of bringing a medicine to market would be prohibitively high and there would be unreasonable delays in access to medicines. In order to promote speedier and more affordable access, medicines have to be licensed for use when there is inevitable uncertainty over whether they might cause rare and/or latent ADRs. Without a foolproof post-licensing monitoring system, such reactions may go undetected for some time, during which patients' health may be seriously compromised.

It is evident that the monitoring system in the UK and elsewhere is very far from perfect. Indeed, it has been argued that post-marketing surveillance is 'the weakest

---

[17] H-G Eichler, 'Safe Drugs and the Cost of Good Intentions' (2009) 360 *New England Journal of Medicine* 1378–80.

[18] BM Psaty and SP Burke, 'Protecting the Health of the Public – Institute of Medicine Recommendations on Drug Safety' (2006) 355 *New England Journal of Medicine* 1753–55.

[19] ibid.

link in the regulatory process'.[20] By relying on ad hoc reporting systems, the database amounts to no more than a series of random case reports, which are inevitably of limited evidential utility. Without knowing how many people are taking a drug, and how many ADRs are *not* reported, case reports amount, in practice, to essentially anecdotal information about the experiences of some patients. Currently, drug safety investigations are rigorous pre-approval, and lax – to say the least – post-approval, when industry efforts are diverted towards marketing rather than research.

If post-approval surveillance is a vital source of safety data that, for a number of reasons, cannot be gathered at the trial stage, this shift in rigour before and after a marketing authorisation is granted is not justifiable. Once a new drug has received a marketing authorisation, there are sound commercial reasons for its manufacturer to stop carrying out research into its safety, and to focus instead on generating publicity and sales. With no incentives to carry out rigorous post-marketing surveillance, and no penalties for failing to do so, it is easy to see why pharmacovigilance has become the 'weak link' in the regulation of medicines. The incentive of receiving a marketing authorisation no longer exists, so it might then be necessary to create a new incentive, or impose penalties for the failure to gather safety data post-licensing. One possibility would be to convert the currently light-touch five year review of the original marketing authorisation into a real review, in which the continuation of the marketing authorisation depends upon the provision of robust safety data generated *after* the medicine was licensed for use. A credible threat that a drug's marketing authorisation will expire after five years unless post-licensing surveillance has established safety and efficacy outside of the small and specially selected trial population may be the only way to ensure that companies carry out the research which is vital to ensure that medicines really are safe and effective when used over long periods of time, by large and mixed patient populations.

Because pre-approval data are regarded as more reliable and rigorous than essentially anecdotal post-approval information about safety and efficacy, they will often represent the 'last word' on a product's safety and efficacy for many years after licensing, despite the fact that the trials which generated these results were carried out in specially selected patient populations treated in highly controlled circumstances. To say that a newly licensed drug has been proved to be safe is then rather misleading, rather the most that can be said is that a newly licensed drug is 'apparently safe based on partial information'.[21]

In order to protect patient safety, pharmacovigilance should be treated as seriously as pre-licensing investigations, but post-licensing trials are not compulsory, and when they are carried out, their purpose tends to be to generate data that can be used in marketing campaigns, rather than to refine the initial assessment of a medicine's safety and efficacy. Relying on voluntary reporting mechanisms, like

---

[20] D Kazi, 'Rosiglitazone and Implications for Pharmacovigilance' (2007) 334 *British Medical Journal* 1233.
[21] DW Light, 'Bearing the Risks of Prescription Drugs' in DW Light (ed), *The Risks of Prescription Drugs* (Columbia UP, 2010) 1–39, 7.

the yellow card scheme, provides a data set which is woefully incomplete and statistically completely unreliable.

There has, unsurprisingly therefore, been substantial criticism of the MHRA's post-licensing surveillance system. The House of Commons Select Committee found that it concentrated its efforts on scrutiny of pre-marketing data, and gave too little attention to the evaluation of drug safety after licensing. Witnesses had suggested to the Committee that the MHRA itself may have a conflict of interest: its responsibility for both pre-marketing investigation *and* post-marketing surveillance means that a subsequent finding that a drug is unsafe may indicate that its initial decision on safety was the wrong one.[22]

At the European level, there have been attempts to strengthen the post-authorisation monitoring of medicinal products by the setting up, in 2006, of the European Network of Centres for Pharmacoepidemiology and Pharmacovigilance (ENCePP), the purpose of which is to facilitate the conduct of multi-centre, independent, post-authorisation studies focusing on safety and on risk-benefit evaluations. ENCePP has agreed a Code of Practice, which commits investigators and study funders to follow certain general principles, including the following:

- The primary purpose of a study shall be to generate data of potential scientific or public health importance and not to promote the sale of a medicinal product.
- The design of the research shall not be aimed towards producing a pre-specified result.
- The results of a study shall always be published, preferably in a peer reviewed journal, or made available for public scrutiny within an acceptable time frame, regardless of the (positive or negative) results and the statistical significance.[23]

The Code is voluntary unless the investigators wish to apply for the ENCePP seal of approval. The purpose of the seal is so that 'Studies carrying the "ENCePP Study" seal will be immediately recognisable to the general public as being conducted in adherence to the ENCePP study principles'.[24] Of course, it is not clear that many members of the public know to look for the ENCePP seal, nor that many will consult its registry of trials.

E Off-label Prescription

A further issue is that a drug might be licensed for one indication, in one subgroup of patients, and then subsequently be used in the treatment of other conditions, or among larger patient groups. Doctors have considerable freedom to prescribe 'off-label', and while, in an ideal world, drug companies would conduct fresh

---

[22] House of Commons Health Select Committee n 15 above, para 302. See also the comments of one of Linsey McGoey's interviewees in L McGoey, 'On the Will to Ignorance in Bureaucracy' (2007) 36 *Economy and Society* 212–35.

[23] For more information see www.encepp.eu/index.html.

[24] See further www.encepp.eu/.

randomised controlled trials (RCTs) in order to apply for a marketing authorisation for any plausible new indication, or for the drug to be used in patient groups other than those in whom it was originally tested, it will obviously be expensive to do this. A drug company is only likely to carry out new RCTs on an already licensed medicine if it can foresee a significantly expanded market for its product if its marketing authorisation is extended to include new indications. Once a medicine is out of patent protection, there is no incentive for any private company to carry out trials into unlicensed indications.

It is not uncommon for both branded and generic drugs to be prescribed off-label for indications other than that for which the original marketing authorisation was granted. Doctors will sometimes act properly in prescribing a drug off-label: if the patient has exhausted other treatment options, trying something else may be justifiable, even if its use for that purpose is not backed up by clinical trial data. In some patient groups, like children, there has historically been no option other than to prescribe off-label because most medicines were not specifically licensed for use in children.

Even when off-label prescription is justifiable, doctors should be aware of the risks of prescribing outside of a drug's licensed indications and they should be frank about these with patients. Patients assume that if a doctor has prescribed them a medicine, it must be known to be appropriate for them, and where this is not the case, the doctor should tell the patient why she is proposing to prescribe off-label, what evidence she has for doing so, and give the patient the option of making an informed decision to take, or not take, a medicine which is not licensed for use in someone like them. Patients who have been prescribed drugs off-label should be monitored especially closely, and doctors should collect and record information about outcomes.[25] Even if the data gathered as a result does not amount to the sort of RCT evidence sufficient to support a label change, the more information that is available about off-label prescription the better.

The MHRA has issued advice to prescribers on the use of unlicensed medicines. It specifies that prescribers should first 'be satisfied that an alternative, licensed medicine would not meet the patient's needs'. They should be satisfied that there is some evidence or experience with use which justifies the decision to prescribe off-label. The reasons for prescribing off-label should be recorded, and patients should be monitored. Although the reasons for prescribing off-label should be explained to patients where there is little evidence to support its use, the MHRA also suggests that it may not be necessary to draw patients' attention to the fact that prescription is outside of the drug's licence 'where current practice supports the use of a medicine outside the terms of its licence'. The MHRA's advice also draws prescribers' attention to the importance of submitting any suspected ADRs to it via the yellow card scheme.[26]

---

[25] R Dresser and J Frader, 'Off-Label Prescribing: A Call for Heightened Professional and Government Oversight' (2009) 37 *Journal of Law, Medicine and Ethics* 476.

[26] MHRA, 'Off-Label Use or Unlicensed Medicines: Prescribers' Responsibilities' (2009) 2 *Drug Safety Update* 6–7.

F The Suppression of Safety Data

The defects in post-marketing safety data considered so far have been the result of haphazard voluntary reporting mechanisms. Doctors do not always report adverse drug reactions in their patients, but this is generally due to a lack of understanding or a lack of time, rather than because they deliberately wish to conceal important safety information from the regulator.

The duties placed on pharmaceutical companies are rather different from the voluntary reporting scheme for doctors. The Medicines for Human Use (Marketing Authorisations) Regulations 1994, as amended, spells out that the manufacturer of a drug has a legal duty to report to the licensing authority 'any suspected adverse reaction, or to submit to the licensing authority any records of suspected adverse reactions'.[27] In addition, anyone who is responsible for pharmacovigilance must 'provide as soon as is reasonably practicable to the licensing authority any other information relevant to the evaluation of the benefits and risks afforded by a medicinal product'.[28] Failure to comply with these requirements is a criminal offence, punishable by up to two years imprisonment.

This more onerous reporting duty generally results in much greater levels of compliance than the voluntary yellow card scheme for healthcare professionals. There have, however, been a handful of cases where it has been alleged that safety data have been deliberately suppressed. In the UK, the most infamous example is the withholding of trial data relating to the use of paroxetine (brand name Seroxat), a selective serotonin reuptake inhibitor (SSRI) antidepressant, in teenagers.

In May 2003, Seroxat's manufacturer, GlaxoSmithKline (GSK) submitted data to the MHRA from two clinical trials (studies 329 and 377) in which paroxetine had been tested in adolescents in the mid-1990s. These data were analysed by the Committee on the Safety of Medicines (CSM), which found that they provided clear evidence (a) that 'there is no good evidence of efficacy in major depressive disorder in the population studied', and (b) that there was 'a clear increase in suicidal behaviour versus placebo'.[29] The MHRA immediately sent an alert to all doctors, specifying that paroxetine should not be prescribed to children.

Because the data in these trials contained information that cast doubt on the safety of paroxetine in paediatric populations, GSK should have submitted them as soon as they became aware of them. As a result the MHRA also launched a criminal investigation. At first sight it might be thought that the case against GSK was a strong one. In early 2004, an internal GSK memo was leaked which appeared to indicate that the failure to disclose the results of studies 329 and 377 had not been an oversight.[30] The leaked document, dated October 1998, stated that 'it

[27] The Medicines for Human Use (Marketing Authorisations) Regulations 1994 Sch 3 para 8.

[28] ibid Sch 3 para 10.

[29] MHRA, *Assessment Report: Paroxetine (Seroxat)* (4 June 2003), available at www.mhra.gov.uk/ Howweregulate/Medicines/Medicinesregulatorynews/CON014153.

[30] W Kondro, 'Drug Company Experts Advised Staff to Withhold Data about SSRI Use in Children' (2004) 170 *Canadian Medical Association Journal* 783.

would be commercially unacceptable to include a statement that efficacy had not been demonstrated, as this would undermine the profile of paroxetine'.

After a painstaking four and a half year investigation by the MHRA, its evidence was passed on to government lawyers, whose advice was both surprising and unequivocal: there could be no prosecution of GSK because 'the legislation was sufficiently unclear as to make a criminal prosecution impossible'.[31] The reason for this was that, at the relevant time, the reporting duties placed upon manufacturers by the Medicines Act were qualified in a number of ways. The duty to notify the MHRA of adverse reactions applied only to adverse reactions 'in the normal conditions of use of the product'. Like many prescription drugs at that time, prescription of paroxetine to children, though common, was in fact off-label, and so ADRs in children were not covered by the Act's reporting requirements. In addition, the data which revealed an elevated risk of suicide did not emerge 'during normal conditions of use', but from clinical trials, so again they were not covered. There *is* an additional duty to report adverse reactions which occur during clinical trials, but at the relevant time this duty applied only to trials conducted in the UK,[32] and this excluded studies 329 and 377.

This case suggests that the duty of candour pharmaceutical companies were assumed to owe to the regulator, backed up by criminal sanctions in case of breach, was, in practice, significantly weaker than the MHRA itself had believed.[33] The relevant Regulations have since been amended, so that the duty to provide 'any other information relevant to the evaluation of the benefits and risks afforded by a medicinal product' now specifically includes 'information arising from use of the product – (i) in a country which is not an EEA State; and (iii) outside the terms of the marketing authorisation, including use in clinical trials'.[34]

More successful than the MHRA's attempted prosecution of GSK was the New York State Attorney Eliot Spitzer's decision to bring a civil action against GSK in June 2004, alleging that it had fraudulently withheld these two clinical studies. In his suit, Spitzer's chief complaint was that trials of paroxetine to treat childhood major depressive disorder (MDD), as well as the safety outcomes of other trials, had been hidden from physicians and thus 'GSK deprived physicians of the information needed to evaluate the risks and benefits of prescribing paroxetine for children and adolescents with MDD'.[35] GSK settled the case, with a payment of $2.5 million, and an agreement to make all of its data on paroxetine public.

There have been other high-profile cases in which there have been suspicions that safety data have been withheld from licensing authorities. Rofecoxib (brand name Vioxx), a medicine used to treat arthritis, was withdrawn from the market

[31] MHRA, *Investigation into GlaxoSmithKline/Seroxat* (MHRA, 6 March 2008), available at www.mhra.gov.uk/Howweregulate/Medicines/Medicinesregulatorynews/CON014153.

[32] Medicines Act 1968 s 31.

[33] L McGoey and E Jackson, 'Seroxat and the Suppression of Clinical Trial Data: Regulatory Failure and the Convenience of Legal Ambiguity' (2009) 35 *Journal of Medical Ethics* 107–12.

[34] Medicines for Human Use (Marketing Authorisations) Regulations 1994, Sch 3, para 6AA.

[35] *People of the State of New York v GlaxoSmithKline* Filed 2 June 2004.

in 2004 on the grounds that it significantly increased the risk of cardiovascular disease. On the basis both of documents released during legal proceedings,[36] leaked emails,[37] and subsequent meta-analyses of the available data,[38] it has been alleged that its manufacturer Merck knew of this risk sometime before the product was withdrawn.[39] An article in *The Wall Street Journal* referred to an internal email in which a senior company doctor revealed that 'the possibility of increased CV [cardiovascular] events is of great concern'; her recommendation was that potential participants with increased risk of cardiovascular disease be excluded from the clinical trials of Vioxx in order to ensure that cardiovascular problems 'would not be evident'.[40] A leaked internal training document, aimed at Merck's sales representatives, was called 'Dodge Ball Vioxx': it apparently instructed them how to 'DODGE!' so-called 'obstacles', such as physicians raising concerns about the cardiovascular effects of Vioxx.[41]

In 1999, Merck had launched the VIGOR (Vioxx Gastrointestinal Outcomes Research) study, involving 8000 patients. The results from this study indicated that rofecoxib had fewer gastrointestinal side effects than its competitor naproxen in the treatment of rheumatoid arthritis. It also showed that patients taking rofecoxib were at increased risk of serious cardiovascular disease. In publishing this study, the additional cardiovascular risk, which Merck in any event put down to a protective effect in the comparator drug,[42] was obscured in a number of ways. For example, Merck employed different termination dates for cardiovascular and gastrointestinal events which enabled myocardial infarctions that occurred in the rofecoxib group in the month after the researchers stopped counting them to be discounted.[43] These data were then widely disseminated.[44] The *New England Journal of Medicine*[45] and other medical journals published articles which appeared to bear out rofecoxib's advantages over naproxen. Merck subsequently carried out another trial, to investigate rofecoxib's potential to prevent recurrent colonic polyps. This trial unequivocally showed increased cardiovascular toxicity and in

[36] Krumholz HM et al, 'What Have We Learnt From Vioxx?' (2007) 334 *British Medical Journal* 120–23.

[37] AW Matthew and B Martinez, 'E-Mails Suggest Merck knew Vioxx's Dangers at Early Stage' *The Wall Street Journal* 1 November 2004, A1.

[38] P Jüni et al, 'Risk of Cardiovascular Events and Rofecoxib: Cumulative Meta-Analysis' (2004) 364 *The Lancet* 2021–29.

[39] L McGoey, 'Pharmaceutical Controversies and the Performative Value of Uncertainty' (2009) 18 *Science as Culture* 151–64.

[40] Matthew and Martinez n 37 above.

[41] ibid.

[42] JE Dalen, 'Selective COX-2 Inhibitors, NSAIDs, Aspirin, and Myocardial Infarction' (2002) 162 *Archives of Internal Medicine* 1091–92.

[43] GD Curfman, S Morrissey and JM Draz, 'Expression of Concern: Bombardier et al., "Comparison of Upper Gastrointestinal Toxicity of Rofecoxib and Naproxen in Patients with Rheumatoid Arthritis"' (2000) 343 *New England Journal of Medicine* 1520–28.

[44] HA Waxman, 'The Lessons of Vioxx – Drug Safety and Sales' (2005) 352 *New England Journal of Medicine* 2576–78.

[45] C Bombardier et al, 'Comparison of Upper Gastrointestinal Toxicity of Rofecoxib and Naproxen in Patients with Rheumatoid Arthritis' (2000) 343 *New England Journal of Medicine* 1520–28.

September 2004 Merck voluntarily withdrew rofecoxib from the market.[46] By this time, more than 80 million patients had taken Vioxx and its annual sales were worth more than $2.5 billion.[47]

II The Consequences of Identifying Drug Safety Hazards

Disclosure of ADRs may not be comprehensive, but when the MHRA is alerted to the existence of a suspected ADR, the next step is to work out what to do with this information. The Commission on Human Medicines (CHM) and its Pharmacovigilance Expert Advisory Group (PEAG) will look at the drug's ADR profile and also consider its benefits in terms of efficacy and the existence of relevant therapeutic alternatives. CHM will then advise the MHRA on whether changes need to be made to the drug's marketing authorisation. Such changes might involve restrictions in use, reduction in dosage or the inclusion of special warnings. These are communicated to healthcare professionals in a number of ways: patient information leaflets and Summaries of Product Characteristics are regularly updated, and doctors and pharmacists receive a monthly drug safety bulletin from the MHRA. Urgent warnings or product recalls will be communicated directly through a drug alert letter/email or via the NHS's Central Alerting System. MHRA drug alerts are classified from 1 to 4 depending upon the risk the product poses to public health. Class 1 is the most critical, it includes serious mislabelling, microbial contamination or the use of incorrect ingredients. A Class 1 alert requires the drug's immediate recall. Class 4 is the least critical and simply advises 'caution in use'.

If the risks of the medicine are judged to outweigh its benefits, and there is no obvious or simple way to minimise these risks, perhaps by setting out contraindications for prescription, withdrawal from the market may be appropriate. This happened in 2010 in relation to rosiglitazone (brand name Avandia), an antidiabetic drug, which had been found to increase the risk of cardiovascular disease. As is evident from this statement from *Drug Safety Update*, withdrawal from the market was in effect a last resort after it was judged impossible to prevent this risk in other ways, for example by identifying the at-risk patient population in advance:

> The UK Commission on Human Medicines has reviewed the available data and has concluded that there is an increased cardiovascular risk for rosiglitazone. It has not been possible to identify additional measures that would reduce the cardiovascular risk or to identify a patient population in whom the benefits continue to outweigh the risks. The

[46] JM Drazen, 'COX-2 Inhibitors – A Lesson in Unexpected Problems' (2005) 352 *New England Journal of Medicine* 1131–32.

[47] EJ Topol, 'Failing the Public Health – Rofecoxib, Merck, and the FDA' (2004) 351 *New England Journal of Medicine* 1707–09.

Commission has therefore concluded that the benefits of rosiglitazone no longer out-weigh its risks.[48]

In practice, very few products are withdrawn as a result of safety concerns. According to the House of Commons Select Committee, 24 prescription drugs were withdrawn on safety grounds in the UK between 1971 and 1992 inclusive (1.1 per year) and 19 were withdrawn between 1993 and 2004 (1.6 per year).[49] It is certainly true that the mere existence of an adverse reaction does not mean that a medicine has become unacceptably unsafe. Aspirin is known to be unsafe in children, but that does not mean that it should not be available to other patients, who benefit enormously from it. It is usually necessary to balance the risks to a minority of patients against the benefits the drug may have for the majority, and so, rather than withdrawing a product which causes adverse reactions in some users, a more appropriate response might be to give a more specific warning about contra-indications for its use. Once the data that indicated that paroxetine (Seroxat) was unsafe in children were disclosed to the MHRA, it issued an imme-diate warning to doctors and changed the product characteristics. Seroxat is still widely prescribed to adults, but the British National Formulary specifies that it should not be prescribed to under-18s.

Of course, it would be a mistake to separate the question of what to do with information gathered through pharmacovigilance from the very real doubts that must exist about the reliability and comprehensiveness of that information. Decisions to withdraw medicines, or to change their mode of administration, may be just as important as the initial decision to grant a marketing authorisation. They are, however, based upon a much less robust evidence base.[50] Decisions to with-draw a drug based upon a handful of case reports may be justifiable: if there is any suggestion that a drug is causing a fatal adverse reaction in some users, it is better to err on the side of caution and withdraw that medicine immediately than to risk more deaths. But it is important to recognise that such a decision is an example of the precautionary principle in action, rather than the result of robust proof that the medicine is unsafe.

III Liability for Drug Injuries

Thus far, this chapter has considered the responsibilities placed on doctors, regu-lators and manufacturers when evidence emerges after licensing which suggests that a medicine may not be safe for all users. It now turns to consider the question of ADRs from the perspective of the injured patient. If someone does suffer an

---

[48] MHRA (2010) 4 *Drug Safety Update* S1.

[49] House of Commons Health Select Committee (2004–05) n 15 above, para 106.

[50] JA Arnaiz et al, 'The Use of Evidence in Pharmacovigilance: Case Reports as the Reference Source for Drug Withdrawals' (2001) 57 *European Journal of Clinical Pharmacology* 89–91.

ADR, might she be able to bring an action against the drug's manufacturer, the prescribing doctor or even the licensing authority which granted the medicine's marketing authorisation? The short and flippant answer in the UK is 'probably not', and in what follows I flesh out the reasons for this.

A Contract

Although not impossible, the chance of a person who has suffered a drug-related injury bringing a successful action in contract law is extremely remote. Very few consumers of prescription medicines will have a contract with the product's manufacturer or its supplier. Consumers do not buy medicines directly from pharmaceutical companies, and when a drug is prescribed under an NHS prescription, the person who takes the medicine will not have a contract either with the pharmacist, or with the prescribing doctor.[51] The only time when a contractual remedy might exist is if the injured consumer purchased the drug privately, or bought it over-the-counter.

For consumers who have directly purchased their medicines, and therefore have a contract with the pharmacist or prescribing doctor, they will have a remedy in contract law if the product does not correspond with its description, or is not of satisfactory quality,[52] perhaps because the medicine was contaminated during the manufacturing process. There is no need to prove fault. Given that rigorous quality control processes must be in place before a medicine can receive a marketing authorisation, manufacturing defects are unusual. Where the consumer has simply suffered an ADR, it will be difficult to establish that there has been a breach of the implied condition of satisfactory quality, especially if the ADR was on the long list of possible side effects on the patient information leaflet.

Under the law of contract, goods must be fit for the purpose for which they are commonly supplied, and if the purchaser tells the supplier that they are purchasing a product for a particular purpose, it must be reasonably fit for that purpose.[53] This means that if a consumer tells a pharmacist that they have a condition, like high blood pressure, which means that the medicine that they are about to purchase is not suitable for them, then arguably it is not reasonably fit for their purpose, and if they are subsequently injured as a result, it is possible that they could bring an action against the pharmacist. In practice, however, pharmacists will generally make sure that, if there is a contraindication to use, inquiries are made of would-be purchasers.

Nevertheless, it is unfortunate that the requirement that drugs are fit for the purpose for which they were purchased is confined to injured patients who happen to have acquired their medicine through a private prescription, or to have purchased it over-the-counter. Very few over-the-counter medicines are likely to

---

[51] *Pfizer Corporation v Minister of Health* [1965] 2 WLR 387.
[52] Sale of Goods Act 1979 ss 14(2) and 14(3), as amended.
[53] Sale of Goods Act ss 14(2B) and 14(3).

cause serious injuries: a medicine will only be classified for direct sale to consumers because there is evidence that it is sufficiently safe. It is prescription medicines that are much more likely to cause injuries, and because hardly any of these are issued under private prescriptions, the Sale of Goods Act is largely irrelevant. In an Australian product liability case against the manufacturer of Vioxx, a claim akin to that which is possible under the UK's Consumer Protection Act 1987, discussed below, ultimately failed. In contrast, the applicant's claim under the Trade Practices Act 1974 succeeded on the grounds that 'because it approximately doubled the risk of heart attack, Vioxx was not reasonably fit for the purpose implicitly made known to [the manufacturer] by the applicant'.[54]

B Negligence

The tort of negligence might look like a more promising route for consumers who have been injured by medicines. It is uncontroversial that manufacturers of products owe their ultimate consumers a duty to take reasonable care to ensure that the product is safe,[55] and so drug companies undoubtedly owe people who take their medicines a duty of care.

The next stage in a negligence action would be to establish that the manufacturer breached their duty of care. The manufacturer's duty is to exercise such care as is reasonable, in all the circumstances. It would not be possible for them to rule out the possibility of anyone suffering an ADR. A manufacturer will act reasonably in putting a product into circulation once clinical trials indicate that it is likely to be safe. It would not be reasonable for manufacturers to carry out clinical trials which go on for so many years and involve so many people that the risk of ADRs could be effectively ruled out. In relation to thalidomide, for example, trials had been carried out on pregnant animals and in humans, and these had indicated that it would be likely to be safe for use in pregnancy. It is possible then that the manufacturer of thalidomide *had* taken reasonable care.

Of course, the prescribing doctor also owes her patient a duty of care. If a GP prescribes a medicine that is contraindicated in the individual for whom it is prescribed, when a reasonable GP would not have done so, then she will be in breach of her duty to her patient. Pharmacists too owe a duty of care to the consumers of the medicines which they prepare. If a pharmacist negligently dispenses the wrong drug, or the wrong dosage, he could be liable for any resulting injury.

In all three cases, even if a breach of duty can be established, it will be necessary to prove that the manufacturer, doctor or pharmacist's breach of duty caused the patient's injuries. This will often be difficult, principally because the person who has taken the medicine will generally be ill, so any deterioration may be the result of their illness rather than the drug they have taken. There is, for example, some

---

[54] *Peterson v Merck Sharpe & Dohme* [2010] FCA 180.
[55] *Donoghue v Stevenson* [1932] AC 562.

evidence that, early in treatment, SSRI antidepressants may increase the risk of suicidal ideation in some users.[56] But because anyone who commits suicide soon after starting to take an SSRI antidepressant will have recently been diagnosed as depressed, it would be difficult to establish that their suicide was a side effect of the drug, rather than their depressed state of mind.[57] Patients will also often be taking many drugs at the same time, so even if it could be established that they had had an adverse reaction, proving that it was the result of one drug rather than another will be difficult.

It is particularly difficult to establish causation when the gist of the claimant's case is that she was not warned of a side effect associated with the drug. In order to prove causation in a failure to warn case, the claimant has to establish that, if she had been warned, she would have chosen not to take the drug and her injuries would have been avoided. The difficulty here is that the claimant now has the benefit of hindsight. A man who was prescribed a statin but not warned that one very rare side effect is alopecia, might have decided to take the statin even if he had been warned. After his hair has fallen out, however, and he knows that he is the unfortunate one patient in a thousand, say, who suffer alopecia as a result of taking this particular statin, of course he is more likely to say that he would have refused to take the drug if he had been warned.

One case in which proving duty, breach and causation was relatively straight-forward was *Prendergast v Sam and Dee Ltd*.[58] Mr Prendergast's doctor had written him a prescription for Amoxil, an antibiotic, which was intended to treat his chest infection. The doctor's handwriting was hard to read, and the pharmacist instead dispensed Daonil, a drug used in the treatment of diabetes. Mr Prendergast took the tablets and suffered permanent brain damage. Both his doctor and the pharmacist were found to have been in breach of their duty of care. Given the dangers of dispensing the wrong drug, in a wholly inappropriate dosage, a reasonable doctor would have ensured that the pharmacist could read his handwriting. The pharmacist too should have realised that it was extremely unlikely that the doctor had meant to write Daonil on the prescription. The prescription was for a short course of Amoxil, to be taken three times a day. In contrast, if the prescription had been for Daonil, it would have been for longer than a week and Daonil is taken only once a day. Diabetics do not pay for their prescriptions, and so the fact that Mr Prendergast did pay for his should have alerted the pharmacist to the fact that he was unlikely to have diabetes. The Court of Appeal refused to overturn the judge's apportionment of liability: the pharmacist was liable to pay 75 per cent of Mr Prendergast's damages, and the doctor 25 per cent.

---

[56] WD Hall, 'How Have the SSRI Antidepressants Affected Suicide Risk?' (2006) 367 *The Lancet* 1959–62

[57] McGoey n 22 above.

[58] *Prendergast v Sam and Dee Ltd*, *The Times* 14 Mar 1989.

C Regulator's Liability

Might it also be possible for an injured patient to bring an action against the regulatory authorities for their failure to ensure that a drug was safe enough? Liability for breach of statutory duty is extremely unlikely. The purpose of the Medicines Act 1968 was to protect public health, and not to provide private law remedies for individual patients. If a claimant wanted to argue that the regulator had been negligent in approving a medicine that subsequently injured them, they would have to first establish that there is a relationship of proximity between them and the regulator, and that it would be fair, just and reasonable to impose a duty of care on the regulator to protect the individual's health. This will generally be impossible.[59]

But even if a claimant did manage to establish that the regulator owed her a duty of care, proving that there had been a breach of that duty will not be easy. The claimant would have to establish that the regulator had acted unreasonably in granting a product a marketing authorisation and given that it only does so after clinical trial data have been analysed by a body of medical experts, namely the Committee on the Safety of Medicines, proving that their collective judgement fell below the standard of care that could be expected of a group of experts would be difficult.

D The Consumer Protection Act 1987

The Consumer Protection Act 1987 implements a European Directive,[60] which was intended to harmonise European product liability regimes. The Act imposes strict liability – that is, liability without fault – on manufacturers and, in certain circumstances, suppliers of defective products which cause physical injury, or property damage greater than €500. Any claim must be brought within three years of the claimant realising that they are injured, and no later than 10 years after the product was first put into circulation. Consumers of medicines who suffer injuries which manifest themselves more than 10 years after the drug received its marketing authorisation will be limited to an action in negligence.

It might be thought that the introduction of liability without fault for consumers injured by defective products might be especially useful for patients who suffer drug-related injuries, but this has not been the case. On the contrary, there have been remarkably few successful cases brought under this piece of legislation and hardly any cases involving medicines. One of the only cases to get as far as the courtroom, *XYZ v Schering Health Care Ltd*,[61] involved a group action by claim-

---

[59] *Smith v Secretary of State for Health (on behalf of the Committee on Safety of Medicines)* [2002] EWHC 200 (QB).

[60] Council Directive of 25 July 1985 on the approximation of the laws, regulations and administrative provisions of the Member States concerning liability for defective products (85/374/EEC) OJ L 210, 7.8.1985, p29

[61] *XYZ v Schering Health Care Ltd* [2002] EWHC 1420 (QB).

ants who had taken different brands of the Combined Oral Contraceptive (COC), and who claimed to have suffered various cardiovascular injuries (which come under the collective description of Venous thromboembolism, VTE). In 1995, the CSM had written to doctors informing them that there were unpublished trials which appeared to show 'around a twofold increase in the risk' of VTE, associated with taking the COC. The manufacturers rejected the CSM's judgement. It was agreed that an action under the Consumer Protection Act would be possible only if there was, in fact, a twofold increase in the risk of VTE associated with these pills. Mackay J analysed the weight of evidence provided by both sides and decided that 'there is not as a matter of probability any increased relative risk of VTE carried by any of the third generation oral contraceptives supplied to these Claimants by the Defendants'. The case therefore collapsed.

i When is a Medicine Defective?

A claimant could only have an action under the Consumer Protection Act if the medicine they have taken is judged to be 'defective', and the Act has a rather odd definition of defect: a product is defective if its safety is not such as persons generally are entitled to expect.[62] If the medicine is contaminated during the manufacturing process, it will be easy to establish that it is not as safe as consumers are entitled to expect, but this sort of defect is rare. It will be much more difficult to prove that the drug is not as safe as persons generally are entitled to expect if the claimant has suffered an ADR.

Of course, consumers do not generally *expect* to be injured by the medicines that they take,[63] so it might be thought that any medicine which causes injury is therefore defective. But the test is not what people do expect, it is what consumers are *entitled* to expect, and persons generally are not entitled to expect that all medicines will be entirely safe for all users. On the contrary, medicines which are potent enough to cure disease or relieve symptoms are likely to cause ADRs in some consumers.

The Act specifies factors relevant to the judgement of what consumers generally are entitled to expect, such as the inclusion of any warnings and what might reasonably be expected to be done with the product,[64] meaning that injuries caused by an overdose will be excluded.[65] The Act also specifies that a product is not to be considered defective because a safer product is subsequently put into circulation.

The dearth of case law makes it difficult to make any evidence-based claims about the Consumer Protection Act's application to cases involving medicines. In *A v National Blood Authority*,[66] a case involving infected blood, the judge held that

---

[62] Consumer Protection Act s 3.
[63] J Stapleton, *Product Liability* (Butterworths, London, 1994) 235.
[64] Consumer Protection Act s 3(2).
[65] R Sykes, *New Medicines, The Practice of Medicine, and Public Policy* (Nuffield Trust, London, 2000).
[66] *A v National Blood Authority* [2001] 3 All ER 289.

consumers were entitled to assume that blood products were safe, even when it was impossible to avoid the risk of infection from an as yet unidentified strain of hepatitis. But blood products are different from medicines, and the judge's findings that people who receive blood transfusions are entitled to expect that the blood will not be infected with hepatitis is not a good precedent for establishing that people who take drugs are entitled to expect that they will never cause adverse reactions.

A similar provision in the Australian Trade Practices Act 1974 was invoked in the action mentioned above, brought in the Australian courts by someone who had suffered a heart attack while taking Vioxx. According to Jessup J:

> the safety of Vioxx was less than what persons generally were entitled to expect because, as a matter of composition, the consumption of Vioxx had the potential to increase the risk of suffering a myocardial infarction, in circumstances which included the absence of any relevant information or warning communicated to the applicant's doctor.[67]

Where a drug causes a serious adverse effect, sufficient to require its withdrawal from the marketplace, it might be relatively straightforward – in the absence of a relevant warning – to establish that it is defective.

Even if a claimant does successfully establish that a drug is defective for the purposes of the Act, the need to prove causation remains. And, as discussed earlier, this can be difficult when the person who has taken the defective product was already ill and perhaps taking a number of other medicines at the same time. Proving, on the balance of probabilities, that it is more likely than not that a medicine was responsible for their poor health outcome will often be challenging.

ii Defences

Even if a claimant is, unusually, able to establish that they took a defective medicine which caused their injuries, the manufacturer might be able to avail itself of one of the defences under the Act. There will, for example, be a defence if the defect is attributable to compliance with a statutory obligation. This is not the same thing as what is known as a 'regulatory compliance' defence, which would mean that there was a defence simply because the manufacturer had properly complied with the licensing regime. Manufacturers have been lobbying for a regulatory compliance defence, and the European Commission is said to be monitoring this issue.[68] A defence also exists if the defendant can prove that the product was never supplied to another, or was not supplied in the course of a business,

---

[67] *Peterson v Merck Sharpe & Dohme* [2010] FCA 180.

[68] European Commission, *Third report on the application of Council Directive on the approximation of laws, regulations and administrative provisions of the Member States concerning liability for defective products (85/374/EEC of 25 July 1985, amended by Directive 1999/34/EC of the European Parliament and of the Council of 10 May 1999)* (14 September 2006). For criticism, see M Mildred, 'Pharmaceutical Products: The Relationship between Regulatory Approval and the Existence of a Defect' (2007) 18 *European Business Law Review* 1276–82.

which means that injuries caused by taking someone else's medication will not be covered. Contributory negligence applies, and so a patient who takes the wrong dose of a drug may be responsible in whole or in part for his or her own injuries.

The most controversial defence is known as the development risks or 'state of the art' defence and is contained in section 4(1)(e):

> it shall be a defence . . . that the state of scientific and technical knowledge at the relevant time was not such that a producer of products of the same description as the product in question might be expected to have discovered the defect if it had existed in his products while they were under his control.

The reason for including this defence was to promote innovation, which it was thought might be stifled if manufacturers had to insure themselves against the possibility of being held strictly liable for undiscoverable defects. Defects which were not discovered during clinical trials are, of course, precisely the sort of defects which are most likely to occur in medicines.[69] It is impossible to detect all rare and latent side effects during clinical trials, and so when these manifest themselves after medicines have been put into circulation, they amount to undiscoverable risks and the manufacturer has a defence. As a result, a similar defence succeeded in the Australian Vioxx case, on the grounds that 'the state of scientific or technical knowledge at the time when Vioxx was supplied to the applicant was not such as would enable the defect to be discovered'.[70]

An action could only succeed under the Consumer Protection Act if the manufacturer knew or should have known of the existence of the risk. If, for example, the drug company was aware of the ADR during the trial process, then it might be liable even if it was not sure at that time that it was caused by the drug. There will also be no defence if, say, the trials had included too few participants, or taken place over an unreasonably short period of time, since it might be argued that producers of similar products could have been expected to discover the risk.

iii Legal Aid

In addition to the difficulties of proving that a medicine is defective, that it caused the claimant's injuries and that the manufacturer knew or should have known of the risk of injury, a further problem is that, in the absence of legal aid, litigation will generally be prohibitively expensive. Because the factual issues are complex, trials involving injuries caused by medicinal products are likely to be lengthy and costly, and will generally involve a number of claimants bringing a claim together as a class action. Very few individuals would be able to afford the legal fees involved in a large class action case. This means that if the Legal Services Commission

---

[69] C Newdick, 'Strict Liability for Defective Drugs in the Pharmaceutical Industry' (1985) 101 *Law Quarterly Review* 405–31.

[70] *Peterson v Merck Sharpe & Dohme* [2010] FCA 180.

decides not to grant legal aid, or to withdraw it, the action will usually have to be dropped.

In recent years, it has become evident that, in practice, an inability to obtain legal aid represents a substantial obstacle to actions against drug companies. Legal aid was refused to claimants who wanted to sue Merck, the manufacturer of Vioxx, discussed earlier, which had been withdrawn after evidence emerged that it caused strokes and heart attacks. It might be thought that the decision to withdraw this drug on safety grounds would stand the claimants in good stead in their claim that Vioxx was defective, and that it had caused their injuries. Certainly, in the US, Merck had set aside $4.85 billion to settle legal claims arising from injuries caused by Vioxx, and as we have seen, a claim also succeeded in Australia. After Vioxx victims were refused legal aid in the UK, they tried to bring actions against Merck in the US, but these were rejected on the grounds that US juries could not be expected to understand another country's system of drug regulation.[71] A lawyer advising the UK claimants admitted to being 'totally stumped': the Vioxx case was, in his view, 'the strongest drug-related case we've seen in the UK for a long time'.[72] In the absence of legal aid, no action was possible.

More recently, in *Multiple Claimants v Sanifo-Synthelabo* (subsequently Sanifo-aventis),[73] legal aid was initially provided, and then withdrawn. A judicial review of that decision led the Legal Services Commission (LSC) to reinstate some funding. Following a number of preliminary hearings and having already provided around £3 million in legal aid, the LSC withdrew any further funding 'at the door of the courtroom' and the case had to be dropped. This case had involved over 100 children who claimed that Epilim, an anti-epileptic drug, was defective within the meaning of the Act. The claimants' mothers had taken Epilim during pregnancy, and the childen's claim was that Epilim is a known teratogen (that is, it damages the fetus in utero), and hence 'defective' under the Consumer Protection Act. The question of liability for birth defects is especially complex and dealt with separately below, but it is noteworthy that Sanifo settled a similar case in the US. The LSC's decision to withdraw legal aid would have been grounded in their lawyers' assessment that there was an insufficiently good chance that the claimants would win their case to justify further public funding of their legal costs. Sanifo's lawyers in the US clearly took a different view of US children's chance of success before a US court.

Legal aid was provided to the litigants in *Bailey v GlaxoSmithKline*, whose argument is that GSK failed to warn patients of the risk of suffering withdrawal symptoms when stopping taking Seroxat. This case is due to be heard in the High Court in 2012.

Towards the end of 2010, the government announced further restrictions on access to legal aid. Personal injury cases, such as those against drug companies for

---

[71] C Dyer and S Boseley, 'US Court Ruling Shuts Door on Drug Claimants' Compensation Hopes' *The Guardian* 7 October 2006.

[72] ibid.

[73] *Multiple Claimants v Sanifo-Synthelabo* [2007] EWHC 1860 (QB).

adverse events, will no longer be covered, on the grounds that 'no win, no fee' (or conditional fee) arrangements are available. Given the costs involved in litigation against drug companies and the fact that claimants in such cases have *never* been successful in court, it is clear that few lawyers would be prepared to enter into a 'no win, no fee' arrangement in relation to this sort of litigation. It is therefore likely that the Seroxat litigation will be the last of its type in the UK.

E Long-term Medication and Pregnancy: A Special Case?

In the absence of robust trial data indicating that drugs can safely be taken during pregnancy, it is extremely common for package inserts to contain warnings either that the medicine should not be taken during pregnancy and by breastfeeding women, or to advise pregnant women to talk to their doctors before taking the medicine. This is seldom because there is robust evidence that the medicine is likely to damage the developing fetus. On the contrary, the problem is usually an absence of evidence of safety, given the understandable reluctance both of drugs companies to carry out clinical trials in pregnant women, and of pregnant women to take part. As with the historical exclusion of children from clinical trials, regardless of how benevolent the motivation for excluding a subgroup of patients from trial participation, the inevitable consequence is that other members of that group suffer from inadequately tested medicines, and this is certainly the case for pregnant women.

When the need for prescription medication arises during pregnancy, the choice a pregnant woman will often face is between receiving treatment which may benefit her but which poses an unknown risk to her fetus, or remaining untreated. If the pregnant woman's condition is relatively mild or trivial, forgoing medication during pregnancy may be annoying, but it is unlikely to have any serious adverse consequences. If, on the other hand, her condition is serious, she may be placed in a very difficult position in which she has to weigh possibly serious harm to herself by remaining untreated with the unknown risk of harm to her fetus.

Long-term medication may raise a particular issue in relation to the risk of birth defects, since it will commonly be prescribed to women who are not pregnant, but who conceive while they are on medication. Unless the woman has stopped taking her long-term medication before she starts trying to conceive, she is likely to be in the position of having taken a drug which poses an unknown risk to the fetus during the time-lag between conception and a positive pregnancy test. Once she finds out she is pregnant, she is then in the difficult position described above: forgo effective treatment or expose the fetus to an unknown risk.

More complicated still are drugs which are addictive or cause serious withdrawal symptoms. In such cases, not only does the woman face a difficult choice, but she may also find it hard or even impossible to stop taking the drug in question. A good example might once again be the antidepressant drug paroxetine

(Seroxat), which is known to cause withdrawal symptoms in some users.[74] There is also evidence that paroxetine is associated with a small but statistically significant elevated risk of congenital birth defects, as well as an increased risk of miscarriage and premature birth.[75] If the pregnant woman has taken paroxetine in the last months of pregnancy, her baby may be born suffering from neonatal withdrawal syndrome.[76]

Paroxetine has been specifically marketed for the treatment of premenstrual dysphoric disorder, which means that women of childbearing age are among its principal users. It could then be argued that the twin risks of addiction and birth defects combine to make information about both risks necessary not just for women who are pregnant when their need for antidepressant medication arises, but also for a significant proportion of all women of childbearing age, in whom pregnancy may be a possibility during the years when they may be taking paroxetine.

If paroxetine was the only effective treatment for depression, then a woman might nevertheless decide that relief of the symptoms of depression was so important to her that it was worth taking it despite these risks, especially if she did not intend to have children in the foreseeable future. But for many women – importantly including those who have no immediate plans to have children – faced with a range of possible treatments for depression, the propensity of one to be addictive and cause birth defects would be material information, which might lead them to favour a different approach to the treatment of their depression, perhaps by opting for some sort of cognitive therapy instead.

F Liability for Birth Defects

Under the Congenital Disabilities (Civil Liability) Act 1976, a child may have a claim for compensation if he is injured as a result of an 'occurrence before its birth', which 'affected the mother during her pregnancy', and which led the child to be born with disabilities which would not otherwise have been present.[77] The Consumer Protection Act 1987 amended the 1976 Act so that it now specifically applies to children whose prenatal injuries are caused by defective products.

The duty owed to the child is a derivative one, and there can be an action only if the defendant (the GP or the manufacturer) might be liable in tort to the parent

---

[74] A Tonks, 'Withdrawal from Paroxetine Can be Severe, warns FDA' (2004) 324 *British Medical Journal* 260; M Lejoyeux and J Ades, 'Antidepressant Discontinuation: A Review of the Literature' (1997) 28 *Journal of Clinical Psychiatry* supplement 7 11–15; M Bloch et al, 'Severe Psychiatric Symptoms Associated with Paroxetine Withdrawal' (1995) 346 *The Lancet* 57.

[75] R Dobson, 'SSRI Use during Pregnancy is Associated with Fetal Abnormalities' (2006) 333 *British Medical Journal* 824; KL Wisner et al, 'Major Depression and Antidepressant Treatment: Impact on Pregnancy and Neonatal Outcomes' (2009) 166 *American Journal of Psychiatry* 557–66; TF Oberlander et al, 'Effects of Timing and Duration of Gestational Exposure to Serotonin Reuptake Inhibitor Antidepressants: Population-Based Study' (2008) 192 *British Journal of Psychiatry* 338–43.

[76] EJ Sanz et al, 'Selective Serotonin Reuptake Inhibitors in Pregnant Women and Neonatal Withdrawal Syndrome: A Database Analysis' (2005) 365 *The Lancet* 482–87.

[77] Congenital Disabilities (Civil Liability) Act 1976 ss 1(1) and 1(2).

in relation to the 'occurrence' which caused the child's injuries. It is not necessary for the parent to suffer any actionable injury. Rather, there will be liability to the child if there was a breach of a duty to the parent which, *if accompanied by injury*, would have given rise to liability.

In October 2009, GSK, the manufacturer of paroxetine, was ordered to pay $2.5 million in damages to an American child whose heart defect was found to be the result of his mother taking paroxetine (brand name Paxil in the US) during pregnancy. Michelle David and her disabled son Lyam Kilker successfully proved that GSK knew of the risk of birth defects associated with paroxetine for some time before it informed the Food and Drug Administration, and that it had therefore been negligent in failing to warn her and prescribing doctors of this risk.[78]

There are, however, reasons to be pessimistic about the likelihood of a success-ful action in the UK for drugs injuries caused during pregnancy under the 1976 Act, as amended by the Consumer Protection Act. The only successful claims under the 1976 Act have been for negligent obstetric care.[79] Of course, the lack of litigation could be explained by the rarity of negligently-caused prenatal harm or the willingness of potential defendants to settle out of court, but given the weight of litigation in the US, it seems unlikely either that prenatal harm does not happen in the UK, or that drugs companies are somehow persuaded to settle cases, rather than fight them.[80]

It would seem obvious that the Consumer Protection Act's amendments to the Congenital Disabilities Act were intended to cover cases where children are born injured as a result of 'products', like medicines, used by their mothers during preg-nancy. In *Multiple Claimants v Sanifo-Synthelabo*,[81] discussed above, the claim was that children had suffered injuries in utero as a result of their mother's epilepsy medication. Before the withdrawal of legal aid, the Court was asked to determine certain preliminary issues, one of which was whether there could have been an 'occurrence' for the purposes of the 1976 Act. Andrew Smith J suggested that the wording of the Act 'does not allow for the possibility that the "occurrence" was by way of an accumulation of the drug within the mother'. Expert evidence would be needed, he concluded, to determine whether the alleged 'transplacental spread' could properly be described as an 'occurrence'. Following the withdrawal of legal aid in this case, this question, perhaps surprisingly, remains unresolved.

G Vaccination Injuries

Unlike most medicines, vaccination is not only intended to benefit the child who is immunised, but also to contribute towards the public health goal of eliminating

---

[78] S Heylman, 'New Paxil Suits Allege Birth Defect Risk' (2007) 43 *Trial* 14.

[79] See, for example, *Peters v University Hospital of Wales NHS Trust* [2002] All ER (D) 29.

[80] *Oxendine v Merrell Dow Pharmaceuticals* 506 A.2d 1100 D.C.,1986; JL Schardein, *Chemically Induced Birth Defects*, 3rd edn (New York, Marcel Dekker, 2000).

[81] *Multiple Claimants v Sanifo-Synthelabo* [2007] EWHC 1860.

certain diseases through population-wide immunisation and the establishment of herd immunity. Babies will benefit from herd immunity to whooping cough before they are old enough to have been vaccinated themselves. The benefits of vaccination are therefore not only to the immunised child but also to children who have not (yet) been vaccinated. Because some vaccination programmes are known to pose a risk of injury to a small number of people, which is believed to be out-weighed by the enormous public health good of herd immunity, it would seem fair to offer some compensation to the handful of individuals whose health may have been compromised for the greater good.

In the 1970s, the Pearson Commission had recommended the setting up of a special strict liability scheme to cover vaccination. Their proposal was never implemented, and an interim scheme, introduced by the Vaccine Damage Payments Act 1979, continues to apply today. Under section 1, a person who has been severely disabled as a result of vaccination against diphtheria, tetanus, whooping cough, poliomyelitis, measles, rubella, tuberculosis, smallpox, mumps, Haemophilus type b infection (hib), or meningitis C, is entitled to a sum of £120,000 for claims made since July 2007 (smaller payments are made for claims before this date).[82]

Applicants must have been vaccinated in the UK since 1948 (in the case of smallpox this was before 1971, when smallpox was eradicated and vaccination ceased). Under section 3(1), claims must be made before the claimant reaches the age of 21. 'Severe disability' is defined as 60 per cent disablement,[83] and the causal link between the vaccine and the disability has to be proved, on the balance of probabilities.[84]

The scheme has not been an overwhelming success, and there have been com-paratively few successful claims. Rates of success vary between different vaccines: a relatively high proportion of claims resulting from the single measles vaccine is successful, compared with very few successful claims in relation to the measles, mumps, and rubella (MMR) vaccine.[85] The disablement threshold might also be said to be problematic. Even if it is possible to calculate the extent of a child's dis-ablement with sufficient accuracy to draw a distinction between a child who is 55 per cent disabled and a child whose disablement reaches the threshold level of 60 per cent, why should the child who is slightly less disabled receive nothing, when the slightly more disabled child might be entitled to £120,000? Nevertheless, given the fact that actions in negligence for injuries caused by medicines are so fraught with difficulty, it must be admitted that – compared with other victims of medi-cines' propensity to cause adverse reactions – children injured through vaccination are comparatively fortunate.

---

[82] Written Ministerial Statement, 3 May 2007. Details at www.dwp.gov.uk.
[83] Vaccine Damage Payments Act 1979 s 1(4).
[84] ibid s 3(5).
[85] S Pywell, 'The Vaccine Damage Payment Scheme: A Proposal for Radical Reform' (2002) 9 *Journal of Social Security Law* 73–93, 83.

IV Conclusion

The Consumer Protection Act, despite its name, has proved to be a remarkably consumer-unfriendly piece of legislation, and there have as yet been no successful cases against pharmaceutical companies. It seems improbable that this is because drugs' manufacturers routinely settle claims in the UK that they are willing to fight in the US. On the contrary, given the lack of success in cases against drug companies in the UK, there would seem to be a greater incentive to taking the case to court in the UK. Because decisions about the provision of legal aid are grounded in the chance of a successful outcome, it is unsurprising that the LSC has withdrawn or withheld funding from class action cases against drug companies. 'No win, no fee' or conditional fee arrangements are popular in other sorts of personal injury cases. Someone who wishes to sue their employer as a result of injuries sustained in the workplace may find it relatively easy to find a lawyer willing to represent them on a conditional fee basis: if they win their claim, the lawyer's costs can be recouped, and this is a sufficiently likely outcome that the lawyer may be happy to take on the case in the knowledge that he may be out of pocket if the case does not succeed. Given how rare, or even non-existent, successful cases against drug companies have proved to be in the UK, it would be understandable if lawyers refused to take on personal injury actions where they would be paid only if their client won their claim.

There is also an important connection between the limits of post-licensing data collection, discussed earlier in this chapter, and the inadequacies of the tort system as a mechanism through which patients who are injured by medicines can seek redress. In countries, like the US, where litigation against drug manufacturers has been much more successful, the information gathered during court proceedings can be fed back to the regulator in order to prompt a label change or other mechanism to protect patient safety.[86] In the UK, this 'feedback loop' is largely absent, given that the chances of a successful claim are slim, at best, and non-existent at worst. As the prospect of obtaining legal aid for class actions against drug companies becomes even more remote, cases are even less likely to get as far as the door of the courtroom, and their information gathering function may disappear altogether.

---

[86] DA Kessler and DC Vladeck, 'A Critical Examination of the FDA's Efforts to Preempt Failure-to-Warn Claims' (2008) 96 *Georgetown Law Journal* 461–95.

5

Marketing

CHAPTER ONE CONSIDERED a number of reasons why medicines are unlike other products, one of which is that, in the case of prescription medicines, the person who chooses which medicine to buy (a) does not pay for it and (b) is not its ultimate consumer. This unusual purchasing model is especially significant when it comes to the advertising of medicines. The story to be told in this chapter is a complex one, but it can be summarised fairly simply: restrictions on the advertising of medicines do not mean that they are not advertised, rather it means that the marketing strategies used to sell medicines are more diffuse, subtle and sophisticated than is the case when a manufacturer is trying to persuade consumers to buy a new shampoo or breakfast cereal. Despite restrictions on advertising, expenditure on marketing and promotional activities accounts for 23 per cent of the industry's turnover in the UK, compared with 17 per cent for research and development.[1]

This chapter starts by considering the rules on advertising which are contained in two sets of regulations, both of which implement EU Directives and their amendments.[2] There is an EU-wide ban on direct to consumer advertising of prescription medicines, but there are also multiple ways in which this restriction can be effectively and sometimes ingeniously overcome. Medicines can be directly advertised to prescribers and suppliers of prescription medicines, and the pharmaceutical industry also has a long history of promoting its products to doctors through gifts and event sponsorship.

I Direct to Consumer Advertising

In the UK, regulations prohibit the issue of any advertisement to the general public which is likely to lead to the use of a prescription-only medicine.[3] The only

---

[1] European Commission, *Executive Summary of the Pharmaceutical Sector Inquiry Report* (EC, 2009), available at http://ec.europa.eu/competition/sectors/pharmaceuticals/inquiry/communication_en.pdf.

[2] The Medicines (Advertising) Regulations 1994 and the Medicines (Monitoring of Advertising) Regulations 1994, as amended.

[3] Medicines (Advertising) Regulations 1994 SI 1994/1932, as amended.

exception is government-controlled vaccination campaigns that have been approved by health ministers: an example would be health promotion campaigns intended to increase take-up of the seasonal flu vaccination among at-risk groups. Pharmacy-available medicines and those on the general sale list can, subject to restrictions on promotional methods that could lead to the unnecessary or excessive use of medicines, be advertised directly to consumers.[4]

In order to police the ban on direct to consumer (DTC) advertising, the Medicines and Heathcare products Regulatory Agency (MHRA)'s Advertising Standards Unit monitors print and broadcast media and the internet and investigates complaints. Complaints can come from members of the public, but are commonly also lodged by pharmaceutical companies, concerned about the promotional activities of their competitors. In a recent Annual Report, for example, the Advertising Standards Unit reported a marked increase in the number of complaints against cosmetic clinics in relation to DTC advertising of botulinum toxin (known as botox) products, used to reduce the appearance of wrinkles.[5] Most of these complaints came from competitor clinics that had already been subject to MHRA action for illegitimately advertising botox.

It is sometimes hard to tell the difference between legitimate disease awareness campaigns and DTC advertising: it is acceptable to raise public awareness of the *existence of treatment*, but it is not acceptable to encourage the *use of a prescription medicine*. Distinguishing between these two sorts of publicity campaigns is not always easy, and becomes especially problematic in the case of online pharmacies, where the whole point is to sell prescription medicines to consumers. The MHRA has issued specific guidance on how 'consumer websites offering medicinal treatment services' can ensure that they do not promote prescription-only medicines (POMs). The home page, for example, must 'avoid direct reference to named POMs, including price information'. If the consumer chooses to access further pages, these 'may contain information on specific medicines provided this is presented in the context of an overview of the treatment options'. There must be no 'special offers on prices', and no use of icons such as 'add to basket', since these promote and invite the purchase of prescription-only medicines.

The only countries which do permit DTC advertising of prescription drugs are the US and New Zealand. But even in these countries, DTC advertising is different from the marketing of most other consumer goods, the purpose of which is to persuade viewers to go out and buy the advertised product for themselves. Prescription drugs are not available for purchase in this way, and so the point of DTC advertising is to 'enlist' potential consumers to visit their doctors and put pressure on them to issue prescriptions.[6] Martin Lipman compares this to TV

---

[4] ibid.

[5] Medicines and Heathcare products Regulatory Agency (MHRA) Advertising Standards Unit, *Delivering High Standards in Medicines Advertising Regulation Fifth Annual Report 2009–2010* (MHRA, 2010).

[6] TS Jost, 'Oversight of Marketing Relationships between Physicians and the Drug and Device Industry: A Comparative Study' (2010) 35 *American Journal of Law and Medicine* 326.

adverts directed at young children who cannot purchase sweets or toys for themselves, rather an intermediary is necessary: 'in one case a parent who has the money and, in the other case, a physician who has the prescription pad'.[7]

Because creating consumer demand, on its own, is not sufficient to increase sales, DTC advertising is only one part of the marketing campaign for a new medicine, in which informing prescribing doctors about the availability of the new product will be at least as important as persuading consumers to ask for it. In the US, DTC advertising represents a fraction (12.5 per cent) of drugs companies' marketing budget, suggesting that even where it is lawful, DTC advertising is not considered to be the most effective way to increase sales of medicines.[8] Indeed, in the US drugs companies were initially opposed to DTC advertising, largely because it was regarded as cheaper and more effective to market products to the gatekeepers to prescription drugs, namely doctors.[9] When the US regulator, the Food and Drug Administration (FDA) lifted its restrictions on DTC advertising in 1997, it quickly became apparent that, in fact, the returns were considerable: it has been estimated that each dollar spent on DTC advertising generates an additional $4.20 in sales.[10]

Given this sort of evidence from the US, it is unsurprising that the pharmaceutical industry is keen to have the EU's ban on DTC advertising lifted, and a number of arguments have been put forward to suggest that this sort of advertising is, in fact, in *patients'* interests. It has, for example, been claimed that DTC advertising provides valuable information to patients, empowering them in their discussions with doctors, and enabling them to take a more active role in the management of their condition.[11] Patients who might not bother to seek medical attention for symptoms that they believe to be trivial or find embarrassing might be encouraged to do so by DTC advertising, and if this facilitates earlier diagnosis and the provision of effective treatment, it could lead to improved health outcomes. DTC advertising is not only intended to reach as yet undiagnosed patients, it is also supposed to act as a reminder for patients who have already been prescribed a particular medicine to ensure that they stick with treatment and remember to visit their doctors to obtain repeat prescriptions.[12]

It has further been argued that the internet is awash with information about drugs, some of which is misleading or inaccurate. Allowing DTC advertising, on

---

[7] MM Lipman, 'Bias in Direct-to-Consumer Advertising and its Effect on Drug Safety' (2007) 35 *Hofstra Law Review* 761.

[8] MA Santoro, 'Introduction to Part II' in Michael A Santoro and Thomas M Gorrie (eds), *Ethics and the Pharmaceutical Industry* (Cambridge University Press, 2005) 127–35.

[9] C Elliott, *White Coat Black Hat: Adventures on the Dark Side of Medicine* (Boston, Beacon Press, 2010) 124.

[10] Kaiser Family Foundation, cited in ibid 124.

[11] S Bonaccorso and JL Sturchio, 'Perspectives from the Pharmaceutical Industry' (2003) 327 *British Medical Journal* 863–86.

[12] JE Calfee, 'Public Policy Issues in Direct-to-Consumer Advertising of Prescription Drugs' (2002) 19 *Journal of Public Policy and Marketing* 174. JE Calfee, C Winston and R Stempski, 'Direct-to-Consumer Advertising and the Demand for Cholesterol-Reducing Drugs' (2002) 45 *Journal of Law and Economics* 673.

this view, enables manufacturers to provide high-quality information to patients, as a corrective to some of the misinformation available on the web.[13]

On the other hand, it could be argued that DTC advertisements are not principally aimed at sick people with unmet needs for medical attention. Rather, their audience is more commonly the 'worried well', and their purpose is to persuade healthy people that they may be presymptomatic and in need of medication to ward off future ill-health. For example, the manufacturer of an anti-osteoporosis drug ran a campaign in the US to persuade middle-aged women to seek out bone-density testing. In fact, bone-density testing is a poor predictor of susceptibility to future fractures; muscle weakness from a lack of exercise is a much more significant factor. Bone-density testing is, however, 'an excellent predictor of the start of drug use'.[14]

Further evidence that DTC advertising is not always directed towards identifying unmet health needs comes from the fact that it tends to be confined to a relatively small subset of prescription drugs. In order to justify the high costs of newspaper and television advertisements, medicines which are advertised directly to the public tend to be expensive drugs which are intended to be prescribed long-term to potentially large patient groups: common examples are treatments for anxiety, obesity, arthritis, impotence, and high cholesterol. Cheap, one-off interventions are generally not advertised, regardless of their potential public health benefits.

Rather than providing objective and high-quality information about the risks and benefits of a particular medicine, Frosch et al found that television DTC advertisements more commonly used 'emotional' appeals to viewers.[15] Characters in advertisements were portrayed as fearful and lacking control over many aspects of their lives before they started taking medication. After taking the advertised product, they are depicted as happy, in control and able to participate again in social activities.[16] Print advertisements in the US are required to provide information about risks and side effects, but these are usually in tiny, almost unreadable print and in language that is difficult or impossible for the average layperson to understand.[17]

DTC advertising may also serve a broader purpose than simply persuading a patient suffering from the symptoms described in the advert to visit their doctor. More subtly and insidiously, it communicates the subliminal message that there is a 'pill for every ill', and that taking medication generally leads to positive outcomes. It can bolster the process of medicalisation, discussed below, whereby

[13] SN Bonaccorso and JL Sturchio, 'For and Against: Direct to Consumer Advertising is Medicalising Normal Human Experience: Against' (2002) 324 *British Medical Journal* 910–11.

[14] B Mintzes, 'For and Against: Direct to Consumer Advertising is Medicalising Normal Human Experience' (2002) 324 *British Medical Journal* 90.

[15] DL Frosch et al, 'Creating Demand for Prescription Drugs: A Content Analysis of Television Direct-to-Consumer Advertising' (2007) 5 *Annals of Family Medicine* 6–13.

[16] ibid.

[17] JR Hoffman and M Wilkes, 'Direct to Consumer Advertising of Prescription Drugs: An Idea whose Time should not Come' (1999) 318 *British Medical Journal* 1301.

people increasingly self-label any difficulties they may be having as *medical* problems, for which it is appropriate to seek out a pharmacological solution. Regular
exposure to DTC advertising also promotes the idea that it is normal and safe to
take prescription drugs both frequently and long-term. If prescription drugs are
advertised in the same way as fizzy drinks or washing powder, consumers may be
encouraged to regard them in the same way as other products, which we choose to
use because they correspond with our lifestyle preferences.[18]

Evidence from the US suggests that the DTC advertising of a drug does increase
the number of prescriptions issued.[19] This fact barely needs stating, of course, since
companies are not going to pay to advertise a product if they do not anticipate
generating any additional income as a result. Some of these additional prescriptions may represent cases of genuine unmet need, but there is a danger that others
will be instances of overprescription, where a doctor is persuaded to prescribe a
medicine as a result of patient demand.[20] Drugs which are only available on prescription, by definition, pose some risks to consumers, otherwise there would be
no reason to restrict their availability. The reason why a drug is classified as prescription-only is precisely because self-diagnosis and self-medication is *not* safe. If
people who would not otherwise be prescribed a medicine take it as a direct result
of DTC advertising, they may be unnecessarily exposed to the risk of adverse reactions. Unnecessary prescriptions will also represent a waste of money, which in the
US will lead to increased insurance premiums, but in the UK would mean a drain
on scarce NHS resources.

There are, on balance, good reasons to resist any move to rescind the current
ban on DTC advertisements for prescription drugs within the EU. Importantly,
however, there are two reasons why this ban may be of decreasing practical significance. First, as discussed in chapter three, in recent years there has been a move
towards the reclassification of many prescription-only drugs, to enable them to be
sold over-the-counter with or without pharmacist supervision. Drugs that are
reclassified in this way *can* be marketed directly to consumers. Adverts for pharmacy and general sale medicines may be used to fix a branded medicine in the
consumer's mind, even if cheaper generic versions are available. Expensive
branded cold and flu 'remedies', for example, generally contain one or more of the
following: paracetamol, phenylephrine (a decongestant), and guaifenesin (an
expectorant). Cheaper versions of all three are available, with exactly the same

---

[18] LJ Weber, *Profits Before People? Ethical Standards and the Marketing of Prescription Drugs*
(Bloomington, Indiana University Press, 2006) 164.

[19] RL Kravitz et al, 'Influence of Patients' Requests for Direct-to-Consumer Advertised Antidepressants:
A Randomised Controlled Trial' (2005) 293 *Journal of the American Medical Association* 1995–2002;
WD Bradford et al, 'How Direct-to-Consumer Television Advertising for Osteoarthritis Drugs Affects
Physicians' Prescribing Behavior' (2006) 25 *Health Affairs* 1371–77; Mintzes B et al, 'Influence of Direct to
Consumer Pharmaceutical Advertising and Patients' Requests on Prescribing Decisions: Two Site Cross
Sectional Survey' (2002) 324 *British Medical Journal* 278–89.

[20] MS Lipsky and CA Taylor, 'The Opinions and Experiences of Family Physicians Regarding Direct-
to-Consumer Advertising' (1997) 45 *Journal of Family Practice* 495–99; TM Schwartz, Consumer-
Directed Prescription Drug Advertising and the Learned Intermediary Rule' (1991) 46 *Food, Drug and
Cosmetics Law Journal* 829.

active doses as in branded cold and flu remedies. But DTC advertising is used to persuade people that the branded medicine is superior. Unlike generic packets of, say, paracetamol, branded cold and flu remedies will have more attractive names and packaging. As more prescription-only drugs are reclassified, this will inevitably be accompanied by an expansion in DTC advertising of branded, non-prescription drugs.

Second, it has proved relatively simple for drugs companies to find ways to reach patients directly, *without* resorting to DTC advertising. It is legal for drugs companies to fund disease awareness campaigns, patient groups and PR campaigns, discussed in the following sections, and all three offer efficient and effective routes for the dissemination of information about prescription medicines *directly to consumers*. Patients are also increasingly likely to seek out information about medicines themselves on the internet, hence bypassing the need for drugs companies to advertise directly to them.

II Selling Diseases

It used to be thought that the market for medicines was inelastic: the only possible consumers being the relatively stable number of people each year who are diagnosed with particular conditions. Now it is evident that there are multiple ways for pharmaceutical companies to expand the market for their products.

In order to sell a new medicine, it can be important first to 'sell' the disease which it is intended to treat. Before the 1960s, for example, clinical depression was assumed to be extremely unusual. Of course, people experienced periods of sadness during their lives, and these would sometimes be extremely debilitating, but few regarded this as a *medical* condition. It was only when amitriptyline was developed in the early 1960s that depression was first promoted as a *clinical* problem, which might be treatable by medication. As part of Merck's marketing strategy for amitriptyline, it distributed 50,000 copies of Frank Ayd's book *Recognising the Depressed Patient* to GPs.[21]

Now, of course, it is evident that the market for antidepressants is huge, and that far from being unusual, if judged by the number of prescriptions written each year, depression is extremely common. Before the 1960s, did huge numbers of people suffer from undiagnosed depressive illness, or since 1960 has a normal, if difficult aspect of human existence been increasingly redefined as a treatable medical condition? Many commentators have suggested that the modern epidemic of depressive illness is part of a trend towards *medicalisation*, that is treating ordinary feelings, like anxiety and sadness, or the normal consequences of ageing, such as baldness or the menopause, as *medical* problems, for which a *medical* solution is

---

[21] Elliott n 9 above, 120.

appropriate. Because the medical solution almost always takes the form of some sort of drug, this process has also been described as *pharmaceuticalisation*.[22]

The process of medicalisation is indubitably not an invention of the pharmaceutical industry, directed solely towards expanding the market for their products. There are multiple reasons for the increasing medicalisation of normal life processes, not least consumer demand for a 'medical fix' for problems like being overweight or feeling overwhelmed by anxiety. Nonetheless, the development of new medicines to treat these new medical conditions clearly facilitates the medicalisation of everyday life.[23] The availability of Ritalin, for example, has undoubtedly had an impact upon the diagnosis of attention deficit hyperactivity disorder (ADHD): parents now seek out a diagnosis in order to access treatment for their children. When oestrogen replacement therapy became available, the symptoms of the menopause were no longer just a nuisance which had to be tolerated, but instead could be represented as a medical problem which could be effectively managed by medication.

In 1992, Lynn Payer accused the pharmaceutical industry of strategic medicalisation, which she labeled 'disease mongering'.[24] Payer explained that the point of disease mongering is 'to convince essentially well people that they are sick, or slightly sick people that they are very ill'.[25] It works precisely because it is part of the wider trend towards medicalisation, with the public increasingly willing both to embrace a medical explanation for social difficulties and to believe that scientific progress will inexorably lead to the development of new medicines to treat every imaginable unwanted symptom.

There are a number of reasons why this drive to find a pharmacological solution to an increasingly wide range of problems is problematic, however. Few drugs are completely safe for all users, and increasing the number of people who are regularly taking medication inevitably increases the number of adverse drug reactions, which is both bad for public health and costly for the NHS. In some cases, medicalisation might also be said to *individualise* problems which do not have an exclusively physiological or organic cause. Childhood depression, for example, might have a range of causes which may be ignored if children are simply prescribed antidepressants. There may be lots of reasons why some women lose interest in sex, and these are glossed over if it is regarded as a medical condition, treatable by a pill which increases blood circulation, but which cannot address some of the more fundamental reasons why some sexual relationships are unfulfilling.

---

[22] SJ Williams, J Gabe and P Davis, 'The Sociology of Pharmaceuticals: Progress and Prospects' (2008) 30 *Sociology of Health and Illness* 813–24; NJ Fox and J Ward, 'Pharma in the Bedroom . . . and the Kitchen. . . . The Pharmaceuticalisation of Daily Life' (2008) 30 *Sociology of Health and Illness* 856–68.

[23] P Conrad and V Leiter, 'Medicalisation, Markets and Consumers' (2004) 45 *Journal of Health and Social Behavior* 158–76.

[24] L Payer, *Disease-mongers: How Doctors, Drug Companies, and Insurers are Making You Feel Sick* (New York, Wiley, 1992).

[25] ibid.

A few conditions are particularly susceptible to strategic pharmaceuticalisation, and these are considered separately in the following sections.

A Sexual Dysfunction

Leonore Tiefer argues that sexual dysfunction is a prime candidate for disease mongering, in part because people are anxious and embarrassed about sex and in part because popular culture has inflated public expectations of sexual satisfaction.[26] Erectile dysfunction (ED), previously known as impotence, was promoted as a common and disabling medical condition as part of the marketing campaign for sildenafil (Viagra). The name change is itself significant: the implication of the word 'impotence' is that the sufferer lacks potency; the term 'erectile dysfunction' is less judgemental and simply suggests that a physiological process is not working properly.

To expand the market for Viagra beyond the relatively small group of men with secondary ED as a consequence of, for example, diabetes or prostate surgery, it had to be recast as a treatment option for men who *occasionally* had difficulties getting or maintaining an erection which Pfizer estimated – on the basis of some rather suspect evidence – to be 'more than half of all men over 40'.[27] Joel Lexchin explains that 'the impression had to be created that ED was of significant concern to many, perhaps even most, men'.[28] In the US, the initial advertising strategy for Viagra was to enlist Robert Dole, a World War II veteran and former senator and presidential candidate to appeal to older men suffering from physical conditions which affected their sexual performance and to send the message that it was not shameful to seek medical help.[29] Later advertising campaigns instead featured younger 'hypermasculine sports figures',[30] and targeted anyone who was disappointed that the constant erections of their teenage years had declined in frequency and potency.

To sell Viagra it was also necessary to emphasise the importance of penetrative sex for a mutually satisfying sexual relationship. Interestingly, however, in their interviews with the female partners of male users of Viagra, Potts et al encountered considerable ambivalence about Viagra's impact upon their own sexual satisfaction.[31] Women resented the pressure to have unwanted sex once their male partner had taken the pill, often without consulting them first: any reluctance they might express about engaging in penetrative sex was not just disappointing for their partners, it often represented a waste of money.

[26] L Tiefer, 'Female Sexual Dysfunction: A Case Study of Disease Mongering and Activist Resistance' (2006) 3 *PLoS Medicine* e178.

[27] J Lexchin, 'Bigger and Better: How Pfizer Redefined Erectile Dysfunction' (2006) 3 *PLoS Medicine* e132.

[28] ibid.

[29] AV Horwitz, 'Pharmaceuticals and the Medicalization of Social Life' in DW Light (ed), *The Risks of Prescription Drugs* (Columbia UP, 2010) 92–115, 105.

[30] ibid.

[31] A Potts et al, 'The Downside of Viagra: Women's Experiences and Concerns' (2003) 25 *Sociology of Health and Illness* 697–719.

The market for Viagra proved to be enormous, and it is unsurprising that there has been considerable interest in developing a 'pink Viagra', for use in women.[32] What, however, is the 'problem' that a female version of Viagra would be treating? While there is a long history of associating female sexual desire with mental instability, in the past it was *excessive* female desire that was treated as pathological. More recently – and some would argue in part as a direct consequence of the possible market for a female Viagra[33] – it is some women's apparent lack of interest in sex which has been medicalised.[34] Hyposexual desire disorder was first included in the Diagnostic and Statistical Manual (DSM) of mental disorders in 1987. In 2000, funded by the pharmaceutical industry, the International Consensus Development Conference on Female Sexual Dysfunction was convened.[35] A resulting journal article, in which the authors declared financial interests or other relationships with 22 drug companies, found the condition to be 'age related, progressive and highly prevalent, affecting 20 per cent to 50 per cent of women'. It recommended more clinical trials.

Of course, a woman's lack of interest in sex would only be susceptible to drug treatment if it has a physiological cause. A variety of theories have been put forward to back up this hypothesis. It has, for example, been argued that women who experience sexual dysfunction have problems with blood flow to their genitals. Another possibility that has been mooted is testosterone deficiency. And finally, a lack of interest in sex has been said to be caused by a chemical imbalance in the brain.[36] A company which produces a medicine that enhances blood flow might explain the problem as one of 'insufficient engorgement'; whereas the manufacturer of a testosterone patch might suggest that the principal cause of female sexual dysfunction is a hormonal imbalance, and so on, leading Moynihan and Mintzes to claim that 'the disease seems designed to fit the drug'.[37]

One commonly reproduced statistic is that 43 per cent of all women suffer from some sort of sexual dysfunction.[38] This figure is almost certainly an overestimate. It was derived from a study in which 1500 women were asked to answer yes or no to whether they had experienced any one of seven problems – including a lack of desire for sex, anxiety about sexual performance, and difficulties with lubrication – for two months or more, during the previous year. If a woman answered yes to one of the questions, they were classified as having sexual dysfunction. In another

---

[32] J Berman et al, 'Effect of Sildenafil on Subjective and Physiologic Parameters of the Female Sexual Response in Women with Sexual Arousal Disorder' (2001) 27 *Journal of Sex and Marital Therapy* 411–20.

[33] R Moynihan, 'The Making of a Disease: Female Sexual Dysfunction' (2003) 326 *British Medical Journal* 45–47.

[34] A Jutel 'Framing Disease: The Example of Female Hypoactive Sexual Desire Disorder' (2010) 70 *Social Science and Medicine* 1084–90.

[35] R Basson et al, 'Report of the International Consensus Development Conference on Female Sexual Dysfunction: Definitions and Classifications' (2000) 163 *Urology* 888–93.

[36] R Moynihan and B Mintzes, *Sex, Lies and Pharmaceuticals: How Drug Companies Plan to Profit from Female Sexual Dysfunction* (Vancouver, Greystone Books, 2010).

[37] ibid 3.

[38] EO Laumann, A Paik, and RC Rosen, 'Sexual Dysfunction in the United States. Prevalence and Predictors' (1999) 281 *Journal of the American Medical Association* 537–44.

study where reported sexual difficulties were only counted if they lasted for more than six months, the figure dropped to 15.6 per cent.[39] A further study found that while 38 per cent of women might qualify for a doctor's diagnosis of sexual dysfunction, only six per cent believed that they had a problem and found it distressing.[40] Yet the '43 per cent' statistic has proved remarkably durable, perhaps because it helpfully (at least for those who might seek to market a drug to treat female sexual dysfunction) suggests a staggering degree of unmet need.

Fluctuations in desire, especially in response to stressful or tiring life events, such as new parenthood, divorce or bereavement, is normal and not evidence that someone has a 'disorder'. Some women may not enjoy sex because the sex that they are having is not, in fact, very enjoyable. The problem may lie with their partner's ability or willingness to satisfy them, or with other aspects of their relationship that they find unsatisfactory, rather than with their blood flow or hormone levels. In the final study mentioned above, most of those women who did report having sexual difficulties believed that this was because of their unsatisfactory relationship, rather than having a physiological cause.[41] Indeed John Bancroft has argued that an inhibition of sexual desire may be a healthy and functional response for women who are experiencing stress, exhaustion or domestic violence.[42] For such women, prescribing a drug to alter their sexual response deflects attention away from the reasons why they do not have happy and fulfilled sexual relationships. Nevertheless, the continual repetition of the 43 per cent prevalence rate is almost certainly part of the strategy to present female sexual dysfunction as common, debilitating *and perhaps potentially treatable*, in order to expand the future market for a pink Viagra.

B Menopause

The menopause is not a disease, it simply marks the end of a woman's reproductive life. It is undoubtedly true that some women find the symptoms of the menopause uncomfortable, embarrassing and painful, and hormone replacement therapy (HRT) has long been marketed as a potential solution. If it was only suitable for women actually going through the menopause, its market – while large – would be more limited than if it could be effectively marketed to pre- and importantly also post-menopausal women. In 2002, the 'Choices Campaign' – funded by a coalition of oestrogen product manufacturers – was launched to 'educate women' about the treatment available to them when going through the menopause. In 2010, a study conducted for the Choices Campaign was reported by the Daily Mail, under the headline 'Why the HRT generation has a fun-filled

---

[39] CH Mercer et al, 'Sexual Function Problems and Help Seeking Behaviour in Britain: National Probability Sample Study' (2003) 327 *British Medical Journal* 426–27.

[40] Cited in Moynihan and Mintzes n 36 above, 57.

[41] ibid 58.

[42] J Bancroft, 'The Medicalisation of Female Sexual Dysfunction: The Need for Caution' (2002) 31 *Archives of Sexual Behaviour* 451–55.

life'.[43] The industry-funded study found that 50 per cent of women on hormone replacement therapy reported improvements in their sex lives since the onset of the menopause, compared with 18 per cent of those not on HRT.

In addition, HRT has been marketed not only for the relief of menopausal symptoms like hot flushes, sweating and vaginal dryness, but also as a way to reduce a woman's risk of suffering from heart disease, osteoporosis, Alzheimer's disease and breast cancer. The theory was that oestregon offered women some protection against a number of common conditions, and hence replacing the oestregon lost at menopause seemed like an obvious way to promote older women's general health and wellbeing. In fact, clinical trials indicated that HRT *increased* the risk of heart disease, breast cancer, stroke and blood clots.[44] Interestingly, however, the response to this new evidence of risk has been to produce safer lower dose formulations, rather than to challenge the medicalisation of the menopause itself. Menopause continues to be regarded as a disorder, but one that is currently awaiting a completely safe medical solution.

C Depression, Anxiety, Shyness and Stress

Depression can be a fatal condition, and there is no doubt that some sufferers are helped by medication. It is, however, a diagnosis with a 'zone of ambiguity' which can, as Carl Elliott puts it, 'be chiselled out and expanded'.[45] In the majority of cases (two-thirds of all prescriptions) anti-depressants are taken by people whose depression is described as 'mild'.[46]

Shyness is a normal human response to certain social situations. Social phobia, social anxiety disorder and avoidant personality disorder, on the other hand, are not part of the 'normal problems of living',[47] but are forms of shyness which are now classified as medical conditions and which can be treated with a number of different drugs, including betablockers, benzodiazepines and selective serotonin reuptake inhibitor (SSRI) antidepressants.[48] In 2003, paroxetine (brand name Seroxat) had its licence extended to treat social anxiety disorder, or extreme shyness, the symptoms of which include fear of public speaking. As Barry Brand, paroxetine's product director in the US put it: 'every marketer's dream is to find an unidentified or unknown market and develop it. That's what we were able to

---

[43] www.dailymail.co.uk/news/article-113427/Why-HRT-generation-fun-filledlife.html#ixzz14ELW0oNZ.

[44] C Stults and P Conrad, 'Medicalisation and Risk Scares: The Case of Menopause and HRT' in Donald W Light (ed), *The Risks of Prescription Drugs* (Columbia UP, 2010) 116–38.

[45] C Elliott, *Better than Well: American Medicine meets the American Dream* (Norton, New York, 2003) 123–24.

[46] C Martinez et al, 'Antidepressant Treatment and the Risk of Fatal and Non-Fatal Self Harm in First Episode Depression: Nested Case-Control Study' (2005) 330 *British Medical Journal* 389.

[47] T Szasz, *The Myth of Mental Illness* (St Albans, Paladin, 1972).

[48] S Scott, 'The Medicalisation of Shyness: From Social Misfits to Social Fitness' (2006) 28 *Sociology of Health and Illness* 133–53.

do with social anxiety disorder'.[49] Social phobia was also marketed aggressively in the US in the immediate aftermath of the terrorist attacks of September 2001, as a condition characterised by feelings of uncontrollable fear and helplessness, for which paroxetine could provide a solution.

It is almost certainly true that some people are so shy that it can make life very difficult indeed, but there will often be a cause for that shyness – lack of self-confidence, for example – which is not treated by resorting to a pharmacological solution. Medication may enable very shy people to engage in social activities with greater ease, but it does not have any impact upon the reasons *why* some people experience crippling shyness in some situations.

It is difficult to diagnose mental conditions like depression and social anxiety disorder. Unlike X-rays and blood tests, diagnosis of these conditions principally consists in the person's own descriptions of their mood, through their answers to checklists of questions. The Burns Depression checklist, for example, contains a list of 25 symptoms and the patient is asked to say whether they have experienced each one 'not at all', 'somewhat', 'a lot', 'moderately' or 'extremely' in the past week. Many of the states of mind on these lists are just a normal part of everyday life – 'difficulty making decisions', for example, or 'feeling tired' – leading inevitably to the risk of over-diagnosis. I filled in the Burns list while writing this chapter, and despite regarding myself as happy and well-adjusted, my diagnosis was one of 'mild depression'.

It is noteworthy that the diagnostic criteria for major depressive disorder – which include low mood, sleep and appetite difficulties, fatigue and lack of concentration – specifically exempt individuals immediately after the death of a close relative, when these 'symptoms' are likely to be normal responses to the shock and sadness of bereavement. Other major life difficulties, which might also prompt feelings of low mood and difficulty sleeping and eating normally, are not excluded, and so it is clearly possible that major depressive disorder will be diagnosed in individuals who are responding normally to stressful experiences like divorce or redundancy. Indeed, where a person's low mood, fatigue and difficulty sleeping result from being in an abusive relationship or being bullied at work, diagnosing her as suffering from major depressive disorder and prescribing medication masks the real cause of her 'low mood' and does nothing to change the social circumstances which are the root cause of her unhappiness.

The use of these checklists may be particularly problematic in children and adolescents, in whom there has been a dramatic increase in the diagnosis of mental health problems and a correspondingly dramatic increase in the use of medication in recent years. If mental problems are diagnosed in teenagers by asking them 'in the past six months, has there been a time when you weren't interested in anything and felt bored or just sat around most of the time?' or 'have there been times when you were very sad?', it is clear that a significant proportion of teenagers who are

---

[49] S Vendantam, 'Drug Ads Hyping Anxiety Make Some Uneasy' *Washington Post* 16 July 2001, A01.

simply experiencing the normal mood fluctuations associated with puberty will be diagnosed as suffering from a mental health disorder.[50]

As disease classifications are broadened, so that more people qualify, the proportion of the population which is considered to be functioning normally inevitably also shrinks.[51] A good example of this 'diagnosis creep' occurred in relation to post-traumatic stress disorder (PTSD), a diagnosis that first emerged to describe the cluster of symptoms – among them, anxiety, depression, substance misuse and personality disorder – experienced by returning Vietnam veterans in the US. Being diagnosed with PTSD enabled these men to receive a disability pension and to avoid social censure.[52] Originally defined as a response to extreme trauma, PTSD is now presented as a normal reaction to a wide range of difficult life experiences. Again, it would be a mistake to lay all of the blame for this on the pharmaceutical industry: some individuals seek to present themselves as victims of trauma in order to obtain compensation for the psychiatric condition they have apparently developed after being involved in or witnessing an accident. Nonetheless, it is clear that it is part of the pervasive medicalisation of distress, which both enables and bolsters the pharmaceuticalisation of unhappiness.

In addition to expanding the market for medication, this process of pharmaceuticalisation rests upon the widespread assumption that conditions like depression result from chemical imbalances in the brain, which can be treated effectively using drugs. The 'chemical imbalance' explanation of mental illness is simple, plausible and appealing to patients. If feelings of despair result from a lack of serotonin in the brain, a drug which increases serotonin levels might be able to 'cure' a person's depression, so long as they keep taking the medicine which restores the chemical balance in their brain. In fact, the evidence for the serotonin depletion explanation for depression is weak.[53] Joanna Moncrieff argues that psychiatric drugs are more likely to act as stimulants or sedatives, rather than being 'magic bullets' capable of targeting a disease-specific imbalance: they are, in short, 'psychoactive chemicals which distort normal brain function by producing a state of intoxication'.[54] By reinforcing the idea that drugs can cure feelings of sadness and helplessness by redressing chemical imbalances, Moncrieff suggests that people are encouraged 'to view themselves as powerless victims of their biology',[55] in preference to finding constructive non-chemical ways to cope with life's difficulties.

---

[50] Horwitz n 29 above.

[51] P Conrad and V Leiter, 'Medicalisation, Markets and Consumers' (2004) 45 *Journal of Health and Social Behavior* 158–76.

[52] D Summerfield, 'The Invention of Post-Traumatic Stress Disorder and the Social Usefulness of a Psychiatric Category' (2001) 322 *British Medical Journal* 95.

[53] JR Lacasse and J Leo, 'Serotonin and Depression: A Disconnect between the Advertisements and the Scientific Literature' (2005) 2 *PLoS Medicine* e392.

[54] J Moncrieff, *The Myth of the Chemical Cure: A Critique of Psychiatric Drug Treatment* (Palgrave Macmillan, Basingstoke, 2008) 224.

[55] ibid 221.

D Treating Risk Factors as Diseases

There is a great deal of money to be made if the target population for medicines is not the minority of the population which is in fact ill, but also includes the healthy majority. As Merck's then CEO, Henry Gadsden, candidly admitted to *Fortune* magazine in 1976, it was a pity their potential market was limited to sick people. His dream, he said, was to make drugs for healthy people so that, just 'like Wrigley's chewing gum', they could 'sell to everyone'.[56] His dream is increasingly becoming a reality. A growing number of new treatments are intended to reduce the risk of *future* disease, rather than treating diseases that patients actually have. Preventative medication usually has to be taken long-term, if not indefinitely, making it an extremely profitable and attractive proposition for drugs companies.

High cholesterol levels and high blood pressure are now treated as diseases in their own right – hyper-cholesterolaemia and hypertension – rather than as risk factors for diseases which may, in fact, never materialise. Indeed, pre-hypertension is a new term for people whose blood pressure is, in fact, normal, but who are perceived to be at risk of suffering high blood pressure in the future.[57] Moyniham and Cassels also point to a gradual reduction in what counts as 'high' blood pressure or 'high' cholesterol levels, and therefore an increase in the population for whom drug treatment may be recommended.[58] In 2006, for example, the National Institute for health and Clinical Excellence (NICE) issued new guidance which resulted in statin use being indicated for 3.3 million more patients in England and Wales.[59] Treating ever larger numbers of healthy people with statins may in fact reduce the proportion that will actually benefit from treatment: one trial of pravastatin for primary prevention indicated that for every 10,000 patients treated with statins for five years, 9,755 would receive no benefit at all.[60] To provide prescription drugs to so many people who stand to gain so little from treatment may not be a cost-effective use of NHS resources, and insofar as some consumers may suffer adverse drug reactions, it may pose a risk to patient safety.

Both doctors and patients appear to regard statins as both safe and useful in reducing the risk of heart disease, but the evidence is in fact equivocal. In chapter two, the use of 'surrogate endpoints' in trials was discussed, and statins are a good example of a drug which is successful at lowering blood test numbers for cholesterol, but where trials have not established that they are successful at reducing the numbers of heart attacks and strokes in patients who do not currently suffer from

---

[56] R Moynihan and A Cassels, *Selling Sickness: How the World's Biggest Pharmaceutical Companies are Turning Us All Into Patients* (New York, Nation Books, 2005) ix.

[57] R Moynihan 'Prediseases: Who Benefits from Treating Prehypertension?' (2010) 341 *British Medical Journal* c4442.

[58] Moynihan and Cassels n 56 above, ix.

[59] National Audit Office, *Prescribing Costs in Primary Care: Report by the Comptroller and Auditor General* (NAO, 2007).

[60] N Freemantle and S Hill, 'Medicalisation, Limits to Medicine, or Never Enough Money to Go Around?' (2002) 324 *British Medical Journal* 864.

cardiovascular disease.[61] But because the 'high cholesterol causes heart disease' explanation is simple, plausible and perhaps also more appealing than the evidence-based message that regular exercise is effective in reducing the risk of heart disease, healthy patients tend to be enthusiastic consumers of medicines which are unlikely to benefit them, and which may have some serious, albeit rare side effects. It would furthermore be a mistake to assume that the piece of common sense wisdom that 'high cholesterol needs to be controlled' emerged out of nowhere. Rather, as Howard Brody has pointed out, pharmaceutical companies have invested a great deal of money in order to ensure that everyone 'knows' the dangers of high cholesterol.[62]

Once people reach middle age, the chance that they are at risk of high cholesterol, high blood pressure or osteoporosis becomes so great that virtually everyone over the age of 50 is a candidate for some sort of long-term medication. This inevitably means that a great deal of money is spent on drugs which *slightly* reduce the risk of future ill-health, often for people who are demanding, articulate and healthy. Ironically, then, increased resort to preventative medication may end up diverting healthcare spending away from the poor and the sick towards the healthy and wealthy.[63]

E Disease Awareness Campaigns

Disease awareness campaigns might involve non-branded advertising campaigns, briefing journalists (see further below) and providing internet-based resources. Again these can be used to draw attention to a condition, and to the availability of effective treatment for it. The aim of disease awareness campaigns is to encourage people to visit their GP in order to find out whether they have an as yet undiagnosed disorder, for which drug treatment is available. Providing the public with unbranded information about a condition does not count as DTC advertising, but where there is only one medicine to treat it, promoting the *condition* to the public comes very close to direct promotion of that product.

The MHRA has issued a specific guidance note on disease awareness campaigns, in order to ensure that they do not fall foul of the prohibition of direct marketing of medicinal products to consumers. The guidelines are clear that disease awareness campaigns 'should not promote the use of a particular medicinal product or products', and they spell out that 'campaigns which aim to stimulate demand by the public for a specific medicine or specific medicines' are likely to be considered promotional. The guidance also notes that campaigns where there is only one, one leading or few medicinal treatments 'potentially draw attention to one medicinal product'. In these circumstances, the MHRA suggests that 'particular care' is

---

[61] H Brody, 'The Commercialisation of Medical Decisions: Physicians and Patients at Risk' in DW Light (ed), *The Risks of Prescription Drugs* (Columbia UP, 2010) 70–90, 76.

[62] ibid, 77.

[63] House of Commons Select Committee, *The Influence of the Pharmaceutical Industry* Fourth Report of Session 2004–05 para 165.

required to avoid breaching the regulations which prohibit DTC advertising, although it does not specify exactly what 'particular care' should entail.

There have, perhaps unsurprisingly, been instances of unbranded disease awareness campaigns taking place at the same time as branded promotions to doctors of a new product. In 2003, for example, Novartis ran a disease awareness campaign which was intended to encourage the public to visit their doctor to ask about fungal nail infections:

> Over 1,000,000 people in the UK suffer from a fungal nail infection . . . The infection can spread to other nails, other parts of your body and to other people, and it won't go away without effective treatment from your GP. . . . Please note, although it may be possible to buy treatments for fungal nail infection over-the-counter at your pharmacy, the most effective ones are only available from your doctor.[64]

This campaign did not mention by name one of the only prescription drugs available to treat fungal nail infections: terbinafine (brand name Lamisil), manufactured by Novartis. It is not a coincidence, however, that around the same time GPs were sent promotional literature about the use of Lamisil in the treatment of fungal nail infections.[65]

Quick et al draw attention to a 'disease awareness' campaign sponsored by Pfizer (the manufacturer of Lipitor), and launched in France at the same time as publication, in *The Lancet*, of the Anglo-Scandinavian Cardiac Outcomes Trial-Lipid Lowering Arm study, which established that atorvastatin (Lipitor) reduced the incidence of major cardiovascular events.[66] The public campaign was designed to be shocking. A print advertisement showed a corpse in a morgue, with the caption: 'A simple blood cholesterol test could have avoided this'. A television advert showed a young and apparently healthy man collapsing at a birthday party. As he is taken away in an ambulance, a voice says 'You may think you're healthy, but too much cholesterol in your blood can cause a heart attack'.

This was an unbranded campaign, but its aim was clear: to broaden the take-up of cholesterol testing and statin use. High cholesterol levels are, after all, only one factor of many that may increase the risk of cardiovascular disease. A public health campaign directed towards reducing the risk of cardiovascular disease would stress the importance of stopping smoking, eating healthily, taking regular exercise and reducing alcohol intake: it would not imply that statin use alone can prevent heart attacks in middle age.

In 2003, GlaxoSmithKline (GSK) launched an awareness campaign for 'restless legs syndrome', described as 'a little known and often misdiagnosed disorder'. The campaign claimed that restless legs syndrome affects '10 per cent of the population and that it can have as great an impact on quality of life as type 2 diabetes, hyper-

---

[64] T Jackson, 'Regulator Spells out Rules on Disease Awareness Campaigns' (2003) 326 *British Medical Journal* 1219.

[65] B Mintzes, 'Disease Mongering in Drug Promotion: Do Governments Have a Regulatory Role?' (2006) 3 *PLoS Medicine* e198.

[66] JD Quick et al, 'Ensuring Ethical Drug Promotion – Whose Responsibility?' (2003) 362 *The Lancet* 747.

tension and acute myocardial infarction'. Newspapers printed articles about the misery endured by sufferers and their partners (the urge to move one's legs is particularly acute at night), and often mentioned that a treatment – ropinirole (brand name Requip) – was awaiting a licence for the condition.[67] Articles commonly provided a link to the Restless Legs Syndrome Foundation website for more information, without mentioning that this is funded by GSK.[68]

In addition to promoting awareness of specific conditions, disease awareness campaigns can serve a broader purpose of simply fixing in the public's mind the idea that it is a good idea to visit to your GP if you have *any* undiagnosed symptoms. The message that treatment is available for a wide range of conditions is a way of tapping into what a leaked pharmaceutical company document described as the 'missing millions' – in the UK this is the estimated two million citizens who do not currently present to their GP or take prescription medication – and who therefore represent a significant marketing opportunity.[69]

III Patient Groups

The pharmaceutical industry also attempts to influence prescribing practices by funding and supporting patient groups. Patient groups are often charities, in need of funding, and without donations from industry many of them might not be economically sustainable. It has, therefore, been argued that industry collaboration with patient groups can be a 'win-win-win' situation:

> First, patients become informed; second, advocacy groups can get help with fundraising and developing business plans from pharma companies; and lastly, pharma companies can get advocacy quotes in a launch press release praising new patient therapies.[70]

The HIV/AIDS pandemic saw the rise of patient advocacy groups who lobbied for more clinical trials, faster drug approval times and increased funding for medicines. Unlike the drug companies themselves, patient groups are much more sympathetic and effective advocates of goals which are often strikingly similar to those of medicines' manufacturers.

Despite the fact that the Association of the British Pharmaceutical Industry (ABPI) Code of Practice requires companies to disclose donations to patient groups, Jones found that only around 40 per cent of its members' websites disclosed financial and in-kind support for consumer groups. In total, 488 grants were disclosed, to 246 patient groups.[71] Most companies funded between one and

---

[67] J Revill, 'Restless Legs Keep 6m Awake' *The Observer* 19 September 2004.

[68] S Woloshin and LM Schwartz, 'Giving Legs to Restless Legs: A Case Study of How the Media Helps Make People Sick' (2006) 3 *PLoS Medicine* e17.

[69] House of Commons Select Committee, n 63 above, para 253.

[70] M Durand, 'Pharma's Advocacy Dance' (2006) *Pharmaceutical Executive* 1.

[71] K Jones, 'In Whose Interest? Relationships between Health Consumer Groups and the Pharmaceutical Industry in the UK' (2008) 30 *Sociology of Health and Illness* 929–43.

10 groups, but nine companies, among them the largest in the sector, each funded 20 or more groups.

Of course, industry funding of patient groups could simply be an example of what is referred to as corporate social responsibility, whereby businesses 'put something back' into the community, often by funding philanthropic activities. The danger, however, is that industry-funded patient groups may be mobilised to lobby for the wider availability of pharmacological interventions.[72] Evidence that this may be the case comes from internal industry documents which the House of Commons Health Select Committee was told refer to patient organisations as 'ground troops' for lobbying government.[73]

There have even been cases where new patient lobbying organisations have been set up by drug companies. Biogen, which manufactures two leading drugs for the treatment of multiple sclerosis, set up *Action for Access* to lobby the NHS to provide wider access to beta-interferon treatment for multiple sclerosis, and Schering Healthcare, another beta-inteferon manufacturer, set up *MS Voice* for the same purpose. Both were shut down after the MHRA judged them to breach direct marketing prohibitions.[74]

The Rarer Cancers Forum is certainly not a 'front' organisation, but its manifesto encourages supporters to lobby Primary Care Trusts (PCTs) and Parliament to provide better access to treatment for the 50 per cent of cancer patients whose cancer is described as 'rarer', meaning it is not breast, colon, lung or prostate. Its funding comes from a long list of companies (AstraZeneca, Bayer Healthcare, Bristol-Myers Squibb Pharmaceuticals, Celgene, Idis Healthcare, GlaxoSmithKline, Merck Sharp and Dohme, Novartis Oncology, PharmaMar, Pfizer and Roche), which might stand to benefit from increased funding for cancer drugs.

Drug companies can also fund websites which are intended to provide information to patients. Breastcancer.org, for example, provides information on symptoms, diagnosis, treatments and managing day-to-day matters like nutrition and personal relationships. Its list of 'corporate partners' includes most of the major drug companies. Of course, breast cancer patients may benefit from this sort of information, and this could be a simple example of corporate social responsibility. There is, however, a risk that industry funding may influence the content of patient information websites. John Read analysed whether the content of the top 50 websites devoted to schizophrenia differed according to whether or not they were industry-funded.[75] He found that the industry-funded websites were more likely to stress bio-genetic causes, rather than psychosocial explanations, for schizophrenia. They were more likely to espouse medication as the solution; to link violence

---

[72] ibid.

[73] House of Commons Select Committee n 63 above, Ev. 139.

[74] A Herxheimer, 'Relationships between the Pharmaceutical Industry and Patients' Organizations' (2003) 326 *British Medical Journal* 1208. See also R Moynihan, 'US Seniors Group Attacks Pharmaceutical Industry "Fronts"' (2003) 326 *British Medical Journal* 351.

[75] J Read, 'Schizophrenia, Drug Companies and the Internet' (2008) 66 *Social Science and Medicine* 99–109.

to coming off medication, and 'to portray schizophrenia as a debilitating, devastating and long-term illness'.[76]

IV Public Relations

'Public relations' (PR) is a euphemistic term for marketing in disguise. A print or television advertisement is clearly and obviously intended to persuade its viewers to buy the featured product. Subject to statutory restrictions on making false or misleading claims, advertisers exercise a great deal of control over the content of adverts. PR campaigns, in contrast, target consumers and purchasers via third parties, such as the print media. Because PR relies on independent commentators to communicate the 'message', the advertiser has less control over content. This, however, is more than compensated for by the credibility of a marketing message transmitted by a trusted communicator. It has been estimated that an article in a newspaper or magazine is 10 times more likely to be trusted as a source of information than a product advertisement.[77] As David Catlett points out, 'The power of public relations often goes unnoticed because it does not call attention to itself in the same way as advertising. . . . But that is precisely why it can be so effective.'[78]

PR may be *more* effective and efficient than DTC advertising: it does not look like marketing; it is often less expensive and consumers find it more credible. Of course, just because a promotional claim is contained in a press release is not sufficient to ensure that it will not be treated as advertising and potentially breach the regulations which prohibit direct to consumer marketing. The MHRA's Blue Guide provides that:

> Press releases e.g. at the time of launch should not be used as a mechanism to promote prescription only medicines. Information on prescription only medicines which is provided to the lay press, television or radio or by press releases must be factual and non-promotional, where appropriate putting the treatment in the context of the effects of the disease. It should not encourage the general public to ask their GP to prescribe the product.

The MHRA considers that press releases should be genuinely newsworthy rather than having the intention of promoting a product. The use of brand names should be kept to a minimum and the tone and content of the press release must be factual and not sensationalised.

Specialist public relations and marketing agencies often manage this process. One of them, Ogilvy, which claims to 'represent all top ten global pharmaceutical companies', explains on its website what it can offer the industry:

---

[76] ibid.

[77] C White, 'Publish and be Pampered' (2003) 327 *British Medical Journal* 348.

[78] D Catlett 'Public Relations and its Role in Pharmaceutical Brand Building' in T Blackett and R Robins (eds), *Brand Medicine: The Role of Branding in the Pharmaceutical Industry* (Houndmills, Palgrave 2001) 130–40, 132.

On a worldwide basis, we have demonstrated our ability to generate top-tier print and broadcast media coverage. This includes generating attention for landmark publications, regulatory milestones, publicizing breaking news at major medical meetings and managing issues with products as they arise.[79]

In addition to generating media coverage, PR agencies build relationships with patient advocacy groups in order to communicate more effectively and credibly with the 'consumers' of medicines. Ogilvy's website again explains:

Advocates play an important role in healthcare communications. They lend credibility to campaigns and can help better reach the consumer on a grassroots level. Over the years, Ogilvy PR healthcare has partnered with numerous advocacy groups to ensure our messages are heard by regulators, physicians and consumers.[80]

PR communications strategies usually start with a non-branded message, intended to increase the audience's awareness of a disorder, often stressing that it is both more common and its effects more serious than the reader might have supposed. One of the first and most basic techniques of marketing is to generate a sense of need, anxiety and dissatisfaction. A key message is that something you previously regarded as merely inconvenient is in fact worthy of medical attention. This has been described by industry insiders as 'condition branding',[81] but it also looks rather like the process of disease mongering described earlier in this chapter.

The second stage is to introduce the message that treatment for this worrying and common disorder has, until recently, been inadequate, but that this is about to change with the development of a new treatment option. Moynihan et al describe a confidential draft document leaked from In Vivo Communications. It describes a three year 'medical education programme' which is intended to create the perception that irritable bowel syndrome (IBS) is a 'credible, common and concrete disease', as part of the marketing strategy for GSK's new drug to treat IBS, alosetron hydrochloride (brand name Lotronex).[82]

V The Relationship between Doctors and the Pharmaceutical Industry

A Advertising

The ban on direct advertising only applies to consumers. Pharmaceutical companies are allowed to advertise their products directly to 'persons qualified to

---

[79] www.ogilvypr.com/en/content/healthcare-more/.

[80] ibid.

[81] R Angelmar et al, 'Building Strong Condition Brands' (2007) 7 *Journal of Medical Marketing* 341–51.

[82] R Moynihan et al, 'Selling Sickness: The Pharmaceutical Industry and Disease Mongering' (2002) 324 *British Medical Journal* 886–91.

prescribe or supply' prescription drugs, the majority of whom are doctors and pharmacists. Leaving aside drugs prescribed in hospitals, 771.5 million prescriptions were dispensed by community pharmacies in 2008–9, so it is not surprising that influencing GP prescribing behaviour is a key marketing goal.[83]

There are a number of ways in which drugs companies advertise to prescribing doctors (and increasingly nurse prescribers too). Drugs companies take out advertisements in medical journals and magazines. Indeed medical journals are dependent upon income from this sort of advertising because most journals do not accept advertising from the manufacturers of consumer goods, like watches, cars or perfume.[84] It is interesting that dependency on advertising which may skew prescribing practices is believed to be ethically superior to advertising which may persuade doctors to make foolish choices about spending their *own* money on luxury products.

Regulation of this 'direct to professional' advertising takes place in two ways. First, there is self-regulation through the ABPI Code of Practice, which is drawn up in consultation with the British Medical Association (BMA), the Royal Pharmaceutical Society of Great Britain and the MHRA and is administered at arm's length by the Prescription Medicines Code of Practice Authority (PMCPA). The PMCPA monitors advertisements and other promotional materials to ensure compliance with the Code and deals with complaints. In 2009, the PMCPA received 92 complaints, 82 of which were investigated (some were withdrawn or found to lie outside the scope of the Code). A breach was found to have occurred in 62 cases (75 per cent). Most complaints were made by doctors, but a significant proportion (20 per cent) came from other pharmaceutical companies, concerned about their competitors' activities.

If the PMCPA judges that the Code has been breached, the company must provide both an undertaking that the activity found to be in breach has ceased, giving details of the action taken, and an assurance that all possible steps have been taken to avoid a similar breach in the future. In some cases, the company can be required to issue a corrective statement and, in the most serious cases, suspension or expulsion from membership of the ABPI is possible. Details of all PMCPA investigations and their outcomes are published on their website.[85]

Second, the MHRA has a role in ensuring that advertising complies with the legal restrictions in the Medicines Act, the Medicines (Advertising) Regulations 1994 and the Medicines (Monitoring of Advertising) Regulations 1994, as amended. It issues the regularly updated *Blue Guide* to advertising and promotion of medicines in the UK, in order to explain the regulations' requirements and to provide additional clarification on interpretation. The MHRA also produces specific guidance notes, an example would be the guidance on disease awareness campaigns, considered above.

---

[83] NHS Information Centre, *General Pharmaceutical Services in England 1999–2000 to 2008–09* (NHS Information Centre, 2009).

[84] A Fugh-Berman, K Alladin, and J Chow, 'Advertising in Medical Journals: Should Current Practices Change?' (2006) 3 *PLoS Medicine* e130.

[85] www.pmcpa.org.uk/?q=completedcases.

The Monitoring Regulations permit the MHRA to require sight of advertisements prior to issue, and it does this – generally for no more than six months – where there has previously been a breach of regulations; where a product has been reclassified, and, perhaps most significantly, whenever a new active substance is being advertised for the first time. In 2008–09 the MHRA vetted advertising prior to issue for 55 medicines.

The MHRA also monitors published advertising materials to check compliance and it handles complaints about medicines' advertising, again publishing the results of its investigations on its website, and taking enforcement action against the producers of non-compliant materials. The MHRA can compel the publication of a corrective statement where advertising has been found to be in breach of the Regulations. This happened only twice in 2008–09. Since breach of most of the Regulations is a criminal offence, it can also consider prosecution. In 2007, for example, Martin Simon Hickman, who ran an illegal online pharmacy, was jailed for a number of offences including selling unlicensed and counterfeit medicines and advertising Viagra.[86]

Because the Regulations prohibit the advertising of unlicensed medicinal products, advertising a new medicine to doctors before it has received a marketing authorisation is unlawful. Under regulation 3A of the Medicines (Advertising) Regulations 1994, as amended, any advertisement for a medicinal product must:

- comply with the particulars listed in the summary of product characteristics (SPC) (this makes it unlawful to promote 'off-label' use);
- encourage rational use by presenting the medicine objectively and without exaggerating its qualities; and
- not be misleading.

Schedule 2 to these Regulations sets out a number of pieces of information which must be included in any advertisement: it must specify one or more of the licensed indications and give information about dosage and method of use. It is not necessary to reproduce all of the information contained in the patient information leaflet verbatim, but a summary of the medicine's side effects, any necessary precautions and contraindications is required, as is the product name and licence number and a list of its active ingredients. Advertising which states or implies that a product is 'safe' is unacceptable, since no medicine can be expected to be 100 per cent safe. On the other hand, claims that a drug is well-tolerated or has a well-established safety profile are acceptable, provided they are supported by evidence.

In practice, the information contained in journal advertisements for drugs is often incomplete, most commonly it fails to include accurate data about risks and side effects. One review of 109 full-page pharmaceutical advertisements found that if a physician relied only on the information in these advertisements, 44 per cent of them would lead to improper prescribing.[87]

---

[86] N Keeling, 'Viagra Empire Run from Prison' *Manchester Evening News* 29 May 2007.
[87] MS Wilkes, BH Doblin, and MF Shapiro, 'Pharmaceutical Advertisements in Leading Medical Journals: Experts' Assessments' (1992) 116 *Annals of Internal Medicine* 912–19.

Although doctors often claim not to be influenced by advertisements, it would seem odd for drug companies to waste money on them if they did not work. Doctors may be right that they do not make prescribing decisions based exclusively on advertisements in medical journals, but they are wrong if they think that that is how this sort of advertising functions. An advertisement for a medicine will seldom be a doctor's first or only exposure to a product; they are instead an 'adjunctive influence . . . designed to reinforce other promotional efforts'.[88] And the evidence suggests that doctors *are* influenced by advertisements,[89] and that they can lead them to prescribe less appropriately and more expensively.[90] Advertising to doctors can be an especially cost-effective form of print advertising: newspaper and magazine advertisements aimed at individual consumers will have to reach multiple consumers in order to generate multiple purchases. In contrast, *one* influenced doctor may write hundreds of prescriptions for the advertised product.

In addition to direct advertising, in the UK there are approximately 8,000 drug company representatives who visit GP surgeries to provide information about medicines to doctors. They are essentially salesmen and women, but to many doctors they are also one of the principal sources of information about new drugs.[91] 'Drug reps', as they are known, are often young, good-looking, well-groomed and friendly. As with other salesmen and women, the first task is to get a 'foot in the door', and to this end, they will commonly bring cakes or other 'treats' for overworked and underpaid reception staff.

Drug representatives are permitted to hand out free samples of a medicine, in order to give prescribers experience in dealing with it, but this is expected to be done only in exceptional circumstances. The *Blue Guide* specifies that samples should be supplied only in response to a written request and that any one recipient must receive a limited number of samples in any one year, which the most recent version of the ABPI Code of Practice sets at 10.[92]

In the US, sales representatives' use of free samples is more common. Because doctors can use these samples to treat their poorer or uninsured patients, the distribution of free samples is popular with doctors and patients alike. They are, however, a marketing technique, designed to persuade doctors of the benefits of a new medicine, so that they are more likely to prescribe it to patients who are insured or able to pay the full price. The apparent generosity of handing out free samples may also function in the same way as the gift-giving considered in the next section, by creating subconscious feelings of indebtedness.

Sales representatives must not promote potential 'off-label' uses of a medicine. Of course, hinting that a medicine might have uses beyond those specified in its

---

[88] Fugh-Berman et al n 84 above.

[89] TJ Wang, JC Ausiello and RS Stafford, 'Trends in Antihypertensive Drug Advertising 1985–1996' (1999) 99 *Circulation* 2055–57.

[90] N Othman, A Vitry and EE Roughead 'Quality of Pharmaceutical Advertisements in Medical Journals: A Systematic Review' (2009) 4 *PLoS Medicine* e6350.

[91] House of Commons Select Committee (2004–05) n 63 above para 77.

[92] Association of the British Pharmaceutical Industry *Code of Practice* (ABPI, 2011) cl 17.2.

marketing authorisation could be extremely lucrative, since it is a simple way to increase the potential market for a new drug, without having to carry out expensive clinical trials in order to prove to the satisfaction of the regulator that the drug is efficacious for this new indication. In recent years, there have been a number of cases in the United States where drug companies have been fined for this sort of off-label marketing. Olanzapine (brand name Zyprexa) was licensed for use in the treatment of acute and long-term bipolar disorder and schizophrenia. Eli Lilly initially denied allegations that its sales representatives had marketed Zyprexa to primary care physicians as a treatment for dementia, for which it was not licensed, and for the treatment of patients who did not meet the full diagnostic criteria for schizophrenia and bipolar disorder, but who suffered from what was described as 'complicated mood'.[93] Subsequently, Eli Lilly admitted that it had been guilty of promoting Zyprexa for unlicensed indications, and agreed to pay a criminal fine of $515 million. A year later, a subsidiary of Pfizer agreed to pay $1.3 billion in criminal fines for systematically promoting off-label use of Bextra, its COX-2 inhibitor, to physicians.[94]

It could be argued that part of the problem lies with doctors' almost unfettered clinical discretion to prescribe drugs off-label, discussed further in chapter four. When a patient has exhausted all of the licensed treatment options, it may be acceptable for their doctors to try a drug which has not been licensed to treat their condition, if they have some grounds for thinking it might work. But this should be exceptional, given that the evidence base will often be no more than anecdotal. In addition, patients should have the right to know if their doctor is proposing to prescribe a medicine for an unlicensed indication. Indeed it is hard to see how a patient gives informed consent to taking a medicine unless they are told that there is no robust evidence that it is either safe or effective for patients with their condition.

B Gifts and Sponsorship

In *Good Medical Practice*, its core guidance to doctors, the General Medical Council advises doctors that:

> If you have financial or commercial interests in organisations providing healthcare or in pharmaceutical or other biomedical companies, these interests must not affect the way you prescribe for, treat or refer patients.[95]

There is nevertheless a long history of drug companies offering gifts, hospitality, travel and other perks to doctors. Mike Shooter, then President of the Royal College of Psychiatrists, explained the problem particularly well:

---

[93] GI Spielmans, 'The Promotion of Olanzapine in Primary Care: An Examination of Internal Industry Documents' (2009) 69 *Social Science and Medicine* 14–20.

[94] KB O'Reilly, 'Pfizer Pays Record $2.3 Billion in Off-Label Drug Marketing Settlement' *American Medical News* 14 September 2009.

[95] General Medical Council, *Good Medical Practice* (GMC, 2006) para 75.

Personal enticements – the mugs, pens and desk-top toys – are usually accepted unwittingly or without a second thought as the psychiatrist tours the trade stands; yet it all helps to advertise the company's products. Walking into some consultants' rooms is like entering a shrine to one firm or another, and one has to ask what message that conveys to patients about the objectivity of the advice they are about to be offered. Other enticements - free holidays, free trips to conferences and first-class travel – are more blatant both in hand-out and receipt. I cannot be the only person to be sickened by the sight of parties of psychiatrists standing at the airport desk with so many perks about them that they might as well have the name of the company tattooed across their foreheads.[96]

Regulation 21(1) of the Medicines (Advertising) Regulations 1994, as amended, provides that:

> where relevant medicinal products are being promoted to persons qualified to prescribe or supply relevant medicinal products, no person shall supply, offer or promise to such persons any gift, pecuniary advantage or benefit in kind, unless it is inexpensive and relevant to the practice of medicine or pharmacy.

Given that breach of regulation 21(1) is a criminal offence, it is clearly important to know what counts as 'inexpensive' and 'relevant to the practice of medicine or pharmacy'. The *Blue Guide* specifies that 'inexpensive' means worth less than £6 (a figure which can be regularly updated) and that these inexpensive gifts will be 'relevant' if they have a clear business use: examples given are pens, notepads, calculators, computer accessories, diaries, calendars, surgical gloves, tissues and coffee mugs.

Regulation 21(1) does not prevent the offer of hospitality at events purely for professional or scientific purposes under the conditions laid down under regulation 21(2), which include that the hospitality should be strictly limited to the main objective of the meeting and should not be offered to persons who are not health professionals, such as the healthcare professional's partner or children. Regulation 21(3) provides that hospitality can also be offered to health professionals at meetings or events held to promote medicines, provided it is strictly limited to the main purpose of the meeting or event. Hospitality should be 'at a reasonable level,' although clearly that simply begs the question of what counts as a reasonable (or indeed unreasonable) level of hospitality.

Interestingly, the rules in the ABPI's Code of Practice are more restrictive than the *Blue Guide*. From January 2011, it has specified that only small gifts that can be passed on and used by patients are allowed. Pens and notebooks bearing a company but not a medicine's name can still be provided at conferences and workshops. Hospitality must only be offered if it is in connection with a scientific meeting. The Code spells out in considerable detail what is and is not acceptable, for example:

> Many items given as promotional aids in the past are no longer acceptable. These include coffee mugs, stationery, computer accessories such as memory sticks, diaries, calendars

---

[96] M Shooter, 'Dancing with the Devil? A Personal View of Psychiatry's Relationships with the Pharmaceutical Industry' (2005) 29 *Psychiatric Bulletin* 81–83.

and the like . . . Items such as toys and puzzles intended for children to play with may no longer be provided. . . . A story-book for young patients about a product or a disease could be provided for relevant patients.[97]

C Continuing Medical Education

As part of the move to ensure that qualification to practice as a doctor is not something that is examined once, at the moment of registration at the start of their career, doctors are now required to continue their medical education after they have qualified. This means that they must take part in a set number of accredited activities each year, such as attending training days or workshops. More than half of the costs of this continuing medical education have historically come from the pharmaceutical industry.[98]

Despite the fact that this sponsorship has generally come from companies' *marketing* budgets, in the past many doctors viewed industry funding of educational events and materials as relatively unproblematic.[99] This view seems to be changing. In 2009, the Royal College of Physicians' working party recommended that all industry funding of continuing education should cease. It recommended that the ABPI and its members could establish a pooled fund to invest in medical education in order to 'unlink' funding from specific companies and reduce the perception and possibility of commercial influence and bias. The latest version of the ABPI Code of Practice does not go this far, however, and simply states that continuing professional education should comply with the Code's provisions on hospitality, that is, events must be held in appropriate venues, and any hospitality offered should be secondary to the main purpose of the event.[100] An all-expenses-paid continuing professional development course which took place over a long weekend at a luxury golf resort, for example, would not be appropriate, whereas offering a sandwich lunch to attendees at an educational event in a teaching hospital would, according to the Code, be unproblematic.

Steinman et al analysed 8000 pages of documents released following litigation in the US concerning the promotion of gabapentin (brand name Neurontin) in order to track the scope of Pfizer's marketing campaign.[101] Interestingly, it found that one strategy was to fund educational programmes through 'unrestricted educational grants' to for-profit medical education companies. Because the grants were unrestricted, control over the content of these programmes was formally relinquished. On the other hand, the advantage to Pfizer was that these programmes did not therefore count as marketing. In addition to this making the

---

[97] ABPI Code of Practice n 92 above, cl 18.

[98] House of Commons Select Committee n 63 above, para 73.

[99] N Hawkes, 'Continuing Medical Education: What Price Education?' (2008) 337 *British Medical Journal* a2333.

[100] ABPI Code of Practice n 92 above, cl 19.1.

[101] MA Steinman et al, 'The Promotion of Gabapentin: An Analysis of Internal Industry Documents' (2006) 145 *Annals of Internal Medicine* 284–97.

events more credible with doctors, this also enabled the medical education companies to discuss off-label uses of gabapentin, which would not have been permissible if this had been categorised as explicitly promotional activity. One of the disclosed company documents stated that educational programmes were a tactic to support 'growth opportunity' in off-label use.

There is a fundamental conflict between the profit imperative of pharmaceutical companies and the goals of medical education. It is not realistic to expect the manufacturer of a drug who stands to make a fortune if it is a success, and to lose a fortune if it is not, to be entirely objective about its risks and benefits. In contrast, in continuing medical education, doctors need neutral information about a range of treatment options, including non-drug options. It could, however, be argued that designing marketing tools which resemble the ways in which doctors learn and develop their expertise – workshops, conferences, symposia in which the keynote speakers are other doctors (albeit doctors, known as 'opinion leaders', who have been paid honoraria by the sponsoring drug company) – is an extraordinarily sophisticated and effective marketing strategy.

Using trusted 'opinion leaders' is a well-established promotional technique which is successful in much the same way as PR because it does not look like marketing. If a drugs company's message can be delivered by a trusted, independent expert, it will have much more impact than if it comes from a sales representative or an advertisement. Doctors are persuaded to act as 'key opinion leaders' because it is flattering to be asked and the honoraria, or speaking fees, may be tempting. The ABPI Code of Practice insists that compensation for consultants' services must be 'reasonable' and must be declared,[102] neither of which prevents the payment of considerable sums of money to senior doctors in return for chairing meetings and speaking at them. In an interesting new twist, there is evidence that *patients* too are sometimes credible authorities whose influence over others is being targeted by drug companies. Patients who have an influential online presence – through social networking sites or from blogging – can be an especially valuable way to communicate with other patients about the merits of a new drug.

D The Size of the Gift Makes a Difference

One of the most interesting assumptions behind the regulation of gifts and sponsorship is that the size of a gift makes a difference to the degree of influence it exerts over the beneficiary.[103] Unlike generous payments and lavish hospitality, the provision of small gifts, which can be used by patients, or pens and note pads handed out at meetings and modest hospitality are assumed to be unproblematic.

---

[102] ABPI Code of Practice n 92 above, cl 20.
[103] TA Brennan et al, 'Health Industry Practices that Create Conflicts of Interest: A Policy Proposal for Academic Medical Centers' (2006) 295 *Journal of the American Medical Association* 429. See also American Medical Association, *Ethical Opinion E-8.061, Gifts to Physicians from Industry* (AMA, 2007); E Wager, 'How to Dance with Porcupines: Rules and Guidelines on Doctor's Relations With Drug Companies' (2003) 326 *British Medical Journal* 1196.

However, this assumption fails to take into account social science evidence about the obligations which are subconsciously created by gift-giving.[104]

Due to the fact that it is generally perceived to be rude to reject kind gestures, it is relatively easy to impose a sense of indebtedness on recipients, and thus influence their subsequent actions. The powerful impulse people experience to reciprocate whenever they receive a gift, however small, has even been said to operate at the neurobiological level,[105] engaging 'the brain's reward and decision-making circuitry' and operating 'below the detection and overt control of higher cognition'.[106]

One of the reasons doctors are so resistant to allegations of bias is that they wish to refute any suggestion that they would *consciously* and *deliberately* decide to prescribe a particular medicine because they had received gifts or other benefits from its manufacturer. As Bert Spilker memorably put it, critics of gifts to doctors 'fear that physicians are so weak and lacking in integrity that they would "sell their souls" for a pack of M&M candies and a few sandwiches and doughnuts.'[107] And of course it is true that a doctor is not going to deliberately make prescribing decisions out of their profound gratitude for a new pencil or a tasty lunch. But this is to misunderstand how bias works. The whole point is that it is *not* deliberate.

Succumbing to a conflict of interest is not the preserve of a 'few bad apples', rather it is much more likely to be completely unintentional.[108] Social science research into the effects of conflicts of interest indicates that individuals are invariably *unaware* that 'their judgments are subject to an unconscious and unintentional self-serving bias'.[109] Even when individuals with conflicts of interest are striving to be objective, they unwittingly weigh evidence in a biased way. This means that, while admirable, individual doctors' commitment to objectivity and professionalism is not sufficient to eliminate the effects of bias. As Dana and Loewenstein put it, 'by subtly affecting the way the receiver evaluates claims made by the gift giver, small gifts may be surprisingly influential'.[110]

In short, even very small gifts create both an expectation of reciprocity and the potential for subconscious bias, and the evidence that they influence prescribing behaviour is overwhelming.[111] There is clear evidence that doctors who receive benefits from pharmaceutical companies, and who listen to their sales representa-

---

[104] D Katz, AL Caplan and JF Merz, 'All Gifts Large and Small: Toward an Understanding of the Ethics of Pharmaceutical Industry Gift-Giving' (2003) 3 *American Journal of Bioethics* 39–46.

[105] Association of American Medical Colleges and Baylor College of Medicine, Department of Neuroscience and Computational Psychiatry Unit, *The Scientific Basis of Influence and Reciprocity: A Symposium* (Association of American Medical Colleges, 2007).

[106] Association of American Medical Colleges, *Industry Funding of Medical Education Report of an AAMC Task Force* (AMA, 2008).

[107] B Spilker, 'The Risks and Benefits of a Pack of M&Ms' (2002) 21 *Health Affairs* 543–44.

[108] DM Cain and AS Detsky, 'Everyone's a Little Bit Biased (Even Physicians)' (2008) 299 *Journal of the American Medical Association* 2893–95.

[109] J Dana and G Loewenstein, 'A Social Science Perspective on Gifts to Physicians from Industry' (2003) 90 *Journal of the American Medical Association* 252–55.

[110] ibid.

[111] C Elliot, 'The Drug Pushers' (2006) 297 *The Atlantic Monthly* 82–93; AS Brett, W Burr and J Moloo, 'Are Gifts from Pharmaceutical Companies Ethically Problematic? A Survey of Physicians' (2003) 163 *Archives of Internal Medicine* 2213–18.

tives' sales pitches, are more likely to prescribe its products.[112] In a meta-analysis of 538 studies, Wazana found conclusive evidence that attending sponsored continuing medical education events and accepting funding for travel or accommodation were associated with increased prescription rates of the sponsor's medication, and that attending presentations given by pharmaceutical industry speakers was associated with subsequent non-rational prescribing.[113]

The latest version of the ABPI Code is a step in the right direction: no longer will doctors' surgeries be full of mugs and post-it notes emblazoned with advertisements for drugs. But the Code does not go so far as to ban the provision of all branded products to doctors, nor does it eliminate industry-funded educational provision. It is perhaps time to recognize that banning doctors from receiving any benefits at all from companies who profit from their prescribing behaviour is the only way to eliminate subconsciously biased prescribing decisions.

E Doctors' Claims not to be Influenced

In spite of the weight of evidence that the marketing of medicines to doctors is effective, doctors are commonly convinced that they are *not* influenced by the industry's marketing techniques. Doctors often believe themselves to be too intelligent to fall for something as crass as advertising. Interestingly, however, Chren found that while most doctors (61 per cent) were certain that they themselves were immune to the marketing efforts of pharmaceutical companies, the vast majority (84 per cent) believed that their colleagues *were* influenced.[114] As Carl Elliott explains:

> The pharmaceutical industry has managed this debate skillfully, pouring vast resources into gifts for doctors while simultaneously reassuring them that their integrity prevents them from being influenced.[115]

But doctors' perceived integrity and imperviousness to outside influences is not sufficient. If doctors really were immune to its promotional activities, it is hard to see why the pharmaceutical industry would spend so much money on them.

In their research into doctors' relationships with drug companies, Doran et al categorised their interviewees into three 'types' depending on their interactions with the pharmaceutical industry: avoiders (10 per cent), confident engagers (50 per cent) and ambivalent engagers (40 per cent).[116] Avoiders thought the very

[112] C Watkins et al, 'Characteristics of General Practitioners who Frequently See Drug Industry Representatives: National Cross Sectional Study' (2003) 326 *British Medical Journal* 1178–79.

[113] A Wazana, 'Physicians and the Pharmaceutical Industry: Is a Gift Ever Just a Gift?' (2000) 283 *Journal of the American Medical Association* 373–80.

[114] M Chren, 'Interactions between Physicians and Drug Company Representatives' (1999) 107 *American Journal of Medicine* 182–83.

[115] Eliott n 111.

[116] E Doran et al, 'Empirical Uncertainty and Moral Contest: A Qualitative Analysis of the Relationship between Medical Specialists and the Pharmaceutical Industry in Australia' (2006) 62 *Social Science and Medicine* 1510–19.

fact that the intention of marketing was to change their clinical practice by influencing their prescribing decisions was enough to render any contact with drug companies problematic. Aware of the possibility of subliminal influence, avoiders decided it was preferable to have no contact at all: one of their interviewees stated: 'Advertising affects people who are arrogant enough to think it doesn't . . . which I think involves most of the medical profession'.[117]

Confident engagers regarded the perks provided by the drugs companies as fair compensation for their time, and commonly took the view that awareness of any potential conflict of interest enabled them to take steps to counteract it. In between lay the ambivalent engagers who were aware of the risks of exposure to promotional activities, but had decided the benefits outweighed the dangers.

In 1998, Stelfox et al studied 70 articles which appeared in the six months following publication of a meta-analysis which had suggested a link between calcium-channel antagonists and heart disease, in order to find out whether there was an association between authors' published positions on the safety of calcium-channel antagonists and their financial relationships with the pharmaceutical industry.[118] Their results were striking: 96 per cent of the supportive authors had financial relationships with manufacturers of calcium-channel antagonists, compared with 60 per cent of the neutral authors and 37 per cent of the critical authors. In only two of the 70 articles were the authors' potential conflicts of interest disclosed. Stelfox et al also investigated whether the supportive authors were more likely to have financial relationships with *other* pharmaceutical companies, and again the results were unambiguous: 100 per cent of the supportive authors, as compared with 67 per cent of the neutral authors and 43 per cent of the critical authors, had financial relationships with at least one pharmaceutical manufacturer.[119]

If doctors prescribe drugs that they otherwise would not as a result of drugs companies' successful marketing campaigns, it is important to remember that the costs will be borne by patients and by the NHS. No drug is risk-free, and so prescribing more frequently creates safety risks for patients who may suffer adverse drug reactions (ADRs). Inappropriate prescribing will impose costs on the NHS: money will be wasted on unnecessary medicines and on treating avoidable ADRs. This makes doctors' claims to be impervious to advertising especially troubling: if I am foolish enough to believe an advertiser's claim that spraying myself with a perfumed body spray will make me irresistible to members of the opposite sex, the only person who loses out when my purchase turns out to have been a waste of money is me. In contrast, a doctor's marketing-influenced decision to prescribe an expensive new drug has no costs for the doctor herself, but may be risky for patients and unnecessarily expensive for the NHS.

Disclosure, as we saw in chapter two, is regarded as one way to 'manage' potential conflicts of interest. From January 2011, the ABPI Code has required drug

---

[117] ibid.
[118] HT Stelfox et al, 'Conflict of Interest in the Debate over Calcium-Channel Antagonists (1998) 338 *New England Journal of Medicine* 101–16.
[119] ibid.

companies to declare all payments to doctors, including speaker fees, payments for membership of advisory boards and for consultancy and sponsorship for attendance at meetings. It could, however, be argued that disclosing receipt of benefits is not sufficient to stop it influencing prescribing behaviour. We would not allow judges to receive even very small gifts from people who are due to appear before them, and perhaps it is time to similarly ban drugs companies from giving any financial or other benefits to doctors.

VI Conclusion

It should not be surprising that the pharmaceutical industry wants to promote its products to prescribing doctors and to consumers. Prescribing decisions, however, are unlike foolish decisions to buy expensive, branded perfumes and face creams. Prescription drugs are, by definition, not safe enough for self-medication to be acceptable. Inappropriate prescriptions may be risky for patients, and they also impose unnecessary costs on the NHS. It is therefore important that the decision to prescribe a medicine is grounded in a doctor's judgement that, based on objective evidence of safety and efficacy, the medicine is clinically indicated for a particular patient. Some marketing may just raise awareness amongst doctors and patients, and therefore might help to meet previously unmet clinical needs. But where marketing skews prescribing decisions – and the evidence that it does is overwhelming – the costs are borne by individual patients and by the NHS, while the profits accrue to the drug companies.

One of the most straightforward reforms would be to institute a ban on direct funding of continuing medical education, patient groups and disease awareness campaigns. In all three cases, the better model would be for drug companies to be allowed to contribute to pooled funds. In the case of education, drug company money could be donated to a fund which is used to subsidise workshops and courses, but where a drug company is not allowed to be an identifiable funder of an individual event, which undoubtedly represents a prime opportunity for advertising and product promotion.

The same system might apply to patient groups. Drug companies could be allowed to contribute to a centrally administered pooled fund, to which patient groups could apply for resources – in the same way as they might apply for funds from other charitable foundations. Drug companies would not then be allowed to choose specific patient groups to fund, according to whether they might be persuaded to lobby for their funder's medicine. Disease awareness campaigns too could be the preserve only of the Department of Health. If a drug company wishes to contribute to disease awareness funding – as part of their corporate social responsibility agenda – then again they should be able to do so, but only if their funds are not tied to indirect promotion of their products.

Of course, it remains to be seen whether drug companies would enthusiastically embrace a pooled approach to the funding of doctors' education, patient groups and disease awareness campaigns. If funding were to cease, this might offer evidence that unbranded funding is of no interest to the marketing departments of pharmaceutical companies, but it might also leave a hole in the funding of valuable activities like patient support groups and continuing medical education. That, however, is not a good reason to leave these indirect marketing strategies unregulated. Other professions have to cover the cost of their own continuing professional education, and if industry-funded continuing education is acknowledged to be marketing in disguise, patients and the NHS would benefit if doctors' educational resources ceased to be tied to the promotion of drugs.

More difficult still is the problem of PR, and the extraordinary effectiveness of promotional activities that can enlist journalists as vectors for what is essentially a marketing message. It is not just pharmaceutical companies who engage in sophisticated PR exercises. Charities, public bodies and other companies understand that providing busy journalists with pre-packaged 'stories' is an easy way to get their preferred message across in a credible and accessible format. While the MHRA can continue to monitor the media to try to detect illicit cases of advertising, in practice, the PR approach to the marketing of prescription medicines is likely to prove difficult, if not impossible, to control. It might then be important to educate the public to be as wary about relying on media reports as they are of advertisements, and to ensure that the messages contained in the media are challenged and scrutinised in order to detect cases when news stories are simply adverts in disguise.

6

Funding and Access to Medicines in the UK

I N THIS CHAPTER, the focus is on the funding of prescription medicines.
Medicines which are available on the general sale list, such as paracetamol or
ibuprofen, are generally relatively cheap. Some pharmacy-available medicines
are more expensive: the morning-after pill, for example, costs around £20, but it
is also available free of charge on prescription and so consumers who decide to
purchase it for themselves are paying for the greater convenience of obtaining it
over-the-counter.

It is in relation to prescription medicines that funding becomes an exceptionally
complex and important issue, both in the United Kingdom and worldwide. This
chapter will address the question of funding and access to medicines within the
UK. It is, however, important to acknowledge that funding of, and access to medicines is an issue of global importance, especially in low-income countries, and
especially in relation to neglected diseases. As a result, the following chapter will
briefly discuss questions of access to medicines in parts of the world where they
may be desperately needed, but essentially unaffordable.

In 2009, it was estimated that the NHS spent a total of £11.9 billion on drugs,[1]
which is more than £32.6 million every day. Generic medicines are often relatively
inexpensive, whereas new branded medicines can cost a great deal of money. New
cancer drugs, in particular, are often particularly expensive: for example lapatinib
(brand name Tyverb) used in combination with capecitabine (Xeloda) for the
treatment of advanced or metastatic HER2-positive breast cancer, costs over
£25,000 per patient per year. The key challenge for regulation is then to ensure that
patients benefit from access to effective medicines while containing costs within
the NHS. This might be done in a number of ways: from explicit rationing to simply reducing wastage (many of us have left-over prescription drugs in our bath-
room cabinets and this represents a waste of NHS resources estimated to amount
to about £800 million per year[2]).

This chapter begins by briefly considering the reasons why some prescription
medicines are so expensive. It then turns to describe the principal mechanism
through which the costs of medicines have been controlled in the UK, namely the

---

[1] Simon Burns MP, Hansard HC Deb, 25 October 2010, c124W.
[2] National Audit Office, *Prescribing Costs in Primary Care: Report by the Comptroller and Auditor General* (NAO, 2007).

Pharmaceutical Price Regulation Scheme. The coalition government has announced that this Scheme, which limits the profits pharmaceutical companies can make, will be replaced from January 2014 by what is known as value-based pricing, which is intended to ensure that the price of a medicine reflects its value to patients.

Even with a regulated price structure, of whatever sort, the unrestricted pre-scribing of every potentially beneficial medicine would be unaffordable for the NHS, and so it is also important to consider how NHS resources are rationed. The Labour government set up the National Institute for health and Clinical Excellence (NICE) in 1999, in order to ensure that rationing decisions were consistent across England and Wales, and grounded in objective evidence of cost-effectiveness. The Scottish Medicines Consortium (SMC) does not have the same 'teeth' as NICE and simply makes recommendations to Health Boards, which are still free to make their own decisions about the availability of new medicines. In Wales, the All Wales Medicines Strategy Group (AWMSG) gives advice on the prescribing of non-NICE appraised drugs for Wales.

Not every medicine is appraised by NICE or the SMC or AWMSG, and patients can apply to have non-approved medicines funded exceptionally by their local Primary Care Trust (PCT) via the 'exceptional case review' process. Where a patient has had their application for exceptional funding turned down, it is then possible for them to apply for judicial review of this decision, or, if they can afford it, to 'top-up' their care by paying for the expensive medicine themselves or pur-chasing insurance for that purpose.

In 2010, along with its controversial reorganisation of the NHS to give general practitioners and GP consortia a greater role in the commissioning of services, the coalition government committed itself to making a number of important changes in the way drugs would be funded in the future. In addition to value-based pricing, it announced the setting up of a new cancer drugs fund (of £200 million per year), and plans to alter the role of NICE in decisions about the funding of medicines within the NHS. Initially, the government had suggested that it would simply remove NICE's powers to decide on a drug's availability within the NHS, but in its consultation on the move to value-based pricing, it envisages a role for NICE, which mainly involves providing advice, rather than making final judgements. Even with the introduction of value-based pricing, removing centrally imposed limits upon doctors' ability to prescribe extremely expensive drugs may lead to a new postcode lottery and might even prove to be unaffordable. The Health Secretary Andrew Lansley has promised that 'we will move to an NHS where patients will be confident that, where their clinicians believe a particular drug is the right and most effective one for them, then the NHS will be able to provide it for them', suggesting that rationing of expensive medicines is no longer necessary, and clinical effectiveness can plausibly be the only relevant criteria.[3] Whether this is, in practice, compatible with a universal health service that is free at the point of use, remains to be seen.

[3] DJ Webb, 'Value-Based Medicine Pricing: NICE Work?' (2011) 377 *The Lancet* 1552–53.

I The Costs of Prescription Medicines

The market in medicines is not an entirely free one. One of the ways in which it is restricted is by awarding intellectual property rights to the manufacturer of any new medicine which is sufficiently innovative to qualify for patent protection.[4] Once a manufacturer has applied for, and been granted, a patent for a novel chemical compound, it has the right to prevent others from making, using, importing or selling the invention without permission for 20 years, after which time patent protection will be lost and other manufacturers can make and sell generic versions of the same medicinal product.

As described in chapter three, it is important to remember that the manufacturer will generally not enjoy 20 years of 'on the market' patent protection. It is common for as much as 10 years of patent protection to expire while the product is being tested, and hence manufacturers may in practice enjoy the exclusive right to sell the medicine for 10 years rather than 20. This means that the research and development (R&D) costs of the new medicine must be recouped, and any profits made, during the 10 years or so when the manufacturer has the exclusive right to sell it. If it costs $800 million to develop a new medicine,[5] it is clear that this investment will be justifiable only if there can be a considerable mark-up on the medicine during the 10 years when its developer is able to profit from it.

The patent system undoubtedly creates incentives towards developing drugs which are capable of making a great deal of money during this limited profit 'window'. This, as discussed in chapter three, distorts research priorities away from the development of entirely new (and therefore risky) compounds, and away from the development of treatments for rare conditions (where the market is always going to be small), towards the development of 'me-too' drugs for conditions, like high blood pressure, where the potential market is enormous.

A further way in which the market for prescription medicines is not really like other markets is that while the choice of which medicine to prescribe is made by the patient's doctor, the purchaser will generally be the NHS. This has a number of consequences. First, because the NHS is – with the exception of the tiny proportion of private prescriptions – a monopoly purchaser, it has been able to exert some pressure on the prices charged by pharmaceutical companies. Second, doctors may be relatively insensitive to, or even unaware of price when deciding upon what medicines to prescribe. In 2002, a joint study by the Department of Health and the Association of the British Pharmaceutical Industry (ABPI) investigated GPs' knowledge of the relative prices of drugs within five therapeutic classes. Doctors were right about 50 per cent of the time, which is consistent with simply guessing.[6] In 2007, the Office of Fair Trading (OFT) again found that GPs' ability

---

[4] Patents Act 1977 s 1.

[5] See further, chapter 2.

[6] Office of Fair Trading, *The Pharmaceutical Price Regulation Scheme: An OFT Market Study* (OFT, 2007) para 2.48, available at www.oft.gov.uk/shared_oft/reports/comp_policy/oft885.pdf.

to rank the cost of branded drugs within six common therapeutic areas 'proved no better than chance'.[7]

For most patients, prescription medicines are 'free', and even when patients do contribute towards the costs of the medicine via the prescription charge (which applies to only 12 per cent of all prescriptions), this will seldom cover the real costs of the medicine.[8] If both prescribers and consumers of medicines are relatively insensitive to price, containing costs within the NHS may depend on finding ways to influence both the prices drugs companies are allowed to charge and doctors' prescribing behaviour.

II The Pharmaceutical Price Regulation Scheme

A What is the Pharmaceutical Price Regulation Scheme?

The Pharmaceutical Price Regulation Scheme (PPRS) was set up in 1957 to control the prices of branded, licensed medicines. It applies throughout the UK and has a number of objectives, some of which may be in tension with one another. It is intended to 'deliver value for money for the NHS by securing the provision of safe and effective medicines at reasonable prices', while at the same time promoting 'a strong and profitable pharmaceutical industry'.[9] As well as delivering certainty and predictability to both the NHS and industry,[10] it is also intended to reward innovation which may lead to the development of valuable new treatments.[11]

The PPRS is a voluntary agreement entered into by the UK Health Departments and the pharmaceutical industry, represented by its trade association the ABPI, and it is renegotiated every five years. The Scheme has two main components. First, profit controls set a maximum level for the profits that a company may earn from the supply of branded drugs to the NHS. Second, price controls place restrictions on companies' freedom to increase their prices, and price cuts are agreed whenever the Scheme is renegotiated. For example, in the latest PPRS, published in 2009, provision was made for two separate price cuts: one of 3.9 per cent in February 2009 and a further cut of 1.9 per cent in January 2010.[12] Given that the UK represents a fairly small proportion (three per cent) of the global market in drugs, it might be thought that the UK's rules on drugs pricing would be of comparatively little importance to companies whose principal market is the US, but

---

[7] ibid 23.

[8] NAO n 2 above.

[9] Department of Health, *Pharmaceutical Price Regulation Scheme 2009* (DH, 2009) paras 2.1.1 and 2.1.12.

[10] ibid para 2.1.4.

[11] ibid para 5.1.

[12] ibid para 7.3.

this would be a mistake. In fact, around 25 per cent of the global pharmaceutical market explicitly reflects or references UK prices.[13]

The effectiveness of the PPRS was evaluated by the OFT in 2007. The OFT was critical of the profits cap, on the grounds that it dulled the incentives to increase profits by producing more valuable drugs and by cutting internal costs. The maximum profit earned by a company that has produced innovative and highly effective drugs is exactly the same as that which can be earned by a company whose products are not very useful.[14] As a result, the OFT concluded that a pricing scheme that could offer incentives for innovation would lead to better outcomes both for patients and for the NHS.

The OFT also found that the UK profits cap was relatively ineffective, in part because of the global nature of the industry: verifying the 'costs' which are submitted as part of each company's annual financial return is almost impossible when these costs are distributed across many countries. In addition, because the margin of allowable profits had increased to 140 per cent over target, repayments of excess profits have, in fact, been negligible (amounting to only 0.01 per cent of revenues).[15]

In conclusion, the OFT found that the only really effective component of the PPRS was the periodic renegotiation of price cuts, and again, it found that these took no account of the value of different drugs to patients. A producer of especially beneficial medicines will have to reduce its prices by the same proportion as manufacturers of medicines that do not offer the same health benefits. Like the profits cap, this does not create an incentive towards innovation, rather it treats innovators and non-innovators alike.

The OFT was also concerned that giving companies the freedom to set initial prices, with limits on subsequent increases and negotiated future price cuts generated an incentive to set the initial price sufficiently high to compensate for the anticipated forthcoming reductions. This, they argued, has become a 'strategic game', with firms attempting to second guess the level of future price cuts when setting initial prices, and the Department of Health trying to work out the extent to which initial prices have been over-inflated when subsequently setting the level of cuts.

As a result of these criticisms, the OFT recommended abolition of the PPRS in its present form and its replacement by value-based pricing, a model which is considered in detail below. While this recommendation was not accepted by the Department of Health at the time, the most recent PPRS, published in 2009, did contain some changes, namely flexible pricing and patient access schemes, designed to ensure that prices better reflect the value of medicines.[16]

---

[13] I Kennedy, *Appraising the Value of Innovation and Other Benefits: A Short Study for NICE* (NICE, 2009) available at www.nice.org.uk/media/98F/5C/KennedyStudyFinalReport.pdf.
[14] S Thornton, 'Drug Price Reform in the UK: Debunking the Myths' (2007) 16 *Health Economics* 981–92.
[15] OFT n 6 above, para 4.34.
[16] DH n 9 above paras 6.4–6.5.

i Flexible Pricing

The 2009 PPRS provides for 'flexible pricing', which means that a company is able to increase or decrease its original list price, by a maximum of 30 per cent, in the light of new evidence of efficacy, or if a new indication emerges which increases the value the medicine offers to NHS patients. Adrian Towse explains how this works in practice:

> The pharmaceutical company would set their NHS price and offer a large discount, NICE would appraise that discounted price, the company will do more clinical trial work, and they would then have the right to go back to NICE and say 'we always thought it was better and now we have the evidence to show this, can we now withdraw our discount?'[17]

Flexible pricing necessarily depends upon there being considerable confidence in the trial results submitted as part of the application to increase prices. NICE would therefore need to be sure that it had access to *all* trial data, not just the data which the pharmaceutical company chooses to disclose in order to support its application to raise a drug's price. Currently, NICE does not have the same right as the MHRA to demand access to *all* the trial data and so it would be vitally important to ensure that an application to increase the price of a drug was not based upon cherry-picked data, in which only positive results are submitted to justify a higher price.

ii Patient Access Schemes

The most recent PPRS specified that patient access schemes should be the exception rather than the rule, but it nevertheless foresaw a role for these schemes within the NHS. The point of patient access schemes is to facilitate earlier patient access to medicines that do not meet the NICE cost-effectiveness threshold. For example, a company might offer discounts or rebates linked to patient response, or it might agree to gather further evidence, and to a price reduction if evidence of cost-effectiveness is not established.

The first such scheme specifically approved by NICE was the Velcade response scheme, incorporated into the appraisal of bortezomib (Velcade) for the treatment of multiple myeloma.[18] The agreement was that patients who have responded well after 12 weeks of treatment would have their continued treatment funded by the NHS, whereas patients who have not responded would stop taking bortezomib, and its manufacturer would refund the cost of their treatment to date, which would be about £12,000 each.

Schemes can also be privately negotiated between manufacturers and NHS suppliers. For example, following NICE's rejection of Tyverb in October 2009, its

---

[17] Quoted in N Siva, 'The Drug Price is Right – or is it?' (2009) 373 *The Lancet* 1326–27.

[18] S Williamson, 'Patient Access Schemes for High-Cost Cancer Medicines' (2010) 11 *The Lancet Oncology* 111–12.

manufacturer GlaxoSmithKline (GSK) announced that it had negotiated a scheme with 26 hospitals in which it planned to waive the cost of the first three months of each patient's treatment, on condition that the PCT pays for the treatment after that time. While this might look generous, it might also represent a sensible marketing strategy: once a group of NHS patients are taking a medicine and are happy with it, it becomes easier for the manufacturer to lobby for wider NHS availability, on grounds of fairness.[19]

Patient access schemes are extremely labour and resource intensive for the NHS: patients must be closely monitored and their responses recorded, and rebates must be specifically applied for. Chapter four discussed the importance of gathering safety and efficacy data after a drug has been licensed, in order to ensure that the drug works and has tolerable side effects not only in a specially selected group of trial participants, but also in the patient population as a whole. It could be argued that patient access schemes, in practice, devolve responsibility for gathering this sort of post-launch data to the NHS.[20] Patient access schemes, while clearly not randomised clinical trials, involve the NHS rather than the drug's manufacturer meeting the costs of gathering information about effectiveness 'in the real world', from which the manufacturer is then able to profit.

The PPRS specifies that:

> Any scheme should be operationally manageable for the NHS without unduly complex monitoring, disproportionate additional costs and bureaucracy. Any burden for the NHS should be proportionate to the benefits of the scheme for the NHS and patients.[21]

It is, however, by no means clear that all patient access schemes have, in fact, only imposed burdens on the NHS proportionate to the benefits to patients. For example, a risk sharing scheme was set up after the National Institute for Health and Clinical Excellence recommended against use of beta interferon (brand names Avonex, Betaseron, and Rebif) and glatiramer acetate for the treatment of multiple sclerosis (MS).[22] Under the scheme, patients were closely monitored, and the agreement was that prices would be reduced if patient outcomes were worse than predicted. All UK MS patients with relapsing remitting MS were eligible, and between 5000 and 7000 were expected to join. This made it a significant and expensive cohort study of effectiveness, funded by the NHS, rather than the drug company which would then be able to benefit from any evidence of efficacy. James Raftery estimates that the costs of hiring additional nurses, monitoring patients and paying for the drugs in this scheme cost the NHS approximately £50 million per year.[23]

[19] A Jack, 'GlaxoSmithKline Sidesteps NICE by Negotiating with Individual Hospitals' (2009) 339 *British Medical Journal* b4406.

[20] House of Commons Health Committee, *Top-Up Fees Fourth Report of Session 2008–09*, available at www.publications.parliament.uk/pa/cm200809/cmselect/cmhealth/194i/194i.pdf.

[21] DH n 9 above, para 6.26.

[22] NICE, *Multiple Sclerosis – Beta Interferon and Glatiramer Acetate Technology Appraisal 32* (NICE, 2002), available at www.nice.org.uk/Guidance/TA32.

[23] J Raftery, 'Multiple Sclerosis Risk Sharing Scheme: A Costly Failure' (2010) 340 *British Medical Journal* c1672.

To make matters worse in the beta interferon scheme, outcomes – if judged by the level of disability and rate of disease progression – *were* significantly worse than predicted,[24] and in fact, were worse than in untreated patients,[25] but prices were not, in fact, reduced. This was because these drugs work by preventing relapses, which is a different thing from reducing disability: treated patients may have had fewer relapses but this did not alter their disease progression. Moreover, because relapses happen relatively infrequently,[26] it is hard to tell whether or not having a relapse in two years is due to an effective medicine or just good luck. As a result of these methodological difficulties, Alasdair Compston suggests that 'attempts to force drug companies to repay costs would be likely to trigger complex legal arguments'.[27]

The scheme was a success from the point of view of manufacturers, however, who were permitted to sell their drugs at full price to the NHS *despite* NICE's decision that they were insufficiently cost-effective. But from the point of view of the NHS, and of other patients whose treatment may have suffered because of the opportunity cost of this scheme, it was 'a costly failure'.[28] In its consultation on the move to value-based pricing, the Department of Health has announced that it plans to discontinue the 2009 PPRS Patient Access Scheme arrangements for new medicines.[29]

III Value-Based Pricing

In a normal consumer market, the price that purchasers of goods are prepared to pay reflects the value of those products to them. If a product is overpriced, consumers will not buy it, and unless its price is reduced, the market for the product will collapse. The market in prescription drugs does not work like this. Patients within the NHS generally do not care what the drugs they have been prescribed cost, whereas the NHS has a keen interest in ensuring that it is getting value for money for the drugs it prescribes.

At the time of writing, the point at which drugs are assessed to see whether they are cost-effective enough to justify purchase within the NHS is by a NICE appraisal. If this takes place at all, it will occur sometime after a new drug has reached the marketplace. This means that there is often a time-lag between a new drug receiv-

---

[24] M Boggild et al, 'Multiple Sclerosis Risk Sharing Scheme: Two Year Results of Clinical Cohort Study with Historical Comparator' (2009) 339 *British Medical Journal* b4677.

[25] C McCabe et al, 'Continuing the Multiple Sclerosis Risk Sharing Scheme is Unjustified' (2010) 340 *British Medical Journal* c1786.

[26] N Scolding, 'The Multiple Sclerosis Risk Sharing Scheme' (2010) 340 *British Medical Journal* c2882.

[27] A Compston, 'Commentary: Scheme has Benefited Patients' (2010) 340 *British Medical Journal* c2707.

[28] House of Commons Health Committee n 20 above.

[29] Department of Health, *A New Value-Based Approach to the Pricing of Branded Medicines* (DH, 2010) para 4.33.

ing a marketing authorisation and the publication of NICE guidance on whether it offers value for money. During this time there is no formal prohibition on pre-scribing the new drug, although it is common for those responsible for commissioning services to delay decisions about funding until the publication of NICE guidance, creating what is known as a period of 'NICE blight'. The rapid increases in prescribing after a positive NICE appraisal suggest that funding bodies use 'the absence of compulsion to avoid funding',[30] and that in practice it is more common for NICE guidance to lift prior restrictions on prescribing than it is for it to impose new ones.

The other consequence of the current system of post-licensing NICE appraisal is that it does not appraise and compare every medicine, but concentrates instead on evaluating new and expensive drugs. If there are lots of drugs which have not been subject to any cost-effectiveness evaluation, it is impossible to know whether they represent value for money for the NHS. As a result, it has been suggested that the NICE system of appraisals could be supplemented by a shorter appraisal of cost-effectiveness prior to *every* medicine's launch.[31] This is sometimes referred to as value-based pricing, and since it would include less controversial and expensive medicines than those which are appraised by NICE, a lighter-touch assessment might be justifiable and make an extension of NICE's role practicable.[32]

In advocating reform of the PPRS in order to introduce some sort of value-based pricing, the OFT considered two possible models. First, ex post value-based pricing would involve companies setting the initial price of a new drug, but the drug's maximum list price would be reset regularly – every five years or so – in response to evidence of cost-effectiveness. Second, ex ante value-based pricing would involve negotiations over price before a new product is launched, which would again be subject to ex post reviews as more evidence emerges. For obvious reasons, the pharmaceutical industry tends to prefer the former model: not only does it preserve their freedom to set prices at the time of a product's launch, but the absence of pre-market negotiations enables new drugs to reach the market more quickly. Ex post assessment also strengthens the bargaining position of the manufacturer, and weakens that of the payer, because the payer's ultimate sanction, refusing to purchase the product at all, is much less credible once the medi-cine is being prescribed to satisfied patients.[33]

The OFT, in contrast, favoured the ex ante model, arguing that rapid negotia-tions could be put in place in order not to unduly delay a new medicine's launch. According to the OFT, early-stage cost-effectiveness assessment could, in fact, benefit both companies and patients by increasing the volume and rate of take-up of cost-effective new medicines, while at the same time the NHS would benefit from ensuring that the NHS pays value-reflective prices at all times.[34]

[30] M Summerhayes and P Catchpole, 'Has NICE been Nice to Cancer?' (2006) 42 *European Journal of Cancer* 2881–86.
[31] Thornton n 14 above.
[32] ibid.
[33] OFT n 6 above, para 5.120.
[34] ibid para 5.122.

In its consultation on its decision to introduce value-based pricing, the government has accepted that value-based pricing should be introduced at a drug's launch, rather than being something that is negotiated later. The proposed scheme would work as follows:

> The manufacturer would have freedom to propose a price for a new medicine and provided this translated into a figure equal to or less than the basic cost effectiveness threshold, that price would be accepted for the NHS. If, however, the manufacturer considered that a higher price was warranted, they would need to provide robust evidence demonstrating that the new medicine merited a higher weighting in terms of burden of illness, therapeutic innovation and improvement, or clinical and wider societal benefits.[35]

The most obvious problem with this is that value-based pricing of new medicines requires reliable estimates of cost-effectiveness to be available at the time of launch. Indeed the Department of Health's consultation claims that 'The value-based pricing model will be based on a robust assessment of the evidence relating to a new medicine's value to patients and society.'[36]

This is problematic, however, because evidence from phase III trials, while important, has significant limitations, which were discussed in detail in chapter four. Because clinical trials do not offer evidence of effectiveness 'in the real world', but only in specially selected trial populations, it is probably *impossible* to take definitive decisions about cost-effectiveness at the time of a drug's launch. Indeed, the Department of Health's consultation admits that 'long-term data will be needed to demonstrate relative performance with complete confidence and such data may not be available at the time a product comes to market'. Any judgement about a medicine's cost-effectiveness prior to launch is therefore inevitably provisional, and there would have to be flexibility to alter the ex ante prices once more evidence becomes available. According to the Department of Health, 'one approach might be to set a price that is supported by the evidence available at launch, but to allow prices to be adjusted as better evidence becomes available'.

In reality, if the decision was subsequently taken that a drug was not cost-effective enough to justify its initial price, either patients would have to be taken off medication that they might be happy with, or the manufacturer would have to lower its price. Neither patients nor drug companies are likely to welcome these outcomes. Of course, if the post-launch evidence base might lead to price reductions, this represents an extremely powerful *disincentive* to pharmaceutical companies to carry out further research,[37] unless there was at least an equally good chance that post-launch clinical trials might enable them to increase their prices.

It could be argued that the OFT's criticism of the PPRS's inability to ensure that the prices of medicines reflect their value, which has been embraced by the

---

[35] DH n 29 above, para 5.5.
[36] ibid para 5.8.
[37] SC Griffin et al, 'Dangerous Omissions: The Consequences of Ignoring Decision Uncertainty' (2011) 20 *Health Economics* 212–24.

coalition government, misses the point that there are other parts of the system that exert this sort of pressure, namely decisions about whether a medicine can be prescribed within the NHS. Because pharmaceutical companies know that, in order to generate profits from selling their medicines to the NHS, they need to satisfy NICE's cost-effectiveness threshold, discussed below, this will create an incentive to setting prices at a level which is likely to offer the NHS sufficient value for money to justify a positive NICE appraisal.[38]

In addition, it could be argued that the whole notion of value-based pricing is, to many economists at least, something of a tautology. The value of a product – or what purchasers are prepared to pay for it – is inevitably already one factor that determines a medicine's price. If a pharmaceutical company released a new branded painkiller where the only active ingredient was paracetamol, and set the price at £50 per packet instead of the 16 pence I pay in my local supermarket, it can safely be predicted that its market would be non-existent. But value is not the only determinant of price; the costs of development and production also have a role to play. The OFT's proposals have therefore been widely criticised by health economists for suggesting that prices should solely reflect demand-side value, rather than additionally reflecting the costs of supply.[39]

Adrian Towse, Director of the Office of Health Economics, is also critical of value-based pricing's exclusive focus on *price* as a way of ensuring that drugs represent value for money, and instead suggests that it would be more sensible to take *volume* into account as well.[40] When more evidence of efficacy emerges, it may establish that a drug works for a subset of all patients, but works less well, or not at all, in others. This sort of evidence does not necessarily justify making the drug cheaper, but might be better dealt with by restrictions on prescribing to ensure that it is only prescribed to the subgroup of patients in whom it is likely to represent good value for money.

The OFT also suggested that in cases where it is genuinely impossible to take an informed view of a medicine's cost-effectiveness at launch, a risk sharing agreement could be negotiated, in which the company and the NHS would agree upon a price, subject to claims of clinical effectiveness being realised. Repayments would be due to the NHS if evidence of cost-effectiveness sufficient to justify this price is not forthcoming, and there would be reimbursement to the company if the originally agreed price is subsequently revised upwards.[41] Of course, the danger here is that the original price will be deliberately inflated in order to compensate for any anticipated subsequent reductions.[42]

---

[38] T Keyworth and G Yarrow, *Review of the Office of Fair Trading's Market Study of the Pharmaceutical Price Regulation Scheme* (Regulatory Policy Institute, Oxford, 2007).
[39] ibid.
[40] A Towse, 'If it Ain't Broke, Don't Price Fix It: The OFT and the PPRS' (2007) 16 *Health Economics* 653–65.
[41] OFT n 6 above, para 5.58.
[42] PP Barros, 'The Simple Economics of Risk-Sharing Agreements between the NHS and the Pharmaceutical Industry' (2011) 20 *Health Economics* 461–70.

In addition to the availability of robust data, value-based pricing would also require an agreed method for judging cost-effectiveness. The OFT recommended the 'quality adjusted life year' or QALY approach, considered in more detail below, but it is worth noting at this stage that this is itself controversial, and the success of value-based pricing will be largely contingent upon the location of a satisfactory cost-effectiveness threshold.[43] The coalition government has not yet committed itself to a particular cost-effectiveness measure, and mentions the QALY approach as 'one (but not the only) option'.[44]

It is also important to remember that the impact of value-based pricing on the total drugs budget may be far less significant than increasing the proportion of generic prescribing within the NHS. In the UK doctors already prescribe generic medicines more frequently than in most other developed countries. An alternative (or supplement) to value-based pricing might be taking further steps to increase generic prescribing rates. This could be done by automatic generic substitution (see chapter three for an explanation of why this was recently rejected by the Department of Health). And, more controversially still, the patent life on medicines could be reduced.[45]

IV The National Institute for health and Clinical Excellence (NICE)

The National Institute for health and Clinical Excellence (NICE) is a special health authority which was set up in 1999. It has a number of functions – including issuing good practice guidance on the management of different conditions – but it is most well known for its role in resource allocation within the NHS. Through its programme of appraisals, NICE determines whether a medicine should be available within the NHS, on an unrestricted basis, or only in certain categories of patients, or only in research or not at all. Of the 367 decisions made by NICE between 1 March 2000 and 30 June 2010, 67 per cent involved straightforward approval, 16 per cent of decisions were that the treatment should be available only in certain circumstances; six per cent permitted the use of the treatment but only in research, and in 11 per cent of cases, the guidance was that the treatment should not be prescribed.[46]

Directions were issued to health authorities in 2002 that any treatments which have been approved by NICE should normally be available to patients within three

---

[43] K Claxton, 'OFT, VBP: QED?' (2007) 16 *Health Economics* 545–58.

[44] DH n 29 above, para 4.7.

[45] D Taylor and T Craig, 'Value Based Pricing for NHS Medicines: Magic Bullet, Counterfeit Treatment or the Mixture as Before?' (2009) 4 *Health Economics, Policy and Law* 515–26.

[46] J Wise, 'NICE Recommended Four in Five Drugs it Evaluated in Past Decade' (2010) 341 *British Medical Journal* c3935.

months,[47] and the government was explicit that 'scarce resources is [sic] not a good reason for failure to implement NICE guidance'.[48] This funding guarantee does not give patients a *right* to treatments which have received a positive appraisal from NICE. There is no duty on doctors to prescribe treatments that NICE has judged to be sufficiently cost-effective. And despite the funding guarantee, implementation of NICE guidance remains variable.[49] The Audit Commission found that only 25 per cent of PCTs could verify that implementation of NICE technology appraisals, in fact, took place within three months.[50] If a treatment is rejected by NICE, this does not mean that there is a legal prohibition on its use within the NHS, although in practice, very few health authorities have been prepared to deviate from NICE guidance.

A Comparative Cost-effectiveness and Disinvestment

NICE does not assess every medicine or other technology, rather, for obvious and understandable reasons, the treatments it decides to appraise – with advice from the Department of Health and the Horizon Scanning Centre at the University of Birmingham – have tended to be new and expensive branded medicines, rather than drugs, including generic drugs, which have been in use within the NHS for many years. This has a number of consequences. First, because of the prioritised funding for NICE-approved medicines, it skews funding towards new medicines, and away from lower-tech interventions and preventative and primary care. Second, it means that NICE has tended to neglect the equally important question of when the NHS should *stop* providing cost-ineffective but well-established medicines.[51] NICE cannot then ensure that only the most cost-effective medicines are provided within the NHS, since this would necessarily be a *comparative* exercise, in which all medicines were assessed and ranked. Rather, NICE is only able to judge whether each of the individual drugs it chooses to assess separately meet some threshold level of cost-effectiveness.

In addition, NICE does not control the volume of prescriptions, and so it is possible that a medicine might be judged cost-effective, but the number of prescriptions issued makes it unaffordable for the NHS. If this were to happen, it would be possible for the NHS to be formally advised by government to ignore NICE guidance.

---

[47] Department of Health, *Directions to Health Authorities, Primary Care Trusts and NHS Trusts in England* (DH, 2001).

[48] Department of Health, *Government Response to the Health Committee's 2nd Report of Session 2001–02 on National Institute for Clinical Excellence* (DH, 2002) 9.

[49] TA Sheldon et al, 'What's the Evidence that NICE Guidance has been Implemented? Results from a National Evaluation using Time Series Analysis, Audit of Patients' Notes, and Interviews' (2004) 329 *British Medical Journal* 999.

[50] Audit Commission, *Managing the Implementation of NICE Guidance* (Audit Commission, 2005).

[51] House of Commons Health Select Committee, *National Institute for Health and Clinical Excellence* First Report of Session 2006–07, available at www.publications.parliament.uk.

Third, because there is a duty to fund NICE approved medicines, PCTs have to find the resources for these prioritised medicines from elsewhere in their budgets. The 'opportunity costs' of NICE approval – in the form of cuts to other parts of the health budget – are not formally part of NICE's decision-making process. This has been criticised by economists who argue that it is impossible to make robust efficiency judgements without taking into account the opportunity costs of decisions.[52] Choices about which treatments should be cut in order to meet the obligation to fund NICE-approved drugs are taken locally, and will therefore vary, creating a new postcode lottery of access to non-NICE-approved medicines.[53] While NICE's decisions may be evidence-based and lead to consistency across England and Wales, *disinvestment* decisions, which may be equally significant, are not necessarily evidence-based, and may be haphazard and geographically variable.

Michael Drummond has suggested that this latter problem might be addressed by NICE being asked to suggest disinvestments in the clinical area of a new approved technology: that is, instead of simply saying that drug Y is cost-effective enough to justify NHS provision, at the same time, NICE would also make a recommendation that drug X, previously used in the same patient group, is not cost-effective enough and Y should be preferred.[54] Alternatively, Drummond suggests that NICE could, on a yearly basis, attempt to operate a 'balanced budget' in relation to its recommendations. If the drug budget is static, any decision to approve a new expensive drug in one year would have to be accompanied by recommendations of how to achieve disinvestments to the same value. Or, if the total drugs budget is to increase, new approvals which went beyond the agreed rise in spending would have to be accompanied by guidance on disinvestment to make up the difference.[55]

The government's proposed move to value-based pricing is a partial attempt to remedy this problem by ensuring that *all* new medicines have their cost-effectiveness assessed prior to launch. This already happens in Scotland, where the Scottish Medicines Consortium assesses and makes recommendations on the availability of *all* new drugs; new formulations of existing medicines; and major new indications for established products.[56] The process is much quicker – each appraisal takes approximately four months, compared with over a year for NICE guidance – and it is cheaper. It is also less comprehensive and less transparent: there is, for example, no public consultation or right of appeal. The SMC can recommend that a new drug is unique, and should be available to all patients within three months; or that the drug is an advance on alternatives, and Boards can use their discretion; or that the drug is no better than alternatives, and should not be prescribed to NHS patients.

---

[52] S Birch and A Gafni, 'Economists' Dream or Nightmare? Maximizing Health Gains from Available Resources using the NICE Guidelines' (2007) 2 *Health Economics, Policy and Law* 193–202.

[53] DA Hughes and RE Ferner, 'New Drugs for Old: Disinvestment and NICE' (2010) 340 *British Medical Journal* c572.

[54] M Drummond, 'NICE: A Nightmare Worth Having?' (2007) 2 *Health Economics, Policy and Law* 203–08.

[55] ibid.

[56] www.scottishmedicines.org.uk.

While there might be advantages in having this sort of preliminary guidance available from launch, there are grounds to be sceptical as to whether 'light-touch' appraisals, made when data are at their most sparse, and in the absence of evidence as to how drugs work in real patient populations, is an adequate *replacement* for NICE's robust and comprehensive appraisal system. Indeed, in Scotland itself, because NICE guidance is assumed to be more rigorous, and grounded in a more comprehensive evidence base, if a NICE appraisal contradicts a preliminary SMC recommendation, NICE guidance supersedes the SMC's initial judgement. The Scottish approach could then be said to be a hybrid system, in which a rapid decision at launch is supplemented by more thorough post-launch review. This hybrid system has much to recommend it: it may be feasible to conduct rapid, early review of *all* new medicines, whereas comprehensive and time-consuming cost-effectiveness analysis of all new medicines would be impossible; at the same time, solely relying on these rapid initial evaluations would be problematic, because the evidence gathered post-launch may reveal that the initial assessment was wrong.[57]

B The Process of NICE Appraisal

NICE's approach to rationing is explicit, open and generally transparent. It publishes all of its appraisals on its website, although it is not able to publish all of the evidence upon which its appraisals are based, because pharmaceutical companies commonly specify that this is commercially sensitive and confidential information. NICE does not carry out its own trials, rather it relies on information supplied by manufacturers, and importantly it does not have the same statutory right as the licensing authority, that is the MHRA or EMA, to demand access to *all* relevant evidence.[58]

Most new and expensive drugs effectively undergo a two stage review process in the United Kingdom. First, they must be licensed for use by EMA or the MHRA, and as we saw in chapter three, this judgement is based only on evidence of quality, safety and efficacy. Price is irrelevant. Second, NICE reviews evidence of efficacy *and price* in order to make a judgement about cost-effectiveness.

Normally, NICE only appraises medicines for their licensed indications, but in 2010 it announced that it was planning to appraise the off-label usage of bevacizumab (Avastin) for the treatment of wet macular degeneration, for which it did not have a marketing authorisation.[59] Avastin is licensed for use in the treatment of bowel cancer, but opthamologists in the US had discovered that a single dose could be split into minute quantities, which, when injected directly into the eye,

[57] J Cairns, 'Providing Guidance to the NHS: The Scottish Medicines Consortium and the National Institute for Clinical Excellence Compared (2006) 76 *Health Policy* 134–43.

[58] T Kendall, L McGoey and E Jackson, 'If NICE was in the USA' (2009) 374 *The Lancet* 272–73.

[59] See further NICE's report on the feasibility of appraising the use of bevacizumab (Avastin) to treat eye conditions, available at www.nice.org.uk/newsroom/pressreleases/BevacizumabAvastinToTreatEyeConditions.jsp.

appeared to halt or even reverse a common cause of blindness. The drug company does produce a version of bevacizumab for use in eyes, Lucentis, which costs approximately £750 per dose. Although Avastin is not cheap, splitting a single dose and using it in multiple patients means that its off-label usage is much more cost-effective than the eye-specific version. Unsurprisingly, the companies which manufacture and market Avastin and Lucentis have been critical of this decision.[60]

Much more commonly NICE will be faced with a new treatment which is an improvement on the standard treatment, but which also costs more. The task for NICE is then to determine what increase in health would be likely to be derived from increased expenditure on the new medicine. In working out this incremental cost-effectiveness ratio (ICER), NICE calculates the cost per QALY of each intervention it appraises.[61]

C QALYs and Cost-effectiveness Analysis

QALYs measure both the *amount* and the *quality* of life generated by a treatment: a treatment is beneficial if it offers patients long periods of healthy and active life, and a treatment is cost-effective if the cost-per-QALY is low. QALYs depend on being able to measure a patient's quality of life – taking into account health-related considerations like mobility, self-care, ability to carry out daily activities and the absence of pain, discomfort, anxiety and depression[62] – both before and after treatment, on a scale from 0 (death) to 1.0 (full health). The quality of life scores are then multiplied by the patient's life expectancy, both before and after treatment. The difference between these two numbers will be the amount of QALYs generated by the treatment. The cost per QALY can then be calculated and used to compare the cost-effectiveness of different treatments.

To take a crude example, let us imagine that without treatment X, a patient is likely to live for two years in fairly poor health, say 0.5 on the QALY scale. After receiving treatment X, he is likely to live for five years in perfect health. Before receiving treatment A, this patient's life contains one QALY and after treatment it contains five QALYs. Treatment X therefore offers him four QALYs. If treatment X costs £40,000, its ICER, or cost per QALY, is £10,000.

NICE has consistently refuted the suggestion that it employs a rigid QALY test for affordability. It is clear that cost-effectiveness, while important, is not the only relevant value, and sometimes questions of fairness and equity have a role to play too.[63] For example, orphan medicines are always likely to cost more to produce

---

[60] S Boseley, 'Firms Fight Move to Obtain Cheap Anti-Blindness Drug Avastin' *The Guardian* 2 January 2011.

[61] R Rosser and P Kind, 'A Scale of Values of States of Illness: Is there a Social Consensus' (1978) 7 *International Journal of Epidemiology* 347–58.

[62] The EuroQoL Group, 'EuroQoL: A New Facility for the Measurement of Health Related Quality of Life' (1990) 16 *Health Policy* 199–208.

[63] R Cookson, M Drummond and H Weatherly, 'Explicit Incorporation of Equity Considerations into Economic Evaluation of Public Health Interventions' (2009) 4 *Health Economics, Policy and Law* 261–63.

because their market is so small, but ruling out their approval might mean that patients who suffer from very rare conditions are effectively untreatable within the NHS. Deviations from the normal QALY threshold might then be justified on fairness grounds.[64] Public health goals such as reducing health inequalities might also militate in favour of treatments for conditions which disproportionately affect the most disadvantaged in society.

Nevertheless, despite not operating as an inflexible ceiling, NICE would be unlikely to reject a technology with an ICER ratio less than £20,000 per QALY on the grounds that it costs too much.[65] It might still be rejected, perhaps because evidence for effectiveness in the general population is limited, but this would not be because of its cost per QALY. Treatments which cost between £20,000 and £30,000 per QALY will be considered by NICE, and recommended for NHS provision if there are reasons to justify the expense, such as the absence of alternative treatments for the target population. Treatments which cost more than £30,000 per QALY are generally not acceptable for NHS provision and an exceptionally strong case would have to be made to justify a positive appraisal. An example is riluzole, used in the treatment of motor neurone disease. NICE approved this for use in the NHS despite its cost per QALY estimate of £39,000, on the grounds that the extension of tracheostomy-free survival time was especially valuable to people suffering from motor neurone disease.[66]

QALYs are explicitly egalitarian in the sense that it is irrelevant to whom they accrue: 'a QALY is a QALY is a QALY'.[67] But while it might seem just and non-discriminatory to treat any quality adjusted life year gained from a treatment in the same way, there are also a number of downsides to this approach. First, QALYs that accrue to people who are generally fit and healthy are treated in exactly the same way as QALYs gained by people who are gravely ill or otherwise disadvantaged. Someone with terminal cancer might value an additional year of life much more than a healthy 20-year-old, for whom one more QALY just represents a very slightly longer long life-expectancy.

Second, NICE's cost-effectiveness threshold does not formally draw a distinction between treatments which are genuinely innovative and those which do not offer much or indeed any improvement over existing treatments. The innovative nature of a product can be taken into account by an Appraisal Committee if it is not adequately captured by the QALY measure,[68] but this does not amount to a formal raising of the QALY threshold for innovative drugs which represent what has been called a 'step-change' in terms of outcomes for patients.[69] Of course, the

[64] MF Drummond et al, 'Assessing the Economic Challenges Posed by Orphan Drugs' (2007) 23 *International Journal of Technology Assessment in Health Care* 36–42.

[65] MD Rawlins and AJ Culyer, 'National Institute for Clinical Excellence and its value judgments' (2004) 329 *British Medical Journal* 224.

[66] J Raftery, 'Review of NICE's Recommendations, 1999–2005' (2006) 332 *British Medical Journal* 1266–68.

[67] MC Weinstein, 'A QALY is a QALY is a QALY – Or is it?' (1988) 7 *Journal of Health Economics* 289–90.

[68] Evidence of Sir Michael Rawlins to the House of Commons Health Committee n 20 above, 41.

[69] Kennedy n 13 above, 38.

categorisation of a new drug as a 'step-change' for patients at launch may have to be provisional: a drug may promise much, but when used over time evidence may emerge that it does not represent a radical improvement to existing treatment options. Any incentives to innovation would therefore have to be open to revision in the light of subsequent evidence and perhaps also reimbursement of the enhanced price if this turns out not to have been justified. Nevertheless, it could be argued that NICE's failure to formally reward innovation offers a disincentive to pharmaceutical companies from engaging in ground-breaking, and hence risky trials of entirely new chemical agents,[70] as well as yet another incentive towards the development of 'me-too' drugs, considered in chapter three.

D End of Life Medicines

After a number of effective but very expensive cancer drugs were rejected by NICE, and in response to Mike Richards' report on top-up fees considered later in this chapter, NICE issued supplementary guidance, which applies only to life-extending end of life treatments. It will be of particular significance in relation to a number of new cancer drugs,[71] especially those which are suitable for small subgroups of cancer patients, which because of their small market and high development costs, are often very expensive.[72] It is also fairly common for cancer drugs to prolong life for no more than a few months, thereby providing comparatively few quality adjusted life years to patients.[73] If drugs which offer very short extensions of life also cost a great deal of money, it is not surprising that they tend to fail NICE's cost-effectiveness threshold. As more of these drugs have reached the marketplace, NICE's rejection rate of cancer drugs has increased, from four per cent before 2006 to around 27 per cent in subsequent years.[74]

NICE's supplementary guidance permits Appraisal Committees to give 'greater weight to QALYs achieved in the later stages of terminal diseases' where a treatment is indicated for patients with a life expectancy of less than two years, and is expected to extend their life for at least three months, provided there is no alternative treatment with comparable benefits, and provided the condition is one which only affects small patient populations (ie conditions diagnosed in fewer than 7000 patients a year in the UK).[75] In practice, it is not clear that this guidance will make much difference. James Raftery's analysis of all rejected cancer drugs in the

[70] D Cooksey, *A Report to Government by the Bioscience Innovation and Growth Team* (Department for Business, Enterprise and Regulatory Reform, 2009).
[71] B Jonsson, 'Being NICE is not the Problem!' (2009) 45 *European Journal of Cancer* 1100–02.
[72] House of Commons Health Committee n 20 above, para 89.
[73] T Fojo and C Grady, 'How Much Is Life Worth: Cetuximab, Non – Small Cell Lung Cancer, and the \$440 Billion Question' (2009) 102 *Journal of the National Cancer Institute* 1207–10.
[74] AR Mason and MF Drummond, 'Public Funding of New Cancer Drugs: Is NICE Getting Nastier?' (2009) 45 *European Journal of Cancer* 1188–92.
[75] NICE, *Appraising Life-Extending, End of Life Treatments* (NICE, 2009), available at www.nice.org.uk.

previous ten years suggested that only two would have satisfied this criterion.[76] Despite this more flexible approach to QALYs in end of life treatments, NICE has continued to reject expensive cancer drugs, including lapatinib (brand name Tyverb) for the treatment of advanced breast cancer, which, with a cost per QALY of £59,400, was still judged to be insufficiently cost-effective.[77]

E Social Values and Consultation

NICE employs scientific and clinical experts to carry out its appraisals, but it has also attempted to consider some of the wider social and ethical issues raised by rationing through its Citizen's Council, a representative sample of 30 UK citizens. The Council played a role in the development of NICE's *Social Value Judgements,* which sets out its approach to questions like whether a person's age or their responsibility for their own ill-health should play a role in the rationing of NHS resources.[78] In relation to age, NICE's general principle is that patients should not be denied, or have restricted access to NHS treatment simply because of their age. Age should be relevant only if it is a robust indicator of a patient's likely response to treatment. *Social Value Judgements* also specifies that 'NICE should not produce guidance that results in care being denied to patients with conditions that are, or may have been, dependent on their behaviour'. Again, it is only if the patient's behaviour is likely to make treatment less effective that it might be appropriate to take it into account.

In addition to soliciting public opinion through its Citizens' Council, NICE also gives 'interested parties' — such as patient groups and the pharmaceutical indus-try — a right to make representations and a right of appeal: of its first 130 apprais-als, 47 were appealed. In the previous chapter, the links between patient groups and the pharmaceutical industry were explored, and it is clear that, in the context of exerting pressure on NICE, the combination of the drug's manufacturer and relevant patient groups (which may, in fact, be sponsored by the manufacturer) represent a powerful lobbying force.[79]

Ian Kennedy describes how the pharmaceutical industry 'regularly adopts an approach based on the supremacy of the consumer/patient. It is an approach based on individualism. What any individual wants/needs should be provided'.[80] In championing the interest of the patient/consumer, and funding patient groups, the pharmaceutical industry has characterised NICE as a curmudgeonly, scrooge-like organisation, determined to deny sick people access to medicines that would be likely to help them. Patient groups have also sometimes adopted this sort of rhetoric, and the popular press has been quick to take up news stories which

---

[76] J Raftery, 'NICE and the Challenge of Cancer Drugs' (2009) 338 *British Medical Journal* 67.
[77] S Boseley, 'Women Denied Cancer Drug that Could Extend Life' *The Guardian* 21 October 2009.
[78] NICE, *Social Value Judgements,* 2nd edn (NICE, 2008).
[79] K Syrett, 'A Technocratic Fix to the "Legitimacy Problem"? The Blair Government and Health Care Rationing in the United Kingdom' (2003) 28 *Journal of Health Politics, Policy and Law* 715.
[80] Kennedy n 13 above, 19.

demonise NICE. The *Daily Mail* has been a particularly strident critic of NICE, suggesting that its guidance commonly amounts to a 'death sentence' for cancer patients.[81]

It could also be argued that successive governments' commitment to 'patient choice' within the NHS has exacerbated this tendency to regard the individual patient and his needs or wants as the paramount consideration, without taking into account, as NICE must, how providing medicines to one patient group will affect the resources available to others. It is precisely NICE's role to promote the collective *public* interest in an affordable NHS, which would soon collapse if there was no ceiling on the amount of money spent on drugs. It is also noteworthy that industry-funded patient groups have been vigorous in their criticism and lobbying of NICE in order to broaden access to new drugs, but perhaps less assiduous in lobbying drugs manufacturers to lower their prices in order to make them more affordable.[82]

F Judicial Review of NICE Decisions

As a public body, NICE's decisions can be challenged via judicial review. Judicial review is not available to challenge the *merits* of public bodies' decisions, only their procedural legality. Since 1999, NICE has been subject to four judicial review actions, three of which were brought by pharmaceutical companies. In the first case, *Eisai Ltd v The National Institute for Health and Clinical Excellence*,[83] the manufacturer of donepezil (brand name Aricept) challenged NICE's guidance that it should not be funded for patients in the earlier stages of Alzheimer's disease (AD) on the grounds of procedural unfairness, discriminatory effects, and irrationality.

Initially, the cost per QALY of Aricept was estimated to be £94,000. A subsequent calculation reduced this figure to £54,000, and if treatment was confined to patients with moderately severe AD, its cost per QALY further dropped to between £31,000 and £38,000. At first instance, Eisai succeeded only in establishing that NICE's decision-making process had discriminatory effects. NICE guidance had relied upon mini mental-state examination (MMSE) scores in order to judge the severity of a patient's AD. MMSE tests are not reliable in people whose first language is not English and in those with learning difficulties, so NICE's reliance upon MMSE scores was unlawful on the grounds that it might have discriminatory effects for these patients.

Eisai then appealed to the Court of Appeal, claiming that NICE's decision to only disclose 'read only' versions of its economic modelling formulae made it impossible for Eisai to investigate the reliability of NICE's calculations. At first

---

[81] J Hope, 'Drug Denial is Devastating "Death Sentence" for Cancer Patients' *Daily Mail* 7 August 2008.

[82] R Minhas and KCR Patel, 'From Rationing to Rational: The Evolving Status of NICE (2008) *Journal of the Royal Society of Medicine* 101, 436.

[83] *Eisai Ltd v The National Institute for Health and Clinical Excellence* [2008] EWCA Civ 438.

instance this argument had been rejected; drug companies do not have the right to quality assure NICE's decision-making processes. Eisai succeeded on this ground before the Court of Appeal, which agreed that NICE's refusal to release the fully executable version of the model placed pharmaceutical companies at a significant disadvantage in challenging the reliability of NICE's decisions.

The Court of Appeal did not decide that NICE's guidance on Arisept was wrong, however. Giving Eisai access to the functional version of the modelling tool does not alter the judgement that Arisept's cost per QALY for patients with mild AD is too high to justify NHS provision. In August 2009, after the Court of Appeal's decision, NICE reiterated that for people with mild AD, the cost per QALY of acetylcholinesterase inhibitors ranged from £56,000 to £72,000, and this was still too high to make Aricept cost-effective.[84] The following year NICE did change its mind on Aricept and two other acetylcholinesterase inhibitors, however, citing new evidence of the drugs' effectiveness. There had not been a new landmark study, however, and NICE itself had described the evidence base as 'disappointing'. Nevertheless, by adjusting its calculations to give more weight to the costs of caring for someone with AD, the cost per QALY was reduced to £30,000 and NHS provision was judged acceptable.[85]

A second judicial review action was mounted by Bristol-Myers Squibb (BMS), which manufactures abatacept (ABA) for the treatment of rheumatoid arthritis. BMS had given NICE its fully executable electronic spreadsheet, which it had used to estimate ABA's cost per QALY, which it calculated was £25,395. This cost per QALY might be likely to have led to NICE approval. NICE then handed BMS's calculations to its Evidence Review Group (ERG), which queried a number of its assumptions. Using different assumptions, the ERG came up with a cost per QALY of £72,865, which was revised down following consultation with BMS to £37,000–£43,000. BMS sought judicial review of the decision to reject ABA on the grounds that NICE had not disclosed the fully executable model used by its ERG to come up with its cost-effectiveness estimate. This time the claim was rejected, on the grounds that it would have been perfectly possible for BMS to work out how the ERG had come to its decisions, since it *had* fully disclosed the assumptions which underpinned them.

The third judicial review action from a pharmaceutical company against NICE was brought by Servier Laboratories, manufacturer of strontium ranelate (brand named Protelos), a treatment for the prevention of osteoporotic fractures in post-menopausal women.[86] The application for judicial review was backed by an industry-supported patient group, the National Osteoporosis Society. NICE had decided that Protelos should be prescribed only to women who could not tolerate the generic and hence cheap treatment of choice, alendronate. Servier claimed that NICE had failed properly to take into account data derived from a post-hoc

---

[84] Z Kmietowicz, 'NICE Decision on Dementia Drugs was Based on "Common Sense" not Evidence, Expert Says' (2010) 341 *British Medical Journal* c5642.

[85] ibid.

[86] *Servier Laboratories v National Institute For Health and Clinical Excellence* [2010] EWCA Civ 346.

subgroup analysis of a study entitled Treatment of Peripheral Osteoporosis (TROPOS), published in the *Journal of Clinical Endocrinology & Metabolism*. A post-hoc subgroup analysis involves deriving data from a study by separating out the results of certain participants in order to demonstrate something that was not specified in the trial design. NICE had taken the view that this study's results were unreliable for a number of reasons, including the fact that comparisons were not being made between randomly selected groups. In unanimously finding for Servier, the Court of Appeal was especially impressed by the European Medicine's Agency's reliance on the subgroup data when deciding to license Protelos: Smith LJ decided it was fair comment 'that it would be surprising if EMA had accepted results flawed in that way'.

There has been one case in which patients have sought to challenge a NICE guideline. This was not a technology appraisal of a new medicine, but rather a patient care guideline.[87] It is of relevance here, however, because the nature of the complaint of two patients who had been diagnosed with Myalgic Encephalomyelitis (ME) or Chronic Fatigue Syndrome, was that NICE had acted irrationally by giving too little consideration to biomedical (or pharmaceutical) treatments for ME, and had prioritised instead psychosocial treatments, such as cognitive behavioural therapy and graded exercise therapy. They advanced a number of grounds for this claim, many alleging bias or conflict of interest on the part of NICE's expert advisers. All were robustly rejected, and the Court also noted that legal proceedings of this type might serve as a disincentive to healthcare professionals from involving themselves in NICE's decision-making processes in the future.

V Exceptional Case Review

PCTs, and in the future perhaps GP consortia, can refuse to fund expensive medicines which do not have a positive NICE appraisal, but they must not operate a blanket ban. Directions issued to PCTs in 2009 specify that they must set up 'arrangements for the determination of requests for the funding of a health care intervention for an individual, where the Primary Care Trust's general policy is not to fund that intervention'.[88] Where a decision is made to refuse exceptional funding for an individual, a written statement giving reasons must be provided.[89]

In addition to having a mechanism for 'exceptional case review',[90] it must be

---

[87] *R (on the application of Fraser) v National Institute For Health and Clinical Excellence* [2009] EWHC 452 (Admin).

[88] DH, *Direction to PCTs and NHS Trusts Concerning Decisions about Drugs and Other Treatments* (DH, 2009) para 2(3)(b).

[89] ibid para 3.3.

[90] *R v North West Lancashire Health Authority, ex p A and Others* [2000] 1 WLR 977. For commentary, see C Newdick, *Who Should We Treat: Rights, Rationing and Resources in the NHS*, 2nd edn (Oxford University Press, 2005) 100–03.

possible for some patients to actually qualify as exceptional cases.[91] An exceptional case review process requires there to be some agreement about what sort of criteria make a patient's case exceptional. In particular, is exceptionality a purely *clinical* judgement: perhaps the patient cannot tolerate the NICE-approved treatment and hence unless the non-NICE approved treatment is funded, the patient will be effectively untreatable? If this approach is adopted, a particular problem is raised by orphan medicines, which are medicines to treat diseases which occur in very small patient populations. Despite incentives to develop orphan medicines, their small market means that they are likely to be expensive, and where there are few affected patients, it will be very difficult to generate robust and adequately statistically powered clinical trial data. The 'exceptional' circumstances are not then *patient*-specific, but rather the *condition* itself is exceptional. Orphan conditions are, almost by definition, exceptional, so it is difficult to draw a distinction between treatments which will and which will not be candidates for exceptional funding, and this problem is exacerbated by the absence of robust comparative cost-effectiveness data.[92] Giving *all* orphan drugs special status as 'exceptional cases' may enable PCTs to avoid making unpopular decisions, but this would have a significant opportunity cost for other patients whose diseases are common, and hence unexceptional, but whose health needs may be just as great.[93]

In addition to having to work out what makes a patient's case *clinically* exceptional, might a patient be treated as exceptional because of her *social* circumstances? If a candidate for an expensive medicine is the sole carer of a disabled child, for example, could she be treated as 'exceptional' as a result of the additional benefits both to her child, and to publicly funded social services, from enabling her to continue to fulfil her caring responsibilities? On the one hand, it might seem illogical to leave out of account the obvious social and financial benefits which would accrue from restoring a disabled child's carer to full health.[94] On the other hand, this looks very like rationing on the basis of a patient's *social value*, and it would be almost impossible to prioritise patients according to their value to others in a fair and non-discriminatory way. Should we offer expensive medicines to doctors and teachers, but not to the unemployed, for example? Should individuals who actively contribute to their local community receive treatment when people who spend their leisure time watching television do not?

A broad-brush approach, like favouring the parents of dependent children, would also be invidious: not only does it discriminate against the childless, but also someone who does not have children may contribute a great deal more to the health and wellbeing of deprived children through voluntary work than a largely absent or neglectful parent. Even if we decided that it was possible to accurately

---

[91] *R (on the application of Rogers)* v *Swindon Primary Care Trust* [2006] EWCA Civ 392.

[92] C Newdick, 'Accountability for Rationing – Theory into Practice' 33 (2005) *Journal of Law, Medicine and Ethics* 660.

[93] C McCabe, K Claxton and A Tsuchiya, 'Orphan Drugs and the NHS: Should we Value Rarity?' (2005) 331 *British Medical Journal* 1016.

[94] J Glover, *Causing Death and Saving Lives* (Penguin London 1977) 222.

judge the non-health benefits that accrue to society from treating a particular individual, it would be impossible to calculate these without exceptionally intrusive surveillance of patients' private lives.

Exceptional case review committees are at the sharp end of the process of rationing scarce NHS resources. They will generally have before them an application from an extremely ill individual, who is convinced that a new medicine, which they have been told is insufficiently cost-effective to justify NHS provision, would make such a difference to their quality of life or even to their life expectancy, that they ought, exceptionally, to be treated as a special case. Unlike NICE, which makes these decisions at a macro population-wide level, exceptional review committees are making choices about whether an *identifiable individual* should have access to an expensive medicine, in cases where that individual often believes this to be a life and death decision.

It would be hard not to be moved by applications for exceptional case funding, but committees must also take into account the opportunity costs to other patients of exceptionally funding a non-NICE approved medicine. If an application is granted, there will be less in the pot for the treatment of others, and their needs may be just as compelling as the patient who has made the application for exceptional funding. It is obviously the task of the exceptional case review committee to take account of the interests of others, but the patients who might suffer if exceptional case funding is made available are not identifiable individuals, and they do not have an independent voice or representation during the exceptional review process. In addition, exceptional case review itself is not cost-free. Clinicians involved in these decisions are diverted away from patient care, and the costs of the process too inevitably have an opportunity cost to others who might benefit from services provided by the PCT.[95]

The fairness of these review processes, and the criteria upon which they have been based, have been tested in the courts in the cases described in the next section.

VI Judicial Review

If a patient does not succeed in persuading their PCT to exceptionally fund the non-NICE approved medicine, the only remaining option is to challenge this decision on procedural grounds by making an application for judicial review of the PCT's refusal of funding. Challenging funding decisions via judicial review is a relatively recent phenomenon, and it is only within the last few years that applicants have had any success. In the first judicial review actions brought by disgruntled patients, the judiciary were sympathetic towards cash-strapped health authorities

[95] Newdick n 92 above.

and well-meaning Secretaries of State.[96] In the words of Lord Denning: 'The Secretary of State says that he is doing the best he can with the financial resources available to him: and I do not think that he can be faulted in the matter.'[97]

More recently, there have been a handful of cases in which patients have sought to challenge funding decisions, mainly involving expensive cancer drugs, and they have had considerable success in persuading the courts that the 'exceptionality' review process has not operated fairly in their cases. As Chris Newdick has pointed out, exceptional case review committees are not generally made up of lawyers, and this fact – along with the difficulty in ensuring that *any* decision-making process is entirely watertight – means that it has proved relatively straightforward for claimants to identify some procedural impropriety, and hence establish that the review process was procedurally flawed.[98]

In *R (on the application of Rogers) v Swindon Primary Care Trust*,[99] the Court of Appeal found that it was not, in fact, possible to think of any grounds for treating one patient for whom Herceptin was an appropriate clinical treatment differently from any other. The exceptionality review procedure, which the Trust claimed to be operating, was essentially meaningless, and the Trust had acted irrationally.

In contrast, in *R (on the Application of Otley) v Barking and Dagenham NHS Primary Care Trust*,[100] there was nothing wrong with the PCT's exceptionality policy, which Mitting J considered to be 'entirely rational and sensible',[101] but its application to Ms Otley's personal circumstances was irrational. Ms Otley suffered from metastatic colorectal cancer and she had secondary tumours in her liver. She had responded poorly to chemotherapy. Her sister found out about a new drug, Avastin, on the internet. Avastin was not available within the NHS, so Ms Otley decided to pay for five cycles of Avastin herself. Her response was excellent: she experienced minimal side effects; she felt much better and her tumours appeared to have shrunk. Given the fact that there was no other treatment available to Ms Otley, and Avastin might be able to prolong her life, 'on any fair minded view of the exceptionality criteria . . . her case was exceptional'.[102] In addition, Mitting J considered that funding five cycles of Avastin for Ms Otley could not be said to put at risk the Trust's capacity to provide care for other patients.

Of course, even if an applicant succeeds in establishing that a PCT has acted irrationally, this does not necessarily mean that funding for the drug will necessarily be made available. In *R (on the Application of Gordon) v Bromley NHS Primary Care Trust*,[103] Ouseley J found that the basis for the trust's rejection of the application for

---

[96] See, for example, *R v Central Birmingham Health Authority, ex p Walker* (1987) 3 BMLR 32 and *R v Central Birmingham Health Authority, ex p Collier*, Unreported, 6 Jan 1988.

[97] *R v Secretary of State for Social Services, ex p Hincks* (1980) 1 BMLR 93 (CA).

[98] C Newdick, 'Judicial Review: Low-Priority Treatment and Exceptional Case Review' (2007) *Medical Law Review* 236.

[99] *R (on the application of Rogers) v Swindon Primary Care Trust* [2006] EWCA Civ 392.

[100] *R (on the Application of Otley) v Barking and Dagenham NHS Primary Care Trust* [2007] EWHC 1927 (Admin).

[101] ibid [27].

[102] ibid [26].

[103] *R (on the Application of Gordon) v Bromley NHS Primary Care Trust* [2006] EWHC 2462 (Admin).

a trial of Tarceva was not wholly clear, but in sending the decision back he stressed that a new decision, properly explained, might still be to refuse funding:

> I emphasise that the claimant may well find it impossible to challenge a refusal of further funding, even on a trial basis, if the decision is explained and grapples with the relevant issues. . . . I . . . make it clear so that the claimant, whose life is on any view tragically short, does not have unrealistic expectations as a result of the modest success which she has achieved here.[104]

VII Top-Up Payments

If patients fail to persuade their PCT to exceptionally fund the non-NICE approved medicine, their only options are to accept the decision or to try to pay for the medicine themselves. Until 2009, however, it was widely believed that the Department of Health's *Code of Conduct for Private Practice* prohibited NHS in-patients from purchasing additional medicines for use during their NHS care. The Code provided that 'a patient cannot be both a private and an NHS patient for the treatment of one condition during a single visit to an NHS organisation',[105] and most NHS Trusts interpreted this as meaning that a patient who pays for a non-NHS funded medicine has to opt out of NHS care altogether, and become a fully private patient. This means that they have to bear the full costs of their care, including paying for other drugs that would ordinarily be freely available to them,[106] as well as paying in full for nursing care and hospital consultants' time.

This interpretation of the Code put seriously ill patients and their families in an extraordinarily invidious position: they might know, often through research on the internet, that a non-NICE approved medicine is available for their condition. Raising the money, perhaps a few thousand pounds, to pay for it might seem like an attractive option, but if this then results in their exclusion from the NHS, it will be an option only for the very richest members of society.

Mike Richards, the National Clinical Director for Cancer, was commissioned to make recommendations about so-called 'top-up payments' within the NHS. He recommended a number of measures that were intended to reduce the number of affected patients: including, as we saw earlier, modifying cost-effectiveness thresholds for life-prolonging medicines. But acknowledging that this would not eliminate the problem of top-up payments, he also recommended that 'NHS patients should be able to receive additional private drugs as long as these are delivered separately from the NHS elements of their care'.[107]

---

[104] ibid [44]. See also *R (on the application of Ross) v West Sussex Primary Care Trust* [2008] EWHC 2252 (Admin).

[105] Department of Health, *The Code of Conduct for Private Practice: Recommended Standards of Practice for NHS Consultants* (DH, 2004) para 2.13, now superseded.

[106] J Appleby and J Maybin, 'Topping up NHS Care' (2008) 337 *British Medical Journal* 2449.

[107] Department of Health, *Improving Access to Medicines for NHS Patients: A Report for the Secretary of State for Health by Professor Mike Richards* (London, DH, 2008), recommendation 9, 59.

Separate delivery of privately purchased medicines is intended to ensure that NHS resources do not indirectly subsidise private treatment by covering the costs associated with the medicine's delivery. In practice, however, separate delivery might not be in the best interests of patients. If a patient is very sick, a clinically unnecessary journey to a private wing or separate private hospital might be both uncomfortable and stressful. Continuity of care is important for patients, and good practice in the care of cancer patients will often be to deliver 'cocktails' of different medicines at the same time.

Where moving the patient is not appropriate, Richards suggested that it should be possible to 'designat[e] an area of an NHS hospital for the delivery of privately funded treatments'.[108] That may mean delivering privately funded medicines on NHS wards, by temporarily designating an area of the ward as 'private'.[109] This leads to the possibility – which many NHS healthcare professionals find problematic – of two NHS patients in adjoining beds receiving a different standard of care, according to their ability to pay.

It remains to be seen whether the government's announcement of its new cancer fund will obviate the need for top-up payments. The cancer fund will make £200 million available each year to cover drugs not yet approved by NICE and

> drug/indication combinations appraised by NICE and not recommended on the basis of cost effectiveness, or where the recommendations materially restrict access to the treatment to a smaller group of patients than the specifications set out in the marketing authorization.[110]

Following the Richards report on top-up payments, a number of insurance policies which would cover the costs of non-NICE approved cancer drugs emerged. Now the status of these policies is uncertain, given that it is not clear whether the cancer fund will effectively mean that cancer patients are never denied treatment on cost grounds, or whether the costs of new cancer drugs are such that, even with this dedicated increased funding, some patients will still be denied treatment within the NHS and will seek to top-up their NHS care with privately funded medicines.

VIII Conclusion

In 2010, the government announced that when the current PPRS expires in 2014, it plans to replace it with a system of value-based pricing while simultaneously removing NICE's powers to determine the availability of medicines within the

---

[108] ibid, recommendation 10, 59.

[109] R Chafe et al, 'Accessing Unfunded Cancer Drugs in Publicly Funded Hospitals' (2009) 10 *The Lancet Oncology* 306–07.

[110] Department of Health, *The Cancer Drugs Fund: Guidance to Support Operation of the Cancer Drugs Fund in 2011–12* (DH, 2011) para 4.1.

NHS. These decisions would be devolved to doctors, in primary care; this means to GP practices and GP consortia. New drugs could be sold cheaply until evidence of effectiveness becomes available, thus removing the period of NICE blight while NICE carries out its appraisals. But value-based pricing as a substitute for NICE, rather than a supplement, will have a number of serious disadvantages.

First, all value-based pricing does is determine the price that the NHS is willing to pay for a medicine. Unlike NICE, it will not set out restrictions on access. This is a very poor way of controlling total expenditure: a drug's price might be set at, say, £10,000 for one year's supply for one patient, but this is the only control exercised by value-based pricing. If GPs prescribe this drug to all patients with, say, bipolar disorder, rather than confining prescription to the subset of patients with bipolar disorder in whom treatment is cost-effective, regardless of the 'value-based price', this might prove to be a huge drain on NHS resources. Since doctors also have the freedom to prescribe drugs off-label, setting the price of a medicine without limiting the volume of prescriptions is clearly a wholly ineffective way to restrict costs. In contrast, NICE not only determines whether the price of the medicine justifies NHS provision, but it can also set restrictions on availability, so that the drug is prescribed to a limited subset of patients, thus offering a more effective brake on NHS expenditure.

There is also no doubt that delegating decision-making to doctors will lead to a postcode lottery – different practices or consortia will make different decisions – and to patients shopping around to find a practice which will prescribe a medicine that they have initially been denied. How will GP practices or consortia make decisions about what to prescribe and what not to prescribe? One danger is that they may over-rely on promotional information from pharmaceutical companies, which will be more concise, clear and user-friendly than the complex data NICE uses to make its decisions. Even if GP consortia were to engage in sophisticated cost-effectiveness analysis, this would be inefficient and would lose the economies of scale gained if one national body does this once for the whole country.

Giving GPs responsibility for controlling the NHS budget will put them in an impossible position. It will be difficult for doctors to tell patients that effective treatment is available, but that it will not be provided because their practice or consortia, has decided that it is too expensive. When these decisions are taken centrally by a body like NICE, they are taken at the macro population-wide level: Tyverb, for example, was insufficiently cost-effective to justify NHS provision. Doctors, however, make decisions at the micro individual level. If an individual doctor refuses to prescribe Tyverb to patient X because he and his partners believe that offering it to her will mean that the practice has less money to spend on other patients, there is no denying that the patient's doctor has decided not to give effective treatment to an individual patient who could benefit from it. Doctors will not relish this responsibility, and patients will find it hard to understand. As Clare Gerada, president of the Royal College of General Practitioners, explained:

the negative impact for GPs could be patients lobbying outside their front door, saying, 'You've got a nice BMW car but you will not allow me to have this cytotoxic drug that will give me three more months of life'. [111]

Because it is common for patients to be discharged from hospital back to ongoing primary care from their GP, difficulties may also emerge if hospital doctors start patients on medicines that their GP practice says it cannot afford.

The government's pledge to increase patients' access to medicines by removing NICE's powers to limit access, and setting up a £200 million cancer fund, is problematic for a number of reasons, but perhaps the most worrying is that if doctors are free to prescribe medicines that NICE would judge to be insufficiently cost-effective, the NHS is effectively writing a blank cheque to the pharmaceutical industry. This is neither sensible nor affordable.

---

[111] D Campbell, 'Doctors Warned to Expect Unrest Over NHS Reforms' *The Guardian* Friday 19 November 2010.

7

Funding and Access to Medicines: A Global Problem

I N THE PREVIOUS chapter it was evident that even a wealthy country like the United Kingdom will sometimes have to ration potentially life-saving medicines. In the world's poorest countries, the problem is infinitely more acute. Diseases which are considered curable in the West continue to kill people in huge numbers in low-income countries: it has been estimated that 18 million people each year die from easily treatable conditions, which amounts to 50,000 avoidable deaths every day.[1] This is not only a public health issue of global importance, but the failure to provide a decent minimum standard of healthcare has also been said to represent an interference with basic human rights.[2] The World Health Organisation's Constitution states that 'the enjoyment of the highest attainable standard of health is one of the fundamental rights of every human being'.[3] According to the United Nation's Universal Declaration of Human Rights, 'Everyone has the right to a standard of living adequate for the health and well-being of himself and of his family'. The International Covenant on Social, Economic and Cultural Rights enshrines the right 'of everyone to the enjoyment of the highest attainable standard of physical and mental health'.[4] Of course, notwithstanding ongoing debates over the justiciability of social and economic rights,[5] these provisions beg the questions of what counts as 'adequate' and what is meant by 'highest attainable'. It is, however, unarguable that too many people worldwide do not enjoy anything like the 'highest attainable' or even a barely adequate standard of health.

There are many reasons for global health inequalities, such as poor sanitation, a lack of clean water, inadequate nutrition and endemic poverty. It is also true that governments in some low-income countries have failed adequately to protect the health of their citizens: in 2007, the World Medical Association passed a *Resolution On Health And Human Rights Abuses In Zimbabwe*, criticising Robert Mugabe's

---

[1] T Pogge, 'Human Rights and Global Health: A Research Program' (2005) 36 *Metaphilosophy* 182–209.

[2] ibid.

[3] World Health Organisation Constitution, 45th edn (WHO, 2006).

[4] International Covenant on Social, Economic and Cultural Rights art 12 (United Nations (UN), 1966).

[5] C Gearty and V Mantouvalou, *Debating Social Rights* (Hart Publishing, Oxford, 2010).

regime for, among other things, denying healthcare to people deemed to be associated with opposition political parties.[6] A year later, an organisation called Physicians for Human Rights issued a report advocating the investigation of Robert Mugabe's government for crimes against humanity for overseeing and ignoring the breakdown of the nation's healthcare system.[7] The problem of global health inequalities is certainly not limited to inadequate access to drugs. Nevertheless, improving the supply of pharmaceutical products to people in low-income countries has become an especially prominent issue in recent years, and although this book is principally about the regulation of medicines within the UK, it is clear that state and non-state actors in high-income countries like the UK are increasingly concerning themselves with the question of global access to medicines.

In the past, it was common to describe countries as either 'developed' or 'developing'; this simple, binary classification is increasingly problematic because some countries which have been categorised as 'developing', like India and China, are now more accurately described as middle-income countries, or even emerging powers. Brazil, Russia, India, China and more recently South Africa, sometimes referred to as the BRICS countries, are in a radically different position in relation to access to medicines from the world's least developed countries, like Somalia and Bhutan. In some middle-income countries, there are very high levels of inequality, such that a significant proportion of the population still lives in poverty, while other sections of the population are much more affluent. These are also countries which have their own flourishing pharmaceutical industries,[8] and which are emerging markets for medicines, especially as their populations increasingly suffer from non-communicable diseases, like heart disease, diabetes, mental illness and cancer,[9] in addition to infectious and communicable diseases, like HIV/AIDS and TB. Indeed, low and middle-income countries now bear nearly 80 per cent of the global burden of non-communicable diseases.[10] Later diagnosis and worse treatment options mean non-communicable diseases kill more people at an earlier age in low-income countries. As the Global Forum for Health Research has pointed out:

> A long-standing stereotype has held that non-communicable conditions are 'diseases of affluence' characteristic of developed countries, while developing countries mainly suffer from communicable diseases. It is clear that this no longer applies and that a major epidemiological transition has taken place.[11]

[6] Adopted by the 58th World Medical Association (WMA) General Assembly, Copenhagen, Denmark, October 2007 (WMA, 2007).

[7] K Brulliard, 'Zimbabwean Government Denying Human Right to Health, Doctors' Group Says' *Washington Post* 14 January 2009.

[8] JP Ruger, and NY Ng, 'Emerging and Transitioning Countries' Role in Global Health' (2010) 3 *Saint Louis University Journal of Health Law & Policy* 253.

[9] P Farmer et al, 'Expansion of Cancer Care and Control in Countries of Low and Middle Income: A Call to Action' (2010) 376 *The Lancet* 1186–93.

[10] WHO, *Global Status Report on Noncommunicable Diseases 2010: Description of the Global Burden of NCDs, their Risk Factors and Determinants* (WHO, 2011).

[11] Global Forum for Health Research (2005) 1 *Global Forum Update on Research for Health* 10–11.

This chapter begins with a brief description of the reasons why much needed medicines are often unaffordable. Global patent protection and exceptions to it are discussed, as well as innovative schemes to provide incentives to develop medicines for low-income countries. It is no longer true to say that the diseases of the poor are completely ignored by high-income countries. One of the Millenium Development Goals is, 'in cooperation with pharmaceutical companies, to provide access to affordable essential drugs in developing countries'.[12] In June 2011, the British Prime Minister gave a speech in which he committed the UK Government to increase its spending on vaccines for the poor:

> today we come together, because we have the chance to save another four million lives by funding vaccines against diseases like pneumonia and diarrhoea. Frankly the idea of children dying from pneumonia and diarrhoea should be absolutely unthinkable in 2011. . . . Today we can help end that cruel lottery and I am delighted to say that Britain will play its full part. In addition to our existing support for GAVI [Global Alliance for Vaccines and Immunisation] we will contribute £814 million of new funding up to 2015. This will help vaccinate over 80 million children and save 1.4 million lives.[13]

The chapter concludes by considering whether the recent emphasis by governments, international organisations and philanthropists on access to medicines, while laudable and important, might also at times reinforce the idea that pharmaceutical drugs are always a magic bullet, capable of single-handedly eradicating disease. Drugs are important, but it is also crucial that the resources devoted to access to medicines initiatives are not at the expense of effective non-drug public health measures.

I The Problem of Unaffordable Medicines

In order to maximise profits, drug companies invest heavily in the development of medicines that will have large markets in countries which can afford to pay high prices. If investment into drug research and development (R&D) is concentrated on products which are likely to prove profitable, the health needs of countries where the market for expensive new drugs is non-existent will be poorly served. Towards the end of the twentieth century, this was commonly described as the 10/90 gap, whereby health problems which affected 90 per cent of the world population attracted only 10 per cent of the global funding for health research.[14] Although that statistic is now a little out of date, it is still true that research into diseases which primarily affect the world's poor – like sleeping sickness and dengue fever – continue to attract much less commercial investment than research into treatments which will have large markets in the West.

---

[12] Target 8E, available at www.un.org/millenniumgoals/.

[13] D Cameron Speech at Vaccine Summit (13 June 2011), available at www.number10.gov.uk/news/speeches-and-transcripts/2011/06/speech-at-vaccine-summit-64686.

[14] Global Forum for Health Research, *The 10/90 Gap in Health Research* (GCFR, Geneva, 1999).

Because people in low-income countries also suffer from non-communicable diseases which affect people living in richer countries, the unavailability of medicines is not always due to a lack of investment in research. Rather for conditions like cancer and HIV/AIDS, the problem is that drugs that are still within patent protection will be expensive, and in low-income countries, they are likely to be unaffordable. In the UK, someone who is diagnosed as HIV positive will generally have access to effective combination therapy that will significantly delay, or even prevent, the onset of an AIDS-related illness. Providing this is expensive: the average cost of treating an HIV positive person in the UK was estimated to be £18,000 per year in 2006, and this figure is continually rising as people live longer and develop resistance to existing treatments.[15] Low-income countries, which are commonly countries that have been particularly badly affected by the AIDS pandemic, simply do not have the resources to provide treatments that are available in the West, and it is therefore unsurprising that throughout the world, only about a third of all individuals infected with the HIV virus have access to effective antiretroviral therapy.[16]

Of course, one of the principal reasons why drugs are expensive is because – in order to recoup their R&D costs, as well as the R&D costs of drugs that fail during the protracted process of drug development – manufacturers are allowed to hold worldwide patents on new medicines for 20 years. Without patent protection of their successful new medicines, so the argument goes, there might be little incentive to invest in risky and expensive research: if competitors could enter the market with an identical product as soon as a new medicine reaches the marketplace, it might be difficult for the original innovator to cover its costs, let alone make a profit.

The patent system is supposed to promote public health too by providing an incentive to carry out valuable research. In relation to diseases which primarily affect people in low-income countries, this assumption underlying the patent system – that patents provide an incentive to develop useful products – simply does not work. Consumers in poor countries are charged high prices for branded, patented medicines, but the profits that companies make from these sales is not then ploughed back into research capable of meeting the health needs of citizens of low-income countries. On the contrary, patents work as an incentive to produce medicines which will make a profit in high-income countries, and these are generally not medicines that will serve the health needs of the poor. Patent protection might even be said to protect the commercial interests of pharmaceutical innovators at the expense of the health interests of populations in low-income countries. This is especially true in relation to secondary, 'evergreening' patents, discussed in chapter three, where it is by no means clear that there is a public health justification for offering a financial incentive to investigate changes to delivery methods or to drug presentation.

---

[15] S Mandilia et al, 'Rising Population Cost of Treating People Living with HIV in the UK, 1997–2013' (2010) 5 *PLoS One* e15677.

[16] UNAIDS/UNDP/WHO Concerned Over Sustainability and Scale Up of HIV Treatment (WHO, 2011).

One obvious solution to the problem of unaffordable medicines might be to introduce modifications to global patent protection in order to promote earlier access to cheaper generic medicines in countries where they are desperately needed, but where branded, patented drugs simply cost too much. Given that 90 per cent of pharmaceutical companies' revenues come from the US, Europe and Japan,[17] it is not clear that their profits would be dented significantly if earlier generic entry were possible in low-income countries. Indeed, as explained in the next section, there have been initiatives which enable low-income countries to override patent rights on health grounds, but in practice these have not been an overwhelming success. More recently, there has been considerable interest in other mechanisms which alter ordinary market conditions in order to provide incentives to the delivery of medicines to low-income countries.

II TRIPs, Doha and Generics

The World Trade Organisation's (WTO) Agreement on Trade-Related Aspects of Intellectual Property Rights (TRIPs) is a multinational agreement which sets out minimum standards for patent protection within all WTO Member States. Countries which sign up to TRIPs agree to recognise global patents on new drugs for 20 years, during which time cheaper generic equivalents cannot enter the marketplace. TRIPs also sets minimum standards for the existence of effective enforcement procedures and remedies.

Before the TRIPs agreement came into force on the 1st of January 1995, around 40 countries offered no patent protection at all for pharmaceutical drugs, and many offered much less than 20 years.[18] In countries where patents were not recognised, manufacturers could produce generic versions of existing, patent-protected drugs, and sell these cheaply. Stefan Ecks explains how, before it joined the WTO, India did not recognise patents in the active ingredients of pharmaceutical products, which meant 'that any drug molecule, even if patented in other countries, could be reverse-engineered and generically produced in India'.[19] Unsurprisingly, other low-income nations commonly sought to import Indian generic drugs, in preference to purchasing the original branded versions, leading some commentators to describe India as the developing world's pharmacy.[20] Of course, the absence of patent protection in some countries, coupled with other countries' willingness to engage in 'parallel trade' in generic medicines did not protect the commercial interests of powerful companies, which clearly wanted to ensure that there was a worldwide market for their branded products.

[17] A Pollock, 'Transforming the Critique of Big Pharma' (2011) 6 *BioSocieties* 106–18.

[18] World Health Organisation, *Globalisation, TRIPs and Access to Pharmaceuticals: WHO Policy Perspectives on Medicines* (WHO, 2001).

[19] S Ecks, 'Global Pharmaceutical Markets and Corporate Citizenship: The Case of Novartis' Anti-cancer Drug Glivec' (2008) 3 *BioSocieties* 165–81.

[20] Oxfam India, *Oxfam Urges India to Remain 'Pharmacy of the Developing World'* (Oxfam, 2010).

Signing up to TRIPs is a condition of membership of the WTO, and so for many countries, the flexibility they used to enjoy in setting their patent rules in order to meet their citizens' needs has now largely disappeared. Most low-income countries had to implement TRIPs by 2000, but some countries were granted an additional transition period of five years. Least developed countries, as defined by the UN,[21] have until 2013 to implement TRIPs, and until 2016 to provide full patent protection for pharmaceutical products.

One obvious way to increase access to medicines in countries which cannot afford the high prices of expensive branded medicines might be to create except-ions to TRIPs so that low-income countries can access generic versions of expen-sive patented drugs before the 20-year minimum period of patent protection has expired. There are a number of ways in which this might happen. TRIPs has always allowed for what is known as compulsory licensing, according to which a govern-ment grants a licence to a generics manufacturer, without the consent of the patent holder, on condition that the patent holder is given 'adequate remuneration'.[22] Compulsory licensing was not generally intended to be a first step, however, and the assumption was that generics companies would apply for a compulsory licence only after they had tried and failed to negotiate a voluntary licence with the patent holder, on reasonable terms. In cases of national emergency or extreme urgency, this requirement to negotiate first with the patent holder can be waived, and the compulsory licence issued immediately. This means that if a country's health problems could be said to amount to a national emergency – which might be relatively straightforward in the case of an epidemic or pandemic – compulsory licensing enables its government to override patent rights, without any need for prior notice or consultation with the patent holder.

In TRIPs' first years of operation, compulsory licensing did not prove to be an overwhelming success. On the contrary, not only was it seldom utilised, but phar-maceutical companies threatened to take governments which issued compulsory licences to court,[23] and the US government used its considerable economic and political power, and the threat of trading sanctions, to lobby against and even block the introduction of compulsory licences for drugs used in the treatment of HIV/AIDS in South Africa and Thailand.[24] As a result, in 2001 the WTO issued a *Declaration on the TRIPs Agreement and Public Health* at Doha which reaffirmed that:

> The TRIPs Agreement does not and should not prevent Members from taking measures to protect public health. Accordingly, while reiterating our commitment to the TRIPs Agreement, we affirm that the Agreement can and should be interpreted and imple-

---

[21] See further UN High Commissioner for Least Developed Countries: www.un.org/ohrlls/.

[22] Agreement on Trade-Related Aspects of Intellectual Property Rights (TRIPs) art 31.

[23] See further U Schuklenk and RE Ashcroft, 'Affordable Access to Essential Medication in Developing Countries: Conflicts between Ethical and Economic Imperatives' (2002) 27 *Journal of Medicine and Philosophy* 179–95.

[24] NA Bass, 'Implications of the TRIPs Agreement for Developing Countries: Pharmaceutical Patent Laws in Brazil and South Africa in the 21st Century' (2002) 34 *George Washington International Law Review* 191–222.

mented in a manner supportive of WTO Members' right to protect public health and, in particular, to promote access to medicines for all.[25]

The Doha declaration went on to reiterate the right of WTO members to make full use of the provisions within TRIPs which provide the sort of flexibility which might be used to protect public health, in particular, the right to grant compulsory licences and the freedom to determine the grounds upon which such licences are granted.[26] Each member state, according to the Doha declaration,

> has the right to determine what constitutes a national emergency or other circumstances of extreme urgency, it being understood that public health crises, including those relating to HIV/AIDS, tuberculosis, malaria and other epidemics, can represent a national emergency or other circumstances of extreme urgency.[27]

In addition to reminding countries of their right to issue compulsory licences, without prior negotiation, in cases of 'extreme urgency', the Doha declaration also recognised that compulsory licensing could not provide a worldwide solution to the problem of unaffordable medicines.[28] According to the original TRIPs provisions on compulsory licensing, a government could issue a compulsory licence only for a medicine which was intended for domestic use.[29] Countries like South Africa, India, China and Brazil have thriving generics industries,[30] but the world's poorest countries have no manufacturing capacity and hence cannot benefit from domestic-only compulsory licensing. Two years after the Doha meeting, this problem was addressed by the *Implementation of Paragraph 6 Decision*, and since 2003 it has also been possible for medicines produced under compulsory licence to be imported to low-income countries which lack manufacturing capacity.[31]

Compulsory licensing of medicines in cases of extreme urgency, and permitting their importation to countries which cannot make their own cheap medicines, would at first sight look like it might be able to provide a solution to the unaffordability of patented medicines in low-income countries. And there have been times when countries have successfully used the threat of compulsory licensing as a bargaining tool in order to negotiate lower prices for medicines.[32] In practice, however, despite the existence of a means to override patent rights, and despite the WTO's affirmation at Doha that it can and should be used to 'protect public health and, in particular, to promote access to medicines for all', compulsory licences are comparatively rare.

One problem is that the process for obtaining a compulsory licence in one country, for import into another, is extremely cumbersome, and time-consuming.

---

[25] WTO, *Doha Declaration on the TRIPs Agreement and Public Health* (WTO, 2001) art 4.
[26] ibid art 5(b).
[27] ibid art 5(c).
[28] ibid art 6.
[29] TRIPs art 31(f).
[30] VB Kerry and K Lee, 'TRIPs, the Doha Declaration and Paragraph 6 Decision: What are the Remaining Steps for Protecting Access to Medicines?'(2007) 3 *Global Health* 3.
[31] ibid.
[32] Kerry and Lee n 30 above.

Apotex, a Canadian company, was one of the first to try to use the process, in order to produce three drugs used in combination in the treatment of HIV/AIDS, but partly as a result of difficulties in negotiating voluntary licences from the patent holders, it took three years for it to enter into an agreement to supply these drugs to Rwanda.[33] Producing drugs under compulsory licence for export to low-income countries 'is an activity with exceptionally thin margins',[34] and there are few incentives for a manufacturer 'to acquire the capacities and rights to produce and export drugs that they will then have to supply at marginal cost'.[35] It is therefore unsurprising that generics manufacturers have generally not enthusiastically embraced compulsory licensing for export.

Interestingly, however, a disinclination to engage in compulsory licensing is also evident among countries which might benefit from importing medicines produced under compulsory licence. A reason for the delays experienced by Apotex was that many low-income countries were reluctant to be named in their licence application, fearing retribution from more powerful trading nations.[36] Governments in low-income countries tend to be concerned about the impact of compulsory licensing upon their country's reputation as a trading partner.[37] This problem is exacerbated by the negotiation of regional and bilateral free trade agreements (FTAs) – described as TRIPs-plus measures – between richer and poorer countries. Most commonly, these involve the US or the EU negotiating an FTA with a low or middle-income country or countries, in which the poorer countries agree to waive some of their rights under TRIPs in return for import/export agreements. TRIPs-plus measures can include a country agreeing to restrict its use of compulsory licensing, or agreeing to recognise extended periods of data exclusivity,[38] or even to increase the period of patent protection beyond 20 years. TRIPs is, after all, a *minimum* standards agreement and countries which are concerned about finding markets for their goods are free to negotiate away some of the rights they would normally have under TRIPs.[39] According to Médicins sans Frontières, TRIPs-plus agreements 'undermine the Doha Declaration and . . . restrict, if not eliminate, the flexibilities and safeguards it reaffirmed'.[40] There is also no evidence that any perceived trade advantages which might accrue to a country which agrees to a TRIPs-plus FTA will in practice ever be sufficient to outweigh the costs of bargaining away rights under TRIPs.

If compulsory licensing has not been able to overcome the barriers patent rights create for global access to medicines, another possible solution might be the set-

[33] SE Davies, *Global Politics of Health* (Cambridge, Polity, 2010) 169.

[34] KC Shadlen, 'The Political Economy of AIDS Treatment: Intellectual Property and the Transformation of Generic Supply' (2007) 51 *International Studies Quarterly* 559–81.

[35] ibid.

[36] Davies n 33 above, 169.

[37] Kerry and Lee n 30 above; ibid.

[38] Oxfam, *Trading Away Access to Medicines How the European Union's Trade Agenda has Taken a Wrong Turn* (Oxfam, 2009).

[39] Correa, C, 'Implications of Bilateral Free Trade Agreements on Access to Medicines' (2006)84 *Bulletin of the World Health Organisation* 399–404.

[40] Médicins sans Frontières, *Access to Medicines at Risk across the Globe: What to Watch Out For in Free Trade Agreements with the United States* (MSF, 2004).

ting up of patent pools. Patent pools involve two or more patent holders agreeing to share their patents with each other, or with third parties, through the negotiation of licences. They have been used by manufacturers of digital and computer technology for self-interested reasons, in order to ensure that different manufacturers' products are compatible with common file-types, like MP3 files. In relation to pharmaceutical patent pools, the point would be not for large pharmaceutical companies to share their patents with each other, however, but rather to make them available to generics manufacturers in low-income countries. In a pharmaceutical patent pool, patent holders voluntarily contribute their patents to a centrally administered pool, where they are made available under licence to manufacturers, who then pay royalties for early access to information which would otherwise be protected by patent.

The Pool for Open Innovation against Neglected Tropical Diseases (NTD) currently contains 2300 patents useful for the production of medicines for the treatment of neglected tropical diseases, which can be made available to anyone 'with a serious commitment to research and develop medicines for NTDs, including industry, academic researchers, funding agencies, and other third parties who can deliver real benefits for patients in least developed countries'. Patent holders agree not to seek royalties for sales in any countries on the UN's Least Developed Countries (LDC) list. Of course, it is not clear that these countries will actually have any generics manufacturing capacity which can take advantage of this open-access, and so they will only benefit if manufacturers in *other* countries, like India, decide to apply for access to patents for the treatment of NTDs which they then intend to supply to LDCs. If the LDCs cannot afford even these cheaper generic imports, the patent pool will not necessarily have solved the problem.

The Medicines Patent Pool, originally set up by UNITAID, is now a free-standing agency which runs an HIV/AIDS-specific patent pool. The Medicines Patent Pool negotiates with patent holders to voluntarily share their AIDS-related patents. Interested manufacturers can then obtain a licence to develop and produce generic versions of the compounds which would otherwise be protected by patents. The Pool describes its advantages as follows:

> It will provide a win-win-win situation for all parties involved: patent holders get royalties on the sales of resulting generic medicines; generic manufacturers get access to broader markets; and patients can benefit from access to the adapted, affordable and safe medicines they need.[41]

A patent pool is especially valuable in the context of HIV/AIDS because of the need for fixed dose combinations of different compounds combined in one pill. At the time of writing, the Medicines Patent Pool has acquired one patent from the US National Institutes for Health, and it is in negotiations with a number of pharmaceutical companies about donations of their patents.

It is clear that, if it works, earlier entry of generic products – whether through compulsory licensing or patent pools – is capable of making a dramatic difference

---

[41] www.medicinespatentpool.org/.

to the affordability of medicines. As the first antiretroviral therapy (ART) came out of patent protection, the annual cost of a first-line ART regime for low-income countries decreased by around 99 per cent from over $10,000 per person in 2000 to as little as $67 in 2010.[42] This is clearly a success story, but it would be a mistake to think that the existence of generic ART has 'solved' the problem of the unaffordability of treatments for HIV/AIDS. The cheapest generic first-line ART has more and worse side effects than the patent-protected first-line treatment which is currently given to people who are diagnosed as HIV positive in richer countries. Consumers of medicines who suffer side effects are more likely to stop taking their medication, and because ART appears to offer some protection against onward transmission, this increases the risk that they will infect others. Early interruption also contributes to the development of drug resistance. Almost everyone who is receiving ART in low-income countries is receiving first-line antiretroviral treatment.[43] In time, it can be predicted that they will develop resistance to this cheaper generic treatment, and will need to be moved on to more expensive second and third-line treatments. This has been described as a 'treatment timebomb',[44] where the recent gains in worldwide access to HIV treatment may simply disappear if the second and third-line treatments, which are currently still within patent protection, do not become much more affordable.

III Incentives to Develop and Supply Treatments in Low-income Countries

Earlier generic entry in low-income countries, even if it were to become widely practised, does nothing to address the problem that producing drugs specifically to meet the health needs of low-income countries is unlikely to be profitable, especially when compared with the profits that can be made from medicines which are prescribed to large patient groups in richer countries.

Initiatives to improve research into and access to medicines to meet the health needs of low-income countries include both 'push' and 'pull' mechanisms. Push mechanisms are intended to stimulate research by offering grants and other assistance. In contrast, pull mechanisms offer incentives to companies to ensure the commercial profitability of effective medicines and vaccines. In recent years, there has been increased interest in devising novel pull mechanisms which distort normal market conditions so that companies have sound *commercial* reasons to

---

[42] United Nations Development Programme, *Good Practice Guide: Improving Access to Treatment by Utilizing Public Health Flexibilities in the WTO TRIPs Agreement* (UNDP, 2010).

[43] ibid.

[44] All Party Parliamentary Group on AIDS, *The Treatment Timebomb: Report of the Enquiry of The All Party Parliamentary Group on AIDS into Long-Term Access to HIV Medicines in the Developing World* (Parliament, 2009).

develop and supply medicines and vaccines for diseases which principally affect people living in low-income countries.

Since 2000, the Global Alliance for Vaccines and Immunisation (GAVI) has brought together state actors and other donors in order to fund vaccination programmes in low-income countries (defined for these purposes as countries where the annual gross domestic product is less than $1000 per head of population). GAVI has embraced a new initiative known as an Advanced Market Commitment (AMC).[45] One of the first AMCs was launched by GAVI at the G8 summit in L'Aquila in Italy in 2009.[46] It involved governments from a number of G8 countries, and the Gates foundation, offering $1.5 billion in an AMC to fund pneumococcal vaccines.

So how do AMCs work? Rather than forcing companies to allow early generic entry, AMCs preserve originator companies' intellectual property rights, and instead encourage them to invest in vaccines where, under ordinary market conditions, they would have no incentive to do so. In relation to vaccines, there are a number of factors which make R&D especially risky. Most obviously, a vaccine is a one-off injection which, if it works, will obviate the need for future treatment. Vaccines are never likely to be as profitable as treatments which must be taken long-term.

AMCs reward companies that produce valuable vaccines with a guarantee of donor-subsidised future sales, at a price which is determined in advance,[47] with a lower, longer-term 'tail price' which can be charged after the AMC funds run out. If no useful product is developed, donors pay nothing, but if a useful medicine or vaccine is produced, then it can be rolled out in poor countries through donations which, when added to the contribution from the host country, enable the company to be reimbursed at a rate which provides an incentive to pursue research into vaccines which could save lives in low-income countries. Importantly AMCs do not provide a guarantee as to the *volume* of sales: if they did then there would be little incentive for the company to ensure that the medicine produced is, in fact, worth buying.[48] Rather, the donors' subsidy is contingent upon the new medicine or vaccine being something that the low-income nation will be willing to buy, at the heavily subsidised price. The theory is that, as a result of the additional funds provided by donors, and because donors only pay for positive results rather than funding research which might or might not yield a useful product, the market return from developing a successful vaccine will be comparable with the return from developing a drug which can be marketed successfully in the West.[49]

---

[45] M Kremer and R Glennerster, *Strong Medicine: Creating Incentives for Pharmaceutical Research on Neglected Diseases* (Princeton, Princeton University Press, 2004).

[46] AD Usher, 'Dispute Over Pneumococcal Vaccine Initiative' (2009) 374 *The Lancet* 1879–80.

[47] World Bank and GAVI, *AMC Pilot Proposal* (Washington DC, World Bank, 2006), available at www.cgdev.org/doc/ghprn/AMC_Pilot.pdf.

[48] ER Berndt and JA Hurvitz, 'Vaccine Advance-Purchase Agreements for Low-Income Countries: Practical Issues' (2005) 24 *Health Affairs* 653–65.

[49] M Kremer and R Glennerster, 'Incentives for Research on Neglected Disease' (2005) 365 *The Lancet* 753–54.

It would be hard to argue against the wider availability of effective vaccines in low-income countries, and yet a number of commentators have suggested that the 'win-win' image of AMCs may be misplaced.[50] One central problem is that it is impossible to know, in advance, how much it will cost to develop and supply an effective medicine or vaccine, and so setting the advance purchase price may involve no more than guesswork. Companies have an obvious financial incentive to overestimate the costs, because if they underestimate them, they will be out of pocket and the AMC will not have achieved its objective. If the cost per dose is higher than it needs to be, some of the money which both donors and the low-income country invest in the AMC will provide additional profits to the pharmaceutical company, when it could more usefully have been spent on immunising more children. Donald Light explains the problem as follows:

> I estimate that the new pneumococcal vaccines can be manufactured for a sustainable average cost of $1.25 a dose, including the capital costs of manufacturing capacity . . . Thus the $1.5 billion donation could buy 1.2 billion doses of vaccine. The AMC model, however, has set the price at $5 or more (in an appendix it is $7.53), so that only 300 million or fewer children will be inoculated, and 80% of the donations will go towards profits.[51]

It is also worth noting that the funds which are invested in AMCs might be able to vaccine more children for less money if they were diverted towards delivering relatively cheap generic vaccines – for polio, measles, yellow fever and hepatitis, for example – which are nevertheless not standard treatment in low-income countries.[52] AMCs may then skew investment towards patented new vaccines, and away from cheaper, generic ones.

In addition, medicines and vaccines which are funded through AMCs tend to be produced in high-income countries. Providing an incentive for R&D which takes place in richer countries does not address the lack of both R&D and manufacturing capacity in low-income countries. Building infrastructure and offering training might enable low-income countries to make their own vaccines,[53] which is clearly vital in order to provide a longer-term solution to global health inequalities. Instead it might be argued that AMCs preserve a model in which vaccines are produced by highly profitable pharmaceutical companies and are made available to people in low-income countries only through the largesse of Western governments and philanthropists.

AMCs also reinforce the idea that vaccines are a private, commercial good, from which profits can and should be made, rather than seeing them as a public good, where the benefit to society is so overwhelming that the privatised intellectual

[50] L McGoey, 'Entropic Failure in Global Health' (forthcoming); D Light, *Advanced Market Commitments: Current Realities and Alternate Approaches* (Amsterdam, Health Action International Europe/Medico International Publications, 2009).

[51] D W Light, 'Is G8 Putting Profits Before the World's Poorest Children? (2007) 370 *The Lancet* 297–98.

[52] DW Light, 'Saving the Pneumococcal AMC and GAVI' (2011) 7 *Human Vaccines* 1–4.

[53] R Horton and P Das, 'The Vaccine Paradox' (2011) *The Lancet* advance access.

property model is inappropriate. Since it has been estimated that someone with TB will infect up to 50 per cent of his contacts, curing someone of TB is not just a private benefit for the person who is successfully treated, rather it benefits the whole community by reducing others' risk of infection.[54] Certainly, some of the early successes in vaccine research did not require the 'pull' of guaranteed future profitability in order to galvanise research into vaccines to eliminate conditions like smallpox and polio. On the contrary, when asked by a journalist who owned the patent on the first polio vaccine, its inventor Jonas Salk replied: 'well, the people I would say. There is no patent. Can you patent the sun?'[55]

A different type of pull mechanism or incentive scheme is to offer 'priority review vouchers' to reward companies which develop drugs to treat neglected diseases.[56] These have been available in the US since 2007,[57] and some commentators have advocated extending the system to Europe.[58] A priority review voucher would be granted in return for bringing to market a new chemical entity for the prevention or treatment of a neglected tropical disease, including tuberculosis, malaria, cholera and leprosy among others, and any other infectious disease for which there is no market in richer countries and which disproportionately affects poor and marginalised populations.[59] A voucher would entitle the bearer to priority regulatory review of another medicine in the future. It has been estimated that a medicine which undergoes priority review is likely to reach the market about a year sooner than it would otherwise. By extending the period of on-market patent protection by as much as a year, early approval of a blockbuster medicine might be worth several hundred million dollars. If priority review vouchers could be transferred for value, this sort of voucher system would not only encourage research into neglected diseases by large pharmaceutical companies, for whom priority review would be extremely valuable. Rather a small biotech company, or a non-profit organisation, which develops a medicine for a neglected disease could sell the voucher to a pharmaceutical company in return for funds which could be invested into further R&D into neglected diseases. In addition to offering an incentive to companies to produce treatments for neglected diseases, Sonderholm has argued that there would also potentially be health benefits to patients in the West, because potentially valuable new medicines will be available sooner than they would without the priority review voucher system.[60]

There are, however, those who have questioned whether a priority review voucher would, in fact, stimulate a company to pursue research into new drugs for

---

[54] JY Kim et al, 'Tuberculosis Control' in R Smith et al (eds), *Global Public Goods for Health: Health Economics and Public Health Perspectives* (Oxford University Press, 2003) 54–72.

[55] Quoted in SL Cochi, HF Hull and NA Ward NA, 'To Conquer Poliomyelitis Forever' (1995) 345 *The Lancet* 1589–90.

[56] DB Ridley et al, 'Developing Drugs For Developing Countries' (2006) 25 *Health Affairs* 313–24.

[57] Food and Drug Administration, Amendments Act of 2007 § 1102.

[58] DB Ridley and AC Sánchez, 'Introduction of European Priority Review Vouchers to Encourage Development of New Medicines for Neglected Diseases' (2010) 376 *The Lancet* 922–27.

[59] Ridley et al n 56 above, 313–24.

[60] J Sonderholm, 'In Defense of Priority Review Vouchers' (2009) 23 *Bioethics* 413–20.

neglected diseases.[61] One estimate of the value of a priority review voucher has been $322 million,[62] and while this is undoubtedly a significant sum, it may still be much less than the cost of developing a new drug: estimated, albeit controversially, to be approximately $800 million.[63] This objection, according to Sonderholm, could be easily met by offering three priority review vouchers instead of one. But a more fundamental problem may be that a company would have to start research into a neglected disease on the assumption that, at the time when it brings that drug to market, it will also have a potential blockbuster drug waiting in the wings. Given the uncertainties involved in drug development, it is easy to see why a company would not regard the benefits it *might* gain in the future from a priority review voucher to be sufficiently certain to justify investing in research into a neglected disease, which also might fail to lead to a valuable drug and which would then have served no useful commercial purpose at all.

Even if offering three vouchers did provide a sufficient incentive to embark on research into neglected diseases, that is only a straightforward solution if the basic funding model for priority review vouchers is considered unproblematic. Essentially by extending the on-market period of patent protection for new medicines, the costs of priority review schemes are borne by the purchasers of those medicines. In the US, priority review vouchers are paid for by insurance companies, and ultimately payments come from the premiums paid by patients. If such a system were introduced in Europe, in the UK the higher prices paid for medicines that enjoy a longer period of on-market patent protection would be borne by the NHS. Awarding more vouchers would simply increase the cost to the NHS. Within the UK, it could be argued that it would be more equitable for funding for new medicines for neglected diseases to come straightforwardly from the UK's budget for overseas aid, rather than, through the backdoor, from already scarce NHS resources.

In addition, the priority review voucher is provided in return for obtaining a marketing authorisation for a drug for an effective disease, and that certainly does not ensure that the drug is actually made available to the people who need it. Problems in the supply-chain of medicines in low-income countries – inadequate infrastructure or lack of healthcare facilities, for example – remain unaddressed. As a result of what is sometimes called the 'last mile' problem,[64] the *existence* of a new drug which could successfully treat a neglected tropical disease does not automatically translate into better health outcomes in populations affected by that disease.

Another potential downside to priority review vouchers is that they are valuable only if the new drug which the voucher-bearer selects for priority review is straightforwardly approved by the regulatory agency. This sort of scheme therefore takes

---

[61] M Ravvin, 'Incentivizing Access and Innovation for Essential Medicines: A Survey of the Problem and Proposed Solutions' (2008) 1 *Public Health Ethics* 110–23.

[62] Ridley n 56 above.

[63] See further ch 2.

[64] A Banerjee, A Hollis and T Pogge, 'The Health Impact Fund: Incentives for Improving Access to Medicines' (2010) 375 *The Lancet* 166–69.

for granted a licensing system in which it is unlikely that the drug which is reviewed in the future, in return for the investment into neglected diseases, will fail to receive a marketing authorisation. If the licensing authority's decision is to *refuse* to grant the new medicine a marketing authorisation, the purchaser of the voucher would understandably feel short-changed. Moreover, insofar as evidence appears to indicate that truncated review times are associated with the licensing of less safe medicines,[65] there might be additional health risks from schemes which promise to speed up approval times for new drugs.

A further reason for scepticism about recent interest in innovative pull mechanisms to prompt companies to invest in treatments for low-income countries is that there appears to be some evidence that this sort of investment has increased dramatically in recent years *in the absence of these novel commercial incentives.*[66] Greater public understanding of the health crises in low-income countries has created a reputational risk for large pharmaceutical companies, and in their interviews with representatives from multi-national pharmaceutical companies, Moran et al found that:

> all multinational companies engaged in neglected disease R&D stated that current government incentives had played no role in their decision to commence this R&D. They believed that additional new incentives were unlikely to shift the behaviour of firms who had disengaged from neglected disease research, and saw the main role for any new incentives as being 'to support companies who had already decided to do neglected disease R&D for other reasons'.[67]

Moran et al's controversial conclusion was therefore that:

> This offer of temptingly large commercial incentives – for activities that companies now willingly conduct for free or very cheaply – seems highly likely to shift current company activity from a strategic/altruistic approach to a for-profit model, at an additional and probably unsustainable cost to the public purse of many billions across all neglected disease products.[68]

A more revolutionary 'pull' mechanism would be to replace the patent system with cash prizes for companies which produce innovative and effective medicines.[69] One possible prize system is described by James Love as follows:

> The amount each drug is awarded would be decided by a national board, based on evidence submitted by drug developers about the use and health benefits of their products. . . . Every new drug would win something from the prize fund - the amount depending on the extent to which an innovation is expected to improve health. Investing in medically unimportant 'me-too' products or hyping drugs that have little chance of

[65] MK Olson, 'The Risk We Bear: The Effects of Review Speed and Industry User Fees on Drug Safety' (2008) 27 *Journal of Health Economics* 175–200.

[66] M Moran et al, *The New Landscape of Neglected Disease Drug Development* (Wellcome Trust, London, 2005).

[67] ibid.

[68] ibid.

[69] T Hubbard and J Love, 'A New Trade Framework for Global Healthcare R&D' (2004) 2 *PloS Biology* e52.

benefiting patients would no longer be profitable. Parts of the fund would be allocated to particular areas of need, such as neglected diseases, or diseases that affect the developing world.[70]

Of course, the obvious downside with this approach is that evidence of the drug's value appears to come from the prize's potential recipient. Without a requirement for independent assessment of a drug's value, the prize approach would provide a powerful incentive to companies to overestimate their new drug's value. Nevertheless, provided a way could be found to judge value independently, enabling useful drugs to be manufactured by generics companies from the outset, while finding a way to reward genuinely valuable health innovations, may help to alter the distorted R&D incentives produced by the patent system. As Joseph Stiglitz puts it: 'the medical prize fund would ensure that we make the best possible use of whatever knowledge we acquire, rather than hoarding it and limiting usage to those who can afford it, as Scrooge might have done'.[71]

IV Humanitarian, Charitable and Philanthropic Initiatives

A number of international organisations, charities and private philanthropic foundations have sought to address global health inequalities, both separately and in tandem. The World Health Organisation was founded in 1948, with a specific public health mandate. It has promoted the 'essential drugs list', that is drugs which are 'basic, indispensable, and necessary for the health needs of the population'.[72] The list is revised every two years, and currently contains more than 340 drugs, most of which are now out of patent protection. In low-income countries, the essential drugs list helps to direct limited health spending where it is likely to do most good.

Médicins sans Frontières was founded in 1971, and its remit – to provide healthcare services where they are most needed – is much wider than access to medicines. In 1999, it launched its Campaign for Access to Essential Medicines, intended to promote access to affordable existing medicines and vaccines and to stimulate the development of new ones. It has campaigned vigorously against TRIPs-plus trading agreements.

One of the most recent developments, and in quantitative terms at least, one of the most significant, has been the global health agenda of private philanthropists, like the Bill and Melinda Gates Foundation which has invested billions of dollars

---

[70] J Love, 'Fair Prices, Fair Profit' *New Scientist* 10 November 2007.

[71] JE Stiglitz, 'Scrooge and Intellectual Property Rights' (2006) 333 *British Medical Journal* 1279.

[72] World Health Organisation, *The Selection of Essential Drugs: WHO Technical Report Series No. 614* (Geneva, WHO, 1977). See further JA Greene, 'Making Medicines Essential: The Emergent Centrality of Pharmaceuticals in Global Health' (2011) 6 *BioSocieties* 10–33.

in public health initiatives. The Global Fund to Fight AIDS, Tuberculosis and Malaria (known as the Global Fund) was set up in 2002 and has to date received $650 million from the Gates Foundation. The Gates Foundation, along with a number of state and non-state donors, including the UK's Department for International Development, have been major donors to One World Health,[73] which is one of the first non-profit pharmaceutical companies. In practice, in order to develop and supply new medicines, One World Health has often partnered with more conventional pharmaceutical companies: for example, in 2011 it announced that its partnership with Sanofi-Aventis would enable semisynthetic artemisinin, a treatment for uncomplicated malaria, to be 'in the supply chain' by April 2012.[74]

Philanthropic initiatives in global health are not new – the Rockefeller Foundation was set up in 1913 to 'promote the wellbeing of mankind throughout the world'[75] – but the scale of funding from the Gates foundation is unprecedented.[76] As a result, the Gates foundation now has 'a great degree of influence over both the architecture and policy agenda of global health'.[77] Its status as a private foundation, making supererogatory gifts to deserving causes, has enabled it to operate relatively free from external scrutiny and accountability, leading McCoy et al to argue that: 'Grant making by the Gates Foundation seems to be largely managed through an informal system of personal networks and relationships rather than by a more transparent process based on independent and technical peer review'.[78] As with the GAVI AMC, described above, there is also a danger that the Gates Foundation overemphasises the public health benefits of new technological initiatives – a spokesman for the Gates foundation has claimed 'We believe our contribution is to help find technology-based solutions'[79] – which could lead to the relative neglect of other major determinants of global health inequalities, such as poor public health delivery systems, war and exploitative trading practices.

In addition to partnering with both public and philanthropic initiatives, pharmaceutical companies have also become major philanthropic players in their own right, and all of the large global companies have schemes whereby they provide cheap medicines to low-income countries,[80] or even donate them free of charge.[81] The Access to Medicines Foundation was set up in order to encourage the pharmaceutical industry to improve transparency and access to medicines through a league table, the latest version of which ranks 27 pharmaceutical companies on

---

[73] See further www.oneworldhealth.org/.
[74] ibid.
[75] www.rockefellerfoundation.org/.
[76] Davies n 33 above, 52.
[77] D McCoy et al, 'The Bill & Melinda Gates Foundation's Grant-Making Programme for Global Health' (2009) 373 *The Lancet* 1645–53.
[78] ibid.
[79] T Yamada, 'Global Health and the Bill & Melinda Gates Foundation' (2009) 373 *The Lancet* 2195.
[80] GlaxoSmithKline Press release: *Millions of Children in the World's Poorest Countries Could Receive Vaccination against Rotavirus Diarrhoeal Disease under New Offer Made by GSK to the GAVI Alliance* (GSK, 2011).
[81] Ecks n 19 above.

their efforts to provide access to medicines, vaccines and diagnostic tests to people living in low and middle-income countries. It also gives individual companies 'report cards' which both identify good practice in individual companies and suggest where there is room for improvement. Coming top, as GlaxoSmithKline did in 2010, is clearly a public relations coup, and the intention behind the Foundation's activities is to use both the stick of exposing poor practice, but more importantly the carrot of good publicity, in order to encourage better practice among pharmaceutical companies.

There may also sometimes be sound commercial reasons for a company to donate medicines in preference to allowing a country's generic manufacturers to manufacture it themselves and sell it cheaply. Stefan Ecks describes how the decision to distribute Glivec, an anti-cancer drug, free of charge in India had a number of commercial advantages for its manufacturer, Novartis. If Indian patients could access Glivec for free, there would be no point in Indian generics manufacturers making a cheap version, and this would help to eliminate the problem of parallel trade. If cheap versions of Glivec were readily available in other countries, it also might be hard to defend its high price in the EU and the US. Giving away an expensive medicine in low-income countries is better for business in the medicine's principal markets – since it fosters an image of the manufacturer as a 'good citizen' – than enabling the low-income country to make the medicine cheaply, which might lead to resentment about unreasonably high prices in high-income countries. In addition, building the goodwill of Indian citizens through this act of corporate generosity might help to produce a vocal lobby of supporters, and this might fortuitously assist Novartis's efforts to obtain patents in the future.

It might seem churlish to criticise schemes which enable medicines to be provided cheaply or given away for nothing in countries where they would otherwise be unaffordable. It could, however be argued, that philanthropic mechanisms for the supply of medicines again preserve the notion that essential medicines are private goods which can be purchased or given, instead of being regarded as a public good, necessary for the attainment of a minimally adequate standard of health.[82] Charitable giving is also essentially voluntary, which means that the generous pharmaceutical company is free to stop giving away medicines in the future, without needing to give reasons. It could further be argued that charitable initiatives may be degrading for recipients, putting them in the position of supplicants, rather than rights-holders.[83] If the donation of medicines to low-income countries effectively stunts the development of local pharmaceutical production facilities, it does not offer a long-term solution to inadequate access to medicines.[84]

Disease-specific schemes, like the GAVI initiative and the Global Fund also adopt what has been described as a 'vertical', or top-down approach to public

---

[82] Greene n 72 above.
[83] Schuklenk and Ashcroft n 23 above.
[84] D Ofori-Adjei and P Lartey, 'Challenges of Local Production of Pharmaceuticals in Improving Access to Medicines' in R Parker and M Sommer (eds), *Routledge Handbook in Global Public Health* (Abingdon, Routledge, 2011) 433–42.

health, and while these are capable of delivering specific benefits – the eradication of smallpox is a good example – they may be much less efficient and effective than a horizontal strategy, where the goal is not to 'parachute' in a particular drug or vaccine, but rather to improve the healthcare infrastructure within a low-income country.[85] Separate disease-specific programmes may create duplication of bureaucracy and do nothing to address the absence or inaccessibility of basic, primary care services.[86] On the contrary, they may sometimes place strain upon already weak health systems.[87] They commonly reflect the donors' concerns, rather than reflecting local demand: sponsoring organisations are able to set objectives and measure results much more easily than where their funding is less directly targeted.[88] It has even been suggested that perceived self-interest of Western donors in avoiding the spread of diseases – like severe acute respiratory syndrome (SARS), pandemic influenza and HIV/AIDS – from low-income to high-income countries is in part responsible for aid programmes' emphasis on infectious and communicable diseases,[89] which can be said to pose a security threat to donor nations, and their relative neglect of equally life-threatening non-communicable diseases.

Vertical, disease-specific programmes can also be inequitable: why should someone with HIV/AIDS receive priority treatment in a country where treatment for cancer, say, is wholly inadequate? In addition, they have a tendency to treat patients as single disease vectors, rather than as people who will have a range of different health needs, often at the same time: providing an HIV positive pregnant woman with antiretroviral drugs to prevent perinatal transmission, while failing to provide the most rudimentary obstetric care, is not a sensible or holistic way to promote infant health.[90] Patient-centred care would not treat patients differently depending upon whether their condition happens to be one which a donor organisation has designated as a priority. Building stable, local health services may not capture the public imagination in the same way as campaigns to eradicate malaria, but it may represent a fairer and more durable way to combat global health inequalities.[91]

It is also important that people in low and middle-income countries have access to *safe and effective* medicines.[92] Rather than just making medicines available, it is also important to put in place measures capable of ensuring that only medicines

---

[85] P Prakongsai et al, 'Can Earmarking Mobilise and Sustain Resources to the Health Sector?' (2008) 86 *Bulletin of the World Health Organisation* 898.

[86] J-P Under, P De Paepe and A Green, 'How do Disease-Control Programmes Damage Health Care Delivery in Developing Countries' in J-P Unger et al (eds), *International Health and Aid Policies: The Need for Alternatives* (Cambridge University Press, 2010) 48–56.

[87] N Spicer and A Walsh, '10 Best Resources on . . . the Current Effects of Global Health Initiatives on Country Health Systems' (2011) *Health Policy and Planning* published online 5 May 2011.

[88] ibid.

[89] Davies n 33 above, 136.

[90] L Garret, 'The Challenge of Global Health' (2007) 86 *Foreign Affairs* 14–38.

[91] LO Gostin, 'Redressing the Unconscionable Health Gap: A Global Plan for Justice' (2010) 4 *Harvard Law & Policy Review* 271.

[92] MP Matsoso et al, 'Medicine Safety and Safe Access to Essential Medicines' in R Parker and M Sommer (eds), *Routledge Handbook in Global Public Health* (Abingdon, Routledge, 2011) 443–50.

which meet some threshold level of safety, quality and efficacy reach patients, and that their safety continues to be monitored through adequate pharmacovigilance measures. Low and middle-income countries do not just need medicines, and healthcare services, but also regulatory systems capable of protecting patient safety.

Moreover, it is ironic that in recent years there has been a significant 'brain drain' of trained healthcare personnel, from low and middle-income countries to high-income countries. It has been estimated that as many as a third of all physicians in developed countries have come from poorer countries.[93] The migration of healthcare workers from poor to rich countries enables high-income countries to fill their vacancies relatively easily at the expense of low and middle-income countries' capacity to provide healthcare services to their citizens. Added to this, patients increasingly travel in the reverse direction, from rich countries like the UK and the US, to poorer countries like India for affordable medical treatment or to avoid long waiting lists, thus potentially further depleting local healthcare resources.[94]

VI Conclusion

One of the dangers of recent initiatives which are intended to tweak normal market conditions in order to both incentivise research capable of addressing the global health burden, and ensure that medicines are made available at affordable prices, is that they may contribute to the process of *pharmaceuticalisation*, or the drive to find a pharmacological solution to health problems, described in chapter five.[95] An overemphasis on the health benefits of drugs may result in the relative neglect of non-pharmacological interventions, like improved sanitation and nutrition and ensuring that people in low-income countries have a reliable supply of clean water. In relation to malaria, for example, if draining marshland and stagnant water can reduce the mosquito population, it might be important to invest in these practices as well as pursuing pharmacological solutions to malaria.[96]

Increasing recognition of the significance of non-communicable diseases, like diabetes, cancer, heart disease and chronic obstructive pulmonary disease, for low and middle-income countries, additionally means that preventative strategies, such as tobacco control, are just as important as delivering affordable medicines.[97]

---

[93] N Daniels, 'International Health Inequalities and Global Justice: Toward a Middle Ground' in S Benatar and G Brock (eds), *Global Health and Global Health Ethics* (Cambridge University Press, 2011) 97–107, 99.

[94] Davies n 33 above, 182–85.

[95] L McGoey, J Reiss, A Wahlberg, 'The Global Health Complex' (2011) 6 *BioSocieties* 1–9.

[96] MF Mrazek and E Mossialos, 'Stimulating Pharmaceutical Research and Development for Neglected Diseases' (2003) 64 *Health Policy* 75–88.

[97] See, for example, World Health Organisation, *Framework Convention on Tobacco Control* (WHO, 2003).

In recent years, it has become clear that some countries – most notably Costa Rica, Cuba and the state of Kerala in India – have had considerable success in improving healthcare delivery despite their relative lack of resources,[98] and the evidence seems overwhelming that investing in public health services, and universal coverage, is much more likely to lead to improved health outcomes than relying upon the private sector to deliver healthcare. The evidence is overwhelming that private provision of healthcare – which is often the norm in low and middle-income countries – is associated with worse health outcomes.[99] The expansion of privatised healthcare favours the more prosperous citizens in low and middle-income countries, but is disastrous for the rural poor.[100]

As a result, investment in public health provision may be a more effective way to improve health than disease-specific aid programmes. More broadly, it might also be important to try to ensure fairer trading conditions, so that Western entrepreneurs do not use their superior bargaining power to drive down the costs of goods which low-income countries seek to export to richer countries. If low-income countries earn more money from fair trading conditions, they will be able to invest in their own health infrastructure in order to improve the standard of healthcare that they are able to provide to their own citizens. As Martin Luther King put it, 'Philanthropy is commendable, but it must not cause the philanthropist to overlook the circumstances of economic injustice which make philanthropy necessary'.[101]

[98] A-E Birn, 'Addressing the Societal Determinants of Health: The Key Global Health Ethics Imperative of Our Time' in S Benatar and G Brock (eds), *Global Health and Global Health Ethics* (Cambridge University Press, 2011) 37–52.

[99] See further the essays in J-P Unger et al (eds), *International Health and Aid Policies: The Need for Alternatives* (Cambridge University Press, 2010).

[100] ibid.

[101] Martin Luther King Jr, *Strength to Love* (London, Collins Fount Paperbacks, 1963).

8

The Future of Medicines I: Pharmacogenetics

ISTORICALLY, DRUGS HAVE generally been developed and prescribed for whole patient populations. In practice, however, different people will respond to the same drug in different ways.[1] Some people are allergic to certain drugs, like penicillin. Patients with poor kidney or liver function may respond differently from healthy individuals. Some medicines work less well if taken at the same time as other drugs, and there is even evidence that ordinary foodstuffs, such as grapefruit juice,[2] have an impact on the absorption of certain medicines. A drug which is effective in some patients may not work well, or at all, for others. Some patients will suffer adverse reactions while others will not, and there are likely to be patients who need a higher or a lower dose than normal. Treatments for conditions such as diabetes, depression and asthma may be effective in only about 60 per cent of patients, and in relation to some treatments for cancer, the figure is as low as 25 per cent.[3]

So why does patient response to medication vary so much? There are multiple relevant factors here – age, gender and the existence of other comorbidities, for example – but in recent years, there has been particular interest in *genetic* differences between patients which affect the ways in which their bodies react to medicines. A number of different genes are involved in the absorption, metabolism and excretion of medicines, and variations in these genes will affect whether a medicine works, and in what dosage.

In addition to identifying genetic variations – sometimes called biomarkers – in individual patients, diseases too may exhibit some genetic variety. This is especially true in relation to cancer. Cancer is not one disease but many, and while in the past cancers were differentiated from each other only in terms of their primary location – liver, breast or prostate, for example – now there is known to be considerable variation *within* different cancers, often as a result of genetic differences in the cancer cells themselves.

Without tests capable of identifying in advance variations in patient response to medication, the prescribing process has historically tended to involve a degree of

---

[1] SE Smith and MD Rawlins, *Variability in Human Drug Response* (London, Butterworths, 1973).

[2] B Ameer and RA Weintraub, 'Drug Interactions with Grapefruit Juice' (1997) 33 *Clinical Pharmacokinetics* 103–21.

[3] Nuffield Council on Bioethics (NCOB), *Pharmacogenetics: Ethical Issues* (NCOB, London 2003) 18.

trial and error: a patient's doctor initially prescribes the medicine she has had most success with in the past, discovers it does not work or has unacceptable side effects, and then tries a different drug, with this process repeated until an effective and tolerable treatment regime is found. Of course, this may delay the patient's access to effective treatment, and will additionally impose costs upon the NHS through the prescription of a number of medicines which turn out to be unacceptable or inefficacious. These costs are particularly significant in the case of antidepressants, which are generally not expected to work straight away. A patient who complains that she has had no relief of her symptoms after three weeks, may be told to continue taking this drug for another three weeks before a definitive judgement can be made that it does not work. This means that depressed patients may have to wait a considerable period of time, perhaps many months, before they and their doctor find a medicine which helps them feel less depressed, and that the NHS has wasted considerable resources – both in GPs' time and in the costs of the drugs themselves – on the prescription of medicines which have not worked at all. Clearly, if it were possible to know *in advance* whether a medicine would be likely to suit a particular patient – in terms of likely effectiveness and tolerability of side effects – there would be considerable advantages both to patients and to the NHS.

What is referred to as pharmacogenetics involves a new approach to the prescription of medicines. Instead of prescribing a drug to a patient *in the hope* that it might suit her, a genetic test could reveal *in advance* whether the drug would be likely to work; what dose would be appropriate, and whether the patient would be likely to suffer any adverse reactions. This is sometimes rather misleadingly referred to as personalised medicine, as if medication was going to be designed to fit each patient's unique needs. In practice, pharmacogenetics would not result in bespoke treatments for individual patients, but instead would enable doctors to categorise patients into different sub-groups, according to whether they are likely to respond well, badly or not at all to a particular medicine or group of medicines. As Adam Hedgecoe put it, 'If we consider the parallel of tailor-made medicine, then what is being proposed is more a case of buying a small, medium or large T-shirt from the Gap rather than being fitted for a Savile Row suit.'[4]

If a drug is metabolised too quickly, for example, it may be broken down and excreted before it is able to have any therapeutic effect, whereas if it is metabolised too slowly, it may achieve a level of concentration in the patient's body which effectively makes it toxic for the patient.[5] An example of the former problem might be the tricyclic antidepressant, amitriptyline, which is metabolised by a particular enzyme (CYP2D6). Some patients are categorised as 'ultra-rapid metabolisers' for CYP2D6, that is, their version of the enzyme will break the drug down so quickly that it will not have much therapeutic effect. If such patients are identified in advance, it would be possible to avoid putting them on an antidepressant which will not work.

[4] A Hedgcoe, *The Politics of Personalised Medicine: Pharmacogenetics in the Clinic* (Cambridge University Press, 2004).

[5] J Van Delden et al, 'Tailor-Made Pharmacotherapy: Future Developments and Ethical Challenges in the Field of Pharmacogenomics' (2004) 18 *Bioethics* 303–21.

It should, however, be noted that the fact that it might be possible to identify the small proportion of patients who will not respond to amitriptyline in advance does not necessarily mean that testing will always routinely precede prescription. Given the costs of testing, the trial and error approach to prescription might still be simpler and cheaper than routine pharmacogenetic testing. This has certainly been the case in relation to warfarin, a cheap anti-coagulant drug, for which pharmacogenetic testing is available. The costs of testing increase the cost of the drug so much that the test is, in practice, seldom used, and poor responders continue to be identified during a process of trial and error prescribing.[6]

Where a pharmacogenetic test can avoid serious adverse reactions, it may be easier to justify the increased costs associated with genetic testing. This is the case in relation to Abacavir, an antiviral medicine used in the treatment of HIV/AIDS. It is well-tolerated by most users, but a small proportion of individuals will experience a potentially fatal hypersensitivity reaction to it, which is thought to correlate with presence of the HLA-B*5701 allele. Testing for this allele can therefore significantly increase the safety of prescribing,[7] and if patients' lives might be at risk from trial and error prescribing of Abacavir, the extra expense is clearly justifiable.

Pharmacogenetic testing may also prove cost-effective where it can accurately target the use of expensive medicines. An example might be trastuzumab (brand name Herceptin), which is a costly drug used in the treatment of breast cancer, and which is effective only for the 25–30 per cent of breast cancer patients in whom the oncogene HER2 is present at abnormally high levels. It is therefore only prescribed to this subset of breast cancer patients, and prescription is always preceded by a diagnostic test which reveals the patient's HER2-status, and hence whether Trastumzumab is both appropriate for her, and cost-effective for the NHS.

If pharmacogenetics can, in cases such as these, improve prescribing practices, by enabling doctors to treat patients from the outset with drugs that are likely to be effective and safe, it is hard to see why it raises any regulatory issues at all. In practice, however, if genetic test-led prescribing represents the future of medicines, there are a number of questions we need to address. First and most obviously, a massive expansion in genetic testing would add a further dimension to the confidentiality of patients' notes. Genetic information is not only sensitive, in the same way as other information about a patient's health status, but it has some distinctive additional features. It is, for example, often predictive rather than diagnostic, so it does not just give information about diseases a patient has now, but also his propensity for *future* ill-health. Furthermore, we share our genes, to some extent, with our close relatives, so that if a person finds out that she has a rare genetic mutation, she inevitably also knows that she inherited it from one or both of her parents and that her siblings are also at risk.

---

[6] SA Fuchs, 'Will the FDA's 2010 Warfarin Label Changes Finally Provide the Legal Impetus for Warfarin Pharmacogenetic Testing?' (2010) 12 *North Carolina Journal of Law & Technology* 99.

[7] S Mallal et al, 'HLA-B*5701 Screening for Hypersensitivity to Abacavir' (2008) 358 *New England Journal of Medicine* 568–79.

Second, the cost implications of pharmacogenetics are uncertain. On the one hand, ensuring that patients have faster access to effective medicines will undoubtedly save money that is currently wasted during the trial and error prescribing process. On the other hand, if a new drug is suitable only for a small subgroup of patients, in order to recoup the costs of its research and development (R&D), it will be expensive. In addition, developing new genetic tests and administering them will itself cost money. Writing a prescription currently takes no more than a minute or two. If a GP instead had to organise a blood test for the patient, send their sample to a laboratory for testing and analysis and see the patient a second time to decide upon an appropriate prescription, the costs to the NHS would be significant. This could also represent a new commercial opportunity for companies which market tests and carry out analysis of genetic results, which may be able to take out patents in the kits, known as platforms or microarrays, used to carry out pharmacogenetic tests. In developing countries, these costs may simply be unaffordable and the gap between the healthcare available in richer and poorer nations may widen even further if it is only patients in high-income countries who are able to benefit from genetically tailored drug treatments.[8]

This leads on to the third concern, namely equity. Drugs which can be developed for relatively large patient subgroups are likely to remain profitable, but some patients may find themselves in subgroups which are so small that developing drugs to treat them would be prohibitively expensive. This problem already exists in relation to 'orphan medicines', but pharmacogenetics would expand the number of affected patients. Not only would patients suffering from rare conditions be included, but also those suffering from extremely common conditions, such as heart disease or cancer, whose genetic profiles rule out the use of the drugs which are effective in the majority of patients.

Fourth, new issues will arise in relation to clinical trials. On the one hand, pharmacogenetics could make participation in trials safer, since it might be possible to identify in advance participants who would be likely to suffer adverse reactions. On the other hand, if drugs are only proved to be safe and effective in certain genetically defined subgroups, doctors will lack robust evidence as to safety and efficacy in other patient groups. A drug might be licensed for use only in a small subgroup of patients, leaving doctors uncertain how to treat patients whose genetic profile is different, but for whom other treatment is not available. Should they risk prescribing a medicine known to be safe and effective only in patients with a different genetic profile from the patient in front of them, or should they leave the patient untreated?

Finally, new questions relating to informed consent and liability for harm might enter the prescribing encounter between the doctor and her patient. Normally, if I visit my doctor complaining of, say, an ear infection, my doctor may or may not offer me antibiotics, and I might or might not agree to take them. If pharma-

---

[8] A Smart, P Martin and M Parker, 'Tailored Medicine: Whom Will it Fit? The Ethics of Patient and Disease Stratification' (2004) 18 *Bioethics* 322–43.

cogenetically tailored treatments for ear infections became available, my doctor could instead say that she would prescribe medication only if I agree to be genetically tested in advance in order to see whether antibiotic X would be likely to work. I may want my ear infection treated, but I might be reluctant to take a genetic test. Could I then ask to be prescribed antibiotic X *without being tested first?* This would be off-label prescription, and raises all of the difficult issues, considered in more detail in chapter four, about the scope of clinical discretion to prescribe under- or untested medication.

In other contexts, we are accustomed to patients having the right *not* to undergo unwanted genetic tests, but if this meant that the prescription of medicines might be unsafe, should the doctor make prescription of medicines dependent upon first agreeing to be tested? If a patient who has refused to be tested goes on to suffer serious side effects, has she effectively waived any right to sue the prescribing doctor or the drug company? All of these complex questions are explored in more detail below.

I The Limitations of Genetic Testing

At the outset, it is important to acknowledge that the information obtained through pre-prescription genetic testing will seldom deliver a clear-cut definitive answer like 'yes, this medicine will be safe and effective for this patient' or 'no, it would be unsafe and ineffective'. Instead of a binary yes/no resolution to a doctor's question as to whether he should prescribe drug X to the patient in front of him, the genetic test results will usually deliver much less certain *probabilistic* information about whether the medicine is *more* or *less likely* to work, or *more* or *less likely* to have intolerable side effects, in a patient with the same genotype as his patient.

A pharmacogenetic test might reveal that a person with this patient's genotype has an 80 per cent chance of suffering a serious adverse side effect with drug X. Let us imagine that another treatment, drug Y, is available which, for someone with this genotype, carries a 20 per cent risk of a different serious adverse side effect. Although it would seem obvious that the second drug should be prescribed rather than the first, remember that if prescribed drug X, the patient has a one in five chance of suffering no ill effects, while if prescribed drug Y, there is a one in five chance she will suffer a serious adverse reaction. Of course, the risk is less, on a macro, population-wide level, but for the individual patient, there is no guarantee that he will not fall into the unlucky minority if he is prescribed drug Y, or the lucky minority if prescribed drug X.

In relation to efficacy too, genetic test results may assist prescribing decisions, but it would be a mistake to assume that they are likely to offer a 100 per cent guarantee of effectiveness. Again, a doctor might be faced with test results that reveal that 70 per cent of patients with this genotype experience an improvement if they take drug A, while 50 per cent who take drug B feel better. Drug A looks like it is more likely to work in this patient than drug B, but the patient may be among the 30 per cent in whom drug A turns out not to work, while they might have ended up in the 50 per cent of patients taking drug B whose condition actually improves as a result.

Relying on pharmacogenetic testing to guide prescribing decisions may then improve drug efficacy and safety on a population-wide level, but for the individual patient there is the possibility that they would be categorised as a poor responder and denied treatment which in fact may have benefited them. Refusing to prescribe a drug to patients who are identified as having an increased risk of suffering an adverse reaction may improve patient outcomes on a national level, but for the individual, who may not in fact suffer any adverse reaction at all, this could lead to the denial of effective treatment.

In addition to the inherent limitations of probabilistic information, in relation to specific genetic tests, it is not uncommon for clinicians to be sceptical about their clinical appropriateness. In particular, as Adam Hedgecoe has pointed out in relation to APOE4 testing in Alzheimer's disease, it is noteworthy that it is those who are most knowledgeable about the condition who are most sceptical about the utility of the test, broadly conceived,[9] while people who know little about Alzheimer's disease are much more enthusiastic and 'gung ho' about the usefulness of a genetic variation which might predict drug responsiveness and disease progression.[10]

Even if it is true that the detection of the APOE4 gene may enable slightly more accurate diagnosis, and will give information about the probable success of one treatment, in the clinic this has to be weighed in the balance with other considerations, such as revealing to the family of the person with dementia that they may also be at increased risk of developing Alzheimer's disease. Hedgecoe's interviewees further pointed out that if the test reveals that only 40 per cent of APOE4 patients will respond to Tacrine, as opposed to 80 per cent in non APOE4 patients, it might still be unfair to deprive these APOE4 patients of treatment that has a 40 per cent chance of helping them. If there is no other treatment available, trial and error prescribing may then be fairer to the individual patient than pharmacogenetic test-led refusals to prescribe.

II An Expansion in Genetic Testing:
Consent and Confidentiality

If a condition of a medicine's licence is that prescription must be preceded by a genetic test which demonstrates whether the patient is in a subgroup for which

---

[9] A Smart, 'A Multi-Dimensional Model of Clinical Utility' (2006) 18 *International Journal for Quality in Health Care* 377–82.

[10] A Hedgecoe, 'From Resistance to Usefulness: Sociology and the Clinical Use of Genetic Tests' (2008) 3 *BioSocieties* 183–94.

prescription is either appropriate or inappropriate, patients being prescribed medication must also give informed consent to genetic testing. In most cases, the only test to be carried out will be to find out whether drug X would be safe and effective, given the patient's genotype. It might therefore be thought that this sort of information is much less sensitive than predictive genetic test results, which reveal a person's susceptibility to future diseases. And it is certainly true that few people would consider that HER2 testing for women with breast cancer raises the same complex ethical issues as testing asymptomatic but at risk individuals for the gene which causes Huntington's disease.[11] The HER2 test simply reveals information about the mutated DNA within a cancerous tumour, rather than potentially informing an asymptomatic individual that they will develop a degenerative and fatal condition in middle age.

There are, however, reasons to be sceptical about whether such a sharp line can be drawn between sensitive predictive genetic testing and less sensitive pharmacogenetic tests. First, a pharmacogenetic test result which reveals that the patient is an unsuitable candidate for *all* of the available treatments for a serious and/or life-threatening condition is information with great significance for the person's future health and/or life-expectancy. It may be just as distressing to be told that your cancer is effectively untreatable as it is to find out that you are at increased risk of suffering from a serious disease in the future. Of course, telling patients that there is nothing that can be done for them – either on clinical or cost grounds – is, in practice, a routine aspect of care in some specialities, like oncology, and so pharmacogenetic test results which reveal that no treatment is suitable do not create an entirely new category of untreatable patients. Nevertheless, if a person's genotype reveals that they are likely to be a poor responder not only for one particular drug, but for a wide range of treatments to which they might need access in the future, this is – like predictive genetic testing – information which might not only be extremely upsetting, but which also might appear valuable to third parties, such as insurers and employers.[12]

Second, some genetic variants which are responsible for variation in response to a medicine may also be responsible for increased susceptibility to disease. Where this is known in advance, a person could be asked to consent to genetic testing and be told that the test in question may reveal not only whether they are a suitable candidate for a particular medicine, but also whether they are at increased risk of, say, colon cancer. It would then be possible for individuals who do not wish to know this to be given sufficient information to make an informed choice about whether the risks of finding out potentially undesirable information about their future ill-health are outweighed by the potential benefits of taking the drug for which the genetic test is a prerequisite.

Difficulties arise, however, where a genetic variant known to influence responsiveness to a medicine is *subsequently* revealed to also increase susceptibility to a

---

[11] A Buchanan et al, 'Pharmacogenetics: Ethical Issues and Policy Options' (2002) 12 *Kennedy Institute of Ethics Journal* 1–15.

[12] See further, E Jackson, *Medical Law*, 2nd edn (Oxford University Press, 2010) 396–400.

serious disease. In such cases, patients who know that they possess a genetic variant which ruled out treating them with a particular drug may subsequently and perhaps inadvertently discover that they are at increased risk of disease. If, for example, a person reads a news story about exciting new research which shows that the genetic variation they know themselves to have is associated with a greatly increased chance of developing colon cancer, they will not have had any choice about receiving this information, or counselling about its implications. This is in stark contrast to normal practice in genetic testing, where non-directive counselling and a commitment to informed consent are the norm.

It is therefore understandable that individuals may be concerned about the wider implications pharmacogenetic testing may have for them, both immediately and in the future. A common concern, for example, is that certain test results may make it harder to obtain insurance. In the UK there is currently a moratorium on the use of genetic test results in setting insurance premiums – and this applies to pharmacogenetic test results too – with one very limited exception of life cover over £500,000, critical illness cover of more than £300,000 and income protection of more than £30,000 per year for patients with the Huntington's gene.[13] But while it would, at the time of writing, not be possible for insurers to gain access to pharmacogenetic test results in order to raise premiums, the voluntary moratorium may not be in place for ever. Although pharmacogenetic test results will generally be of much less predictive value to insurers than more prosaic information, to which they are entitled to demand access – such as whether the individual smokes – the concern that undergoing pharmacogenetic testing could have future implications for a person's insurability is not completely groundless. It is therefore not surprising that some people may be reluctant to consent to pre-prescription genetic testing.

Of course, a patient has the right to refuse genetic testing, but where a test has been devised which is a good predictor of patient response to a new medicine, a refusal to take the test may mean that they receive a much poorer standard of care as a result. If there is no other available therapy, and the test is a condition of prescribing, a doctor would be acting properly in refusing to prescribe, meaning that the patient would receive no treatment at all, despite the availability of a potentially safe and effective treatment. A doctor might have clinical discretion to prescribe the medicine despite the patient's refusal of a genetic test, but this might lead to an avoidable and serious adverse event (liability for which is discussed in more detail below).

III Resource Implications

If pharmacogenetics becomes a routine part of drug prescription, would it lead to cheaper or more expensive medicines? Until more pharmacogenetic drugs are

---

[13] For discussion see ibid 398.

developed, it is impossible to know the answer to this question, since there are plausible reasons both for thinking that costs might rise, and for predicting that they might fall.

If both patients and diseases are increasingly broken down into smaller sub-groups, there will be fewer 'blockbuster' drugs (drugs which earn over $1 billion per year). Since the profitability of a drug depends on the size of its market, the pharmaceutical industry has tended to prioritise research into drugs which have the potential to be 'blockbusters', which will generally be medicines targeted at very large patient populations, and which – like statins or antidepressants – are often intended to be taken long-term.

Pharmacogenetic research will inevitably disrupt this blockbuster-focused business model. It has the potential to be very bad for business, from the point of view of the pharmaceutical industry, since it may expose the limitations of products which are currently widely marketed. The trial and error approach to prescribing may be frustrating for doctors and patients alike, and costly for the NHS, but it ensures that the initial market for a medicine is much larger than it would be if poor responders could be excluded from the outset. By ensuring that drugs are prescribed only for genetically-determined subgroups, pharmacogenetics could fragment and shrink the market for new medicines. Indeed, a drug company might decide during development that the market for a new compound is so small that the potential profits cannot justify the costs of development. If the drug does reach the marketplace, then, since the R&D costs are the same and the market is much smaller, it would seem to follow that the prices will have to be higher than those of blockbuster medicines which can be prescribed to all.

In addition to the drug itself being more expensive, the costs of prescribing would also have to rise to include the cost of the genetic test itself and the cost of taking a sample and having it analysed. If drug prices rise and the costs of prescribing increase as a result of the additional costs of genetic testing, pharmacogenetics could represent a significant drain on already stretched NHS resources.

On the other hand, if it is possible to use knowledge about biomarkers to work out before a clinical trial starts which patients are likely to benefit from a new medicine, and which are likely to suffer unacceptable side effects, trials may involve fewer participants and be both shorter and cheaper, thus reducing a new medicine's R&D costs. It might also be predicted that drugs which might otherwise have been rejected on safety grounds during development could make it to the marketing authorisation stage, subject to a condition that those patients in whom it is unacceptably unsafe are identified by a genetic test before the drug is prescribed.

Currently, it has been estimated that, for every 10,000 chemical compounds which are initially investigated, only about 100 candidate drugs will be identified.[14] Of these, only one will reach the lead compound stage, and there is no guarantee

---

[14] Organisation for Economic Cooperation and Development, *Pharmacogenetics: Opportunities and Challenges for Health Innovation* (OECD, 2009) 19.

that this will make it through the three phases of clinical trials to reach the marketplace. There is also, as we saw in chapter two, an exceptionally high attrition rate of drugs during phases I–III: at each stage more drugs fail than proceed to the next stage. The Organisation for Economic Cooperation and Development has described the attrition rates during drug discovery as 'crippling for the pharmaceutical industry'.[15] Of course, the R&D costs of drugs which have to be abandoned during development are in practice recouped from the sales of the few successful drugs, thus pushing up their prices. If fewer drugs fail during the various stages of drug development, we might expect the prices of drugs which do make it to market to fall.

In addition, if pharmacogenetics leads to more accurate and effective prescribing, there will be considerable cost savings for the NHS since money will not be wasted on prescription drugs which are unsafe or ineffective for the individual user. The trial and error approach to prescribing wastes a great deal of money, both through the prescription of drugs that do not work and through repeated doctor-patient consultations. If this could be eliminated, again there might be substantial cost savings.

The costs of adverse drug reactions are also significant, both to the patient herself and to the NHS. It is impossible to know what proportion of adverse drug reactions might be prevented if it was possible to rule out genetic causes, since patients would still fail to take their medicine exactly according to instructions and suffer drug-drug (or drug-food) reactions. Nevertheless, even though genetic testing could not prevent all adverse reactions to medicines, there would be enormous advantages for patients and for the NHS if the number of adverse drug reactions could be reduced.

It would also be good for both patients and the NHS if it could be predicted prior to prescription that a medicine is not likely to work for a particular patient. Patients would avoid the discomfort and irritation of taking a medicine which has no effect or causes unpleasant side effects. It has even been suggested that the frustration of the trial and error approach to prescribing has broader consequences by reducing patient compliance with future drug regimes, which itself may lead to worse outcomes for patients.[16] More accurate prescribing would also save the NHS money, in relation both to the cost of the drug itself and the cost of the patient's follow-up visit to the GP to report that there has been no improvement.

IV Cost-effectiveness and Orphan Patients

At the time of writing there is some uncertainty about the National Institute of health and Clinical Excellence's (NICE) future role in rationing access to medicines

---

[15] ibid 34.
[16] NCOB n 3 above, para 2.29.

within the NHS. It is, however, clear that the NHS cannot do without some measure of a drug's cost-effectiveness when making decisions about whether it should be publicly funded, and if so, for which patient groups. Once more is understood about genetic variations in patient responses to medicines, it is likely that some genetic subgroups will be larger and more cost-effective to treat than others. To take a grossly simplified example, imagine that drug X works well for 60 per cent of patients suffering from breast cancer; drug Y is safe and effective in 30 per cent of patients, and drug Z works well in five per cent; the remaining five per cent of patients do not respond well to either X, Y or Z, and are effectively untreatable. If we also assume that the R&D costs of each new medicine are roughly similar, it is clear that the market for drug X is substantial, and hence it will be relatively easy for its manufacturer to recoup its costs and make a profit. Drug Y has a fairly large market, and it too may be economically feasible. In contrast, the market for drug Z is small, and in order for its manufacturer to recoup the costs of R&D *and* make a profit, its price is likely to be very high, and certainly much higher than the costs of drugs X and Y.

When NICE (or whoever is charged with evaluating cost-effectiveness) comes to determine whether to approve NHS prescription of drugs X, Y and Z, it is much more likely to find that drugs X and Y meet its QALY threshold than drug Z. Patients who fall within the smaller genetic subgroups are hence more likely to find that the drugs which might work for them are too expensive to prescribe within the NHS. Consider also the five per cent of patients who are not treatable by X, Y or Z. What incentive could there be for a pharmaceutical company to design a medicine which could treat their breast cancer, given that the market is always likely to be small and, within the UK, the chance of it being approved for use in the NHS may be low?

In addition, it is critically important to recognise that genetic variations in the body's capacity to absorb and metabolise drugs will be likely to affect more than one medicine. The patients in the example above who do not respond to drugs X, Y and Z for the treatment of breast cancer might also be poor responders for a wide range of other medicines. The danger here is that whole sections of society, classified according to their genotypes, will be categorised as hard or impossible to treat for a large number of diseases.

In insurance-based healthcare systems, such as the US, labelling an individual as difficult or very expensive to treat would clearly have a significant impact upon their capacity to purchase health insurance. Even in the UK, where private health insurance is not the norm, test results which reveal that an individual is likely to be hard to treat across a wide range of common conditions might be information that the providers of life or critical illness insurance policies would be interested in, should the moratorium on the use of genetic test results in setting insurance premiums be lifted in the future.

There might also be significant psychological consequences for the individual from a test result which reveals not that they are likely to develop a particular disease or condition in the future – as currently happens when at-risk groups undergo testing for, say, the BRCA1 and 2 genes or for Huntington's disease – but, rather, that *whatever* condition they might develop in the future, and however treatable it may be in the population as a whole, there are unlikely to be medicines that will work for them.

The possibility that pharmacogenetics could lead to some patient subgroups essentially being abandoned by drugs companies, on the grounds that designing medicines for them will not be profitable, is analogous to the problem of 'orphan medicines', when special incentives have been introduced to encourage investment in medicines for which the market is too small to be commercially viable. In Europe, there are a number of criteria for orphan designation, one of which is that:

> The medicinal product is intended for the diagnosis, prevention or treatment of a life-threatening, seriously debilitating or serious and chronic condition and without incentives it is unlikely that the revenue after marketing of the medicinal product would cover the investment in its development.[17]

It seems obvious that this definition is likely to cover drugs for what might be called 'orphan populations', for whom effective and safe medicines will simply be unavailable, if the process of drug discovery and development is subject only to market-based incentives. Like diseases, which occur only in small patient groups where the market will always be too small to justify the costs of drug development, state intervention may be necessary to distort the market and create special incentives, to prevent genetically-defined 'orphan populations' being effectively untreatable, whatever condition they might develop in the future.

Genetic variation happens both between and within different racial groups, and it would be a mistake to use race as a simple proxy for genetic variability.[18] Nonetheless, the fairness issues that arise as a result of some people being too difficult or expensive to treat may be exacerbated by the fact that this genetic variability may in some cases correlate, at least in part, with membership of a minority ethnic group.[19]

Indeed it has been argued that one of the most significant ethical issues raised by pharmacogenetics is that it could contribute to the view that race and ethnicity are simple biological categories, rather than being socially and culturally constructed.[20] Clearly, race or ethnicity is a very crude proxy for genetic variation, but insofar as there is any correlation between, for example, being of African origin and being more likely to have a specific genetic variant, it is much cheaper to identify a patient's racial origin than it is to test their genome,[21] and hence there may be a danger that race is, in practice, used as a shorthand for genome variation,

---

[17] Council Regulation (EC) 141/2000 on orphan medicinal products [2000] OJ L 18 of 22.1.2000, art 3.

[18] J Kahn, 'How a Drug becomes "Ethnic": Law, Commerce, and the Production of Racial Categories in Medicine' (2004) 4 *Yale Journal of Health Policy, Law and Ethics* 1–46.

[19] SS Lee and J Race, 'Distributive Justice and the Promise of Pharmacogenomics: Ethical Considerations' (2003) 3 *American Journal of Pharmacogenomics* 385–92.

[20] J Hartigan, 'Is Race Still Socially Constructed? The Recent Controversy over Race and Medical Genetics' (2008) 17 *Science as Culture* 163–93.

[21] J Kahn, 'Beyond BiDiL: The Expanding Embrace of Race of Biomedical Research and Product Development' (2009) 3 *Saint Louis University Journal of Health Law & Policy* 61.

which could then reinforce assumptions about biological differences between people of different racial origins.

V Clinical Trials

A Safer, Smaller Trials?

The traditional model of drug development, described in chapter two, has tended to presuppose that drugs are developed for whole populations. Phase I trials establish whether the compound is safe for a random selection of healthy volunteers, and then phases II and III test the compound in patients suffering from the condition the drug is intended to treat. If, instead, biomarkers could be used to predict drug response and to identify which individuals are most likely to benefit from a new treatment, trial participants could be carefully selected to ensure that the drug is only given to the subgroup of the population in whom it is thought likely to be safe and effective. If variations in drug response can be identified *in advance*, the size and cost of trials might be reduced

Pharmacogenetic analysis could also make trial participation safer for participants, revealing before a trial starts whether they might be likely to suffer adverse side effects or, in the case of phases II and III, whether they would fall within a subgroup which would be more or less likely to benefit from the new treatment, if they receive it. Of course, the obvious downside to carrying out trials only in specific subgroups of patients is that the data generated will only offer evidence of its safety and efficacy in a subset of the population. If the only available medicine for a particular condition has been tested solely in patients with a particular biomarker, doctors may have the clinical discretion to prescribe off-label to patients without this biomarker, but this would plainly be risky, both in terms of the patient's health and the doctor's potential legal liability for any harm that results. Hence targeted clinical trials, while safer, may inevitably reduce the scope of the evidence base upon which prescribing doctors are able to rely.

There is a clear analogy here with the historical exclusion of women, children, the elderly and other minority or marginalised groups from clinical trials.[22] It may be simpler and cheaper to test drugs only in groups of young men – trial data are not then distorted by women's hormonal variations, by comorbidities in the elderly or by practical difficulties in enrolling children – but this inevitably means that the evidence base for prescription in these excluded groups is inadequate. If, in the future, drug labels warn that the drug has not been tested in people with a particular single-nucleotide polymorphism (SNP), this would be akin to the

---

[22] CK Svensson, 'Representation of American Blacks in Clinical Trials of New Drugs' (1989) 261 *Journal of the American Medical Association* 263–65.

currently ubiquitous warnings directed to pregnant women.[23] People with that SNP would then be faced with the dilemma routinely experienced by pregnant women: take a medicine where there is no evidence that it can be safely taken in pregnancy, or forego treatment altogether.

Pharmacogenetic testing could also enable potentially beneficial drugs which cause serious side effects in some users to nevertheless proceed through the various stages of drug development, since it might be possible to ensure that the majority can benefit from the drug while identifying in advance the subgroup for which prescription would be inappropriate. If drugs which are extremely unsafe in some users nevertheless reach the marketplace, the importance of safe prescribing practices would increase. In such cases, self-medication with drugs purchased in online pharmacies could be extremely dangerous.

B Routine Testing in Trials

In addition to testing would-be trial participants in advance in order to tell whether it is safe for them to take the medicine under investigation, it also might become increasingly common for the taking of DNA samples to become routine during clinical trials, even when there is no known pharmacogenetic variation in response. If unexpected differences emerge between participants during the trial, it would then be possible for researchers to go back to the samples provided by the participants in order to investigate whether the variation in response might have a genetic explanation. Indeed, it could be argued that it would probably be sensible to take a DNA sample from *all* clinical trial participants so as not to rule out the possibility of identifying genetic factors which might help to explain any surprising or unexpected results, or long-term side effects.

Making trial participation contingent upon agreeing to have a DNA sample stored could, however, make it difficult for some would-be trial participants to say no to genetic testing. It is clear that, for some participants, trial participation may offer the only opportunity to gain access to a new medicine, which will often be a valuable option for patients who are terminally ill and who have exhausted all other licensed medicines. In relation to phase I trials, chapter two considered the possibility that some poorer people may misrepresent their health status in order to participate in trials where compensation is provided. Again, payments to trial subjects may work as an incentive to agree to genetic testing. If there is an intention to keep and store samples of DNA, the concerns that arise whenever any biobank is set up may apply. For example, should the police be allowed access to it in order to assist with crime detection?

Complete anonymisation of samples may not be possible: in order for the sample to be useful, it would be necessary to have some way of linking it to the trial participant so that if a number of participants suffer an unusual adverse event, perhaps many years after the trial was concluded, it is possible to go back to the stored DNA samples in order to work out whether there might be a genetic cause. This would mean that samples would have to be pseudonymised – where subsequent linkage is possible – but not anonymised. If pseudonymised samples are likely to be stored for a considerable period of time, it will be necessary to determine how specific the consent to storage and use should be. If the participant's consent is only to the use of their sample in the particular trial to which they consented in the first place, it would be impossible to use this sample in a future research project, regardless of how potentially valuable the outcome might be. On the other hand, if research subjects are asked to give generic consent to *any* future research use, subjects may be reluctant to give such a wide authorisation to the use of their identifiable DNA, and it may prove difficult to recruit participants.

C Feedback

A further issue is the extent of the researchers' duty to inform participants about results which they obtain during the trial and which may have implications for the person's health. If a healthy volunteer gives consent to take part in a clinical trial of a new cholerastase inhibitor, for example, and tests reveal that the volunteer has a genetic mutation which predisposes her to early onset Alzheimer's, what are the obligations of the researcher? It might be argued that no tests other than the one specified in the trial protocol should be carried out, and hence this question should not arise. But as described earlier, some genetic variations or biomarkers that affect drug response *also* indicate increased susceptibility to disease.

If the researcher does find out information about a trial volunteer's susceptibility to future ill-health, is there an obligation to inform her? Ideally, when she consented to take part in the trial, she should have been alerted to the fact that the genetic test might reveal information relevant to her health and she should have been given the option to receive feedback or to indicate that she would prefer not to receive any information about her own health.[24]

D Unprofitable Pharmacogenetic Trials

In addition to using pharmacogenetic information in the design of new trials, it is also important to consider carrying out research into genetic differences in patient responses to *existing* medicines, including those that are out of patent protection. If genetic tests could help us understand why fluoxetine (brand name Prozac, but now out of patent protection) works for some depressed patients but not for others, research to identify and design those tests would be important and valuable. Once a medicine can be manufactured generically, however, it is not clear whose

---

[24] G Laurie, 'In Defence of Ignorance: Genetic Information and the Right not to Know' (1999) 6 *European Journal of Health Law* 119–32.

responsibility it should be to carry out research, the outcome of which might be a reduction in the market for a medicine which is produced cheaply by a number of manufacturers. When research can lead to the marketing authorisation of a drug which is protected by a patent, the pharmaceutical industry has a clear financial incentive to invest in clinical trials. This is self-evidently not the case for drugs which are out of patent protection.

It might, therefore, be important to think about circumstances in which another body – the drugs regulator, for example – might be charged with carrying out or funding this sort of research. In turn, this would require decisions to be taken about where the money for non-profitable research should come from. If the Medicines and Healthcare products Regulatory Agency (MHRA) were to be charged with funding this sort of research, its licensing fees would have to go up, and since these are passed on to drugs companies, this would be likely to result in increased prices for drugs where profits *can* be made.

The recognition that genetic differences between people lead to differences in the way in which they respond to the same medicine has a further implication in relation to clinical trials. When submitting an application for a marketing authori-sation, it is common for drugs companies to rely on evidence generated from trials that have taken place in other countries. Insofar as some genetic variations may be more common in some racial groups, data which establishes safety and efficacy in one part of the world does not necessarily offer definitive proof of safety and effi-cacy in another.[25] Some of the genetic variations responsible for differences in patient response to antiviral medication for patients who are HIV positive appear to correlate, to some extent at least, with race.[26] A trial that shows that a new medicine used in the treatment of HIV/AIDS works in a largely Caucasian trial population does not necessarily establish definitive proof of safety and efficacy for use in Africa, and vice versa.

VI Licensing

If clinical trials reveal that a medicine is safe and/or effective only in a subgroup of patients suffering from a particular condition, the MHRA or the European Medicines Agency (EMA) could require a genetic test to precede prescription in all cases, as a condition of that medicine receiving a marketing authorisation. In order to assess whether this should be the case, the licensing authority would require proof that the test is an accurate and reliable predictor of a medicine's safety and/or efficacy. In some ways, this is analogous to current practice in rela-tion to contraindications for a medicine's use. An analogy might be that a doctor

---

[25] HL McLeod, 'Pharmacokinetic Differences between Ethnic Groups' (2002) 359 *The Lancet* 78.

[26] A Telenti, V Aubert and F Spertini, 'Individualising HIV Treatment – Pharmacogenetics and Immunogenetics' (2002) 359 *The Lancet* 722–23.

or nurse should not write a prescription for the oral contraceptive pill without first testing the patient's blood pressure.

The difference is that there are fewer concerns about the safety and confidentiality of information about one's blood pressure than there are in relation to genetic test results and DNA samples. Knowledge of someone's high blood pressure is clearly sensitive personal information, and it does tell you something about their risk of future illness, but recording a person's blood pressure in their notes is much less susceptible to future misuse than storing a non-anonymised sample of their DNA.

It is also important to recognise that the discovery of genetic variation in response to a medicine will not always mean that a genetic test must precede prescription. There may be cases where the chance of effectiveness is slightly reduced in people with a particular genetic variation, but where is still worth prescribing the medicine in order to see if it works. Perhaps drug X is effective in 70 per cent of the population without a particular genetic mutation and 60 per cent of the population with that mutation. Nothing would be gained by a condition that all patients must be tested for this mutation before prescription, because even if the test reveals that they do have the mutation, the drug is still more likely to work than not.

This leads to the further point that greater understanding of genetic variation in drug response does not necessarily mean the end of trial and error prescribing. The costs of genetic testing are not insignificant, and even when a test might reveal clinically useful information, these costs will not necessarily be justified. A good example is the painkiller codeine, which is ineffective in the ten per cent of the population in whom cytochrome P450 (CYP) 2D6 is inactive.[27] Codeine is an inexpensive painkiller, and although it would be possible for it to be available only on prescription following a genetic test which demonstrates whether it will be effective, the downsides of trial and error self-medication of codeine do not justify restricting its availability in this way. A patient who experiences no pain relief after taking codeine will simply try another painkiller. If a genetic test could tell whether a person is likely to experience a trivial side effect, again it may be easier and cheaper to simply prescribe the drug to the whole patient population – with the normal warnings about possible side effects – rather than insist upon the inconvenience and expense of genetic testing.

VII Withdrawn Medicines?

In addition to being part of a new medicine's initial marketing authorisation, a drug company might want to bring forward new evidence that a medicine which

---

[27] P Leman and S Greene, 'Testing Patients to Allow Tailored Drug Treatment' (2005) 3330 *British Medical Journal* 352.

had been withdrawn from the market on safety grounds could in fact receive a new or reinstated marketing authorisation. This could restrict its prescription to the subgroup of patients in whom it is, in fact, safe and effective and prohibit its prescription to those in whom a genetic test reveals, in advance, that it presents an unacceptable risk of harm. It is also possible that a drug company might decide to reinstate research on a compound that was rejected during the development stage on safety grounds, if it can identify genetic factors that may facilitate the identification of patients in whom it presents an unacceptable risk of harm.

If the withdrawn medicine represents the only possible treatment for a condition, such that its withdrawal rendered that condition effectively untreatable, there may be strong incentives, both in terms of profitability and on public health grounds, for pursuing research which enables its reinstatement, on condition that prescription is preceded by a genetic test which can identify those patients in whom it presents an unacceptable risk of serious side effects. However, where there are other possible treatments, known to be safe for all users, there may be little incentive to carry out pharmacogenetic research on withdrawn medicines.

To withdraw a medicine from the market on safety grounds is a dramatic and unusual step (as explained in chapter four, it has happened only 19 times in 11 years) and it will generate negative publicity for the withdrawn medicine among the medical profession, and sometimes among the public too. Doctors and patients are not likely to be keen to prescribe or take a drug that was withdrawn because it posed an unacceptable risk to health, even if they are now reassured that a genetic test can facilitate targeted prescribing. To take an extreme example, it is hard to imagine that any pregnant woman would be willing to take thalidomide in order to alleviate her morning sickness, regardless of whether pharmacogenetic research were to indicate that it could safely be taken in pregnancy by some women. Even if this reluctance was demonstrably irrational, the market for thalidomide as a treatment for morning sickness is clearly going to be vanishingly small, and hence pharmacogenetic research into thalidomide's safety in pregnancy would be a waste of money.

VIII Improved Post-licensing Surveillance?

Allen Roses has suggested that a further possible consequence of pharmacogenetics might be what he calls 'enhanced surveillance' after a drug has reached the market.[28] This would involve the regulatory authority giving a new medicine a provisional marketing authorisation, and then the first few hundred thousand patients to receive prescriptions would have their blood spots stored for future analysis when adverse drug reactions are reported. Enhanced surveillance would

---

[28] AD Roses, 'Pharmacogenetics and Future Drug Development and Delivery' (2000) 355 *The Lancet* 1358–61.

enable genetic variations in response which are not known prior to a medicine's launch to subsequently be discovered, and if appropriate, the medicine's marketing authorisation could be altered to reflect this new information. Roses argues that such a surveillance system 'would be a significant advance for patients, regulatory authorities, and the pharmaceutical industry', since it would facilitate the collection of data from much larger patient groups than ever take part in clinical trials. As a result, according to Roses, 'The identification and characterisation of rare ADRs should thus be more rapid and complete.'

Roses is clearly right that this sort of post-marketing surveillance could generate more complete and useful data on patient safety than clinical trials, but there might be practical difficulties in putting such a system in place. Not only would it require patients to give consent to having a blood spot taken and stored, but also costly arrangements would have to be in place both to enable samples to be stored, retrieved and tested, and to ensure accurate and complete reporting of adverse reactions. Nevertheless, given the inadequacies of clinical trial data, discussed in chapter four, and the fact that post-licensing surveillance has been described as the 'weak link' in the regulatory framework, any mechanism which facilitates the gathering of robust post-licensing safety data should be given serious consideration.

IX Liability for Harm

It is, as described in chapter four, difficult to bring an action against a drug company for the harm caused by an adverse drug reaction. In negligence, there could only be liability if it could be established that the drug manufacturer was in breach of its duty to the claimant to take reasonable care to avoid foreseeable injury. If an adverse reaction in some users is known when the drug is marketed, a simple warning on the package insert and in information provided to prescribing doctors will be enough to show that reasonable care was taken. If the adverse reaction is not known, again it will be relatively straightforward – provided that adequate clinical trials were carried out (which is in any event a prerequisite for receiving a marketing authorisation) – to establish that reasonable care was taken in establishing safety prior to licensing.

Although strict liability is supposed to exist for consumers who are injured by defective products, a drug which causes an adverse reaction in some users is not necessarily defective, because it is widely acknowledged that any chemical compound which has a powerful enough physiological effect to cure disease or relieve symptoms may also cause side effects, some of which can be extremely serious. As we saw in chapter four, whether a drug is defective for the purposes of the Consumer Protection Act 1987 is judged by the consumer expectation test – is it as safe as persons generally are entitled to expect? Of course, no patient actually *expects* to be injured by a medicine, and so it could be argued that any drug which causes an unwanted side effect is defective, and that there should, as a result, be strict liability for all drug injuries. In chapter four, however, it was evident that this is very far from the case in the UK. If anyone who suffered a drug side effect serious enough to amount to a personal injury had a straightforward action against the manufacturer, it might be expected that the UK's courts would be overwhelmed with actions under the Consumer Protection Act 1987. To date there have been *no* successful actions under this Act against drug manufacturers. Consumers generally are not entitled to expect all medicines to be 100 per cent safe, and the advent of pharmacogenetic testing is not going to change this.

If there was no way that the manufacturer could have known about the risk – as will often be the case if there is no warning contained in the product leaflet – it will be able to avail itself of what is known as the development risks defence. If, however, a drug company *knew* that there was genetic variation in the safety of a medicine, but failed to warn doctors or patients, or to suggest or require pre-prescription genetic testing, a consumer who was not warned that the drug might not be safe for them might be able to bring an action against the drug manufacturer, or, if the doctor negligently failed to take notice of such a warning, against the prescribing doctor. The important question would be whether the drug manufacturer could rely on a general warning that the drug causes serious adverse side effects in some users, or whether – if it knows that those users can be identified in advance with pharmacogenetic testing – its duty of care would extend to a specific warning to people known to be at risk of the adverse event. Clearly, if the pharmacogenetic test is an integral part of the marketing authorisation for the product, then there would obviously be a duty to warn prescribing doctors and patients about the necessity of pre-prescription testing. More difficult are cases where the genetic risk is known, but testing is not a prerequisite for on-label prescription.

Such a case has arisen in the US. In *Cassidy v SmithKline Beecham*,[29] a case that was eventually settled out of court, the claim was that the manufacturer of a vaccine against Lyme disease (a tick-borne infectious disease which is especially prevalent in some rural parts of the US) should have recommended that testing for the HLA-DR4+ allele should have preceded vaccination. This is a common mutation, occurring in about 30 per cent of the population, and in patients receiving this vaccine, it triggers the development of untreatable autoimmune arthritis. Because the test costs more than $300, insisting on pre-vaccination testing would have made the vaccine extremely expensive and the market for it would have collapsed. Following the manufacturer's decision to settle this case out of court, the vaccine was withdrawn from the market.

If a medicine *is* licensed for use only when a specific genetic test precedes prescription, a doctor who prescribed the medicine without insisting that the patient undergoes genetic testing is effectively prescribing the medicine off-label. Because the doctor will be responsible for his decision to prescribe off-label, and if harm results, might be sued in negligence, doctors are likely to be very reluctant to pre-

---

[29] *Cassidy v SmithKline Beecham* No 99-10423 (Pa. Ct. of Common Pleas, 1999).

scribe a medicine when its marketing authorisation specifies that it must only be prescribed following a genetic test to patients in whom it is known to be safe.

But what if the patient refuses to undergo genetic testing, but still wishes to be prescribed the medicine? Of course, the first step for the doctor would be to explain why the test is necessary, and to reassure the patient about the confidentiality of the results. If the patient is still adamant that they will not have the test, the doctor certainly does not have to prescribe a medicine which they are concerned may be ineffective or unsafe, but could it ever be acceptable for him to do so? Because it might be expected that if the risks of prescription to someone with the relevant genetic variant are trivial, or the difference in effectiveness marginal, the genetic test would be optional rather than a condition of its marketing authorisation, a doctor should probably rely on the MHRA's or EMA's judgement that the test is sufficiently important that the drug should not be prescribed without it.

If a doctor did prescribe a medicine for which pre-prescription genetic testing is a licence condition without insisting that the patient undergoes the genetic test, then, if the patient does suffer an adverse drug reaction, the question of whether the doctor would be liable to the patient would depend upon whether a reasonable doctor would have chosen to prescribe off-label in such circumstances. If the harm which the genetic test was intended to avoid was serious, it would be very difficult for a doctor to establish that it was reasonable to prescribe the medicine without it. The fact that the patient asked for the medicine in such circumstances is not completely irrelevant; voluntary assumption of the risk of injury *can* operate as a complete defence to an action in negligence, but given the doctor's duty to use his clinical expertise and superior knowledge to protect the patient's wellbeing, it is very unlikely to do so in these circumstances.

A patient who is refused access to a medicine because of his refusal to undergo a genetic test might nevertheless be able to obtain it – or a counterfeit version of it – from one of the increasing number of online pharmacies that appear to be willing to supply prescription-only drugs to anyone who wants to purchase them, and which might also be likely to be willing to sell medicines outside of their licence conditions.

If a pharmacogenetic test is available, but use of it is not a licence condition, a doctor has discretion over whether to insist that the patient undergoes testing before he will prescribe the medicine or not. The fact that the test is not a formal prerequisite suggests that prescription *without* access to the pharmacogenetic test results would not pose an unacceptable risk to health. In such circumstances, a patient's request to be prescribed the drug without undergoing the test may carry more weight when the doctor exercises his discretion than it would when the medicine's licence condition suggests that a failure to be tested is risky.

What if the patient does take the pharmacogenetic test, and it reveals that a drug is unlikely to work or the patient is at a high risk of suffering a serious adverse reaction? If a more effective or safer treatment is available, a doctor would not be acting reasonably – and might be in breach of her duty of care – if she chose instead to prescribe a drug that she knows is unlikely to work or likely to cause a serious adverse reaction. Difficult questions arise, however, if the drug in question is the only available treatment for the patient's condition. It is easy to see why a patient might prefer to take a medicine which has a 10 per cent chance of working rather than remaining untreated, but should doctors always accede to requests like this, especially since there is a 90 per cent chance that the prescription will represent a waste of NHS resources?

More difficult still would be a patient's request to be prescribed a medicine in spite of test results that reveal that she is at increased risk of suffering a serious adverse reaction. Again, if the patient's condition is extremely serious, it is easy to see why she might be willing to run the risk of serious harm in order to receive the only available treatment. If a doctor accedes to this sort of request, again she may find herself liable to the patient if the adverse reaction materialises, and while the patient may be contributorily negligent, a doctor is unlikely to be able to completely absolve herself of responsibility by pointing to the patient's request.

Thus far, this chapter has assumed that the genetic test results used to guide prescription decisions will be accurate, but it is also worth noting that the introduction of a new testing stage into the process of prescribing medicines creates new risks. The patient's sample, or her results, might be mixed up with the sample or results of another patient with a similar name, for example. Mistakes may be made when analysing the patient's DNA[30] and doctors may make simple prescribing errors. Both technical and human error cannot be ruled out, and while clearly systems should be put in place to minimise the likelihood of common mistakes – such as using NHS numbers and other identifiers, as well as names in order to reduce the risk of confusing patients with similar names – it is impossible to be 100 per cent certain that mistakes will never happen. As a result, patients who are wrongly prescribed drugs that should have been ruled out if the test results had been properly handled may also be able to bring actions in negligence, against the doctor or the organisation responsible for testing their sample.

More difficult will be cases where a patient was not prescribed a drug which might have helped her because she was wrongly judged to have a genetic variation which ruled out prescription. If the patient's condition then deteriorates, she might want to bring an action in negligence. The difficulty will lie in establishing that if she *had* been prescribed the drug, her condition would have improved. There is seldom any guarantee that a medicine will work, and it may prove difficult to establish, on the balance of probabilities (ie that it is more likely than not), that if the mistake in the analysis of the genetic tests had not happened, she would have been cured or had her symptoms effectively relieved.

---

[30] C Netzer and N Biller-Andorno, 'Pharmacogenetic Testing, Informed Consent and the Problem of Secondary Information' (2004) 18 *Bioethics* 344–60.

X Conclusion

It is vitally important that the significance of pharmacogenetics is not overstated. Of course, understanding more about why drugs that are safe and effective in some users are unsafe and/or ineffective in others has the potential to radically improve prescribing practices. But not all of these variations are the result of genetic bio-markers. Older people with comorbidities may respond differently from younger people; people whose liver function has been compromised by alcohol misuse will respond differently from people who do not drink. Whenever a genetic 'cause' for a health outcome is discovered, there is often a tendency to engage in both genetic exceptionalism (whereby genetic differences are singled out as special and unique, as opposed to other differences between people – such as their socio-economic circumstances – which have health impacts which are just as significant) and genetic determinism (which involves the belief that our health status is entirely or largely dictated by our genes).

One particular danger in relation to pharmacogenetics is that we overemphasise the role of genetics in causing adverse drug reactions or inefficacy, thereby down-playing or missing other possible causes, such as poor patient compliance or defects in the trial data upon which the drug's marketing authorisation was based. It is common for accounts of the ethical issues raised by pharmacogenetics to raise the problem of sections of society being categorised as hard or impossible to treat. Again, while this is undoubtedly a serious concern, it should not deflect our atten-tion away from other reasons why some sections of society are harder to treat than others. Globally, patients in some parts of the world are 'impossible to treat' because they cannot afford the drugs that might benefit them. And even within the UK, some marginalised sections of society – such as the homeless – are 'hard to treat' simply because it is difficult to register with a GP unless one has a permanent place of residence.

It is also important to recognise that the existence of knowledge of genetic vari-ability in patient response to medicines will not necessarily change current pre-scribing practices. If genetic testing adds significantly to the costs of prescription drugs, the trial and error approach to prescribing may be more convenient and cost-effective than pharmacogenetic prescribing. Within the NHS, the premium prices that might accompany pharmacogenetic prescribing might be worth paying only if the consequences of *not* doing so would be extremely serious. For very expensive drugs, like Herceptin, targeted prescribing is likely to be cost-effective within the NHS. Indeed, it is almost certainly the case that pharmacogenetic testing will be of particular importance in relation to certain conditions, most notably cancer and HIV/AIDS.[31] In relation to cheaper generic drugs, like warfarin and codeine, testing to identify dosage and efficacy is available, but it is not used

---

[31] KK Jain, 'Personalised Medicine for Cancer: From Drug Development into Clinical Practice' (2005) 6 *Expert Opinion on Pharmacotherapy* 1463–76.

routinely, because it would massively increase the cost of cheap and generally effective medication. Poor responders continue to be identified by trial and error prescribing, and this is likely to continue to be the case for many, if not the majority of drugs, regardless of the availability of pharmacogenetic tests. Of course, patients might decide to pay for 'top-up' genetic testing themselves, to reap the benefits of targeted prescribing, and if this were to become routine, we would have a two-tier system for delivering pharmacogenetic medicines, which could exacerbate existing health inequalities.

9

The Future of Medicines II: Enhancement

THERE ARE A number of ways in which medicines can be used as enhancements. Professional athletes might take drugs to build up their muscles or to enhance their ability to train for extended periods of time. Students or professional chess players may hope for increased concentration or memory power. Shift workers could seek a medical solution to the twin difficulties of sleeping during the day and staying awake and alert throughout the night. Balding men might hope that a pill could stimulate hair growth, and someone who wants to lose weight may find a pill that suppresses their appetite more appealing than exercising more and eating less.

This chapter considers the question of whether regulation should draw a distinction between medicines which are intended to treat disease or relieve symptoms and drugs which are instead taken in order to improve upon or enhance 'normal functioning'.[1] It might, for example, be appropriate for treatments which enhance rather than restore wellbeing to be unavailable within the NHS, and be available only to private patients, as commonly happens already in relation to cosmetic, as opposed to reconstructive, plastic surgery. Non-therapeutic medicines might also be subject to a different risk-benefit calculation: where a treatment might be able to cure a life-threatening disease, the presence of serious side effects would not necessarily rule it out on safety grounds. The sort of side effects which are tolerated by cancer patients undergoing chemotherapy treatment would clearly be wholly unacceptable if the treatment was directed towards a more trivial end, such as wrinkle reduction.

Of course, drawing a distinction between therapeutic treatments and enhancements is not straightforward, and nor does it represent some sort of shorthand for drugs which should be widely and freely available, and those which should not. An obvious example is the contraceptive pill, which does the opposite of restoring normal functioning. Its purpose is to enhance women's lives by giving them control over their fertility, yet this enhancement medication is such a public health good that it is one of the only medicines which has never been subject to the prescription charge. Vaccination too does not cure disease but enhances a person's

---

[1] N Daniels, 'Health-Care Needs and Distributive Justice' (1981) 10 *Philosophy and Public Affairs* 146–79.

capacity to fight infection, and further enhances the lives of non-vaccinated individuals by contributing to the establishment of herd immunity.[2]

While the enhancement-therapy distinction is certainly not a bright line boundary, in recent years interest in what might be called cosmetic pharmacology has exercised commentators from a range of disciplines.[3] It has, for example, been maintained that using drugs to achieve certain ends – sporting success, for example, or losing weight – is somehow 'cheating', and that society loses something important if human achievements, which normally take time and effort, are simply the result of taking a pill. This leads on to the question of *why* enhancements effected through medical means are treated differently from other ways in which individuals try to improve themselves, or their children. If parents can employ a private tutor to help their daughter pass her exams, what would be wrong with instead giving her daily doses of cognitive enhancing drugs? Pole-vaulters were able to dramatically increase the height they could vault with the introduction of fibreglass poles.[4] Why is this any different from a pole-vaulter taking anabolic steroids in order to build muscles which also help him to jump higher?

In relation to the law, the question then is whether enhancement medication should be *available*, but only through private prescription, in the same way as botox injections for wrinkle reduction, or whether, in certain circumstances, the use of enhancement medication should be *outlawed*, as currently happens in relation to doping in sporting competitions. Students commonly use caffeine to help them study for longer periods of time, but might other cognitive enhancements be treated as illegitimate attempts to distort the level playing field of competitive examinations?

There are, of course, good reasons to exclude many enhancement medicines from NHS coverage. Given the inevitability of rationing within the NHS, considered in chapter six, it would be hard to justify the routine prescription of medicines which do not fulfil any health need at all. On the other hand, if enhancement medication is freely available to the wealthy and out of reach of the poorer sections of society, existing inequalities of opportunity may be exacerbated. Children whose parents are rich would not only benefit from the nutritional, social and educational advantages they already enjoy over children from deprived backgrounds, but they might also have their ability to concentrate or memorise material chemically enhanced.

Finally, there are commentators who have gone so far as to argue that enhancements could result in a new era of trans- or post-humanism, whereby basic aspects of human nature are altered in order to create 'better' humans, or even a new species altogether. Whether or not new forms of enhancement do, in fact, mark this

[2] J Harris, *Enhancing Evolution: The Ethical Case for Making Better People* (Princeton, 2007) 21.
[3] Of course, debates over the legitimacy of enhancement are not limited to the use of drugs, and commonly encompass other technological advances such as genetic modification, but in this chapter the focus will be on medicines as enhancements.
[4] PJ Whitehouse et al, 'Enhancing Cognition in the Intellectually Intact' (1997) 27 *Hastings Centre Report* 14–22.

sort of break with the natural state of human beings is open to question, but even among those who believe that they do, there is considerable disagreement over whether this move should be celebrated or condemned.

I The Line between Treatment and Enhancement

Much of the debate over medical enhancement appears to assume that it is easy to tell when a drug, or other technology, enhances someone's life rather than cures their disease. Commonly, it is said that a treatment is therapeutic if it is intended to *restore* normal functioning and an enhancement if it is intended to *improve* on normal functioning.[5] This definition is problematic, however, for a number of reasons.

First, it relies upon the existence of a clear and stable definition of what 'normal functioning' entails. As people age, their bodies and their minds become less agile, and so the normal functioning of someone over the age of 85 will not uncommonly involve macular degeneration, osteoporosis, high blood pressure, dementia, and arthritis. Yet, few people would argue that treating these symptoms of ageing was an illegitimate use of NHS resources because it involved going beyond restoring normal functioning. On the other hand, if legitimate state-funded treatment involves reversing the consequences of ageing and restoring someone who is 90 to the normal functioning of, say, a fit and healthy 30-year-old, drugs for male-pattern baldness, wrinkles and ordinary memory loss would all be routinely available within the NHS.

A further difficulty is that human functioning is not simply normal or abnormal; rather *within* the category 'normal functioning' there will be considerable variation. It often makes sense to think of the distribution of human characteristics as a bell curve. At each end of the curve are aberrations – in relation to height, say, there are relatively few men in the UK who are over seven feet tall, and few who are shorter than five feet. In between those extremes, there are a lot of men who are close to the average height of five feet nine inches, and fewer who are towards the edges of the curve. If it is acceptable to give human growth hormone to a child who, without it, may reach a height of four feet, why not give it to someone who is likely to be five feet two, which is both normal *and short*. In relation to IQ (admittedly an imperfect measure of intelligence), again there are a few people whose IQ is lower than 70, who we might classify as having learning difficulties, and a few exceptionally able people whose IQ is over 145, and then there are the majority whose IQ lies somewhere within the 'bell' of the curve. It is normal to have an IQ of 90 and normal to have an IQ of 110, so someone could be enhanced, while still remaining within the category of 'normal'.

---

[5] N Daniels, 'Normal Functioning and the Treatment-Enhancement Distinction' (2000) 9 *Cambridge Quarterly of Healthcare Ethics* 309–22.

In addition to difficulties in establishing what 'normal functioning' means, debates over enhancement also commonly assume that it is easy to tell when a particular characteristic or ability is enhanced. Of course, if a pill enables an athlete to run faster than he could without it, it is fairly obvious that he has been enhanced. But in other contexts, what we mean by being 'better than well' may be less straightforward.[6] In relation to memory, for example, what would a perfect memory entail? It would probably not involve being able to remember everything that has ever happened to us in minute detail. Indiscriminate and perfect recall might be very difficult to live with.[7] On the other hand, to say that a perfect memory entails only remembering pleasant experiences would also be problematic, since it may be important for us to remember bad experiences too in order to learn from them, and to be able to empathise with others.[8]

It would also be a mistake to imagine that more of a beneficial quality will always represent an enhancement. For example, there are disadvantages to being short and advantages to being tall, but only within a relatively normal range. A girl who had reached the height of six feet by the age of 12 would probably regard a pill that was able to *stunt* any further growth as an enhancement.

Insofar as some of the drugs which are currently regarded as enhancements may have risks and cause side effects, it would furthermore be a mistake to assume that long-term medication, designed to alter brain function, is always straightforwardly an enhancement. Methylphenidate (brand name Ritalin), for example, has a number of undesirable and common side effects, including insomnia, nervousness, headache, decreased appetite, abdominal pain and palpitations.[9] There is also some evidence that Ritalin may reduce normal growth rates,[10] and its long-term impact on brain function is still not properly understood. As Turner and Sahakian put it, 'it would be devastating to learn that a dazzling youth of successful cognitive enhancement meant a middle age of premature memory loss and cognitive decline'.[11] 'Enhancement' medication might then, in practice, leave someone worse off than they were before taking it. This has undoubtedly been the case in relation to paroxetine (Seroxat), which has been licensed for use in the treatment of social anxiety disorder. It may enhance someone's ability to cope in social situations, but there is also evidence that it may increase the risk of suicidal ideation in some users,[12] and some people have reported experiencing withdrawal

---

[6] C Elliott, *Better than Well: American Medicine meets the American Dream* (Norton, New York, 2003).

[7] W Dekkers and MO Rikkert, 'Memory Enhancing Drugs and Alzheimer's Disease: Enhancing the Self or Preventing the Loss of it? (2007) 10 *Medicine, Health Care and Philosophy* 141–51.

[8] ibid.

[9] National Institute for Health and Clinical Excellence, *Final Appraisal Determination - Attention Deficit Hyperactivity Disorder - Methylphenidate, Atomoxetine and Dexamfetamine (Review)* (NICE, 2005) para 3.15.

[10] JM Swanson et al, 'Effects of Stimulant Medication on Growth Rates across 3 Years in the MTA Follow-up' (2007) 46 *Journal of the American Academy of Child and Adolescent Psychiatry* 1015–27.

[11] DC Turner and BJ Sahakian, 'Ethical Questions in Functional Neuroimaging and Cognitive Enhancement' (2006) 4 *Poiesis and Praxis* 81–94.

[12] WD Hall, 'How Have the SSRI Antidepressants Affected Suicide Risk?' (2006) 367 *The Lancet* 1959–62.

symptoms when they stop taking it.[13] Paroxetine may be regarded by some as an enhancement, but taking it has certainly not been universally life-enhancing.

A further problem is that most drugs which could plausibly be described as enhancements are often also treatments for medical conditions. Ritalin is prescribed to children with Attention Deficit Hyperactivity Disorder (ADHD), but it is also often taken by students who believe that it helps them concentrate for longer.[14] Modafinil (brand name Provigil) was originally marketed as a treatment for narcolepsy, but it is used 'off-label' by people who wish to benefit from increased wakefulness and alertness, including academics and scientists: a poll conducted by the journal *Nature* found that one in five of its readership had used some sort of cognitive enhancing drug.[15] Viagra is used for the treatment of erectile dysfunction, and is taken recreationally by people who want to enhance rather than restore sexual function.

Memory enhancing drugs might be enhancements if used by students when preparing for examinations, but would be therapeutic treatment for patients suffering from Alzheimer's disease. Somewhere between these two extremes, some degree of memory loss is normal as people grow older. So for a man in his sixties, experiencing some age-related deterioration of memory, is the use of a memory-boosting drug *treatment* (for his age-related physical condition) or an *enhancement* (of his normal age-specific functioning)?

The fact that medicines generally do not come clearly labeled as 'therapy' or 'enhancement' makes it especially difficult to judge whether the risks associated with taking medication are justified by the benefits it brings. At the level of issuing a marketing authorisation, a drug may be safe enough to justify prescription for its clinical indication, and then be prescribed off-label, or acquired illegitimately for use as an enhancement, when its risk-benefit profile may be rather different.

Off-label prescription of enhancement medication raises the question of the prescribing doctor's duty towards his patients. As discussed in chapter four, off-label prescription is more easily justifiable when a person is extremely ill and has exhausted all of the established medicines for his condition. Then the risks associated with prescribing a drug to a patient in whom it is not indicated, and where there is no robust clinical trial data justifying prescription, may be worth taking for even the small chance of a cure or relief of symptoms. Off-label prescription for cosmetic or enhancement purposes, where there is no pressing health need to 'try anything', is much less likely to be a reasonable use of medical discretion.

Just because a person wants to be prescribed Viagra in order to enhance his party lifestyle does not place the doctor under a duty to issue a prescription. On the contrary, doctors are not their patient's handservants and should only prescribe a medicine to a patient if they have grounds for believing (a) that the medicine is an

[13] A Tonks, 'Withdrawal from Paroxetine Can be Severe, Warns FDA' (2002) 324 *British Medical Journal* 260.

[14] SM Outram, 'The Use of Methylphenidate Among students: The Future of Enhancement?' (2010) 36 *Journal of Medical Ethics* 198–202.

[15] B Maher, 'Poll Results: Look Who's Doping' (2008) 452 *Nature* 674–75.

appropriate treatment for the patient's condition, and (b) that the patient does not have any contraindications to its prescription. Decisions to prescribe should be compatible with the fundamental goals of medicine, which, in Miller and Brody's words, include 'avoiding disproportionate risks of harm that are not balanced by the prospect of compensating medical benefits'.[16] In addition, then, to the risk-benefit judgement which is made at the point of licensing a new medicine, the individual doctor should be carrying out his own risk-benefit assessment in relation to each patient. A man who has been left impotent after prostrate surgery is therefore in a different position in relation to a request for Viagra than a man who would like his normal sexual relationship to more closely resemble a porn movie.

Although doctors are not prohibited from issuing off-label prescriptions for medicines, patient request, on its own, does not offer sufficient grounds for doing so. On the contrary, doctors should only issue off-label prescriptions if they have reasonable grounds for believing that the medicine is an appropriate response to the patient's condition. This presents difficulties for doctors, however, since by definition, there are seldom high-quality clinical trials available to support off-label usage. If there were, the drug company would be likely to have used them to justify an application to have additional indications added to the drug's marketing authorisation in order to increase sales.

If a patient is injured as a result of an off-label prescription, it would be possible for her to bring an action in negligence against her doctor. Here the question for the court would be: would a reasonable doctor have prescribed this medicine to this patient? Hence, in order to avoid the possibility of a negligence charge, doctors would be well advised to ensure that they can demonstrate that there was some objective evidence to support their prescribing practices, beyond simply responding to patient demand.

From the point of view of the patient, access to enhancement medication will be more straightforward if they present themselves as suffering from a medical condition. Students who want access to Ritalin may find it easier to obtain, either from an online pharmacy or from a doctor, if they are well versed in the symptoms of ADHD. Whenever diagnosis comes from the patient's description of their symptoms, rather than from a blood test or an X-ray, it may be relatively straightforward to persuade a doctor to prescribe a medicine which is not, in fact, clinically indicated by effectively 'pathologising' oneself. Ironically, then, the use of conventional medicines as enhancements may lead to over diagnosis of the illnesses these medicines are designed to treat.

---

[16] FG Miller and H Brody, 'Enhancement Technologies and Professional Integrity' (2005) 5 *American Journal of Bioethics* 15–17.

II A Pharmacological Fix?

There are multiple ways in which human beings have enhanced their cognitive, sporting and other abilities. Education, literacy and computers are all ways in which we have improved our capacity for complex reasoning and the communication of ideas. It is, for example, believed to be good for children to be read a bedtime story,[17] but this is possible only because of 'unnatural' technological enhancements such as the printing press and artificial light. In the past, there was suspicion of enhancements which we now regard as self-evidently beneficial. An extreme example of this comes from Plato's Phaedrus, in which he tells the story of Thamus, the king of a city in Egypt, who is telling Theuth, who was said to be the inventor of calculation, geometry, astronomy, and writing, what he thinks of these developments. Now we see the ability to write as an unmitigated good. Thamus, on the other hand, did not approve:

> Those who acquire [the ability to write] will cease to exercise their memory and become forgetful; they will rely on writing to bring things to their remembrance by external signs instead of by their own internal resources. What you have discovered is a receipt for recollection, not for memory. And as for wisdom, your pupils will have the reputation for it without the reality: they will receive a quantity of information without proper instruction, and in consequence be thought very knowledgeable when they are for the most part quite ignorant. And because they are filled with the conceit of wisdom instead of real wisdom they will be a burden to society.[18]

Very few human beings live in an unimproved 'state of nature'. Of course, taking enhancing drugs involves ingesting a substance that may physically alter one's body or brain, but that is also true of improved nutrition, which has undoubtedly enhanced human development. Indeed, neural changes can be effected by exercise, sleep and reading, so there is not necessarily anything particularly special about enhancing and altering brain function.

It has, however, been argued that enhancement medication represents an easy shortcut to social or other goods that are normally achieved through dedication and hard work. This objection to enhancement suggests that there is something suspect about effort free achievements: that there should be 'no gain without pain'.[19] Of course, we use easy shortcuts in our daily existence all the time: I flick a switch in order to heat my home; I drive my car to the supermarket rather than struggling home with heavy bags. This criticism of enhancements suggests that there are *certain* ends where the need to work hard is character building and develops

---

[17] Y Kelly et al, 'What Role for the Home Learning Environment and Parenting in Reducing the Socioeconomic Gradient in Child Development? Findings from the Millennium Cohort Study' (2011) *Archives of Disease in Childhood* online prepublication access.

[18] Quoted in N Postman, *Technopoly: The Surrender of Culture to Technology* (London, Vintage Books, 1993) 4.

[19] M Schermer, 'Enhancements, Easy Shortcuts and the Richness of Human Activities' (2008) 22 *Bioethics* 355–63.

virtuous characteristics like courage, perseverance and discipline: taking a pill to lose weight does not involve self-control and willpower, and hence some would regard it as an illegitimate easy shortcut.

A related argument is that an achievement is praiseworthy only if it has involved hard work. If I set out from London to walk to Santiago de Compostela, I will be attempting something which is difficult and challenging, and, if I succeed, I might expect to be congratulated for my efforts. If I fly the same distance, I will not have achieved anything admirable. But of course, that does not mean there is anything *wrong* with flying to Santiago de Compostela. I may want to visit a friend there for the weekend, and an insistence that I walk would rule out my trip. The shortcut enables me to achieve an end – visiting my friend – which is important to me, and it is the end that matters most here, not the means.

The argument that enhancement medication is illegitimate because it represents an easy short cut suggests that in relation to *certain* human accomplishments, the means, in fact, matter more than the end itself. Of course, the person who chooses to walk to Santiago de Compostela regards the *means* of getting there as the most important thing. If they were offered an airline ticket as they set off on their journey, they would reply that the whole point was to walk. In relation to enhancements, however, the 'easy shortcut' criticism suggests that it is not open to people to opt for an easy means – such as taking a pill – because the end (weight loss, say, or improved cognitive abilities) is more important *to them* than the means.

In addition to being condemned on the grounds that they are easy ways to achieve challenging ends, it has also been suggested that using drugs to blunt some of the more difficult experiences in life impoverishes our character development. In order to feel empathy for the pain of others, for example, it has been suggested that it is necessary to have had some experience of pain oneself.[20] Propranolol, used to treat post-traumatic stress disorder (PTSD) by preventing the 'over-consolidation' of painful memories, might make it easier to cope after witnessing a traumatic event, but it is hard to know what the longer-term consequences might be of memory suppression.[21]

This sort of argument – that 'easy pleasures and cheap thrills will . . . make us weak and spineless'[22] – suggests that authentic success or happiness comes only from hard work and suffering. Again, this misses the point that it is not always wrong or inauthentic to achieve something easily. The question of whether the means matter more than the end, or vice versa, will often be a matter of personal preference, and depend on the context and circumstances, rather than on whether it is always necessarily better to struggle in order to achieve our ends.

---

[20] A Chatterjee, 'The Promise and Predicament of Cosmetic Neurology' (2006) 32 *Journal of Medical Ethic* 110–13.

[21] J Bell, 'Propranolol, Post-Traumatic Stress Disorder and Narrative Identity' (2008) 34 *Journal of Medical Ethics* e23.

[22] AL Caplan, 'Good, Better, or Best?' in J Savulescu and N Bostrom (eds), *Human Enhancement* (Oxford University Press, 2009) 199–209, 205.

III Enhancing Sporting Ability and Cheating

Because competitive sport is about winning, marginal improvements in ability are of disproportionate significance: the person who comes fourth in the 100 metre race at the Olympics will have run a fraction of a second slower than the person who wins the gold medal, but this tiny difference in ability – especially compared with the massive difference between every athlete who takes part in the final and the population as a whole – is the difference between being forgotten and being a sporting legend. It is therefore not surprising that the pressure upon elite sportsmen and women to improve their performance, even very slightly, is extreme.

In addition, the use of an enhancement does not just make the enhanced sportsman's performance better, it disadvantages his unenhanced opponents: a sporting competition is a zero-sum game where if one person has a better chance of winning, it is also more likely that his competitors will lose.[23] It is easy to see why, if athletes believe that their opponents are using enhancements, they might find it difficult to resist the temptation to join them. In a 1995 poll, 198 sprinters, swimmers, weightlifters and other athletes (most of whom had competed, or aspired to compete at the Olympics) were asked the following question:

> You are offered a banned performance-enhancing substance, with two guarantees: (1) You will not be caught. (2) You will win. Would you take the substance?

195 athletes said 'yes'; three said 'no'.[24]

More shocking are the answers from the same group of athletes to a second question:

> You are offered a banned performance-enhancing substance that comes with two guarantees: (1) You will not be caught. (2) You will win every competition you enter for the next five years, and then you will die from the side effects of the substance. Would you take it?

More than half of the athletes answered 'yes'.[25]

There is nothing new about sportsmen trying to enhance their performance by ingesting substances that they believe will give them a competitive edge: in Ancient Greece, for example, wrestlers were said to have consumed vast quantities of red meat in order to help build up their muscles and Norsemen apparently took hallucinogenic mushrooms before rowing competitions.[26] Cyclists used to take amphetamines in order to improve their performance: in 1967 the British cyclist Tom Simpson suffered a heart attack on Mont Ventoux during the 13th stage of

---

[23] R Goodman, 'Cognitive Enhancement, Cheating, and Accomplishment' (2010) 20 *Kennedy Institute of Ethics Journal* 145–60.

[24] M Bamberger and D Yaeger, 'Over The Edge' *Sports Illustrated* 14 April 1997.

[25] ibid.

[26] DC Wilson, '"Let Them Do Drugs" a Commentary on Random Efforts at Shot Blocking in the Sports Drug Game' (2006) 8 *Florida Coastal Law Review* 53.

the *Tour de France* after consuming a combination of brandy and amphetamines. It is only since the 1970s that a worldwide list of banned substances and a system of regular testing has been developed. Despite 'doping' now being against the rules and despite routine drug-testing and the threat of disqualification, its use continues to be relatively common.

In part, this is because, even with random testing, the chances of being found out are still not that great, especially for competitors who use drugs occasionally or who take substances that can mask the presence of drugs in their system. In addition, the pace of drug development is rapid, and it is hard for the compilers of the 'banned list' to keep up. Athletes can avoid the risk of being caught by taking drugs that have not yet been banned, or they can take modified versions of drugs which will not show up in a urine test.[27] Blood testing would be more effective than urine testing, but since it involves an invasive procedure with a small risk of harm, there has been resistance to moving towards routine blood testing.

Despite fairly widespread flouting of the rules governing the use of enhancements in sport, competitive sport is nevertheless an interesting test case of the regulation of enhancement techniques, because a system of rules prohibiting their use does exist. The World Anti-Doping Agency (WADA) monitors compliance with its Code and carries out an extensive programme of random testing, both in and out of competition. WADA determines whether a substance should be included on its prohibited list according to whether at least two out of the three following criteria apply:

- the substance or method enhances or has the potential to enhance sporting performance;
- the use of the substance or method represents an actual or potential health risk to the athlete;
- the use of the substance or method violates the 'spirit of sport', defined as a set of core values including 'ethics, fair play and honesty' and 'respect for rules and laws.'

It is not therefore necessary for the enhancement medication to pose any risk at all to the competitor's health, provided it both enhances the competitor and violates the spirit of sport.

Two issues arise from the prohibition on drug taking by athletes. The first is *why* using drugs to increase sporting prowess is against the rules, whereas other strategies, like training at high altitude or adopting a carbohydrate loading diet, are not. It is also worth asking why some substances which enhance performance are banned, while others, like caffeine, which does appear to improve performance in a range of sports, are not.[28] Of course, the rules of any sport are, to some extent, arbitrary. Football teams must have 11 players, and a team that fielded 12 players would be cheating, even though there would be nothing *morally* objectionable to

---

[27] Bamberger and Yaegar above n 24.
[28] V Cakic, 'Smart Drugs for Cognitive Enhancement: Ethical and Pragmatic Considerations in the Era of Cosmetic Neurology' (2009) 35 *Journal of Medical Ethics* 611–15.

football played by 12 players. Most people do not believe the ban on performance enhancing drugs to be entirely arbitrary, however, and certainly the view of the sporting authorities is that some strategies to enhance performance are legitimate, and within the spirit of the game, while others are not. But how do we tell when a drug violates the spirit of sport?

If I were to take erythropoietin (EPO), a performance enhancing drug used by professional cyclists, it would not turn me into a potential winner of the *Tour de France*. EPO, a drug licensed to increase red-cell production in anaemia sufferers, increases the amount of oxygen in the blood which, as with all performance enhancing drugs, *enables* but certainly does not replace longer and more punishing training schedules. Training at high altitude has the same effect – the relative lack of oxygen in the air forces the body to produce more red blood cells – yet this would generally be regarded as evidence of dedication, and hence acceptable, whereas a drug that does exactly the same thing is not.

In addition, roughly five per cent of the population naturally have unusually high levels of EPO: Finnish skier Eeor Mäntyranta, who won three Olympic gold medals in the 1960s, had a genetic mutation which meant that he had 40–50 per cent more red blood cells than normal.[29] He was not disqualified from competition on the grounds of this genetic abnormality, so why not permit athletes who have not been so fortunate in the genetic lottery to use synthetic EPO to raise themselves to the same level as Mäntyranta in order to create a more level playing field?

One reason commonly given for a ban on performance enhancing drugs is that they create an uneven playing field, whereby some competitors have an advantage over others from the start. This argument assumes that, absent drug use, the playing field is indeed level, when it is clearly not. Basketball players who are over seven feet tall have an advantage over shorter players. Swimmers with large feet are able to swim faster than they would if their feet were smaller. And genetic variations between individuals mean that some people may naturally have characteristics – like Eeor Mäntyranta's exceptionally high levels of red blood cells – which others do not.

Aside from the genetic 'lottery', some children happen to be born into families that have the time, willingness and resources to facilitate the sort of gruelling training schedules which are now a prerequisite for sporting success. If you grow up in the Swiss mountains, it will be easier for you to practice your downhill skiing than if you live in Islington. Luck, both genetic and environmental, may determine one's ability to compete in sport at the highest level. Could it then be argued that performance enhancing drugs might, in some circumstances, be able to redress this imbalance and create a more level playing field for all?[30]

An at first sight more compelling reason for the ban on performance enhancing drugs is that using them is logical if what one values in sport is winning prizes, but

---

[29] J Savulescu, 'Enhancement and Fairness' in P Healy and S Rayner (eds), *Unnatural Selection: The Challenges of Engineering Tomorrow's People* (Oxford, Earthscan, 2009) 177–87, 185.
[30] J Savulescu, B Foddy and M Clayton, 'Why We Should Allow Performance Enhancing Drugs in Sport' (2004) 38 *British Journal of Sports Medicine* 666–70.

that this misses the point that what is valuable about sporting achievement is not the medal itself, but the 'internal standards of excellence' to which successful sportsmen and women aspire.[31] On this view, courage, endurance and sheer hard work are the proper ends of sport, and the medal is an acknowledgement that someone has excelled in these internal goods of sport. The point of elite sport is to test the limits of what human beings can achieve through pushing their (unenhanced) bodies to their limits. What is being cheated on this view by a doped athlete is not his competitors, but the sport itself.[32]

This might also help to explain the line drawn between new equipment which enhances performance but is nevertheless permitted and equipment which alters the fundamental nature of the competition, and is not. Whitehouse et al contrast fibreglass poles, which undoubtedly significantly enhance the performance of pole-vaulters, but do not alter the essence of the challenge – to leap over a high bar with the aid of a pole – with someone who turns up to 'run' a marathon wearing roller skates. This person could legitimately compete in a 26.2 mile roller skate race, but this would be a different competition from a marathon.[33] On the other hand, a steroid-enhanced 100 metre race, or an EPO-enhanced *Tour de France* are not fundamentally different from an unenhanced 100 metre race and an unenhanced *Tour de France*. On the contrary, even among sprinters and elite cyclists who have not taken drugs, efforts will have been made through training programmes, and through the elaborate use of special diets and dietary supplements, to achieve the same ends of bulked out muscles or the capacity for extreme endurance.

And if the reality is that sportsmen and women will continue to take performance enhancing drugs, and if the systems used to try to eliminate doping in sport are bound to be incapable of identifying all drug use, it could be argued that what is now being tested is not what unenhanced human bodies are capable of, but rather the ingenuity of drug developers and advisers. The emphasis on drugs as cheating diverts attention away from the question of safety: sportsmen and women have incentives to use drugs that are undetectable, rather than drugs that are safe.

If the health of sportsmen and women is of primary importance, this would militate towards acceptance and regulation of performance enhancing drugs, rather than an outright ban. If a drug can help someone to achieve the sort of narrow advantage over others which makes all the difference in elite sporting competitions, it is unsurprising that many competitors are willing to take considerable risks with their health – as well as risking disqualification if discovered – by taking drugs which they obtain on the black market. In relation to recreational drugs, it is clear that the illegality of heroin and crack cocaine does not stop people taking them, it just makes the drug user less safe. Sharing needles and the use of highly toxic bulking agents pose more of a risk to a heroin addict's health than the drug itself. Similarly, if it is

---

[31] M Schermer, 'On the Argument that Enhancement is "Cheating"' (2008) 34 *Journal of Medical Ethics* 85–88.

[32] ibid.

[33] Whitehouse et al n 4 above.

athletes' safety that is our principal concern, regulation of the supply of performance enhancing drugs might be more effective than prohibition.[34]

IV A Parallel with Education?

Some drugs – such as Ritalin, amphetamines and cocaine – are stimulants, and while they can increase arousal and motivation, they in fact appear to have little impact upon cognitive ability.[35] Other medicines do appear to improve memory function. Modafinil improves wakefulness and alertness and cholinesterase inhibitors, like donepezil, help compensate for impaired neural transmission in Alzheimer's patients by increasing the levels of acetylcholine, which is a neurotransmitter that appears to have a role in maintaining attention and forming new memories.

If, and of course not everyone accepts this, performance enhancing drugs *are* rightly banned in sport, should we apply the same logic to examinations and ban students' use of these sorts of cognitive enhancing drugs? Currently, examination rules do not prohibit using caffeine to help revise late into the night, or the use of beta-blockers to calm nerves. Unlike competitive sport, which does have a list of banned enhancement techniques, this would be a new development in education, where an increasing number of students are taking medication for stress, anxiety, depression or ADHD. Just as examination rules currently prohibit students from taking crib sheets into the examination room, should students also be barred from taking certain drugs, and subjected to random drugs testing, with the threat of disqualification if they test positive?

The argument that chemical enhancements undermine the internal goods of sporting competition could also be applied to education. We value hard work and effort, so it might be argued that taking a pill undermines the dignity of having worked hard to succeed. On the other hand, just as with doping in sport, it is unlikely that a drug would ever be able to *replace* rather than *facilitate* hard work. The idea that one could take a pill and suddenly and miraculously be an expert in ancient Norse literature is fanciful. Cognitive enhancements would only ever be able to prolong the amount of time one spent working, and facilitate recall. Just as a child sent to a good school will still have to work hard to pass exams, students who take pills in order to concentrate for longer will not do well unless they put considerable time and effort into their studies.

Also, in parallel with the ban on performance enhancing drugs, it could also be argued that it would, in practice, be very difficult, if not impossible, to prevent the use of cognitive enhancing drugs by students. Even if a system of urine testing at

---

[34] B Kayser, A Mauron, and A Miah, A, 'Viewpoint: Legalisation of Performance-Enhancing Drugs' (2005) 366 *The Lancet* S21.
[35] BB Quednow, 'Ethics of Neuroenhancement: A Phantom Debate' (2010) 5 *BioSocieties* 153–56.

exam time were put in place,[36] it would be virtually impossible to eliminate the use of drugs taken outside of the exam period.

In relation to the 'level playing field' argument, again it would seem odd to single out drugs as a unique distorter of equality of opportunity in education. There is some evidence from twin studies of the heritability of IQ – so nature does not provide us with a level playing field to begin with – but more importantly still, it is clear that the ability to pass exams is enhanced by a variety of environmental influences, such as parental attitudes to education, extra tuition and better nutrition. Academic success is partly the result of sheer hard work, but it is also down to good fortune in the genetic lottery and is heavily influenced by the socioeconomic status of one's parents. If performance enhancing drugs are to be banned on the grounds that they give some students a competitive advantage over others, might there be grounds for banning private tuition for the same reason?

It could even be argued that, unlike private tuition which undoubtedly exacerbates existing socioeconomic inequalities, cognitive enhancing drugs might – provided they were made widely available – have the opposite effect: there is, for example, some evidence that the greatest improvements in cognitive performance are enjoyed by those with cognitive deficits, and that they may not work, and may even sometimes have deleterious effects, on the cognitively healthy.[37]

V Distributional Justice

Following on from this, one of the most compelling arguments against the use of enhancements is that they are very unlikely to be available to all. Given that the rationing of treatments which are capable of curing disease is now inevitable, it is clear that enhancement medicines are not going to be freely available, to anyone who wants them, within the NHS. If, as seems more likely, access to enhancement medication is heavily restricted within the NHS, and subject to fewer restrictions in the private sector, it seems obvious that it will be used more frequently by people who are already well off, and less frequently by people who are disadvantaged. In short, the benefits of enhancement techniques are very unlikely to be fairly distributed across society (unless one adopts Robert Nozick's definition of fair distribution, according to which, provided one acquired one's greater material assets lawfully and without force, the resulting inequality of assets is fair[38]).

Privately purchased enhancement techniques therefore have the potential to exacerbate existing inequalities. This is not new, the rich already live healthier and longer lives than the poor,[39] but it is sometimes argued that enhancement medi-

---

[36] P Miller et al, 'The Cognition Enhanced Classroom' in P Miller and J Wilsdon (eds), *Better Humans?* (London, Demos, 2006) 79–85.

[37] Cakic n 28 above.

[38] R Nozick, *Anarchy, State and Utopia* (New York, Basic Books, 1974).

[39] S Atkinson, *Health Inequalities in London: Where Are We Now?* (Greater London Authority, 2006).

cine could significantly widen the gulf between the 'haves' and the 'have nots'. Against this, the argument that we should resist permitting enhancement medicines unless we could be certain that they would be made available to all is at odds with other areas of medical treatment in which the inability to treat everyone does not lead us to refuse to countenance treating some. An obvious, but imperfect analogy is organ transplantation.[40] There are insufficient organs available to ensure that everybody who could benefit from an organ transplant receives one. Instead of ruling out transplantation, on the grounds that not all may benefit, this should lead us to strive to ensure that the measures in place to allocate scarce organs are fair and defensible. Of course, there is *absolute* scarcity of organs, and this is rather different from relative inequalities of wealth in society.

A better analogy might then be cosmetic surgery, botox injections, and more prosaically, gym membership, regular facials and high-quality nutrition. Some people look remarkably young for their age, and while this may in part be down to genetic good fortune, it is also sometimes the result of expensive lifestyle adjustments, which are indubitably not available to everyone. We do not ban people from taking steps to enhance their appearance, on the grounds that not everyone is able to do so. If we want to draw a distinction between the unequal distribution of some enhancement techniques which are permissible, and others where their unequal distribution is grounds for prohibition, we need to find a reason why wrinkle reduction injections are qualitatively different from medicines which might make people taller or smarter.

A different sort of argument might focus on the choices not of the people seeking enhancement, but of the doctors offering this sort of service. Rich, healthy people who want to be able to remember more or cycle faster will be both easier and more lucrative to treat than disadvantaged and sick patients. It could then be argued that the medical profession itself should prioritise alleviating pain and restoring health, rather than providing cosmetic pharmacology services to healthy but dissatisfied narcissists. But while we may think less highly of a Harley Street doctor who is using his medical training to inject rich people with botox than we would of his contemporary from medical school who works long hours in a busy NHS hospital, we do not prohibit him from practising.

It could further be argued that enhancements could serve rather than undermine justice and the fair distribution of capacities. Currently, a minority of adults are significantly disadvantaged by cognitive incapacity. If enhancement drugs could help these individuals reach a level of cognitive function which enabled them to have a decent opportunity to lead a flourishing life, natural *inequalities* in the distribution of talents and abilities might be redressed, at least in part.[41] Of course, it may be true that this is an unlikely outcome of the development of enhancement techniques, and that experience suggests that educational enhancements, such as private tuition, are used to improve the abilities of those who are

---

[40] J Harris, 'Enhancements are a Moral Obligation' in J Savulescu and N Bostrom (eds), *Human Enhancement* (Oxford University Press, 2009) 131–54, 147.

[41] Savulescu n 29 above, 183.

already relatively privileged, rather than being used to redress past inequalities. However, the important point to note here is that the tendency for enhancements, of whatever kind, to benefit the 'haves' more than the 'have nots' is not an inherent characteristic of the enhancement. Concerns about distributional injustice should focus upon the multiple ways in which society tends to perpetuate inequality, rather than on the existence of enhancement medicines. We should not be blaming, and banning, the smart pill when the real problem is entrenched social inequality.

VI Coercion

It has further been argued that some people might be coerced into using enhancement medication, most plausibly where their job makes a particular characteristic or trait especially valuable. This has already happened in the US military:[42] for its 1986 air raid on Libya, the United States Air Force allowed aircrew to take sleeping pills in order to sleep before the mission, and to use stimulants to maintain alertness during and afterwards.[43] Enhanced alertness and the ability to concentrate for prolonged periods of time might improve the performance of airline pilots, surgeons and long-distance lorry drivers, and might therefore save the lives of passengers, patients and other road users respectively. Indeed, one study found that pilots who had taken a cholinesterase inhibitor outperformed the pilots who had taken a placebo when faced with an emergency situation. Another study found that having taken donepezil for 30 days enhanced pilots' ability to recall how to perform complex tests on a flight simulator.[44] If there was robust evidence that medication could significantly improve passenger safety, it is easy to imagine pilots coming under some degree of pressure, not to say compulsion, to comply with a recommended enhancement medication regime.

All medicines have side effects, and for drugs that affect brain function, it is perhaps unlikely that one ability will be straightforwardly enhanced without also affecting other brain activity, perhaps negatively. For example, dexamphetamine – a stimulant drug which has been used by the United States military – can eradicate fatigue. It might therefore be thought that it could prove helpful for surgeons

---

[42] H Greely et al, 'Towards Responsible Use of Cognitive-Enhancing Drugs by the Healthy' (2008) 456 *Nature* 702–05.

[43] TM Gibson, 'The Bioethics of Enhancing Human Performance for Spaceflight' (2006) 32 *Journal of Medical Ethics* 129–32. Employers' use of enhancement medication to 'improve' their employees' performance was given a horrifying new twist in 2011, when the International Criminal Court's Chief Prosecutor, Luis Moreno-Ocampo, announced that there was evidence that Viagra had been distributed to Libyan troops loyal to Muammar Gaddafi as part of an official policy sanctioning the use of rape in order to suppress the population. See further O Bowcott, 'Libya Mass Rape Claims: Using Viagra would be a Horrific First' *The Guardian* 9 June 2011.

[44] JA Yesavage, 'Donepezil and Flight Simulator Performance: Effects on Retention of Complex Skills' (2002) 59 *Neurology* 123–25.

carrying out long and difficult operations. Dexamphetamine can also lead to overconfidence, however, which is, as Warren et al point out, undoubtedly 'an undesirable quality in a surgeon making management decisions under stressful circumstances'.[45]

Pressure to take medication might also be exerted within schools, perhaps by head teachers insisting that disruptive students take stimulant drugs, like Ritalin, or face expulsion.[46] Given that this sort of medicine is not risk-free, it seems invidious to give children or their parents the choice between taking potentially risky medication or being barred from education. Intuitively, however, many people would be more sympathetic to making immunisation to diseases like measles a prerequisite to school entry. In some US schools, admission is contingent upon evidence that children have received certain vaccinations, and there have been calls for the measles, mumps and rubella (MMR) vaccine to be made compulsory in the UK.[47] The difference between compulsory medication and compulsory vaccination might be explained in part by the fact that childhood vaccination is generally safe and recommended by virtually all reasonable medical practitioners, whereas there are more risks and uncertainty attached to stimulant treatment for children with disruptive behaviour patterns. In addition, it might be argued that mind-altering drugs represent a greater interference with the child's freedom of thought and action than a vaccine jab.

More generally, it has been argued that in a society where pharmacological enhancement became the norm, it would be difficult to remain unenhanced. Some athletes take performance enhancing drugs because they know that athletes against whom they must compete will be doing so. Similarly, if one is competing with the cognitively enhanced for university places or for jobs, it may be difficult to resist the conclusion that, if everyone else is doing it, one would be disadvantaged if one chose not to take enhancement medication.

VII Prescription Drug Abuse

As well as being used to enhance performance, prescription drugs can also be taken, in the same way as other recreational drugs like alcohol, cannabis, cocaine and ecstasy, in order to enhance the user's sense of wellbeing. In recent years, there has been a dramatic increase in the number of people using medicines recreationally, rather than to treat ill-health. Stimulants, like methylphenidate (Ritalin), are used as an 'upper' in the same way as cocaine, while narcotic pain relievers, like

---

[45] OJ Warren et al, 'The Neurocognitive Enhancement of Surgeons: An Ethical Perspective' (2009) 152 *Journal of Surgical Research* 167–72.

[46] JM Appel, 'When the Boss Turns Pusher: A Proposal for Employee Protections in the Age of Cosmetic Neurology' (2008) 34 *Journal of Medical Ethics* 616–18.

[47] J Shepherd, 'MMR Jab Should be Compulsory for All Children Starting School, Expert Says' *The Guardian* 3 June 2009.

oxycodone (brand name Oxycontin), are used as 'downers', in the same way as cannabis and heroin.[48]

Prescription drugs are perceived to be safer than illegal recreational drugs – and of course, it is true that drugs manufactured by pharmaceutical companies are not going to be bulked out with toxic substances like household bleach or detergent in the same way as illegal drugs. But the assumption that the non-medical use of prescription drugs is safe and non-addictive is plainly wrong, and both overdose from and addiction to prescription drugs has been described as 'a public health epidemic'.[49] Prescription drugs are easy to obtain and may be comparatively cheap. There is evidence that they are increasingly used both in preference to illegal drugs,[50] and in combination with them, to moderate the effects (perhaps by alleviating anxiety or the feelings experienced during 'comedown') or to enhance and accentuate the 'high'.[51]

The problem of prescription drug abuse is particularly prominent in the US.[52] In 2011, Gil Kerlikowske, Director of the Office of National Drug Control Policy in the US gave evidence to the US Senate's Crime and Terrorism Committee in which he described prescription drug abuse as 'the fastest-growing drug problem in the United States'.[53] In the US, the number of people who took prescription drugs for a non-medical purpose for the first time is now about the same as the number of first-time marijuana users,[54] and the US's 2009 National Survey on Drug Use and Health estimated that over seven million Americans had misused opioid painkillers in the previous month.[55]

Prescription drug abuse is also undoubtedly a worldwide phenomenon. In the UK 1.5 million people are addicted to prescription and over-the-counter drugs including benzodiazepine tranquillisers and sleeping pills, and there is a thriving black market in drugs like diazepam (brand name Valium).[56] It has been estimated

---

[48] E Pilkington, 'Pharmageddon: How America Got Hooked on Killer Prescription Drugs' *The Guardian* 9 June 2011.

[49] Centers for Disease Control, *Prescription Drug Overdoses: An American Epidemic* (CDC, 2011), available at www.cdc.gov/about/grand-rounds/archives/2011/01-February.htm.

[50] M McCarthy, 'Prescription Drug Abuse Up Sharply in the USA' (2007) 369 *The Lancet* 1505–06.

[51] KK Rigg and GE Ibañez, 'Motivations for Non-Medical Prescription Drug Use: A Mixed Methods Analysis' (2010) 39 *Journal of Substance Abuse Treatment* 236–47.

[52] In April 2011, the Obama administration announced a national plan with the goal of reducing prescription drug abuse by 15% within five years, through a combination of measures, including better education both for doctors to spot substance abuse, and for the public, to raise awareness of the importance of safe disposal of unused prescription drugs, and targeting 'soft touch' prescribers, sometimes described as 'pill mills'. See further White House, *Epidemic: Responding to America's Prescription Drug Abuse Crisis* (White House, 2011), available at www.whitehousedrugpolicy.gov/publications/pdf/rx_abuse_plan.pdf.

[53] Statement of R Gil Kerlikowske to the Senate Committee on the Judiciary, Subcommittee on Crime and Terrorism, 'Responding to the Prescription Drug Epidemic: Strategies for Reducing Abuse, Misuse, Diversion' (24 May 2011), available at http://kyl.senate.gov/legis_center/subdocs/052411_Kerlikowske.pdf.

[54] US Substance Abuse and Mental Health Services Administration, *Results from the 2009 National Survey on Drug Use and Health: National Findings* (SAMHSA, 2010).

[55] ibid.

[56] The All Party Parliamentary Drug Misuse Group, *An Inquiry into Physical Dependence and Addiction to Prescription and Over-the-Counter Medication 2007–2008* Parliamentary Session.

that between one and three per cent of the population of Canada abuse prescription opioids.

Many people who abuse prescription drugs obtain or take them from people they know, to whom they may have been legitimately prescribed, and, although it could not provide a complete solution to the problem, prescribing smaller quantities of drugs which are known to be used recreationally, and educating patients about the importance of safe disposal of unused prescription drugs might at least mean that there are fewer 'leftover' opioid painkillers in circulation.[57] Of course, this would do nothing to address the problem of offshore online pharmacies, which, as we saw in chapter three, are willing to supply Valium and Ritalin to anyone without a prescription.

VIII Transhumanism and Posthumanism: Utopia or the End of History?

A Posthumanism

Since to enhance something is to improve it or make it better or greater, it is in some ways hard to see why anyone could object to human beings enhancing themselves.[58] It is, however, noteworthy that the question of the legitimacy or otherwise of enhancement techniques has attracted the negative attention of a number of academics whose work is not normally concerned with medical or bioethical issues, most notably political scientists Francis Fukayama, Jurgen Habermas and Michael Sandel, in addition to that of bioethicists like Leon Kass.[59] Each of these writers approaches the question of enhancement in a different way, expressing different concerns, but they all share the general assumption that embracing enhancement technologies would be inadvisable or even dangerous, principally because it would mean altering something that is inherently good about human nature.

There are a number of problems with the claim that enhancement should be resisted because it involves interfering with human nature. First, and most fundamentally, what is 'human nature' (or as Fukayama puts it: 'Factor X'[60])? Human beings evolved gradually from our primate ancestors, and it would be very hard to

---

[57] In the US, the Secure and Responsible Drug Disposal Act 2010 was introduced in order to ensure that safe and secure drug disposal programmes are able to take possession of controlled substances for the purposes of disposal.

[58] A Chan and J Harris, 'In Support of Human Enhancement' (2007) 1 *Studies in Ethics, Law, and Technology* 10.

[59] A Buchanan, 'Enhancement and the Ethics of Development' (2008) 18 *Kennedy Institute Ethics Journal* 1–34, 17.

[60] F Fukuyama, *Our Posthuman Future: Consequences of the Biotechnology Revolution* (New York, Farrar, Strauss and Giroux, 2002) 149.

identify the moment when one of them suddenly and miraculously was endowed with a distinctively *human* nature.[61] Even if we could agree that most human beings now share a number of characteristics, such as the capacity for language and cognition, what would it mean to say that human nature was being corrupted by treatments which *improve* cognitive abilities or prolong life? Human beings have been trying to improve their lot for thousands of years, and it would be odd if in the first decades of the twenty-first century we had reached both the pinnacle, and the end-point of this evolutionary and developmental process.

In part as a result of vaccination programmes and medicines like penicillin, life expectancy has risen dramatically in the last 100 years. If this progress continues, we might expect the average person to live to be well over 100 within the next few decades. The ageing process is the result of accumulated molecular damage, and research on animals suggests that it is possible to slow this process down by manipulating hormonal signals and cellular pathways in order to enable cells throughout the body to 'buffer' the toxic effects of environmental and other sources of damage.[62] Oshlanksy et al argue that it will soon be possible to delay ageing by about seven years, so that, at the age of 50, an averagely healthy person would have the health profile of a normal 43-year-old, while someone who is 60 would be as healthy as a 53-year-old, and so on.[63]

Would longer life spans and the ability to delay the ageing process interfere with human nature, or are they just part of man's continual and non-static interaction with his environment? In the context of debates over enhancements, what is interesting is that research into the prevention or cure of age-related diseases, like Alzheimer's, stroke, cancer or arthritis, is almost universally celebrated. Whereas the prospect of delaying ageing and significantly prolonging lifespans, in a more general and non-specific way, is often greeted with concern about pressure on the earth's resources and dwindling opportunities for young people. In fact, however, delayed ageing and longer lifespans will generally come about only because previously untreatable degenerative conditions become curable.[64]

Second, the 'don't mess with human nature' line of argument rests on the assumption that unenhanced human nature is necessarily preferable. But of course medical treatment in general is intended to interfere with the normal state of human existence. Michael Sandel is critical of the desire for 'mastery over nature', and the consequent failure to be 'open to the unbidden'.[65] Ordinary medical treatment involves both these things: we want to master nature precisely in order *not* to be open to 'unbidden' pain and disease. Sandel claims that medical treatment,

---

[61] J Hughes, 'Beyond Human Nature' in P Healy and S Rayner (eds), *Unnatural Selection: The Challenges of Engineering Tomorrow's People* (Oxford, Earthscan, 2009) 51–59, 52.

[62] SJ Olshansky et al, 'In Pursuit of the Longevity Dividend' in P Healy and S Rayner (eds), *Unnatural Selection: The Challenges of Engineering Tomorrow's People* (Oxford, Earthscan, 2009) 94–102, 99.

[63] ibid 100.

[64] Harris, n 2 above, 59–71.

[65] M Sandel, 'The Case against Perfection What's Wrong with Designer Children, Bionic Athletes, and Genetic Engineering' (2004) 292 *Atlantic Monthly* 50–62.

conventionally understood, 'honours human nature', and permits flourishing.[66] It is, however, hard to see how such a sharp line can be drawn between medical treatment (which on Sandel's view is acceptable) and medical enhancement (which on his view is unacceptable). Enhancing a person's immune system, by vaccination or by other means, enables them to resist disease. Does this 'honour nature' or display an illegitimate tendency towards mastery over it?

Imagine that a new drug treatment for Alzheimer's disease, or for age-related macular degeneration, resulted not only in the stemming of memory or sight loss, but also radically improved the patient's memory or vision. A person could then have been treated *and enhanced* at the same time, and it would seem odd to rule out the new treatment for dementia or blindness on the grounds that it might leave the patient with greatly improved memory or vision, rather than simply returning her to a normal state.

Sandel also makes the slightly counter-intuitive claim that social solidarity is created by our sense that our natural talents, or their opposite, are the result of luck, rather than deliberate choice. Nature, as Julian Savulescu has pointed out, 'allots capabilities with no eye to fairness'.[67] On the contrary, the genetic, environmental and social lotteries which determine, at least in part, how our lives will turn out are extremely *unfair*. Sandel argues that those of us who have done well in the unequal distribution of material resources and natural talents recognise our serendipitous good fortune, and this makes us more likely to feel solidarity with those who have not been so lucky.

If, on the other hand, our capacities were the result of the deliberate efforts we had made to enhance ourselves, Sandel argues that we might hold those who have failed to enhance themselves responsible for their disadvantaged state and that, as a result, social solidarity would break down. Sandel's sense that he himself has been exceptionally fortunate in the social and genetic lotteries of life may prompt his feelings of sympathy and generosity towards people who have been less fortunate. This is, however, not a universal response to inequality. In the UK, the coalition government's resurrection of the distinction between the deserving poor (hard-working families) and the undeserving (welfare scroungers)[68] suggest that enhancement techniques would not destroy social cohesion which inevitably results from feelings of solidarity with those who are less fortunate than ourselves. Holding people responsible for their fate would not be a new development, entirely the result of biomedical enhancement techniques.

Habermas makes a slightly different claim, namely that having been enhanced by one's parents would make people feel alienated from their true selves. Again, this is slightly odd given all the efforts parents already make to shape their children's opportunities and life chances. A parent who insists that her child practices his violin for four hours a day may be curtailing the child's opportunity to pursue other interests. A parent who feeds her child too much junk food is restricting

---

[66] ibid 57.
[67] Savulescu n 29 above, 182.
[68] R Williams, 'The Government Needs to Know How Afraid People Are' *New Statesman* 9 June 2011.

that child's development. Parents are generally free to make choices about their children's diet and education which can both adversely and positively affect the rest of their lives. None of us can realistically believe that we are the sole authors of our life histories – we have all been shaped by our parents and by the education we received – but equally, that does not mean that we have no agency at all.[69] If a child is pushed towards academic success – by intensive tutoring or by being fed smart pills – it is still possible for her to drop out altogether or to decide to devote her energies to non-academic pursuits, like sport or gardening. If parental attempts to exercise too much control over their children's futures are a problem, this is neither new nor the result of new enhancement techniques, the problem, in short, is 'bad parenting, not bad technology'.[70]

Sandel's argument that it is good to be 'open to the unbidden' and bad to strive for 'mastery over nature' is also made with particular relevance to parental attempts to 'improve' their offspring. It is undoubtedly true that unconditional parental love is good for children, but this is not incompatible with striving to give one's children every advantage that one can. A parent who does everything they can to find a cure for their child's disease is not thereby indicating that their love for their child is conditional upon him being healthy. Parents who will love their children only if they display certain characteristics, such as good health or academic success, and will reject them if they do not, are displaying what Lewens calls 'a defect of character'.[71] A parent who seeks to improve her child's life chances is not, however, the same thing as a parent who will necessarily reject a child whose life does not turn out well.

The claim that enhancement medication might alienate human beings from their authentic selves is also made in a report from the President's Council on Bioethics 'Beyond Therapy', whose principal author was Leon Kass. A drug like Prozac, the report argued, not only alters mood, but also separates individuals from the experiences and thoughts associated with those moods, thus challenging their very identity. The argument is not that it is good to be depressed, but rather that sometimes feeling troubled is a normal part of the human condition. If Prozac makes someone less fretful about the emptiness of consumerist culture, Carl Elliott suggests that it may make it easier for them live happily in the US, but enhancing our capacity to tolerate vapid materialism does not necessarily make this sort of cosmetic psychopharmacology desirable.[72] A more extreme example still might be a drug which bleached a person's skin colour: having a whiter skin might 'enhance' someone's ability to live successfully in a racist society, but regarding skin-lightening medication as a 'solution' to the difficulties of encountering prejudice and discrimination in one's daily life is addressing the wrong target.

---

[69] CAJ Coady 'Playing God' in J Savulescu and N Bostrom (eds), *Human Enhancement* (Oxford University Press, 2009) 181–97.

[70] Caplan n 22 above, 209.

[71] T Lewens, 'Enhancement and Human Nature: The Case of Sandel' (2009) 35 *Journal of Medical Ethics* 354–56.

[72] C Elliott, 'The Tyranny of Happiness: Ethics and Cosmetic Psychopharmacology' in E Parens (ed), *Enhancing Human Traits: Ethical and Social Implications'* (Washington, Georgetown University Press, 1998) 177–88.

In a related argument, it has been maintained that enhancement would lead to the creation of a new species of post-humans, who would be superior to ordinary humans, and who would therefore be likely to discriminate against them, at best, and enslave or exterminate them, at worst.[73] Indeed, Daniel Wikler has suggested that, in an age of cognitive enhancement, the bar at which we decide that someone lacks the ability to make good decisions for themselves might be raised so that people who we now categorise as 'normal' might be regarded as cognitively deficient and in need of paternalistic interventions.[74] Society is currently organised so that people of low to average ability, both cognitively and physically, can cope with the challenges of daily life. If, Wikler argues, the cognitively and physically enhanced arranged society to suit themselves, the 'normals' might find life increasingly difficult.

As Allen Buchanan explains, what these critics of enhancement have in common is the assumption that human enhancement would be a private good for the enhanced individuals, who would be cleverer or more athletic or more beautiful than they would have been without the use of the enhancement, but that it would be a public disaster. What they miss, in Buchanan's view, is the possibility that enhanced productivity might have social or collective benefits, and that enhancement is not necessarily a zero-sum affair in which one person is necessarily enhanced at the expense of another. Literacy, for example, is an enhancement where the benefits are both private and public, and where there is not a finite amount of literacy to go round, such that rich people's ability to converse with each other necessarily implies that the poor are confined to more primitive forms of communication. On the contrary, the greater the proportion of the population which is literate, the better it is for society as a whole.

B Transhumanism

Almost in a mirror image of the conservative critique of enhancements, transhumanists have argued that enhancements enable human beings to conquer our natural deficiencies and improve upon normal species functioning.[75] Transhumanists reject 'nature as a general criterion of the good',[76] pointing out that there is, in fact, much to be improved upon in the experiences and actions of unenhanced human beings. Nature's 'gifts', on this view, include cancer, starvation and dementia, and the human natures of some of our fellow humans are a propensity to 'murder, rape, genocide, cheating, torture [and] racism'.[77] For transhumanists, human nature is 'a

---

[73] Fukuyama n 60 above.

[74] D Wikler, 'Paternalism in the Age of Cognitive Enhancement' in J Savulescu and N Bostrom (eds), *Human Enhancement* (Oxford University Press, 2009) 342–55.

[75] J Savulescu, 'New Breeds of Humans: The Moral Obligation to Enhance' (2005) 10 *Reproductive Biomedicine Online* (Suppl 1) 36–39.

[76] N Bostrom, 'In Defense of Posthuman Dignity' (2005) 19 *Bioethics* 202–14.

[77] ibid.

work-in-progress . . . that we can learn to remould in desirable ways'.[78] Rather than viewing changes to human nature as necessarily alienating, transhumanists argue that, while some changes might be for the worse, others might make our lives infinitely more satisfying. We cannot yet know what it would be like to be post-human, but that does not necessarily mean that post-humanity is to be feared.

If a new breed of enhanced 'transhumans' were to emerge, again it would not necessarily lead to ordinary 'normals' being discriminated against or terrorised. Nick Bostrom, for example, points out that the current differences between the cognitive and physical abilities of different human beings, which are admittedly very great indeed, do not rule out the possibility of treating everyone with appropriate dignity. Of course, discrimination against the weak and the vulnerable exists, but this is an argument not against enhancement, but against intolerance and prejudice.

Erik Parens has argued that both critics of enhancement techniques and enthusiasts share a concern with what he calls 'authenticity', but that they have different understandings of what this entails.[79] Those who adopt what he refers to as the 'gratitude' framework believe that we should be grateful for our life and its gifts, and this leads them to question the legitimacy of interfering too much with human capabilities. In contrast, invoking the 'creativity' framework suggests that we should use our creativity to transform that gift for the better. Parens suggests that these are not mutually exclusive positions, and that most of us, in fact, move between them in our responses to enhancements. So, for example, very few people believe that human beings should not use their creativity to try to cure disease. On the other hand, most of us would think that we would lose something valuable if we abandoned all intimate relationships and simply took a pill to simulate the experience of intimacy.

Here the critical issue is that what counts as an enhancement will sometimes involve a degree of subjective judgement, rather than being a self-evident, objectively determinable fact. I may find the prospect of an unselective memory, with perfect recall of every embarrassing or painful moment in my life a bleak and unwelcome prospect. Others may find this appealing. Some drugs which are intended to make us 'better than well' – immunity to cancer, for example – may be almost universally regarded as enhancements; in relation to others, reasonable people may disagree.

IX Conclusion

In something of an anticlimax, the question of whether or not a medicine enhances or treats, in addition to being a difficult judgement to make in a wide range of

---

[78] N Bostrom, 'Human Genetic Enhancements: A Transhumanist Perspective' (2003) 37 *Journal of Value Inquiry* 493–506.

[79] E Parens, 'Toward a More Fruitful Debate about Enhancement' in J Savulescu and N Bostrom (eds), *Human Enhancement* (Oxford University Press, 2009) 155–80, 174.

circumstances, is in many ways an irrelevance. When any new medicine is licensed for use in humans, the important question is whether it is safe and whether it works. In relation to safety, few drugs are completely safe for all users and the important question is then whether the medicine's benefits outweigh its risks, and this – rather than whether we categorise it as treatment or enhancement – remains the critical issue. A pill which slightly improved a person's memory, but which carried the risk of very serious side effects, similar to those experienced by patients undergoing chemotherapy, for example, would fail this risk-benefit calculation, since a marginal improvement to memory is much less beneficial than the possibility of halting the progression of cancer.

More difficult than the question of whether a drug was acceptably safe would be the question of efficacy. Many of the medicines which might be categorised as enhancements are developed initially as treatments for disease or dysfunction. Clinical trials will be directed as establishing proof of efficacy in the patient population for which a marketing authorisation is sought. Efficacy may then be established prior to licensing for *on-label* usage, but the use of the same medicine as an enhancement will commonly be off-label, and hence there will not be robust clinical trial data demonstrating efficacy when taken as an enhancement. If a medicine was to be marketed solely as an enhancement, it could receive a marketing authorisation based upon proof that it did, in fact, enhance performance, but this is likely to be exceptional.

More commonly, the medicine will be licensed for use for one purpose and, in fact, used for an additional purpose: it will be what Lev et al describe as a 'dual use intervention'.[80] Two issues arise here. First, off-label prescription is generally believed to lie within the acceptable margin of clinical discretion. Restricting the use of licensed medicines as enhancements would then require some restrictions on this clinical discretion. Of course, doctors' clinical discretion is limited by their duty of care towards their patients. A decision to prescribe possibly long-term medication in the absence of robust evidence as to safety and efficacy should be taken only if the doctor reasonably believes that the benefits are likely to outweigh the potentially unknown risks in the individual patient.

Of course, if a pharmaceutical company knows that a medicine is likely to be widely prescribed for an off-label use, it might be argued that they should be under a duty to carry out clinical trials in order to establish proof of efficacy for the off-label use, rather than profiting from prescriptions which are grounded only in anecdotal evidence.

In practical terms, however, the rise of online pharmacies makes it impossible to guarantee that there will be effective restrictions on access to prescription medicines, once licensed for use. This in turn raises a number of broader issues which arise if self-medication with drugs which are intended to be available only on prescription becomes commonplace. If a person whose high blood pressure presents

---

[80] O Lev, FG Miller and EJ Emanuel, 'The Ethics of Research on Enhancement Interventions' (2010) 20 *Kennedy Institute of Ethics Journal* 101–13.

a contraindication to, say, the use of Ritalin suffers serious side effects as a result of their foolish decision to purchase it on the internet, they are likely to expect treatment for those side effects within the NHS. Self-medication may therefore pose a health risk to individuals and impose costs on society.

Second, it is difficult to see how a medicine's enhancement potential could be relevant to a decision to license it as a treatment for an established condition. We would not want to rule out treatments for dementia because they might also be taken by students or professional chess players. Although a medicine's safety when misused *can* be one relevant factor when deciding whether to grant a marketing authorisation, the misuse of pharmaceutical drugs is common and if the potential for misuse is always a sufficient reason for refusing a marketing authorisation, few medicines would reach the marketplace.

Using pills to enhance oneself, rather than to treat disease, has a great deal in common with the use of surgical or other techniques for cosmetic purposes.[81] There are risks associated with surgery, and with less invasive cosmetic procedures like botox injections, and although cosmetic interventions will sometimes confer valuable health benefits – as in the case of reconstructive surgery for burns victims – other 'benefits' may seem trivial or silly. Nevertheless, increasing numbers of people are willing to pay for cosmetic procedures themselves, and to submit themselves to both known risks and potentially unknown longer-term consequences. There is also, inevitably, unequal access to cosmetic interventions. In terms of the medical profession itself, it could again be argued that using one's medical skills and training to carry out 'tummy tucks' may be lucrative, but it does not represent the pinnacle of medical achievement.

If cosmetic or enhancement pharmacology becomes simply another branch of cosmetic healthcare provision, it might be important to regulate aspects of the provision of enhancement medication which have received relatively little attention in debates about the ethics of enhancement, but which experience with cosmetic surgery suggests may be of particular importance, such as policing and regulating misleading advertising and unqualified practitioners.[82] People who seek out access to enhancement medication should be able to tell whether a clinician is properly qualified, and they should be given all the information that they need about risks and benefits so that their decision to take enhancement medication is an informed one. If cosmetic pharmacology is inevitable, we should strive to ensure that it is as safe as possible.

---

[81] A Chatterjee, 'Cosmetic Neurology and Cosmetic Surgery: Parallels, Predictions, and Challenges' (2007) 16 *Cambridge Quarterly of Healthcare Ethics* 129–37.

[82] National Confidential Enquiry into Patient Outcome and Death (NCEPOD) *On the Face of it: A Review of the Organisational Structures Surrounding the Practice of Cosmetic Surgery* (NCEPOD, 2010).

Concluding Remarks

A S SHOULD BE clear by now, the system of medicines regulation is far from perfect. The purpose of this short conclusion is to draw together a number of criticisms that this book has made of the current regulatory system in order to suggest some priorities for reform. I do not mean to imply that sweeping and comprehensive legal change would be easy, or even feasible. Rather, and much more modestly, these concluding remarks are intended to flag up particular issues which may warrant further investigation.

If we are going to have a special regulatory framework for medicines, then as a starting point it seems obvious that all medicinal products should have to meet the same exacting standards of proof of quality, safety and efficacy. This does not mean that all medicinal products must necessarily be chemically synthesised compounds. On the contrary, there is no reason why the producer of a herbal remedy, which wishes to make a medicinal claim for it, should not go through the same process as other drug manufacturers of having to establish (a) that it is safe, and (b) that it works. Some complementary remedies may pass these tests, others will not, but if safety and efficacy cannot be proven, medicinal claims must not be made.

Put simply, producers of complementary and alternative medicines which cannot prove safety and efficacy should not be allowed to market their products as if they were medicines, capable of altering disease progression or alleviating symptoms. This would probably not be a popular move, because it is clear that some consumers like taking alternative medicines, and even derive benefit from them. Reports of improvements after taking homeopathic remedies are not evidence that they work, however. Instead people may experience a powerful placebo effect when their ailments are taken seriously by a sympathetic practitioner. I would be in favour of subjecting *all* medicinal products to the same licensing regime, but it is also important to recognise that conventional medicine may have some lessons to learn from the popularity of alternative and complementary medicine. Harnessing the placebo effect of warmth and empathy while pretending that homeopathy works is misleading, and should be outlawed. But acknowledging that warmth and empathy may promote recovery could help to improve health outcomes in conventional medical settings.

In relation to clinical trials, the legacy of research abuses – such as the Nazi's horrific experiments on human subjects and the shameful exploitation of poor and vulnerable people like the US citizens at Tuskegee whose syphillis was left untreated – has been a regulatory system which emphasises the importance of a subject's voluntary and informed consent to participation. This has had a number of consequences, such as an ethical review process which focuses upon questions that arise in the recruitment of research subjects. Until recently, this has left comparatively neglected questions of conflict of interest and publication bias.

It is increasingly recognised that the pharmaceutical industry's involvement in clinical trials creates a potential conflict of interest. Clinical trials are no longer carried out by academic scientists for whom the outcome 'this does not work' is just as interesting as 'this looks promising'. Instead the pharmaceutical industry can make huge profits if trials show positive results, and huge losses if they are negative and the investment to date has been a waste of money. Given this financial interest in the results of trials, it is not surprising that the industry now exercises considerable control over how trials are run, employing specialist private companies both to carry out trials for them, and to disseminate the results. As sub-contractors of the drug company, hoping to ensure repeat business for themselves, these companies also have a clear financial incentive in ensuring that results are positive and that they receive positive coverage in the medical press. As a result, it may be unsurprising that there is evidence of the under-reporting of negative data and the multiple reporting of positive data. In practice, because this can distort the evidence base which is used to make licensing, funding and prescribing decisions, it has significant implications for public health and for NHS resources.

The most effective way to deal with this problem might be to wrest control of clinical trials away from the manufacturers of medicinal products and give responsibility instead to an independent regulatory body. This would require a dramatic shift in the organisation of clinical trials and it would undoubtedly be difficult to effect overnight. More prosaically, it might be important to shift the emphasis of ethical review processes away from their almost exclusive focus on issues that arise in the planning of a trial towards issues that arise subsequently, such as selective publication. If failure to publicly disseminate trial data were treated as straightforward research fraud, and ethical review committees were given the resources and the sanctions necessary to police publication bias, it might be possible to focus more attention on the distortions in the evidence base that may be prompted by endemic conflicts of interest.

In order to maximise the chance of obtaining positive results, companies that run clinical trials may try to specially select the trial population, in order to recruit people in whom it is easiest to demonstrate safety and efficacy. This has a knock-on effect when it comes to the licensing of medicines, because it means that trial data may show no more than that a new medicine appears to be safe and effective when taken for a short period of time by carefully chosen volunteers. This does not necessarily mean that the drug either works or is safe in the longer term, or when taken by real patients who may have comorbidities and/or be taking other medicines at the same time, and who might also be likely to smoke, drink, use drugs, become pregnant or be under 16. It is also important to recognise that proving efficacy may simply mean proving that the medicinal product works better than a placebo: that is, that it is better than nothing. There is no need for it to be an improvement on existing and well-tolerated medicines, thus facilitating the development of more and more 'me-too' drugs. It would be possible to amend the regulations so that they require new medicines to offer a demonstrable therapeutic or safety advantage over existing ones. Of course, manufacturers might argue that a new medicine may only be recognised as an improvement some time after it is marketed. This, however, could be an argument for more rigorous and extensive clinical trials, or, at the very least, for more honest labelling. Rather than expecting the first patients to take a new medicine to be uninformed guinea pigs, they need to be told in clear and uncertain terms about the limitations of the evidence base, especially if another well-tolerated and effective medicine is available for their condition.

It is common for a new medicine to reach the marketplace with only about 10 more years of patent protection left in place. Unsurprisingly then, companies may engage in a variety of techniques to try to extend the de facto period of patent protection. Some are dubious and might be outlawed if the 'novelty' prerequisite for patent protection were more rigorously enforced. It is understandable that a new chemical compound should receive a patent, but it is surely harder to justify patenting the particular colour combination of the capsule's plastic casing. Multiple patents for one product facilitate the launching of preventative patent infringement actions, in order to delay generic entry. Agreements in which the manufacturer of a branded medicine effectively bribes a generics manufacturer to delay marketing its cheaper version may be win-win arrangements for both companies, but they impose a significant cost on publicly funded healthcare systems, are anti-competitive and should be rigorously policed.

The inherent limitations of trial data also mean that the moment at which a medicine receives a marketing authorisation should not be treated as the moment at which definitive and final evidence of safety and efficacy is available. On the contrary, post-licensing monitoring, and even post-licensing trials are vitally important in order to gather evidence of a medicine's safety and efficacy profile in the real world. Unfortunately, however, pharmacovigilance appears to be the weak link in regulation. A small minority of adverse reactions is reported to the regulator, and drug companies are understandably more interested in trials that expand the indications for a product than they are in gathering information which may cast doubt upon its safety and efficacy when used long-term in real patient populations.

One relatively straightforward way to modify the set of incentives which encourage trials for new indications in order to expand the market for the product, and discourage the gathering of post-licensing safety and efficacy data would be to ensure that marketing authorisations are time-limited. A medicine could therefore only continue to be licensed for use five years after it received its initial marketing authorisation if robust evidence of its safety and efficacy in its post-licensing phase were presented to the regulator. There is currently a five-year review, but this is generally regarded as a formality. Not only could this be converted into a real hurdle to be overcome, but also it would be possible for review to happen more than once. More intensive and/or more frequent review would not be cost-free, but nor is the status quo in which medicines for which the evidence base may be weak continue to be prescribed to patients for whom they may not work or may be unsafe.

The lack of teeth in post-marketing surveillance is compounded in the UK by the difficulties faced by injured patients seeking to bring personal injury actions against drug manufacturers. In theory, in addition to the possibility of a claim in negligence, consumers should benefit from strict (no fault) liability when they are injured by defective products. In practice, it has proved virtually impossible to successfully pursue drugs manufacturers in the courts, a problem compounded by the withholding and withdrawing of legal aid from a number of class actions. Not only might this leave injured patients uncompensated, but it also means that the safety signals which might otherwise be picked up from legal claims go unnoticed. At the time of writing, it seems unlikely that there will be increases to the legal aid budget in the UK, but it is surely inequitable that global pharmaceutical companies routinely compensate injured US patients while leaving similarly situated UK citizens uncompensated.

The ban on direct to consumer advertising within the EU is under pressure not only from companies lobbying to have it rescinded, but also from the multiple ways in which products can be effectively marketed indirectly to consumers, without falling foul of the regulations. Indeed, when marketing does not look like advertising – but comes instead in the guise of a disease awareness campaign, a patient information website or even a newspaper or magazine article – it is likely to be more effective than when it straightforwardly looks like an attempt to sell something. Addressing the sophisticated marketing message which is euphemistically described as 'public relations' is difficult. More straightforward, however, would be a ban on direct funding of disease awareness campaigns, sources of patient information and patient groups. It would be possible to force philanthropic drug company funding to be pooled, so that it cannot be tied to product-specific campaigns or given to patient groups which can be mobilised to lobby for the availability of particular medicines within the NHS. Indirect promotion, where a non-branded campaign is in practice directed towards the promotion of an identifiable product, should be treated in the same way as direct to consumer advertising: that is, it should be banned.

It would also be relatively straightforward to address the pharmaceutical industry's relentless promotion of its products to the medical profession. It might be unpopular, but there should be no funding of continuing medical education, free gifts and hospitality which is tied to particular brands or products. If drug companies wish to engage in the funding of medical education, as part of their corporate social responsibility agenda, this should again be mediated through a pooled fund in which the contributions of individual companies are merged and the indirect promotion of particular products is not possible.

Prescription medicines are expensive, and there is no easy way to ensure their affordability within the NHS. The National Institute for health and Clinical

Excellence (NICE) has been a world leader in instituting a rigorous system of evidence-based cost-effectiveness appraisal of new and expensive medicines. It is not perfect, and much more attention needs to be paid to disinvestment decisions. Nevertheless, the current government's decision, which at the time of writing is still in the planning stage, to downgrade its status and move towards a value-based pricing system does not look as though it would be likely improve the NHS's ability to ensure that it does not waste money on medicines that are insufficiently cost-effective.

In a book of this size, it is impossible to do justice to the rich and diverse literature addressing global health inequalities, and in particular, unequal access to medicines. It is, however, vitally important that we overturn two common misconceptions about access to medicines in low and middle-income countries. First, the assumption that the poorest people in the world suffer principally from infectious diseases is no longer true: instead, they bear most of the global burden of non-communicable diseases like cancer, heart disease and diabetes. Malaria prevention is important, but so too is tobacco control. Second, high-profile initiatives aimed at improving access to medicines in low and middle-income countries have tended to adopt a single-disease top-down approach. Eradicating malaria may sound like a more stirring and momentous goal than building infrastructure, but all the evidence suggests that strengthening poor countries' public health systems is more effective than parachuting in disease-specific aid campaigns. It is also important to challenge aid programmes which leave untouched the impact of TRIPs and TRIPs-plus free trade agreements on the ability of low and middle-income countries to meet their citizens' health needs.

Pharmacogenetics raises some important and as yet unanswered questions about how an expansion of genetic testing might affect the costs of medicines. It might make medicines safer and cheaper, but equally there are grounds for thinking that the costs of prescribing might rise. Categorising patients according to their genotype might also raise a number of difficult issues, not least the problem of discovering that some people are effectively untreatable for a wide range of conditions.

Medicines are already used by many people as enhancements rather than treatment, a trend which is exacerbated by the rise of e-pharmacies willing to supply prescription medication to anyone who wishes to purchase it. If off-label use of medicines for enhancement purposes is likely to become more common, the most important issue may be consumer safety, rather than moral judgements about whether it might be cheating or represent an illegitimate 'quick fix'. Because medicines that are used as enhancements are also usually treatments for conditions, this raises the question of the legitimacy of off-label prescription and the responsibility of drug companies to carry out trials for new indications. Enhancement medication – with a few notable exceptions like the contraceptive pill – is unlikely to be routinely available on the NHS, leading to concerns about unequal access. It is, however, worth questioning whether unequal access to smart pills is qualitatively different from unequal access to private tuition and the other advantages affluent parents are able to offer their children.

Concluding Remarks

Finally, regulating medicines presents a diverse series of challenges, many of which are beyond the scope of laws governing the licensing and supply of medicinal products. Medicines regulation cannot be expected to solve health inequalities, or determine what to do about patients who are rendered untreatable by developments in pharmacogenetics. What it can do, however, is face head on the way in which gaps in some areas of regulation, or a lack of teeth in others, have become comprehensively exploitable by those whose principal interest is in selling more drugs.

Bibliography

Abadie, R, *The Professional Guinea Pig: Big Pharma and the Risky World of Human Subjects* (Duke University Press, 2010).

Abraham, J, 'Sociology of Pharmaceuticals Development and Regulation: A Realist Empirical Research Programme' (2008) 30 *Sociology of Health and Illness* 869–85.

Abraham, J and Lewis, G, 'Harmonising and Competing for Medicines Regulation: How Healthy Are the EU's Systems of Drug Approval?' (1999) 48 *Social Science and Medicine* 1655–67.

——, *Regulating Medicines in Europe* (London, Routledge, 2000).

Abraham, J and Reed, T, 'Reshaping the Carcinogenic Risk Assessment of Medicines: International Harmonisation for Drug Safety, Industry/Regulator Efficiency or Both?' (2003) 57 *Social Science & Medicine* 195–204.

Academy of Medical Sciences, *Safer Medicines* (The Academy of Medical Sciences, 2005).

Advertising Standards Unit MHRA, *Delivering High Standards in Medicines Advertising Regulation Fifth Annual Report 2009–2010* (MHRA, 2010).

Al-Marzouki, S, et al, 'Selective Reporting in Clinical Trials: Analysis of Trial Protocols Accepted by *The Lancet*' (2008) 372 *The Lancet* 201.

All Party Parliamentary Drug Misuse Group, *An Inquiry into Physical Dependence and Addiction to Prescription and Over-the-Counter Medication 2007–2008* Parliamentary Session.

All Party Parliamentary Group on AIDS, *The Treatment Timebomb: Report of the Enquiry of The All Party Parliamentary Group on AIDS into Long-Term Access to HIV Medicines in the Developing World* (Parliament, 2009).

Als-Nielsen, B, et al, 'Association of Funding and Conclusions in Randomised Drug Trials' (2003) 290 *Journal of the American Medical Association* 921–28.

Ameer B and Weintraub RA, 'Drug Interactions with Grapefruit Juice' (1997) 33 *Clinical Pharmacokinetics* 103–21.

American Medical Association (AMA), *Ethical Opinion E-8.061, Gifts to Physicians from Industry* (AMA, 2007).

Angell, E, Sutton, A, Windridge K and Dixon-Woods, M, 'Consistency in Decision-Making by Research Ethics Committees: A Controlled Comparison' (2006) 32 *Journal of Medical Ethics* 662–64.

Angell, M and Relman, AS, 'Patents, Profits and American Medicine: Conflicts of Interest in the Testing & Marketing of New Drugs' (2002) *Daedalus* 102–11.

Angelmar, R, et al, 'Building Strong Condition Brands' (2007) 7 *Journal of Medical Marketing* 341–51.

Antes, G and Chalmers, I, 'Under-Reporting of Clinical Trials is Unethical' (2003) 261 *The Lancet* 978–79.

Appel, JM, When the Boss Turns Pusher: A Proposal for Employee Protections in the Age of Cosmetic Neurology (2008) 34 *Journal of Medical Ethics* 616–18.

Appelbaum, PS, Roth, LH and Lidz, C, 'The Therapeutic Misconception: Informed Consent in Psychiatric Research' (1982) 5 *International Journal of Law and Psychiatry* 319–29.

Appleby, J and Maybin, J, 'Topping Up NHS Care' (2008) 337 *British Medical Journal* 2449.

Arnaiz, JA, et al, 'The Use of Evidence in Pharmacovigilance: Case Reports as the Reference Source for Drug Withdrawals' (2001) 57 *European Journal of Clinical Pharmacology* 89–91.

Arruñada, B, 'Quality Safeguards and Regulation of Online Pharmacies' (2004) 13 *Health Economics* 329–44.

Ashcroft, R, 'Equipoise, Knowledge and Ethics in Clinical Research and Practice' (1999) 13 *Bioethics* 314–26.

Association of American Medical Colleges, *Industry Funding of Medical Education Report of an AAMC Task Force* (AMA, 2008).

Association of American Medical Colleges and Baylor College of Medicine, Department of Neuroscience and Computational Psychiatry Unit, *The Scientific Basis of Influence and Reciprocity: A Symposium* (Association of American Medical Colleges, 2007).

Association of the British Pharmaceutical Industry (ABPI), *Report of Seminar Medicines; Tried and Tested – or an Unknown Risk?* (2 November 2000), available at www.abpi.org. uk/amric/tried_&_tested.pdf.

——, *Annual Report 2009–10* (ABPI, 2010).

——, *Code of Practice* (ABPI, 2011).

Atkinson, S, *Health Inequalities in London: Where Are We Now?* (Greater London Authority, 2006).

Audit Commission, *Managing the Implementation of NICE Guidance* (Audit Commission, 2005).

Avorn, J, *Powerful Medicines: The Benefits, Risks, and Costs of Prescription Drugs* (New York, Knopf, 2004) 365.

Baarts, C and Pedersen, IK, 'Derivative Benefits: Exploring the Body through Complementary and Alternative Medicine' (2009) 31 *Sociology of Health and Illness* 31 719–33.

Backstrom, M, Mjorndal, T and Dahlquist, R, 'Under-Reporting of Serious ADRs in Sweden' (2004) 13 *Pharmacoepidemiology and Drug Safety* 483–87.

Bamberger, M and Yaeger, D, 'Over the Edge' *Sports Illustrated* 14 April 1997.

Bancroft J, 'The Medicalisation of Female Sexual Dysfunction: The Need for Caution' (2002) 31 *Archives of Sexual Behaviour* 451–55.

Banerjee, A, Hollis, A and Pogge, T, 'The Health Impact Fund: Incentives for Improving Access to Medicines' (2010) 375 *The Lancet* 166–69.

Barnes, J, 'Quality, Efficacy and Safety of Complementary Medicines: Fashions, Facts and the Future. Part II: Efficacy and Safety' (2003) 55 *British Journal of Clinical Pharmacology* 331–40.

Barros, PP, 'The Simple Economics of Risk-Sharing Agreements between the NHS and the Pharmaceutical Industry' (2011) 20 *Health Economics* 461–70.

Bass, NA, 'Implications of the TRIPs Agreement for Developing Countries: Pharmaceutical Patent Laws in Brazil and South Africa in the 21st Century' (2002) 34 *George Washington International Law Review* 191–222.

Basson, R, et al, 'Report of the International Consensus Development Conference on Female Sexual Dysfunction: Definitions and Classifications' (2000) 163 *Urology* 888–93.

Baylis, F, 'The Olivieri Debacle: Where were the Heroes of Bioethics?' (2004) 30 *Journal of Medical Ethics* 44–49.

Beecher, HK, 'Ethics and Clinical Research' (1966) 274 *New England Journal of Medicine* 1354–60.

Bibliography

Bekelman JE, et al, 'Scope and Impact of Financial Conflicts of Interest in Biomedical Research' (2003) 289 *Journal of the American Medical Association* 454–56.

Bell, J, 'Propranolol, Post-Traumatic Stress Disorder and Narrative Identity' (2008) 34 *Journal of Medical Ethics* e23.

Belton, K, et al, 'Attitudinal Survey of Adverse Drug Reaction Reporting by Medical Practitioners in the United Kingdom' (1995) 39 *British Journal of Clinical Pharmacology* 223–26.

Bentley, JP and Thacker, PG, 'The Influence of Risk and Monetary Payment on the Research Participation Decision Making Process' (2004) 30 *Journal of Medical Ethics* 293–98.

Berman, J, et al, 'Effect of Sildenafil on Subjective and Physiologic Parameters of the Female Sexual Response in Women with Sexual Arousal Disorder' (2001) 27 *Journal of Sex and Marital Therapy* 411–20.

Berndt, ER and Hurvitz, JA, 'Vaccine Advance-Purchase Agreements for Low-Income Countries: Practical Issues' (2005) 24 *Health Affairs* 653–65.

Bero, L, et al, 'Factors Associated with Findings of Published Trials of Drug-Drug Comparisons: Why Some Statins Appear More Efficacious than Others' (2007) 4 *Public Library of Science* 1–10.

Bessell, TL, et al, 'Quality of Global E-Pharmacies: Can We Safeguard Consumers?' (2002) 58 *European Journal of Clinical Pharmacology* 567–72.

Bhat, SB and Hegde, TT, 'Ethical International Research on Human Subjects Research in the Absence of Local Institutional Review Boards' (2006) 32 *Journal of Medical Ethics* 535–53.

Birch, S and Gafni, A, 'Economists' Dream or Nightmare? Maximizing Health Gains from Available Resources using the NICE Guidelines'2 (2007) *Health Economics, Policy and Law* 193–202.

Birn, A-E, 'Addressing the Societal Determinants of Health: The Key Global Health Ethics Imperative of Our Time' in S Benatar and G Brock (eds), *Global Health and Global Health Ethics* (Cambridge University Press, 2011) 37–52.

Bloch, M, et al, 'Severe Psychiatric Symptoms Associated with Paroxetine Withdrawal' (1995) 346 *The Lancet* 57.

Blumenthal, D, et al, 'Withholding Research Results in Academic Life Science: Evidence from a National Survey of Faculty' (1997) 277 *Journal of the American Medical Association* 1224–28.

Bodenheimer, T, 'Uneasy Alliance – Clinical Investigators and the Pharmaceutical Industry' (2000) 342 *New England Journal of Medicine* 1539–44.

Boggild, M, et al, 'Multiple Sclerosis Risk Sharing Scheme: Two Year Results of Clinical Cohort Study with Historical Comparator' (2009) 339 *British Medical Journal* b4677.

Boissel, JP, et al, *Critical Literature Review on the Effectiveness of Homoeopathy: Overview of Data from Homoeopathic Medicine Trials: Homoeopathic Medicine Research Group Report to the European Commission* (Brussels, 1996) 195–210.

Bombardier, C, et al, 'Comparison of Upper Gastrointestinal Toxicity of Rofecoxib and Naproxen in Patients with Rheumatoid Arthritis' 343 (2000) *New England Journal of Medicine* 1520–28.

Bonaccorso SN and Sturchio JL, 'For and Against: Direct to Consumer Advertising is Medicalising Normal Human Experience: Against' (2002) 324 *British Medical Journal* 910–11.

Bonaccorso, S and Sturchio, JL, 'Perspectives from the Pharmaceutical Industry' (2003) 327 *British Medical Journal* 863–86.

Boozang, KM, et al, *Conflicts of Interest in Clinical Trial Recruitment & Enrollment: A Call for Increased Oversight* White Paper for the Center for Health & Pharmaceutical Law & Policy, Seton Hall Law School (November 30, 2009).

Boseley, A, 'Women Denied Cancer Drug that Could Extend Life' *The Guardian* 21 October 2009.

Boseley, S, 'Firms Fight Move to Obtain Cheap Anti-Blindness Drug Avastin' *The Guardian* 2 January 2011.

Bostrom, N, 'Human Genetic Enhancements: A Transhumanist Perspective' (2003) 37 *Journal of Value Inquiry* 493–506.

——, 'In Defense of Posthuman Dignity' (2005) 19 *Bioethics* 202–14.

Bourgeois, FT, Murthy, S and Mandl, KD, 'Outcome Reporting Among Drug Trials Registered in ClinicalTrials.gov' (2010) 153 *Annals of Internal Medicine* 158–66.

Bowcott, O, 'Libya Mass Rape Claims: Using Viagra Would be a Horrific First' *The Guardian* 9 June 2011.

Bradford, WD, et al, 'How Direct-to-Consumer Television Advertising for Osteoarthritis Drugs Affects Physicians' Prescribing Behavior' (2006) 25 *Health Affairs* 1371–77.

Braithwaite, J, *Corporate Crime in the Pharmaceutical Industry* (London, Routledge, 1984).

Bremer, S and Hartung, T, 'The Use of Embryonic Stem Cells for Regulatory Developmental Toxicity Testing In Vitro – The Current Status of Test Development' (2004) 10 *Current Pharmaceutical Design* 2733–47.

Brennan, TA, et al, 'Health Industry Practices that Create Conflicts of Interest: A Policy Proposal for Academic Medical Centers' (2006) 295 *Journal of the American Medical Association* 429.

Brett, AS, Burr W and Moloo, J, 'Are Gifts from Pharmaceutical Companies Ethically Problematic? A Survey of Physicians' (2003) 163 *Archives of Internal Medicine* 2213–18.

British Pharmacopoeia Commission Secretariat of the Medicines and Healthcare products Regulatory Agency (MHRA), *The British Pharmacopoeia 2011: The Leading Global Standards for UK Pharmaceutical and Medicinal Products* (MHRA, 2011).

Brody, H, 'The Commercialisation of Medical Decisions: Physicians and Patients at Risk' in DW Light (ed), *The Risks of Prescription Drugs* (Columbia UP, 2010) 70–90.

Brown, WA, 'The Placebo Effect' (1998) 278 *Scientific American* 90–95.

Brulliard, K, 'Zimbabwean Government Denying Human Right to Health, Doctors' Group Says' *Washington Post* 14 January 2009.

Bryant, J and Powell, J, 'Payment to Healthcare Professionals for Patient Recruitment to Trials: A Systematic Review' (2005) 331 *British Medical Journal* 1377.

Buchanan, A, et al, 'Pharmacogenetics: Ethical Issues and Policy Options' (2002) 12 *Kennedy Institute of Ethics Journal* 1–15.

Buchanan, A, 'Enhancement and the Ethics of Development' (2008) 18 *Kennedy Institute Ethics Journal* 1–34.

Burroughs, VJ, 'Racial and Ethnic Inclusiveness in Clinical Trials in Ethics and the Pharmaceutical Industry' in Michael A Santoro and Thomas M Gorrie (eds), *Ethics and the Pharmaceutical Industry* (Cambridge University Press, 2005).

Busfield, J, 'Pills, Power, People: Sociological Understandings of the Pharmaceutical Industry' (2006) 40 *Sociology* 297–314.

Cain, DM and Detsky, AS, 'Everyone's a Little Bit Biased (Even Physicians)' (2008) 299 *Journal of the American Medical Association* 2893–95.

Cairns, J, 'Providing Guidance to the NHS: The Scottish Medicines Consortium and the National Institute for Clinical Excellence Compared' (2006) 76 *Health Policy* 134–43.

Cakic, V, 'Smart Drugs for Cognitive Enhancement: Ethical and Pragmatic Considerations in the Era of Cosmetic Neurology' (2009) 35 *Journal of Medical Ethics* 611–15.

Calfee, JE, 'Public Policy Issues in Direct-to-Consumer Advertising of Prescription Drugs' (2002) 19 *Journal of Public Policy and Marketing* 174.

Calfee, JE, Winston, C and Stempski, R, 'Direct-to-Consumer Advertising and the Demand for Cholesterol-Reducing Drugs' (2002) 45 *Journal of Law and Economics* 673.

Campbell, D, 'Doctors Warned to Expect Unrest Over NHS Reforms' *The Guardian* Friday 19 November 2010.

Caplan, AL, 'Good, Better, or Best?' in J Savulescu and N Bostrom (eds), *Human Enhancement* (Oxford University Press, 2009) 199–209, 205.

Carpenter, DP, 'The Political Economy of FDA Drug Review' (2004) 23 *Health Affairs* 52–63.

Carse, A and Little, MO, 'Exploitation and the Enterprise of Medical Research' in Jennifer S Hawkins and Ezekiel J Emanuel, *Exploitation and Developing Countries: The Ethics of Clinical Research* (Princeton UP, 2008) 206–45, 214.

Cartwright, N, 'Are RCTs the Gold Standard?' (2007) 2 *BioSocieties* 11–20.

Catlett, D, 'Public Relations and its Role in Pharmaceutical Brand Building' in T Blackett and R Robins (eds), *Brand Medicine: The Role of Branding in the Pharmaceutical Industry* (Houndmills, Palgrave 2001) 130–40.

Cave, E, 'Seen but Not Heard? Children in Clinical Trials' (2010) 18 *Medical Law Review* 1–27.

Cekola, J, 'Outsourcing Drug Investigations to India: A Comment on US, India and International Regulation of Clinical Trials in Cross-Border Pharmaceutical Research' (2007) 28 *North Western Journal of International Law and Business* 125.

Centers for Disease Control (CDC), *Prescription Drug Overdoses: An American Epidemic* (CDC, 2011).

Chafe, R, et al, 'Accessing Unfunded Cancer Drugs in Publicly Funded Hospitals' (2009) 10 *The Lancet Oncology* 306–07.

Chalmers, I, 'Underreporting Research is Scientific Misconduct' (1990) 263 *Journal of the American Medical Association* 1405–08.

——, 'From Optimism to Disillusion About Commitment to Transparency in the Medico-Industrial Complex' (2006) 99 *Journal of the Royal Society of Medicine* 337.

Chan, A-W, et al, 'Empirical Evidence for Selective Reporting of Outcomes in Randomised Trials: Comparison of Protocols to Published Articles' (2004) 291 *Journal of the American Medical Association* 2457–65.

Chan, S and Harris, J, 'In Support of Human Enhancement' (2007) 1 *Studies in Ethics, Law, and Technology* 10.

Charuvastra, A and Marder, SR, 'Unconscious Emotional Reasoning and the Therapeutic Misconception' (2008) 34 *Journal of Medical Ethics* 193–97.

Chatterjee, A, 'Cosmetic Neurology and Cosmetic Surgery: Parallels, Predictions, and Challenges' (2007) 16 *Cambridge Quarterly of Healthcare Ethics* 129–37.

——, 'The Promise and Predicament of Cosmetic Neurology' (2006) 32 *Journal of Medical Ethic* 110–13.

Chren, M, 'Interactions between Physicians and Drug Company Representatives' (1999) 107 *American Journal of Medicine* 182–83.

Chuang-Stein, C, Beltangady, M, Dunne M and Morrison, B, 'The Ethics of Non-Inferiority Trials' (2008) 371 *The Lancet* 895–96.

Cho, MK and Bero, LA, 'The Quality of Drug Studies Published in Symposium Proceedings' (1996) 124 *Annals of Internal Medicine* 485–89.

Claxton, K, 'OFT, VBP: QED?' (2007) 16 *Health Economics* 545–58.

Coady, CAJ, 'Playing God' in J Savulescu and N Bostrom (eds), *Human Enhancement* (Oxford University Press, 2009) 181–97.

Cochi SL, Hull HF and Ward NA, 'To Conquer Poliomyelitis Forever' (1995) 345 *The Lancet* 1589–90.

Cohen-Kohler, JC, Forman, L and Lipkus, N, 'Addressing Legal and Political Barriers to Global Pharmaceutical Access: Options for Remedying the Impact of the Agreement on Trade-Related Aspects of Intellectual Property Rights (TRIPS) and the Imposition of TRIPs-Plus Standards' (2008) 3 *Health Economics, Policy and Law* 229–56.

Coleman, CH, 'Rationalizing Risk Assessment in Human Subject Research' (2004) 46 *Arizona Law Review* 1–51.

Collier, J and Iheanacho, I, 'The Pharmaceutical Industry as an Informant' (2002) 360 *The Lancet* 1405–09.

Committee for Medicinal Products for Human Use, *Points to Consider on Switching between Superiority and Noninferiority* (EMA, 2000).

Compston, A, 'Commentary: Scheme has Benefited Patients' (2010) 340 *British Medical Journal* c2707.

Conrad, P and Leiter, V, 'Medicalisation, Markets and Consumers' (2004) 45 *Journal of Health and Social Behavior* 158–76.

Conroy, S, McIntyre J and Choonara, I 'Unlicensed and Off-Label Drug Use in Neonates' (1999) 80 *Archives of Disease in Childhood Fetal and Neonatal Edition* F142–F145.

Conroy, S, et al, 'Survey of Unlicensed and Off-Label Drug Use in Paediatric Wards in European Countries' (2000) 320 *British Medical Journal* 79–82.

Cooksey, D, *A Report to Government by the Bioscience Innovation and Growth Team* (Department for Business, Enterprise and Regulatory Reform, 2009).

Cookson, RM, Drummond, M and Weatherly, H, 'Explicit Incorporation of Equity Considerations into Economic Evaluation of Public Health Interventions' (2009) 4 *Health Economics, Policy and Law* 261–63.

Correa, C, 'Implications of Bilateral Free Trade Agreements on Access to Medicines' (2006) 84 *Bulletin of the World Health Organization* 399–404.

Council for International Organisations of Medical Sciences (CIOMS), *International Ethical Guidelines for Biomedical Research Involving Human Subjects* (CIOMS, 2002).

Cucherat, M, et al, 'Evidence of Clinical Efficacy of Homeopathy: A Meta-Analysis of Clinical Trials' (2000) 56 *European Journal of Clinical Pharmacology* 27–33.

Curfman, GD, Morrissey, S and Draz, JM, 'Expression of Concern: Bombardier et al., "Comparison of Upper Gastrointestinal Toxicity of Rofecoxib and Naproxen in Patients with Rheumatoid Arthritis"' (2000) 343 *New England Journal of Medicine* 1520–28.

Cutler, DM, 'The Demise of the Blockbuster?' (2007) 356 *New England Journal of Medicine* 1292–93.

D'Agostino, RB, Massaro, JM and Sullivan, LM, 'Non-Inferiority Trials: Design Concepts and Issues – The Encounters of Academic Consultants in Statistics' (2003) 22 *Statistics in Medicine* 169–86.

Daemmrich, A, and Krücken, G, 'Risk versus Risk: Decision-Making Dilemmas of Drug Regulation in the United States and Germany' (2000) 9 *Science as Culture* 505–34.

Dalen, JE, 'Selective COX-2 Inhibitors, NSAIDs, Aspirin, and Myocardial Infarction' (2002) 162 *Archives of of Internal Medicine* 1091–92.

Dana, J and Loewenstein, G, 'A Social Science Perspective on Gifts to Physicians from Industry' (2003) 90 *Journal of the American Medical Association* 252–55.

Daniels, N, 'Health-Care Needs and Distributive Justice' (1981) 10 *Philosophy and Public Affairs* 146–79.

——, 'Normal Functioning and the Treatment-Enhancement Distinction' (2000) 9 *Cambridge Quarterly of Healthcare Ethics* 309–22.

——, 'International Health Inequalities and Global Justice: Toward a Middle Ground' in S Benatar and G Brock (eds), *Global Health and Global Health Ethics* (Cambridge University Press, 2011) 97–107.

Davies, SE, *Global Politics of Health* (Cambridge, Polity, 2010).

De Angelis, C, et al, 'Clinical Trial Registration: A Statement from the International Committee of Medical Journal Editors' (2004) 351 *New England Journal of Medicine* 1250–51.

DeCosta, A, et al, 'Community Based Trials and Informed Consent in Rural North India' (2004) 30 *Journal of Medical Ethics* 318–23.

Dekkers, W and Rikkert, MO, 'Memory Enhancing Drugs and Alzheimer's Disease: Enhancing the Self or Preventing the Loss of It? *(2007)*10 *Medicine, Health Care and Philosophy* 141–51.

Department of Health (DH), *Directions to Health Authorities, Primary Care Trusts and NHS Trusts in England* (DH, 2001).

——, *Government Response to the Health Committee's 2nd Report of Session 2001–02 on National Institute for Clinical Excellence* (DH, 2002).

——, *The Code of Conduct for Private Practice: Recommended Standards of Practice for NHS Consultants* (DH, 2004).

——, *The Expert Group on Phase One Clinical Trials: Final Report* (DH, 2006), available at www.dh.gov.uk.

——, *Improving Access to Medicines for NHS Patients: A Report for the Secretary of State for Health by Professor Mike Richards* (DH, 2008).

——, *Pharmaceutical Price Regulation Scheme 2009* (DH, 2009).

——, *Direction to PCTs and NHS Trusts Concerning Decisions about Drugs and Other Treatments* (DH, 2009).

—— *A New Value-Based Approach to the Pricing of Branded Medicines* (DH, 2010).

——, *Consultation on the Proposals to Implement "Generic Substitution" in Primary Care: Analysis of Responses for Department of Health* by Greenstreet Berman (DH, 2010).

——, *The Proposals to Implement "Generic Substitution" in Primary Care, Further to the Pharmaceutical Price Regulation Scheme (PPRS) 2009* (DH, 2010).

——, *The Cancer Drugs Fund: Guidance to Support Operation of the Cancer Drugs Fund in 2011–12* (DH, 2011).

Dewey, J, *The Later Works 1925–1953: Volume 1 1925 Experience and Nature* JA Boydston (ed) (Southern Illinois UP, 1988).

Dickersin, K, et al, 'Factors Influencing Publication of Research Results' (1992) 267 *Journal of the American Medical Association* 374–78.

Dimasi, JA and Paquette, C, 'The Economics of Follow-On Drug Research and Development: Trends in Entry Rates and the Timing of Development' (2004) 22 *Pharmacoeconomics* Suppl 2:1–14.

Dixon-Woods, M, Angell, E, Ashcroft,RE and Bryman A,'Written Work: The Social Functions of Research Ethics Committee letters' (2007) 65 *Social Science and Medicine* 792–802.

Dixon-Woods, M, et al, 'What do Research Ethics Committees Say about Application to do Cancer Trials?' (2008) 9 *Lancet Oncology* 700–01.

Djulbegovic, B, et al, 'The Uncertainty Principle and Industry-Sponsored Research' (2000) 356 *The Lancet* 635–38.

Dobson, R, 'SSRI Use during Pregnancy is Associated with Fetal Abnormalities' (2006) 333 *British Medical Journal* 824.

Dorn, SD, et al, 'A Meta-Analysis of the Placebo Response in Complementary and Alternative Medicine Trials of Irritable Bowel Syndrome' (2007) 19 *Neurogastroenterology and Motility* 630–37.

Drazen, JM, 'COX-2 Inhibitors – A Lesson in Unexpected Problems' (2005) 352 *New England Journal of Medicine* 1131–32.

Dresser, R and Frader, R, 'Off-Label Prescribing: A Call for Heightened Professional and Government Oversight' (2009) 37 *Journal of Law, Medicine and Ethics* 476.

Drummond, MF, et al, 'Assessing the Economic Challenges Posed by Orphan Drugs' (2007) 23 *International Journal of Technology Assessment in Health Care* 36–42.

Drummond, M, 'NICE: A Nightmare worth Having?' (2007) 2 *Health Economics, Policy and Law* 203–08.

Durand, M, 'Pharma's Advocacy Dance' (2006) *Pharmaceutical Executive* 1.

Dyer, C and Boseley, S, 'US Court Ruling Shuts Door on Drug Claimants' Compensation Hopes' *The Guardian* 7 October 2006.

Ecks, S, 'Global Pharmaceutical Markets and Corporate Citizenship: The Case of Novartis' Anti-cancer Drug Glivec' (2008) 3 *BioSocieties* 165–81.

Edmond, G, 'Judging the Scientific and Medical Literature: Some Legal Implications of Changes to Biomedical Research and Publication' (2008) 28 *Oxford Journal of Legal Studies* 523–561.

Edmonds, P, Dermot, D and Oglialoro, C, 'Access to Important New Medicines' (2000) 13 *European Business Journal* 146–58.

Ekelund, M and Persson, B, 'Pharmaceutical Pricing in a Regulated Market' (2003) 85 *Review of Economics and Statistics* 298–306.

Elland, I, et al, 'Attitudinal Survey of Voluntary Reporting of Adverse Drug Reactions' (1999) 48 *British Journal of Clinical Pharmacology* 623–27.

Elliott, C, *Better than Well: American Medicine Meets the American Dream* (Norton, New York, 2003).

——, 'Pharma Goes to the Laundry: Public Relations and the Business of Medical Education' (2004) 34 *Hastings Center Report* 18–23.

——, 'The Drug Pushers' (2006) 297 *The Atlantic Monthly* 82–93.

—— 'The Mild Torture Economy' (2010) 32 *London Review of Books* 26–27.

——, 'The Tyranny of Happiness: Ethics and Cosmetic Psychopharmacology' in E Parens (ed), Enhancing Human Traits: Ethical and Social Implications' (Washington, Georgetown University Press, 1998) 177–88.

——, *White Coat Black Hat: Adventures on the Dark Side of Medicine* (Boston, Beacon Press, 2010).

Emanuel, EJ, 'Addressing Exploitation: Reasonable Availability versus Fair Benefits' in Jennifer S Hawkins and Ezekiel J Emanuel, *Exploitation and Developing Countries: The Ethics of Clinical Research* (Princeton UP, 2008) 286–313.

Engelberg, AB, Kesselheim, AS and Avorn, J, 'Balancing Innovation, Access, and Profits – Market Exclusivity for Biologics' (2009) 361 *New England Journal of Medicine* 1917–19.

Epstein, RA, *Overdose: How Excessive Government Regulation Stifles Pharmaceutical Innovation* (New Haven, Yale University Press, 2006).

Ernst, E, 'Complementary and Alternative Medicine: What the NHS Should be Funding?' (2008) 58 *British Journal of General Practice* 208–09.

——, 'We Must Give Patients the Evidence on Complementary Therapies' (2006) 333 *British Medical Journal* 308.

Ernst, E and Cassileth, BR, 'The Prevalence of Complementary/Alternative Medicine in Cancer: A Systemic Review' (1998) 83 *Cancer* 777–82.

European Commission (EC), *A stronger European-based pharmaceutical industry for the benefit of the patient – a call for action* (EC, 2003).

——, *Third Report on the Application of the Directive* (EC, 2006).

——, *Pharmaceutical Sector Inquiry Report* (EC, 2009).

——, *Executive Summary of the Pharmaceutical Sector Inquiry Report* (EC, 2009).

European Medicines Agency (EMA), *European Medicines Agency Policy on Access to Documents (Related to Medicinal Products for Human and Veterinary Use)* (EMA, 2010).

European Ombudsman, *Draft Recommendation of the European Ombudsman in his Inquiry into Complaint 2560/2007/BEH against the European Medicines Agency* (7 June 2010).

Evans, R and Boseley, S, 'The Drugs Industry and its Watchdog: A Relationship too Close for Comfort' *The Guardian* 4 October 2004.

Eysenbach,G, 'Online Prescribing of Sildanefil (Viagra) on the World Wide Web' (1999) 1 *Journal of Medical Internet Research* E10.

Fagerlund, N and Rasmussen, SB, 'AstraZeneca: The First Abuse Case in the Pharmaceutical Sector' (2005) 3 *EC Competition Policy Newsletter* 54–56.

Falit, B, 'The Path to Cheaper and Safer Drugs: Revamping the Pharmaceutical Industry in the Light of GlaxoSmithKline's Settlement' (2005) 33 *Journal of Law, Medicine and Ethics* Spring 174.

Fanning, J and Glover-Thomas, N, 'Take this Medicine: The Legality of Prescription Incentive Schemes' (2010) 18 *Medical Law Review* 417.

Farahani, P, et al, 'Clinical Data Gap between Phase III Clinical Trials (Pre-Marketing) and Phase IV (Post-Marketing) Studies: Evaluation of Etanercept in Rheumatoid Arthritis' (2005) 12 *Canadian Journal of Clinical Pharmacology* e254–e263.

Farmer, P, et al, 'Expansion of Cancer Care and Control in Countries of Low and Middle Income: A Call to Action' (2010) 376 *The Lancet* 1186–93.

Featherstone, K, and Donovan JL, 'Random Allocation or Allocation at Random? Patients' Perspectives of Participation in a Randomised Controlled Trial' (1998) 317 *British Medical Journal* 1177–78.

——, 'Why Don't They Just Tell Me Straight, Why Allocate it?' The Struggle to Make Sense of Participating in a Randomised Controlled Trial' (2002) 55 *Social Science and Medicine* 709–19.

Ferguson, P, *Drug Injuries and the Pursuit of Compensation* (London, Sweet & Maxwell, 1996).

Ferguson, PR, 'Clinical Trials and Healthy Volunteers' (2008) 16 *Medical Law Review* 23–51.

Ferner, RE, 'Controversy over Generic Substitution' (2010) 340 *British Medical Journal* c2548.

Fisher, JA, 'Co-ordinating "Ethical" Clinical Trials: The Role of Research Coordinators in the Contract Research Industry' (2006) 27 *Sociology of Health and Illness* 678–94.

——, *Medical Research for Hire: The Political Economy of Pharmaceutical Clinical Trials* (Rutgers University Press, 2009).

Fitten, LJ, 'The Ethics of Conducting Research with Older Psychiatric Patients' (1993) 8 *International Journal of Geriatric Psychiatry* 33–39.

Fitzgerald, DW, et al, 'Comprehension during Informed Consent in a Less-Developed Country' (2002) 360 *The Lancet* 1301–02.

Flanagin, A, et al, 'Prevalence of Articles with Honorary Authors and Ghost Authors in Peer-Reviewed Medical Journals' (1998) 280 *Journal of the American Medical Association* 222–24.

Fojo, T and Grady, C, 'How Much Is Life Worth: Cetuximab, Non – Small Cell Lung Cancer, and the $440 Billion Question' (2009) 102 *Journal of the National Cancer Institute* 1207–10.

Fox, NJ and Ward, J, 'Pharma in the Bedroom . . . and the Kitchen. . . . The Pharmaceuticalisation of Daily Life' (2008) 30 *Sociology of Health and Illness* 856–68.

Franck L, Chantler C and Dixon M, 'Should NICE Evaluate Complementary and Alternative Medicine?' (2007) 334 *British Medical Journal* 506–07.

Freemantle, N and Hill, S, 'Medicalisation, Limits to Medicine, or Never Enough Money to Go Around?' (2002) 324 *British Medical Journal* 864.

Friedberg, M, et al, 'Evaluation of Conflict of Interest in Economic Analyses of New Drugs Used in Oncology' (1999) 282 *Journal of the American Medical Association* 1453–57.

Frosch, DL, et al, 'Creating Demand for Prescription Drugs: A Content Analysis of Television Direct-to-Consumer Advertising' (2007) 5 *Annals of Family Medicine* 6–13.

Fuchs, SA, 'Will the FDA's 2010 Warfarin Label Changes Finally Provide the Legal Impetus for Warfarin Pharmacogenetic Testing?' (2010) 12 *North Carolina Journal of Law & Technology* 99.

Fugh-Berman, A, Alladin, K and Chow J, 'Advertising in Medical Journals: Should Current Practices Change?' (2006) 3 *PLoS Medicine* e130.

Fukuyama, F, *Our Posthuman Future: Consequences of the Biotechnology Revolution* (New York, Farrar, Strauss and Giroux, 2002) 149.

Garret, L, 'The Challenge of Global Health' (2007) 86 *Foreign Affairs* 14–38.

Gearty, C and Mantouvalou, V, *Debating Social Rights* (Hart Publishing, Oxford, 2010).

General Medical Council (GMC), *Consent to Research* (GMC, 2010).

——, *Good Medical Practice* (GMC, 2006).

Gibson, TM, 'The Bioethics of Enhancing Human Performance for Spaceflight' (2006) 32 *Journal of Medical Ethics* 129–32.

Glass, HE and Dalton, DW, 'Profiles of Phase IV Investigators and Subsequent Prescribing of the Study Drug' (2006) 17 *Journal of Pharmaceutical Marketing and Management* 3–17.

Global Forum for Health Research (GCFR), *The 10/90 Gap in Health Research* (GCFR, Geneva, 1999).

——, (2005) 1 *Global Forum Update on Research for Health* 10–11.

Glover, J, *Causing Death and Saving Lives* (London, Penguin, 1977).

Glover-Thomas, N and Fanning, J, 'Medicalisation: The Role of E-Pharmacies in Iatrogenic Harm' (2010) 18 *Medical Law Review* 28–55.

Goldacre, B, 'Benefits and Risks of Homoeopathy' (2007) 370 *The Lancet* 1672–73.

Goodman, R, 'Cognitive Enhancement, Cheating, and Accomplishment' (2010) 20 *Kennedy Institute of Ethics Journal* 145–60.

Goozner, M, *The $800 Million Pill: The Truth Behind the Cost of New Drugs* (Berkeley, University of California Press, 2004).

Gostin, LO, 'Redressing the Unconscionable Health Gap: A Global Plan for Justice' (2010) 4 *Harvard Law & Policy Review* 271.

Bibliography

Gøtzsche, P, et al, 'Constraints on Publication Rights in Industry-initiated Clinical Trials' (2006) 295 *Journal of the American Medical Association* 1645–46, 1646.

Gøtzsche, PC and Jørgensen, AW, 'Opening up Data at the European Medicines Agency' (2011) 342 *British Medical Journal* d2686.

Grady, C 'Ethics of Vaccine Research' in AS Iltis (ed), *Research Ethics* (London, Routledge, 2006) 22–31.

Grant Thompson, W, *The Placebo Effect and Health: Combining Science and Compassionate Care* (Amherst, NY, Prometheus Books, 2005).

Gray, G and Flynn P, 'A Survey of Placebo Use in a General Hospital' (1981) *General Hospital Psychiatry* 199–203.

Greely, H, et al, 'Towards Responsible Use of Cognitive-Enhancing Drugs by the Healthy' (2008) 456 *Nature* 702–05.

Greene, JA, 'Making Medicines Essential: The Emergent Centrality of Pharmaceuticals in Global Health' (2011) 6 *BioSocieties* 10–33.

Griffin, SC, et al, 'Dangerous Omissions: The Consequences of Ignoring Decision Uncertainty' (2011) 20 *Health Economics* 212–24.

Griffin, JP, 'Venetian Treacle and the Foundation of Medicines Regulation' (2004) 58 *British Journal of Clinical Pharmacology* 317–25.

Hall, WD, 'How Have the SSRI Antidepressants Affected Suicide Risk?' (2006) 367 *The Lancet* 1959–62.

Harris, J, *Enhancing Evolution: The Ethical Case for Making Better People* (Princeton, 2007).

——, 'Enhancements are a Moral Obligation' in J Savulescu and N Bostrom (eds), *Human Enhancement* (Oxford University Press, 2009) 131–54.

Hartigan, J, 'Is Race Still Socially Constructed? The Recent Controversy over Race and Medical Genetics' (2008) 17 *Science as Culture* 163–93.

Hasford, J, et al, 'Physicians' Knowledge and Attitudes Regarding the Spontaneous Reporting System for Adverse Drug Reactions' (2002) 55 *Journal of Clinical Epidemiology* 945–50.

Hawkes, N, 'Continuing Medical Education: What Price Education?' (2008) 337 *British Medical Journal* a2333.

Healy, D, 'Shaping the Intimate: Influences on the Experience of Everyday Nerves' (2004) 34 *Social Studies of Science* 219–45.

Healy, D and Cattell, D, 'Interface between Authorship, Industry and Science in the Domain of Therapeutics' (2003) 183 *British Journal of Psychiatry* 22.

Hedgecoe, A, 'From Resistance to Usefulness: Sociology and the Clinical Use of Genetic Tests' (2008) 3 *BioSocieties* 183–94.

——, *The Politics of Personalised Medicine: Pharmacogenetics in the Clinic* (Cambridge University Press, 2004).

Heeley, E, et al, 'Prescription-Event Monitoring and Reporting of Adverse Drug Reactions' (2001) 358 *The Lancet* 1872–73.

Henry, D and Lexchin, J, 'Patent law' (2003) 361 *The Lancet* 1059.

Herxheimer, A, 'Relationships between the Pharmaceutical Industry and Patients' Organizations' (2003) 326 *British Medical Journal* 1208.

Heylman, S, 'New Paxil Suits Allege Birth Defect Risk (2007) 43 *Trial* 14.

Hill, Z, et al, 'Informed Consent in Ghana: What do Participants Really Understand?' (2008) 34 *Journal of Medical Ethics* 48–53.

Hoffman, JR and Wilkes, M, 'Direct to Consumer Advertising of Prescription Drugs: An Idea Whose Time Should Not Come' (1999) 318 *British Medical Journal* 1301.

Hope, J, 'Drug Denial is Devastating "Death Sentence" for Cancer Patients' *Daily Mail* 7 August 2008.

Hopewell, S, et al, 'Publication Bias in Clinical Trials due to Statistical Significance or Direction of Trial Results' (2009) 1 *The Cochrane Library* 1–26.

Horton, R, 'The Dawn of McScience' (2004) 51 *New York Review of Books* 7–9.

Horton, R and Das, P, 'The Vaccine Paradox' (2011) *The Lancet* advance online access.

Horwitz, AV, 'Pharmaceuticals and the Medicalization of Social Life' in DW Light (ed), *The Risks of Prescription Drugs* (Columbia UP, 2010) 92–115, 105.

House of Commons Health Select Committee, *National Institute for Health and Clinical Excellence* First Report of Session 2006–07.

——, *The Influence of the Pharmaceutical Industry* Fourth Report of Session 2004–05.

——, *Top-Up Fees* Fourth Report of Session 2008–09.

House of Commons Science and Technology Committee, *Evidence Check 2: Homeopathy* Fourth Report of Session 2009–10.

House of Lords Select Committee on Science and Technology, *Complementary and Alternative Medicine* Sixth Report of Session 1999–2000.

Hrachovec, B and Mora, M, 'Reporting of 6-Month vs 12-Month Data in a Clinical Trial of Celecoxib' (2001) 286 *Journal of the American Medical Association* 239–89.

Hróbjartsson, A, 'Clinical Placebo Interventions are Unethical, Unnecessary and Unprofessional' (2008) 19 *Journal of Clinical Ethics J* 66–9.

Hubbard, T and Love J, 'A New Trade Framework for Global Healthcare R&D' (2004) 2 *PloS Biology* e52.

Hughes DA, 'Less is More: Medicines that Require Less Frequent Dosing Improve Adherence, but are they Better?' (2006) 24 *Pharmacoeconomics* 211–13.

Hughes, DA and Ferner, RE, 'New Drugs for Old: Disinvestment and NICE' (2010) 340 *British Medical Journal* c572.

Hughes, J, 'Beyond Human Nature' in P Healy and S Rayner (eds), *Unnatural Selection: The Challenges of Engineering Tomorrow's People* (Oxford, Earthscan, 2009) 51–59.

Iheanacho, I, 'Drug Regulation: A Sometimes Unhealthy Coalition' (2010) 340 *British Medical Journal* c2613.

Ingelfinger, FJ, 'Informed (but Uneducated) Consent' (1972) 287 *New England Journal of Medicine* 466.

International Committee of Medical Journal Editors, *Uniform Requirements for Manuscripts Submitted to Biomedical Journals: Writing and Editing for Biomedical Publication* (October 2008).

Jack, A, 'GlaxoSmithKline Sidesteps NICE by Negotiating with Individual Hospitals' (2009) 339 *British Medical Journal* b4406.

——, 'Perils for Pill Pushers' *The Financial Times* 22 September 2010.

Jackson, E, 'Informed Consent and the Impotence of Tort' in S McLean (ed), *First Do No Harm* (Aldershot, Ashgate, 2006) 273–86.

Jackson, E, *Medical Law*, 2nd edn (Oxford University Press, 2010).

Jackson, T, 'Regulator Spells Out Rules on Disease Awareness Campaigns' (2003) 326 *British Medical Journal* 1219.

Jain, KK, 'Personalised Medicine for Cancer: From Drug Development into Clinical Practice' (2005) 6 *Expert Opinion on Pharmacotherapy* 1463–76 .

Jarernsiripornkul, N, et al, 'Patient Reporting of Adverse Drug Reactions: Useful Information for Pain Management?J (2003) 7 *European Journal of Pain* 219–24.

Johansen, HK and Gøtzsche P, et al, 'Constraints on Publication Rights in Industry-initiated Clinical Trials' (2006) 295 *Journal of the American Medical Association* 1645–46, 1646.

Johansen, HK and Gøtzsche PC, 1Problems in the Design and Reporting of Trials of Antifungal Agents Encountered during Meta-analysis' (1999) 282 *Journal of the American Medical Association* 1752–59.

Jones, K, 'In whose Interest? Relationships between Health Consumer Groups and the Pharmaceutical Industry in the UK' (2008) 30 *Sociology of Health and Illness* 929–43.

Jones, MJ, 'Internet-Based Prescription of Sildenafil: A 2104-Patient Series' (2001) 3 *Journal of Medical Internet Research* E2.

Jones, TC 'Call for a New Approach to the Process of Clinical Trials and Drug Registration' (2001) 322 *British Medical Journal* 92.

Jonsson, B, 'Being NICE is not the Problem!' (2009) 45 *European Journal of Cancer* 1100–02.

Joppi, R, Bertele, V and Garattini, S, 'Disappointing Biotech' (2005) 331 *British Medical Journal* 895.

Jost, TS, 'Oversight of Marketing Relationships between Physicians and the Drug and Device Industry: A Comparative Study' (2010) 35 *American Journal of Law and Medicine* 326.

Jüni, P, et al, 'Risk of Cardiovascular Events and Rofecoxib: Cumulative Meta-Analysis' (2004) 364 *The Lancet* 2021–29.

Jutel, A, 'Framing Disease: The Example of Female Hypoactive Sexual Desire Disorder' (2010) 70 *Social Science and Medicine* 1084–90.

Kahn, J, 'Beyond BiDiL: The Expanding Embrace of Race of Biomedical Research and Product Development' (2009) 3 *Saint Louis University Journal of Health Law & Policy* 61.

——, 'How a Drug becomes "Ethnic": Law, Commerce, and the Production of Racial Categories in Medicine' (2004) 4 *Yale Journal of Health Policy, Law and Ethics* 1–46.

Kaptchuk, TJ, et al, 'Components of Placebo Effect: Randomised Controlled Trial in Patients with Irritable Bowel Syndrome' (2008) 336 *British Medical Journal* 999–1003.

Katz, D, Caplan, AL and Merz, JF, 'All Gifts Large and Small: Toward an Understanding of the Ethics of Pharmaceutical Industry Gift-Giving' (2003) 3 *American Journal of Bioethics* 39–46.

Kayser, B, Mauron, A and Miah, A, 'Viewpoint: Legalisation of Performance-Enhancing Drugs' (2005) 366 *The Lancet* S21.

Kazi, D, 'Rosiglitazone and Implications for Pharmacovigilance' (2007) 334 *British Medical Journal* 1233.

Keeling, N, 'Viagra Empire Run from Prison' *Manchester Evening News* 29 May 2007.

Kelly, Y, et al, 'What Role for the Home Learning Environment and Parenting in Reducing the Socioeconomic Gradient in Child Development? Findings from the Millennium Cohort Study' (2011) *Archives of Disease in Childhood* online pre-publication access.

Kendall, T, McGoey, L and Jackson, E, 'If NICE was in the USA' (2009) 374 *The Lancet* 272–73.

Kennedy, I, *Appraising the Value of Innovation and other Benefits: A Short Study for NICE* (NICE, 2009).

Kerry, VB and Lee, K, 'TRIPs, the Doha Declaration and Paragraph 6 Decision: What are the Remaining Steps for Protecting Access to Medicines?' (2007) 3 *Global Health* 3.

Kessler, DA, et al, 'Therapeutic-Class Wars – Drug Promotion in a Competitive Marketplace' (1994) 331 *New England Journal of Medicine* 1350–53.

Kessler, DA and Vladeck, DC, 'A Critical Examination of the FDA's Efforts to Preempt Failure-to-Warn Claims' (2008) 96 *Georgetown Law Journal* 461–95.

Keyworth, T and Yarrow, G, *Review of the Office of Fair Trading's Market Study of the Pharmaceutical Price Regulation Scheme* (Regulatory Policy Institute, Oxford, 2007).

Kim, KY, et al, 'Tuberculosis Control' in R Smith et al (eds), *Global Public Goods for Health: Health Economics and Public Health Perspectives* (Oxford University Press, 2003) 54–72.

Kjaergard, L and Als-Nielsen, B, 'Association between Competing Interests and Authors' Conclusions: Epidemiological Study of Randomised Clinical Trials Published in the BMJ' (2002) 325 *British Medical Journal* 249.

Kleijnen, J Knipschild, P and ter Riet, G, 'Clinical Trials of Homoeopathy' (1991) 302 *British Medical Journal* 316–23.

Kmietowicz, Z, 'NICE Decision on Dementia Drugs was Based on "Common Sense" not Evidence, Expert Says' (2010) 341 *British Medical Journal* c5642.

Kondro, W, 'Drug Company Experts Advised Staff to Withhold Data about SSRI Use in Children' (2004) 170 *Canadian Medical Association Journal* 783.

Kramer, L, 'The FDA' s Callous Response to AIDS' *The New York Times* 23 March 1987 A19.

Kremer, M and Glennerster, R, 'Incentives for Research on Neglected Disease' (2005) 365 *The Lancet* 753–54.

Kremer, M and Glennerster, R, *Strong Medicine: Creating Incentives for Pharmaceutical Research on Neglected Diseases* (Princeton, Princeton University Press, 2004).

Kravitz, RL, et al, 'Influence of Patients' Requests for Direct-to-Consumer Advertised Antidepressants: A Randomised Controlled Trial' (2005) 293 *Journal of the American Medical Association* 1995–2002.

Krimsky, S, et al, 'Financial Interest of Authors in Scientific Journals: A Pilot Study of 14 Publications' (1996) 2 *Science and Engineering Ethics* 395–410.

Krimsky, S and Rothenberg, L, 'Financial Interest and its Disclosure in Scientific Publications' (1998) 280 *Journal of the American Medical Association* 25–26.

Krumholz HM, et al, 'What Have We Learnt from Vioxx?' (2007) 334 *British Medical Journal* 120–23.

Lacasse, JR and Leo, J, 'Serotonin and Depression: A Disconnect between the Advertisements and the Scientific Literature' (2005) 2 *PLoS Medicine* e392.

Laine, C, et al, 'Clinical Trial Registration: Looking Back and Moving Ahead' (2007) 147 *Annals of Internal Medicine* 275–77.

Laumann, EO, Paik, A and Rosen, RC, 'Sexual Dysfunction in the United States. Prevalence and Predictors' (1999) 281 *Journal of the American Medical Association* 537–44.

Laurance, J, 'Magic is Acceptable' (2010) 375 *The Lancet* 885.

Laurie, G, 'In Defence of Ignorance: Genetic Information and the Right not to Know' (1999) 6 *European Journal of Health Law* 119–32.

Lee, SS and Race, J, 'Distributive Justice and the Promise of Pharmacogenomics: Ethical Considerations' (2003) 3 *American Journal of Pharmacogenomics* 385–92.

Lee, CJ, Lee, LH and Lu, CH, *Development and Evaluation of Drugs: From Laboratory through Licensure to Market* (CRC Press, 2003).

Lee, TH, ' "Me-Too" Products – Friend or Foe?' (2004) 350 *New England Journal of Medicine* 211–21.

Lejoyeux, M and Ades, J, 'Antidepressant Discontinuation: A Review of the Literature' (1997) 28 *Journal of Clinical Psychiatry* supplement 7 11–15.

Leman, P and Greene, S, 'Testing Patients to Allow Tailored Drug Treatment' (2005) 3330 *British Medical Journal* 352.

Lemmens, T, 'Leopards in the Temple: Restoring Scientific Integrity to the Commercialised Research Scene' (2004) 32 *Journal of Law, Medicine and Ethics* 641–57.

Lemmen, T and Elliott, C, 'Justice for the Professional Guinea Pig' (2001) 1 *American Journal of Bioethics* 51–53.

Leppard, D, 'Elephant Man Drug Victims Told to Expect Early Death' *The Sunday Times* 30 July 2006.

Lev, O, Miller, FG and Emanuel, EJ, 'The Ethics of Research on Enhancement Interventions' (2010) 20 *Kennedy Institute of Ethics Journal* 101–13.

Lewens, T, 'Enhancement and Human Nature: The Case of Sandel' (2009) 35 *Journal of Medical Ethics* 354–56.

Lexchin, J, 'Bigger and Better: How Pfizer Redefined Erectile Dysfunction' (2006) 3 *PLoS Medicine* e132.

Lexchin, J, et al, 'Pharmaceutical Industry Sponsorship and Research Outcome and Quality: Systematic Review' (2003) 326 *British Medical Journal* 1167–70.

Lexchin, J and O'Donovan, O, 'Prohibiting or 'Managing' Conflict of Interest? A Review of Policies and Procedures in Three European Drug Regulation Agencies' (2010) 70 *Social Science and Medicine* 643–47.

Lichtenberg, F and Philipson, T, 'The Dual Effects of Intellectual Property Regulations: Within- and between-Patent Competition in the US Pharmaceuticals Industry' (2002) 45 *Journal of Law and Economics* 643–72.

Lie, RK, et al, 'The Standard of Care Debate: The Declaration of Helsinki versus the International Consensus Opinion' (2004) *Journal of Medical Ethics* 190–93.

Light, DW, 'Is G8 Putting Profits before the World's Poorest Children? (2007) 370 *The Lancet* 297–98.

Light, D, *Advanced Market Commitments: Current Realities and Alternate Approaches* (Amsterdam, Health Action International Europe/Medico International Publications, 2009).

Light, DW, 'Bearing the Risks of Prescription Drugs' in DW Light (ed), *The Risks of Prescription Drugs* (Columbia UP, 2010) 1–39.

——, 'Toward Safer Prescribing and Better Drugs in DW Light (ed), *The Risks of Prescription Drugs* (Columbia UP, 2010) 140.

——, 'Saving the Pneumococcal AMC and GAVI' (2011) 7 *Human Vaccines* 1–4.

Linde, K and Melchart, D, 'Randomised Controlled Trials of Individualised Homeopathy: A State-of-the-Art Review' (1998) 4 *Journal of Alternative and Complementary Medicine* 371–88.

Linde, K, et al, 'Impact of Study Quality on Outcome in Placebo-Controlled Trials of Homeopathy' (1999) 52 *Journal of Clinical Epidemiology* 631–36.

Lipman, MM, 'Bias in Direct-to-Consumer Advertising and its Effect on Drug Safety' (2007) 35 *Hofstra Law Review* 761.

Lippert, MC, et al, 'Alternative Medicine Use in Patients with Localised Prostate Cancer Treated with Curative Intent' (1999) 86 *Cancer* 2642–48.

Lipsky, MS and Taylor, CA 'The Opinions and Experiences of Family Physicians Regarding Direct-to-Consumer Advertising' (1997) 45 *Journal of Family Practice* 495–99.

Liu, EH, et al, 'Use of Alternative Medicine by Patients Undergoing Cardiac Surgery' (2000) 120 *Journal of Thoracic and Cardiovascular Surgery* 335–41.

Lock, S and Wells, F, 'Preface to the Second Edition' in S Lock and F Wells (eds), *Fraud and Misconduct in Medical Research* (BMJ Publishing Group, London, 1996) xi–xii.

London, AJ, 'Equipoise and International Human Subjects Research' (2001) 15 *Bioethics* 312–32.

Love, J, 'Fair Prices, Fair Profit' *New Scientist* 10 November 2007.

Lurie, P and Wolfe, SM, 'Unethical Trials of Interventions to Reduce Perinatal Transmission of the Human Immunodeficiency Virus in Developing Countries' (1997) 337 *New England Journal of Medicine* 853–56.

Lustgarten, A, 'Drug Testing Goes Offshore' *Fortune* (8 Aug 2005).

Lynöe, N, et al, 'Obtaining Informed Consent in Bangladesh' (2001) 344 *New England Journal of Medicine* 460–61.

Maher, B, 'Poll Results: Look Who's Doping' (2008) 452 *Nature* 674–75.

Mallal, S, et al, 'HLA-B*5701 Screening for Hypersensitivity to Abacavir' (2008) 358 *New England Journal of Medicine* 568–79.

Mangset, M, et al, ' "I Don't Like that, it's Tricking People too Much . . .": Acute Informed Consent to Participation in a Trial of Thrombolysis for Stroke' (2008) 34 *Journal of Medical Ethics* 751–56.

Mann, H, 'Research Ethics Committees and Public Dissemination of Clinical Trial Results' (2002) 360 *The Lancet* 406–08.

Martin, RM, et al, 'Underreporting of Suspected Adverse Drug Reactions to Newly Marketed ("Black Triangle") Drugs in General Practice: Observational Study' (1998) 317 *British Medical Journal* 119–12.

Martinez C, et al, 'Antidepressant Treatment and the Risk of Fatal and Non-Fatal Self Harm in First Episode Depression: Nested Case-Control Study' (2005) 330 *British Medical Journal* 389.

Mason, AR and Drummond, MF, 'Public Funding of New Cancer Drugs: Is NICE Getting Nastier?' (2009) 45 *European Journal of Cancer* 1188–92.

Mathieu, S, et al 'Comparison of Registered and Published Primary Outcomes in Randomised Controlled Trials' (2009) 302 *Journal of the American Medical Association* 977–84.

Matsoso, MP, et al, 'Medicine Safety and Safe Access to Essential Medicines' in R Parker and M Sommer (eds), *Routledge Handbook in Global Public Health* (Abingdon, Routledge, 2011) 442–50.

Matthew, AW and Martinez, B, 'E-mails Suggest Merck knew Vioxx's Dangers at Early Stage' *Wall Street Journal* 1 November 2004 A1.

Mayor, S, 'More than Half of Drugs Sold Online are Fake or Substandard' (2008) 337 *British Medical Journal* a618.

McCabe, C, Claxton, K and Tsuchiya, A, 'Orphan Drugs and the NHS: Should we Value Rarity?' (2005) 331 *British Medical Journal* 1016.

McCabe, C, et al, 'Continuing the Multiple Sclerosis Risk Sharing Scheme is Unjustified' (2010) 340 *British Medical Journal* c1786.

McCarthy, M, 'Prescription Drug Abuse up Sharply in the USA' (2007) 369 *The Lancet* 1505–06.

McCoy, D, et al, 'The Bill & Melinda Gates Foundation's Grant-Making Programme for Global Health' (2009) 373 *The Lancet* 1645–53.

McGoey, L, 'On the Will to Ignorance in Bureaucracy' (2007) 36 *Economy and Society* 212–35.

——, 'Pharmaceutical Controversies and the Performative Value of Uncertainty' (2009) 18 *Science as Culture* 151–64.

——, 'Entropic Failure in Global Health' (forthcoming).

McGoey, L and Jackson, E, 'Seroxat and the Suppression of Clinical Trial Data: Regulatory Failure and the Convenience of Legal Ambiguity' (2009) 35 *Journal of Medical Ethics* 107–12.

McGoey, L, Reiss, J and Wahlberg, A, 'The Global Health Complex' (2011) 6 *BioSocieties* 1–9.

McLeod, HL, 'Pharmacokinetic Differences between Ethnic Groups' (2002) 359 *The Lancet* 78.

Medicins Sans Frontieres (MSF), *Access to Medicines at Risk across the Globe: What to Watch Out For in Free Trade Agreements with the United States* (MSF, 2004).

Medicines and Healthcare products Regulatory Agency (MHRA), *Assessment Report: Paroxetine (Seroxat)* (MHRA, 2003).

——, *The Homeopathic National Rules Scheme: Brief Guidance for Manufacturers and Suppliers* (MHRA, 2006).

——, *A Guide to what is a Medicinal Product* (MHRA Guidance Note 8, revised 2007).

——, *Investigation into GlaxoSmithKline/Seroxat* (MHRA, 2008).

——, *Medicines Act Advisory Bodies Annual Report 2009* (MHRA, 2009).

——, 'Off-Label Use or Unlicensed medicines: Prescribers' Responsibilities' (2009) 2 *Drug Safety Update* 6–7.

——, (2010) 4 *Drug Safety Update* s1.

——, *Healthcare Professional Reporting: Adverse Drug Reactions* (MHRA, 2010).

——, *Unlicensed Herbal Remedies Made up to Meet the Need of Individual Patients: Section 12(1) of the Medicines Act 1968* (MHRA, 2011).

——, *Placing a Herbal Medicine on the UK Market* (MHRA, 2011).

Melander, H, et al, 'Evidence B(i)ased Medicine – Selective Reporting from Studies Sponsored by Pharmaceutical Industry: Review of Studies in New Drug Applications' (2003) 326 *British Medical Journal* 1171–73.

Mercer, CH, et al, 'Sexual Function Problems and Help Seeking Behaviour in Britain: National Probability Sample Study' (2003) 327 *British Medical Journal* 426–27.

Mildred, M, 'Pharmaceutical Products: The Relationship between Regulatory Approval and the Existence of a Defect' (2007) 18 *European Business Law Review* 1276–82.

Miller, FG and Brody, H, 'Enhancement Technologies and Professional Integrity' (2005) 5 *American Journal of Bioethics* 15–17.

Miller, FH, 'Trusting Doctors: Tricky Business When it Comes to Clinical Trials' (2001) 81 *Boston University Law Review* 423.

Miller, PB and Lemmens, T, 'The Human Subjects Trade: Ethical and Legal Issues Surrounding Recruitment Incentives' (2003) 31 *Journal of Law, Medicine and Ethics* 398–418.

Miller, P, et al, 'The Cognition Enhanced Classroom' in P Miller and J Wilsdon (eds), *Better Humans?* (London, Demos, 2006) 79–85.

Mintzes, B, 'For and Against: Direct to Consumer Advertising is Medicalising Normal Human Experience' (2002) 324 *British Medical Journal* 90.

——, 'Disease Mongering in Drug Promotion: Do Governments Have a Regulatory Role?' (2006) 3 *PLoS Medicine* e198.

Mintzes, B, et al, 'Influence of Direct to Consumer Pharmaceutical Advertising and Patients' Requests on Prescribing Decisions: Two Site Cross Sectional Survey' (2002) 324 *British Medical Journal* 278–79.

Moodley, K, Pather M and Myer, L, 'Informed Consent and Participant Perceptions of Influenza Vaccine Trials in South Africa' (2005) 31 *Journal of Medical Ethics* 727–32.

Moran, M, et al, *The New Landscape of Neglected Disease Drug Development.* (London, Wellcome Trust, 2005).

Morgan, SG, et al, '"Breakthrough" Drugs and Growth in Expenditure on Prescription Drugs in Canada' (2005) 331 *British Medical Journal* 815.

Moynihan, R, 'US Seniors Group Attacks Pharmaceutical Industry "fronts"' (2003) 326 *British Medical Journal* 351.

Moynihan, R, 'The Making of a Disease: Female Sexual Dysfunction' (2003) 326 *British Medical Journal* 45–47.

——, 'Prediseases: Who Benefits from Treating Prehypertension?' (2010) 341 *British Medical Journal* c4442.

——, and Cassels, A, *Selling Sickness: How the World's Biggest Pharmaceutical Companies are Turning us all into Patients* (New York, Nation Books, 2005).

Moynihan, R and Mintzes, B, *Sex, Lies and Pharmaceuticals: How Drug Companies Plan to Profit from Female Sexual Dysfunction* (Vancouver, Greystone Books, 2010).

Moynihan, R, et al, 'Selling Sickness: The Pharmaceutical Industry and Disease Mongering' (2002) 324 *British Medical Journal* 886–91.

Nathan, DG and Weatherall, DJ, 'Academic Freedom in Clinical Research' (2002) 347 *New England Journal of Medicine* 1368–71.

National Audit Office (NAO), *Prescribing Costs in Primary Care: Report by the Comptroller and Auditor General* (NAO, 2007).

National Confidential Enquiry into Patient Outcome and Death (NCEPOD), *On the Face of it: A Review of the Organisational Structures Surrounding the Practice of Cosmetic Surgery* (NCEPOD, 2010).

National Institute for Health and Clinical Excellence (NICE), *Multiple Sclerosis – Beta Interferon and Glatiramer Acetate Technology Appraisal 32* (NICE, 2002).

——, *Final Appraisal Determination – Attention Deficit Hyperactivity Disorder – Methylphenidate, Atomoxetine and Dexamfetamine (Review)* (NICE, 2005).

——, *Social Value Judgements*, 2nd edn (NICE, 2008).

——, *Appraising Life-Extending, End of Life Treatments* (NICE, 2009).

Netzer, C and Biller-Andorno, N, 'Pharmacogenetic Testing, Informed Consent and the Problem of Secondary Information' (2004) 18 *Bioethics* 344–60.

Newdick, C, 'Strict Liability for Defective Drugs in the Pharmaceutical Industry' (1985) 101 *Law Quarterly Review* 405–31.

——, 'Accountability for Rationing – Theory into Practice' 33 (2005) *Journal of Law, Medicine and Ethics* 660.

——, 'Judicial Review: Low-Priority Treatment and Exceptional Case Review' (2007) *Medical Law Review* 236.

——, *Who Should We Treat: Rights, Rationing and Resources in the NHS*, 2nd edn (Oxford University Press, 2005).

NHS Information Centre, *General Pharmaceutical Services in England 1999–2000 to 2008–09* (NHS Information Centre, 2009).

Noah, L, 'The Coming Pharmacogenomics Revolution: Tailoring Drugs to Fit Patients' Genetic Profiles' (2002) 43 *Jurimetrics Journal* 1–28.

Nozick, R, *Anarchy, State and Utopia* (New York, Basic Books, 1974).

Nuffield Council on Bioethics (NCOB), *The Ethics of Research Related to Healthcare in Developing Countries* (NCOB, London, 2002).

——, *Pharmacogenetics: Ethical Issues* (NCOB, London, 2003).

Nundy, S, Chir, M and Gulhati, CM, 'A New Colonialism? – Conducting Clinical Trials in India' (2005) 352 *New England Journal of Medicine* 1633–36.

O'Reilly, KB, 'Pfizer Pays Record $2.3 Billion in Off-Label Drug Marketing Settlement' *American Medical News* 14 September 2009.

Oberlander, TF, et al, 'Effects of Timing and Duration of Gestational Exposure to Serotonin Reuptake Inhibitor Antidepressants: Population-Based Study' (2008) 192 *British Journal of Psychiatry* 338–43.

Bibliography

Office of Fair Trading (OFT), *The Pharmaceutical Price Regulation Scheme: An OFT Market study* (OFT 2007).

Ofori-Adjei, D and Lartey, P, 'Challenges of Local Production of Pharmaceuticals in Improving Access to Medicines' in R Parker and M Sommer (eds), *Routledge Handbook in Global Public Health* (Abingdon, Routledge, 2011) 433–42.

Olshansky, SJ, et al, 'In Pursuit of the Longevity Dividend' in P Healy and S Rayner (eds), *Unnatural Selection: The Challenges of Engineering Tomorrow's People* (Oxford, Earthscan, 2009) 94–102, 99.

Olson, MK, 'Pharmaceutical Policy Change and the Safety of New Drugs' (2002) 45 *The Journal of Law and Economics* 615–42.

——, 'The Risk we Bear: The Effects of Review Speed and Industry User Fees on Drug Safety' (2008) 27 *Journal of Health Economics* 175–200.

Organisation for Economic Cooperation and Development (OECD), *Pharmacogenetics: Opportunities and Challenges for Health Innovation* (OECD, 2009).

Othman, N, Vitry, A and Roughead, EE, 'Quality of Pharmaceutical Advertisements in Medical Journals: A Systematic Review' (2009) 4 *PLoS Medicine* e6350.

Outram, SM, 'The Use of Methylphenidate among Students: The Future of Enhancement?' (2010) 36 *Journal of Medical Ethics* 198–202.

Oxfam, *Trading Away Access to Medicines How the European Union's Trade Agenda has Taken a Wrong Turn* (Oxfam, 2009).

Oxfam India, *Oxfam Urges India to Remain "Pharmacy of the Developing World"* (Oxfam, 2010).

Pace, C, et al, 'Quality of Parental Consent in a Ugandan Malaria Study' (2005) 95 *American Journal of Public Health* 1184–89.

Pappworth, MH, *Human Guinea Pigs: Experimentation on Man* (Beacon Press, Boston, 1967).

Parens, E, 'Toward a More Fruitful Debate about Enhancement' in J Savulescu and N Bostrom (eds), *Human Enhancement* (Oxford University Press, 2009) 155–80.

Payer, L, *Disease-Mongers: How Doctors, Drug Companies, and Insurers are Making you Feel Sick* (New York, Wiley, 1992).

Perlis, RH, et al, 'Industry Sponsorship and Financial Conflict of Interest in the Reporting of Clinical Trials in Psychiatry' (2005) 162 *American Journal of Psychiatry* 1957–60.

Petryna, A, *When Experiments Travel Clinical Trials and the Global Search for Human Subjects* (Princeton University Press, 2009).

Pich, X, et al, 'Role of a Research Ethics Committee in Follow-Up and Publication of Results' (2003) 361 *The Lancet* 1015–16.

Pilkington, E, 'Pharmageddon: How America Got Hooked on Killer Prescription Drugs' *The Guardian* 9 June 2011.

Pirmohamed, M, et al, (2004) 'Adverse Drug Reactions as Cause of Admission to Hospital: Prospective Analysis of 18,820 Patients' (2004) 329 *British Medical Journal* 15–19.

PLoS Medicine Editors, 'Increased Responsibility and Transparency in an Era of Increased Visibility' (2010) 7 *PLoS Medicine* e1000364.

Pogge, T, 'Human Rights and Global Health: A Research Program' (2005) 36 *Metaphilosophy* 182–209.

Pollock, A, 'Transforming the Critique of Big Pharma' (2011) 6 *BioSocieties* 106–18.

Postman, N, *Technopoly: The Surrender of Culture to Technology* (London, Vintage Books, 1993).

Potts, A, et al, 'The Downside of Viagra: Women's Experiences and Concerns' (2003) 25 *Sociology of Health and Illness* 697–719.

Prakongsai, P, et al, 'Can Earmarking Mobilize and Sustain Resources to the Health Sector?' (2008) 86 *Bulletin of the World Health Organisation* 898.

Prayle, D and Brazier, M, 'Supply of Medicines: Paternalism, Autonomy and Reality' (1998) 24 *Journal of Medical Ethics* 93–98.

Psaty, BM and Burke, SP, 'Protecting the Health of the Public – Institute of Medicine Recommendations on Drug Safety' (2006) 355 *New England Journal of Medicine* 1753–55.

Psaty, BM and Rennie, D, 'Clinical Trial Investigators and Their Prescribing Patterns' (2006) 295 *Journal of the American Medical Association* 2787–90.

Pywell, S, 'The Vaccine Damage Payment Scheme: A Proposal for Radical Reform' (2002) 9 *Journal of Social Security Law* 73–93, 83.

Quednow, BB, 'Ethics of Neuroenhancement: A Phantom Debate' (2010) 5 *BioSocieties* 153–56.

Quick, JD, et al, 'Ensuring Ethical Drug Promotion – Whose Responsibility?' (2003) 362 *The Lancet* 747.

Raftery J, 'Multiple Sclerosis Risk Sharing Scheme: A Costly Failure' *(2010)* 340 *British Medical Journal* c1672.

——, 'NICE and the Challenge of Cancer Drugs' (2009) 338 *British Medical Journal* 67.

——, et al, 'Payment to Healthcare Professionals for Patient Recruitment to Trials: Systematic Review and Qualitative Study' (2008) 12 *Health Technology Assessment* 1–128.

——, 'Review of NICE's Recommendations, 1999–2005' (2006) 332 *British Medical Journal* 1266–68.

Ranzini, A, Allen, A and Lai, YL, 'Use of Complementary Medicines and Therapies among Obstetric Patients' (2001) 97 *Obstetrics & Gynecology* S46.

Rao, JN and Sant Cassia, LJ, 'Ethics of Undisclosed Payments to Doctors Recruiting Patients in Clinical Trials' (2002) 325 *British Medical Journal* 36.

Ravvin, M, 'Incentivizing Access and Innovation for Essential Medicines: A Survey of the Problem and Proposed Solutions' (2008) 1 *Public Health Ethics* 110–23.

Rawlins, M, 'Pharmacovigilance: Paradise Lost, Regained or Postponed?' (1994) 29 *Journal of the Royal College of Physicians of London* 1.

Rawlins, MD and Culyer, AJ, 'National Institute for Clinical Excellence and its value judgments' (2004) 329 *British Medical Journal* 224.

Read, R, 'Schizophrenia, Drug Companies and the Internet' (2008) 66 *Social Science and Medicine* 99–109.

Reichman, JH, 'Rethinking the Role of Clinical Trial Data in International Intellectual Property Law: The Case for a Public Goods Approach' (2009) 13 *Marquette Intellectual Property Law Review* 1.

Rennie, D, 'Trial Registration A Great Idea Switches From Ignored to Irresistible' (2004) 292 *Journal of the American Medical Association* 1359–62.

Rennie, D, Yank V and Emanuel, L, 'When Authorship Fails: A Proposal to Make Contributors Accountable' (1997) 278 *Journal of the American Medical Association* 579–85.

Resch, K, Hill, S and Ernst, E, 'Use of Complementary Therapies by Individuals with Arthritis' (1997) 16 *Clinical Rheumatology* 391–95.

Reverby, SM, '"Normal Exposure" and Inoculation Syphilis: A PHS "Tuskegee" Doctor in Guatemala 1946–48' (2011) 23 *Journal of Policy History* 6–28.

Revill J, 'Restless Legs Keep 6m Awake' *The Observer* 19 September 2004.

Ridker, PM and Torres, J, 'Reported Outcomes in Major Cardiovascular Clinical Trials Funded by For-Profit and Not-for-Profit Organisations 2000–2005' (2006) 295 *Journal of the American Medical Association* 2270–76.

Ridley, DB, et al, 'Developing Drugs for Developing Countries' (2006) 25 *Health Affairs* 313–24.

Ridley, DB and Sánchez, AC, 'Introduction of European Priority Review Vouchers to Encourage Development of New Medicines for Neglected Diseases' (2010) 376 *The Lancet* 922–27.

Rigg, KK and Ibañez, GE, 'Motivations for Non-Medical Prescription Drug Use: A Mixed Methods Analysis' (2010) 39 *Journal of Substance Abuse Treatment* 236–47.

Rising, K, Bacchetti, P and Bero, L, 'Reporting Bias in Drug Trials Submitted to the Food and Drug Administration: Review of Publication and Presentation' (2008) 5 *PLoS Medicine* e217.

Rochon, PA, et al, 'Evaluating the Quality of Articles Published in Journal Supplements Compared with the Quality of those Published in the Parent Journal' (1994) 272 *Journal of the American Medical Association* 108–13.

Roses, AD, 'Pharmacogenetics and Future Drug Development and Delivery' (2000) 355 *The Lancet* 1358–61.

Ross, JS, et al, 'Trial Publication after Registration in ClinicalTrials.Gov: A Cross-Sectional Analysis' (2009) 6 *PLoS Medicine* e1000144.

Rosser, R and Kind, P, 'A Scale of Values of States of Illness: Is there a Social Consensus' (1978) 7 *International Journal of Epidemiology* 347–58.

Ruger, JP and Ng, NY, 'Emerging and Transitioning Countries' Role in Global Health' (2010) 3 *Saint Louis University Journal of Health Law & Policy* 253.

Safer, J, 'Design and Reporting Modifications in Industry-Sponsored Comparative Psychopharmacology Trials' (2002) 190 *Journal of Nervous and Mental Disease* 583–92.

Sample, I, 'E Coli Outbreak: German Organic Farm Officially Identified' *The Guardian* 19 June 2011.

Sandel, M, 'The Case against Perfection What's Wrong with Designer Children, Bionic Athletes, and Genetic Engineering' (2004) 292 *Atlantic Monthly* 50–62.

Sandhill, R, 'Prescription Drugs: Legal and Lethal' *The Sunday Times* 24 February 2008.

Santoro, MA, 'Introduction to Part II' in Michael A Santoro and Thomas M Gorrie (eds), *Ethics and the Pharmaceutical Industry* (Cambridge University Press, 2005) 127–35.

Sanz, EJ, et al, 'Selective Serotonin Reuptake Inhibitors in Pregnant Women and Neonatal Withdrawal Syndrome: A Database Analysis' (2005) 365 *The Lancet* 482–87.

Saver, RS, 'Medical Research and Intangible Harm' (2006) 74 *University of Cincinnati Law Review* 941.

Savulescu, J, 'Two Deaths and Two Lessons: Is it Time to Review the Structure and Function of Research Ethics Committees?' (2002) 28 *Journal of Medical Ethics* 1–2.

——, 'New Breeds of Humans: The Moral Obligation to Enhance' (2005) 10 *Reproductive Biomedicine Online* (Suppl 1):36–9.

——, 'Enhancement and Fairness' in P Healy and S Rayner (eds), *Unnatural Selection: The Challenges of Engineering Tomorrow's People* (Oxford, Earthscan, 2009) 177–87, 185.

——, Chalmers, I and Blunt, J, 'Are Research Ethics Committees Behaving Unethically? Some Suggestions for Improving Performance and Accountability' (1996) 313 *British Medical Journal* 1390.

Savulescu J, Foddy, B and Clayton, M, 'Why we should Allow Performance Enhancing Drugs in Sport' *(2004)* 38 *British Journal of Sports Medicine* 666–70.

Schafer, A, 'Biomedical Conflicts of Interest: A Defence of the Sequestration Thesis – Learning from the Cases of Nancy Olivieri and David Healy' (2004) 30 *Journal of Medical Ethics* 8–24.

Schardein, JL, *Chemically Induced Birth Defects*, 3rd edn (New York, Marcel Dekker, 2000).

Schermer, M, 'Enhancements, Easy Shortcuts and the Richness of Human Activities' (2008) 22 *Bioethics* 355–63.

——, 'On the Argument that Enhancement is "Cheating"' (2008) 34 *Journal of Medical Ethics* 85–88.

Schuklenk, U and Ashcroft, RE, 'Affordable Access to Essential Medication in Developing Countries: Conflicts between Ethical and Economic Imperatives' (2002) 27 *Journal of Medicine and Philosophy* 179–95.

Schwartz, TM, Consumer-Directed Prescription Drug Advertising and the Learned Intermediary Rule' (1991) 46 *Food, Drug and Cosmetics Law Journal* 829.

Scolding, N, 'The Multiple Sclerosis Risk Sharing Scheme' (2010) 340 British Medical Journal c2882.

Scott, S, 'The Medicalisation of Shyness: From Social Misfits to Social Fitness' (2006) 28 *Sociology of Health and Illness* 133–53.

Sered, S and Agigian, A, 'Holistic Sickening: Breast Cancer and the Discursive Worlds of Complementary and Alternative Practitioners' (2008) 31 *Sociology of Health and Illness* 616–31.

Shadlen, KC, The Political Economy of AIDS Treatment: Intellectual Property and the Transformation of Generic Supply' (2007) 51 *International Studies Quarterly* 559–81.

Shang, A, et al, 'Are the Clinical Effects of Homoeopathy Placebo Effects? Comparative Study of Placebo-Controlled Trials of Homoeopathy and Allopathy' (2005) 366 *Lancet* 726–73.

Shapiro, D, Wenger, N and Shapiro, M, 'The Contributions of Authors of Multiauthored Biomedical Research Papers' (1994) 271 *Journal of the American Medical Association* 438–42.

Sharples, FMC, van Haselen, R and Fisher, P, 'NHS Patients' Perspective on Complementary Medicine: A Survey' (2003) 11 *Complementary Therapies in Medicine* 243–48.

Sheldon, TA, et al, 'What's the Evidence that NICE Guidance has been Implemented? Results from a National Evaluation using Time Series Analysis, Audit of Patients' Notes, and Interviews' (2004) 329 *British Medical Journal* 999.

Shepherd, J, 'MMR Jab should be Compulsory for all Children Starting School, Expert says' *The Guardian* 3 June 2009.

Shooter, M, 'Dancing with the Devil? A Personal View of Psychiatry's Relationships with the Pharmaceutical Industry' (2005) 29 *Psychiatric Bulletin* 81–83.

Shuchman, M, 'Delaying Generic Competition – Corporate Payoffs and the Future of Plavix' (2006) 355 *New England Journal of Medicine* 1297–300.

Silverman, GK, et al, 'Failure to Discount for Conflict of Interest when Evaluating Medical Literature: A Randomised Trial of Physicians' (2010) 36 *Journal of Medical Ethics* 265–70.

Simes, J, 'Publication Bias: The Case for an International Registry of Clinical Trials' (1986) 4 *Journal of Clinical Oncology* 1529–41.

Sismondo, S, 'How Pharmaceutical Industry Funding Affects Trial Outcomes: Causal Structures and Responses' (2008) 66 *Social Science and Medicine* 1909–14.

Sismondo, S and Doucet, M, 'Publication Ethics and the Ghost Management of Medical Publication' (2010) 24 *Bioethics* 273–83.

Siva, N, 'The Drug Price is Right – or is it?' (2009) 373 *The Lancet* 1326–27.

Smart, A, 'A Multi-Dimensional Model of Clinical Utility' (2006) 18 *International Journal for Quality in Health Care* 377–82.

Smart, A, Martin, P and Parker, M, 'Tailored Medicine: Whom Will it Fit? The Ethics of Patient and Disease Stratification' (2004) 18 *Bioethics* 322–43.

Smith, R, 'Medical Journals Are an Extension of the Marketing Arm of Pharmaceutical Companies' (2005) 2 *PLoS Medicine* e138.

Smith, SE and Rawlins, MD, *Variability in Human Drug Response* (London, Butterworths, 1973*)*.

Snowdon, C, Garcia, J and Elbourne, D, 'Making Sense of Randomisation; Responses of Parents of Critically Ill Babies to Random Allocation of Treatment in a Clinical Trial' (1997) 45 *Social Science and Medicine* 1337–55.

Soint, E, 'The Search for Wellbeing in Alternative and Complementary Health Practices' (2006) 28 *Sociology of Health and Illness* 330–49.

Sonderholm, J, 'In Defense of Priority Review Vouchers' (2009) 23 *Bioethics* 413–20.

Spicer, N and Walsh, A, '10 Best Resources on . . . the Current Effects of Global Health Initiatives on Country Health Systems' (2011) *Health Policy and Planning* published online 5 May 2011.

Spielmans, GI, 'The Promotion of Olanzapine in Primary Care: An Examination of Internal Industry Documents' (2009) 69 *Social Science and Medicine* 14–20.

Spilker, B, 'The Risks and Benefits of a Pack of M&Ms' (2002) 21 *Health Affairs* 543–44.

Stapleton, J, *Product Liability* (Butterworths, London, 1994).

Stein, MS and Savulescu, J 'Welfare versus Autonomy in Human Subjects Research, (2011) 38 *Florida State University Law Review* 303.

Steinbrook, R, 'Gag Clauses in Clinical-trial Agreements' (2005) 352 *New England Journal of Medicine* 2160–62.

Steinman, MA, et al, 'The Promotion of Gabapentin: An Analysis of Internal Industry Documents' (2006) 145 *Annals of Internal Medicine* 284–97.

Stelfox, HT, et al, 'Conflict of Interest in the Debate over Calcium-Channel Antagonists' (1998) 338 *New England Journal of Medicine* 101–06.

Stiglitz, JE, 'Scrooge and Intellectual Property Rights' (2006) 333 *British Medical Journal* 1279.

Stults, C and Conrad, P, 'Medicalisation and Risk Scares: The Case of Menopause and HRT' in Donald W Light (ed), *The Risks of Prescription Drugs* (Columbia UP, 2010) 116–38.

Summerfield, D, 'The Invention of Post-Traumatic Stress Disorder and the Social Usefulness of a Psychiatric Category' (2001) 322 *British Medical Journal* 95.

Summerhayes, M and Catchpole, P, 'Has NICE been Nice to Cancer?' (2006) 42 *European Journal of Cancer* 2881–86.

Suñe-Martin P and Montoro-Ronsano JB, 'Role of a Research Ethics Committee in Follow-Up and Publication of Results' (2003) 361 *The Lancet* 2245–46.

Svensson, CK, 'Representation of American Blacks in Clinical Trials of New Drugs' (1989) 261 *Journal of the American Medical Association* 263–65.

Swanson, JM, et al, 'Effects of Stimulant Medication on Growth Rates across 3 Years in the MTA Follow-Up' (2007) 46 *Journal of the American Academy of Child and Adolescent Psychiatry* 1015–27.

Sykes, R, *New Medicines, The Practice of Medicine, and Public Policy* (Nuffield Trust, London, 2000).

Syrett, K, 'A Technocratic Fix to the "Legitimacy Problem"? The Blair Government and Health Care Rationing in the United Kingdom' (2003) 28 *Journal of Health Politics, Policy and Law* 715.

Szasz, T, *The Myth of Mental Illness* (St Albans, Paladin, 1972).

Taylor, D, 'Fewer New Drugs from the Pharmaceutical Industry' (2003) 326 *British Medical Journal* Feb 2003; 326: 408–40.

Taylor, D and Craig, T, 'Value Based Pricing for NHS Medicines: Magic Bullet, Counterfeit Treatment or the Mixture as Before?' (2009) 4 *Health Economics, Policy and Law* 515–26.

Taylor, T, *The Anatomy of the Nuremberg Trials: A Personal Memoir* (New York, Little Brown, 1993).

Teff, H 'Regulation under the Medicines Act 1968: A Continuing Prescription for Health' (1984) 47 *Modern Law Review* 303–23.

Telenti, A, Aubert, V and Spertini, F, 'Individualising HIV Treatment – Pharmacogenetics and Immunogenetics' (2002) 359 *The Lancet* 722–23.

The EuroQoL Group, 'EuroQoL: A New Facility for the Measurement of Health Related Quality of Life' (1990) 16 *Health Policy* 199–208.

Thomas KJ, Coleman, P and Nicholl, JP, 'Trends in Access to Complementary or Alternative Medicines via Primary Care in England: 1995–2001 Results from a Follow-Up National Survey' (2003) 20 *Family Practice* 5757.

Thornton, S, 'Drug price reform in the UK: debunking the myths' (2007) 16 *Health Economics* 981–92.

Tiefer, L, 'Female Sexual Dysfunction: A Case Study of Disease Mongering and Activist Resistance' (2006) 3 *PLoS Medicine* e178.

Tilburt, JC, et al, 'Prescribing "Placebo Treatments": Results of National Survey of US Internists and Rheumatologists' (2008) 337 *British Medical Journal* a1938.

Tonks, A, 'Withdrawal from Paroxetine can be Severe, Warns FDA' (2004) 324 *British Medical Journal* 260.

Topol, EJ, 'Failing the Public Health – Rofecoxib, Merck, and the FDA' (2004) 351 *New England Journal of Medicine* 1707–09.

Towse, A, 'If it Ain't Broke, don't Price Fix it: the OFT and the PPRS' (2007) 16 *Health Economics* 653–665

Tramèr, MR, 'Aspirin, Like all other Drugs, is a Poison: We do not Know who Should be Given what Dose and for How Long' (2000) 321 *British Medical Journal* 1170.

Tramèr, MR, et al, 'Impact of Covert Duplicate Publication on Meta-Analysis: A Case Study' (1997) 315 *British Medical Journal* 635.

Trotter, G, 'Interpreting Scientific Data Ethically: A Frontier for Research Ethics' in Iltis, AS (ed), *Research Ethics* (Routledge, 2006) 165–77, 169.

Trouiller, P, et al, 'Drug Development for Neglected Diseases: A Deficient Market and a Public-Health Policy Failure' (2002) 359 *The Lancet* 2188–94.

Turner, DC and Sahakian, BJ, 'Ethical Questions in Functional Neuroimaging and Cognitive Enhancement' (2006) 4 *Poiesis and Praxis* 81–94.

Turner, EH, et al, 'Selective Publication of Antidepressant Trials and its Influence on Apparent Efficacy' (2008) 358 *New England Journal of Medicine* 253.

Turner, S, et al, 'Adverse Drug Reactions to Unlicensed and Off-Label Drugs on Paediatric Wards: A Prospective Study' (1999) 88 *Acta Paediatrica* 965–68.

Unger, J-P, et al (eds) *International Health and Aid Policies: The Need for Alternatives* (Cambridge University Press, 2010).

UK Health Departments, *Governance Arrangements for Research Ethics Committees* (DH, 2011)

United Nations Development Programme (UNDP), 'Good Practice Guide: Improving Access to Treatment by Utilizing Public Health Flexibilities in the WTO TRIPS Agreement' (UNDP, 2010).

US Substance Abuse and Mental Health Services Administration (SAMHSA), *Results from the 2009 National Survey on Drug Use and Health: National Findings* (SAMHSA, 2010).

Usher, AD, 'Dispute over Pneumococcal Vaccine Initiative' (2009) 374 *The Lancet* 1879–80.

Van Delden, J, et al, 'Tailor-Made Pharmacotherapy: Future Developments and Ethical Challenges in the Field of Pharmacogenomics' (2004) 18 *Bioethics* 303–21.

Vandenbroucke JP, 'Without New Rules for Industry-Sponsored Research, Science Will Cease to Exist'. Rapid response on bmj.com 14 December 2005.

Vendantam, S, 'Drug Ads Hyping Anxiety Make Some Uneasy' *Washington Post* 16 July 2001, A01.

Vincent, C and Furnham, A, *Complementary Medicine: A Research Perspective* (Chichester; Wiley, 1997).

Villanueva, P, et al, 'Accuracy of Pharmaceutical Advertisements in Medical Journals' (2003) 361 *The Lancet* 27–32.

Wachbroit, R, 'Assessing Phase I Clinical Trials' (2010) 9 *Law, Probability and Risk* 179–86.

Wager, E, et al, 'How to Do It: Get Patients' Consent to Enter Clinical Trials' (1995) 311 *British Medical Journal* 734.

Wager, E, 'How to Dance with Porcupines: Rules and Guidelines on Doctor's Relations with Drug Companies' (2003) 326 *British Medical Journal* 1196.

Wang, TJ, Ausiello, JC and Stafford, RS, 'Trends in Antihypertensive Drug Advertising 1985–1996' (1999) 99 *Circulation* 2055–57.

Warren, OJ, et al, 'The Neurocognitive Enhancement of Surgeons: An Ethical Perspective' (2009) 152 *Journal of Surgical Research* 167–72.

Watkins, C, et al, 'Characteristics of General Practitioners who Frequently See Drug Industry Representatives: National Cross Sectional Study' (2003) 326 *British Medical Journal* 1178–79.

Waxman, HA, 'The Lessons of Vioxx – Drug Safety and Sales' (2005) 352 *New England Journal of Medicine* 2576–78.

Waxman, J, 'Shark Cartilage in the Water' (2006) 333 *British Medical Journal* 1129.

Wazana, A, 'Physicians and the Pharmaceutical Industry: Is a Gift Ever Just a Gift?' (2000) 283 *Journal of the American Medical Association* 373–80.

Webb, DJ, 'Value-Based Medicine Pricing: NICE Work?' (2011) 377 *The Lancet* 1552–53.

Weber, LJ, *Profits before People? Ethical Standards and the Marketing of Prescription Drugs* (Bloomington, Indiana University Press, 2006).

Weinfurt, KP, et al, 'Disclosure of Financial Relationships to Participants in Clinical Research' (2009) 361 *New England Journal of Medicine* 916.

——, 'Views of Potential Research Participants on Financial Conflicts of Interest: Barriers and Opportunities for Effective Disclosure' (2006) 21 *Journal of General Internal Medicine* 901–06.

Weinstein, MC, 'A QALY is a QALY is a QALY – Or is it?' (1988) 7 *Journal of Health Economics* 289–90.

White, C, 'Publish and be Pampered' (2003) 327 *British Medical Journal* 348.

White, J, 'Corporate Manipulation of Research: Strategies are Similar across Five Industries' (2010) 67 *Stanford Law and Policy Review* 105.

Whitehouse, PJ, et al, 'Enhancing Cognition in the Intellectually Intact' (1997) 27 *Hastings Centre Report* 14–22.

Wikler, D, 'Paternalism in the Age of Cognitive Enhancement' in J Savulescu and N Bostrom (eds), *Human Enhancement* (Oxford University Press, 2009) 342–55.

Wilkes, MS, Doblin, BH and Shapiro MF, 'Pharmaceutical Advertisements in Leading Medical Journals: Experts' Assessments' (1992) 116 *Annals of Internal Medicine* 912–19.

Williams, SJ, Gabe, J and Davis, P, 'The Sociology of Pharmaceuticals: Progress and Prospects' (2008) 30 *Sociology of Health and Illness* 813–24;

Williams, R, 'The Government Needs to Know How Afraid People Are' *New Statesman* 9 June 2011.

Williamson, S, 'Patient Access Schemes for High-Cost Cancer Medicines' (2010) 11 *The Lancet Oncology* 111–12.

Wilson, DC, '"Let Them Do Drugs" a Commentary on Random Efforts at Shot Blocking in the Sports Drug Game' (2006) 8 *Florida Coastal Law Review* 53.

Wise, J, 'NICE Recommended Four in Five Drugs it Evaluated in Past Decade' (2010) 341 *British Medical Journal* c3935.

Wisner, KL, et al, 'Major Depression and Antidepressant Treatment: Impact on Pregnancy and Neonatal Outcomes' (2009) 166 *American Journal of Psychiatry* 557–66.

Woloshin, S and Schwartz, LM, 'Giving Legs to Restless Legs: A Case Study of How the Media Helps Make People Sick' (2006) 3 *PLoS Medicine* e17.

World Bank and GAVI, *AMC Pilot Proposal* (World Bank, Washington DC, 2006).

World Health Organisation (WHO), *Effective Medicines Regulation: Ensuring Safety, Efficacy and Quality*, WHO Policy Perspectives on Medicines, WHO/EDM/2003.2 (WHO, Geneva, 2003).

——, *Framework Convention on Tobacco Control* (WHO, Geneva, 2003).

——, *Globalization, TRIPS and Access to Pharmaceuticals: WHO Policy Perspectives on Medicines* (WHO, Geneva, 2001).

——, *The Selection of Essential Drugs: WHO Technical Report Series No. 614* (WHO, Geneva, 1977).

World Medical Association (WMA), *Declaration of Helsinki: Ethical Principles for Medical Research Involving Human Subjects* (6th version adopted at the 59th WMA General Assembly, Seoul, South Korea Oct 2008), available at www.wma.net.

World Trade Organisation (WTO), *Doha Declaration on the TRIPs Agreement and Public Health* (WTO, 2001).

Wynia, M and Boren, D, 'Better Regulation of Industry-Sponsored Clinical Trials is Long Overdue' (2009) 37 *Journal of Law, Medicine and Ethics* 410.

Yamada, T, 'Global Health and the Bill & Melinda Gates Foundation' (2009) 373 *The Lancet* 2195.

Yesavage, JA, et al, 'Donepezil and Flight Simulator Performance: Effects on Retention of Complex Skills' (2002) 59 *Neurology* 123–25.

INDEX

Introductory Note

References such as '178–9' indicate (not necessarily continuous) discussion of a topic across a range of pages. Wherever possible in the case of topics with many references, these have either been divided into sub-topics or only the most significant discussions of the topic are listed. Because the entire work is about 'medicines' the use of this term (and certain others which occur constantly throughout the book) as an entry point has been restricted. Information will be found under the corresponding detailed topics.